The African Diaspora

*Columbia Studies in International
and Global History*

J'aime la couleur, by Cheri Samba, 2003

Patrick Manning

The African Diaspora

≡ A HISTORY THROUGH CULTURE ≡

Columbia University Press | New York

Columbia University Press

Publishers Since 1893

New York   Chichester, West Sussex

Copyright © 2009 Patrick Manning

Paperback edition, 2010

All rights reserved

A Caravan book. For more information, visit www.caravanbooks.org.

Library of Congress Cataloging-in-Publication Data

Manning, Patrick, 1941–

The African diaspora : a history through culture / Patrick Manning.

   p.   cm. — (Columbia studies in international and global history)

Includes bibliographical references and index.

ISBN 978-0-231-14470-4 (cloth : alk. paper) — ISBN 978-0-231-14471-1
(pbk. : alk. paper) — ISBN 978-0-231-51355-5 (e-book)

   1. African diaspora—History.   2. Africa—Civilization.   3. Blacks—
History.   I. Title.

DT16.5.M35   2009

909'.0496—dc22

2008026555

Columbia University Press books are printed on permanent
and durable acid-free paper.

This book is printed on paper with recycled content.
Printed in the United States of America

c 10 9 8 7 6 5 4

p 10 9 8 7

Designed by Lisa Hamm

References to Internet Web sites (URLs) were accurate at the time of writing.
Neither the author nor Columbia University Press is responsible for URLs
that may have expired or changed since the manuscript was prepared.

For Robin Kilson
brilliant historian of the black experience
ardent bibliophile
fearless critic
dear friend

Contents

Maps

Graphs and Tables

Illustrations

Color illustrations follow page 202. Illustrations with italic page numbers are reproduced in the color insert.

Preface

T he history of Africans and people of African descent, a complex story in itself, lies at the center of the history of all humanity. The tale of modernity cannot fairly be told without full attention to the African continent and peoples of African descent. This book recounts the history of black people in the six centuries since 1400, as their world brought them global connections, enslavement, industrialization, and urbanization. Rather than being a history of specific regions or nations, this is a history of the interconnections of people throughout Africa, the Americas, most of Europe, and much of Asia. The Atlantic Ocean, the Mediterranean Sea, and the Indian Ocean, rather than separating people into isolated groups, are seen in this volume as fluid pathways to and from the continents and islands where Africans have migrated and voyaged, voluntarily and under duress, for many centuries and up to the present day.

Since this is a story of overlapping and connected lives, I have written it for an overlapping and connected set of audiences. Most basically, the book is for those who seek to inform themselves on the relationships among black communities and who have an interest in viewing the modern world with an appreciation for the experience and outlook of people throughout Africa and the African diaspora.

Dividing potential readers according to their relationship to schooling, I will assert that, first, the book is written for undergraduate students encountering this material perhaps for the first time—students around the world who read in English. For these students, I hope the book will open new vistas about the breadth of connections in the historical past. If the quantity of detail in the book appears daunting at times, I hope it will remind readers of how much has actually occurred in the past and of how the student as historian must have the confidence to select those details that help him or her develop clear interpretations of the past. Second, the book is written for historical professionals at graduate and postgraduate levels, who may wish to focus in more detail on the interpretive arguments and nuances. For this audience, more familiar with the concepts I present, I also hope the book will show the advantages of exploring history on a scale this broad. Third, the book is intended for general readers from black and other communities who are interested in the development of the modern world as experienced by black people. The conflicts and transformations addressed in this book are those of the real world, and I hope readers of various backgrounds and professions will find the interest and the patience to explore this history of the African diaspora. And even while the history of Africans on the continent and in the diaspora is the principal focus here, the narrative has substantial implications for world history more broadly and for modernity.

The same group of potential readers can be divided according to areas of primary interest. The first general topic is the history of black peoples. This volume presents a broad overview of that history wherever blacks have been and are now—in Africa, the Americas, Asia, Europe, and the islands—and the connections of those communities to one another and to other communities. The second general topic is world history. The story of the African diaspora addresses one-sixth of humanity over the past six centuries. The analysis here of the dynamics of interaction across the large part of the world in which black people have lived identifies a set of patterns that may have been representative in many ways of the world as a whole.

The third general topic is modernity. While some debates about the miraculous birth and the special nature of the modern world are couched in obscure academic language, this topic is important to all who wish to understand the African diaspora. Modernity is the condition of life today and in the recent past—a condition filled with triumphs, complexities, and disasters in industry, science, government, and communication, bringing progress, oppression, capitalism, and inequality. Modernity is a condition that is deeply felt and almost universally experienced. Too often, however, it is defined narrowly and then explained in such a fashion as to exclude black people from it. Modernity is the overall ethos of the modern world, in economic, social, cultural, and other realms; it is an exhilarating but difficult situation. The *experience* of modernity is unmistakable, and it is conveyed in songs and literature in every language. The *explanation* of modernity, however, is open to question. Some explanations treat modernity as a break from the past, achieved by a few: this approach emphasizes the unique insights and accomplishments of genius and privilege and divides the world into the traditional and the modern. Other explanations emphasize the continuity of recent times with the more distant past and argue that the modern world was constructed through the efforts and interactions of many; such explanations divide the world into the masses and the elite and treat the elite as the beneficiaries but not necessarily the creators of modernity.

I propose an interactive view of modernity, to reveal the important place of black people in construction of the modern world. My view contrasts with the leading sociological interpretations of modernity and the leading historical interpretations of the modern world, which consign Africa and the African diaspora to the footnotes.[1] These interpretations virtually leave Africans, the African diaspora, slavery, race, and emancipation out of their interpretations—not simply because of respect for traditional interpretation or disregard for black history but as a result of flaws in their historical logic. They give too much attention to societies, nations, kingdoms, empires, and urban centers, and not enough attention to diasporas, networks, mixes, hinterlands, and exchanges on the roads between centers. Despite the dynamics of the world of today, the static worship of central places still reigns supreme in the academic conceptualization of society. Only when connective approaches to the past are given analytical parity with central places and ruling classes will we have a history of the past and an understanding of our present that acknowledges the acts of all our ancestors in creating our world. In short, to appreciate the history of the modern world, we need to treat diasporas with the same importance as nations.

Many skilled writers on the black world decline to celebrate modernity, focusing critically on the negative aspects of global transformation as reflected in enslavement, racial discrimination, and cultural deprivation.[2] Their concerns are appropriate, as these are the stories that are usually marginalized in the leading interpretations of modernity. Yet the same stories, seen from another angle, reveal black achievements in education, cultural production, and political leadership. The experience of black people is central to understanding the achievements and missteps that continue to shape modernity. But understanding modernity means addressing the choice of whether the modern world is considered to be uniquely complex—cut off from the traditional past and from those who live today in a world of the past—or whether it is seen as another stage in our evolving history. In these pages, life under the condition of modernity is seen as widely shared and sharply different from the times before, yet it is tied to those earlier times by a million strands of continuity, evolutionary change, strife, and destruction.

The advent of modernity—which involved triumphs and arguably unbearable costs—cannot be accurately understood or imaginatively and comprehensively engaged without a responsible narration of the role played in its making by African peoples and the African continent as a whole.

The key element of the book's organization involves treating Africa and the African diaspora as a whole. Rather than break the world of black people into localized regions and study each one individually, this volume encompasses large areas of the black world and emphasizes connections and interactions among them. The chapters are organized chronologically rather than regionally, and each chapter contrives to address most areas of the black world. More precisely, the analysis treats the African continent—its many regions and the details of its life—as equal in importance to the diaspora of Africans overseas. As will be argued in the chapters to come, the dynamics, conflicts, and discoveries of the African continent have been on a par with those of the Americas and the Old World diaspora.

The interpretation sustains five themes throughout the book. The first theme, encompassing the others, is the connections that held together the African diaspora as a global community of mutual identification. The remaining, more specific themes are the discourse on race, the changes in economic life, the patterns of family life, and the evolution of popular culture. These five themes, explored through sequential chapters, are braided together to show the changing character of the social struggles that dominated each successive period of history throughout the African diaspora from 1400 to 2000.

The cover illustration, Romare Bearden's *She-ba* (1970), anticipates several of the themes of this book. Bearden's collage, a decidedly modern work in its form, resonates with the heritage of the ages. The queen's dignity—her link to the welfare of her community—offers a vision of leadership viewed favorably on the African continent and in the New World diaspora. The image also evokes notions of family, culture, continuity, and visions of the future. Further, since the biblical Sheba is often linked not only to the Nile Valley but to Saba in South Arabia, this New World image makes a link to the Old World diaspora as well as the African continent. In this and other illustrations in the book, I have sought to present works and images created by black people. In certain cases, especially in chapter 2, I have selected views of diaspora blacks created by people outside their community. Otherwise, I have given priority to images conveying interpretive statements from black people about their world.

I believe that some remarkable patterns of the past emerge from studying history at this scale. It may seem surprising—to readers used to studying history at the local level—to hear an argument that the histories of North America, South America, southern Africa, West Africa, the Ottoman Empire, and India could be substantially similar. Yet, in the mid-nineteenth century, slavery was under attack in all of these areas and, along with this renunciation of slavery, former slaves were rising to positions of responsibility in government. In addition, at the opening of the twentieth century, while slavery was abolished or nearly so, new forms of discrimination—again, in all of these regions of the world—had removed almost all black people from those positions of responsibility in government. This is just one of the many striking historical parallels throughout the black world that await discovery.

In assembling this story of the global interactions and changes in the experience of black people, I have been guided by some big questions about the past and the future. First, the past:

Why did world slavery grow to such an extent in the modern era?
What have been the social contributions of black communities?
How did black communities create their cultural advances?

There are answers to these queries, but they cannot be compressed into a multiple-choice test. The chapters ahead take up the search for answers in many ways.

At the same time, looking ahead is equally important in motivating our study of history. So here are some big questions about the future that have influenced the organization of this book:

Will social equality ever be possible?
Should reparations be granted for past injustice?
Will racism end?
What is the future of black identity?

These questions, like those about the past, lie just beneath the surface of the narrative and analysis in the chapters to come. In the epilogue, I return to them and offer my responses.

This book focuses on the drama, the transformation, the agony, and the renewal in the lives of Africans at home and abroad. Further, the book demonstrates that the African diaspora—a vast dispersal of black people across the African continent, the Americas, the European and Asian continents, and the islands of the great seas—adds up to a large and representative part of the human population, and its activities add up to a large part of human history. This story of African experiences confirms the interconnections that have linked human populations across the world. Tracing those experiences across time reveals that the issues of today—modernity, democracy, equality, progress—have been fought over in different ways over time. These past struggles were not simply archaic battles, however. On the contrary, they established patterns that continue to influence many aspects of life in the present world.

Acknowledgments

My first acknowledgment is to the people of Africa and the African diaspora, alive and among the ancestors, who created the experience of which I offer this chronicle. Taking up the task of recounting their past, with attention to honor and to truth, brought me excitement and anxiety. Writing it has brought me to look into the lives of black people throughout the world, and it has pulled together many aspects of my own academic life. I was encouraged ahead, despite the complexity of this task, by the thought that a broad overview of the African diaspora and its successive transformations will reaffirm some previously recognized patterns and will convey some new and global dimensions of issues that are commonly discussed mainly in national terms. I have sought to express my interpretation in explicit terms. I am comforted by the knowledge that others are now writing at this breadth, to ensure that there will be debates on the interpretation of the African diaspora, rather than an authorized story.

I offer my thanks to Bruce Borland for leading me through the exercise of proposing the book. Several readers of the manuscript helped me to close off some of its paths and open others. The list begins with special appreciation to Robin Kilson for the repeated and sometimes hilarious sessions of debate, critical reading, and bibliographical hints, with which she helped me to revise substantial sections of the manuscript, especially the epilogue. Of my other colleagues in African-American Studies at Northeastern University, I have benefited from the insights of the late Jordan Gebre-Medhin, Robert L. Hall, Ronald Bailey, Kwamina Panford, and William F. S. Miles. Kim D. Butler and Mamadou Diouf read the manuscript with great insight and gave me the encouragement to make substantial modifications in organization and in argument. Colleagues in four other departments provided spirited responses to drafts of individual chapters: the department of history at the University of the West Indies, St. Augustine, Trinidad (with special thanks to department chair Brinsley Samaroo and to Bridget Brereton and Claudius Fergus); the department of history and archaeology of the University of the West Indies, Mona, Jamaica (with special thanks to department chair Swithin Wilmot and to Glen Richards); the department of African and African-American Studies at Harvard University (with special thanks to Emmanuel Akyeampong, Evelyn Brooks Higginbotham, and Henry Louis Gates); and the department of history at the University of Pittsburgh (with thanks to Alejandro de la Fuente, George Reid Andrews, Seymour Drescher, and Marcus Rediker). Kim Alan Pederson edited and commented on the manuscript with a level of skill and insight I have come to depend on.

In addition, I offer my deep appreciation to Susan Manning, my companion in life, whose warmth and generosity have provided the appropriate mix of calmness and excitement, critique and reassurance.

The African Diaspora

⚌ 1 ⚌

Diaspora

Struggles and Connections

People of sub-Saharan Africa <u>have migrated, in wave after wave, to other regions of the world.</u> The initial movements—beginning seventy thousand years ago—involved settlement of the Old World tropics; this was followed by occupation of Eurasia, Oceania, and the Americas. In the last few millennia, as societies and civilizations grew up throughout the world, Africans have continued to migrate and settle overseas. For the black people of sub-Saharan Africa, this "sunburst" of settlement beyond their homeland has brought particularly close linkages to Egypt, other parts of North Africa, and Arabia. Further settlements across the waters of the Indian Ocean, the Mediterranean Sea, and the Atlantic Ocean brought African settlers to Asia, Europe, and the Americas. It is a sad reality that, from the fifteenth through the nineteenth centuries, most African migrants beyond the continent were forced to travel and to serve as slaves. But in slavery and in freedom, African migrants and their descendants made their mark. Culture and commerce have flowed steadily and ties of personal attachment have been established and maintained among the regions of Africa and the African diaspora. In the twenty-first century, those earlier migrations and cultural interactions of people of African descent retain as much significance as ever.

This volume narrates the last six centuries of connections among black people in Africa and throughout overseas regions and provides some background on earlier times. It is a complex tale of cultural development, enslavement, colonization, struggles for liberation, and construction of modern society and identity. At the same time, this work poses and attempts to address some of the important questions that still face us as a result of the African diaspora. The analytical framework that shapes the chronological narrative presented here relies on five central themes: diaspora and its connections, the discourse on race, economic transformations, family life, and cultural production.

Diaspora

The analysis of diasporas—the migrations that brought them about and the dynamics of these dispersed communities—has become a significant topic in the work of historians, sociologists, and other scholars.[1] Social scientists today use the term "diaspora" to refer to migrants who settle in distant lands and produce new generations, all the while maintaining ties of affection with and making occasional visits to each other and their homeland. The diaspora of Africans takes its place alongside the diasporas of Chinese, South Asians, Jews, Armenians, Irish, and many other ethnic or regional groupings. Diasporas can be large or small: the Jamaican diaspora lies within the African diaspora; the Palestinian diaspora within the larger Arab diaspora. They are new and old. More than two thousand years ago, for example, a Polynesian diaspora launched the settlement of many central Pacific islands.

"Diaspora" is an ancient term, long used almost exclusively in reference to the dispersion of Jewish people around the world. An interesting history of the term comes out of the diffusion of Jewish and Greek populations in the ancient world. From the time of the Babylonian captivity, Jews had been divided between their Palestinian homeland and Babylonia, and after they were freed from enslavement in Babylon they spread from Mesopotamia to the Mediterranean shores. Jewish populations held onto their religion, but they tended to embrace the local language. For instance, many adopted Greek, and thus it was that the Greek-speaking Jews of Alexandria, the great commercial city of the Egyptian coast, decided in roughly 200 BCE to support a translation of the Hebrew Bible into Greek. This translation, the Septuagint, used the Greek term "diaspora" (from the sowing or dispersal of seeds) to translate several Hebrew terms that described the scattering of Jews outside the Jewish homeland. As Jews continued to scatter voluntarily and involuntarily through Europe, North Africa, and Asia, the term "diaspora" moved with them. With the rise of Christianity, the Septuagint and the term "diaspora" entered the Greek and Latin versions of the Christian Bible.

How did the term "diaspora" begin to be applied to the experience of Africans? According to two of the founders of African diaspora studies, George

Shepperson and Joseph E. Harris, the term was used and perhaps coined at the time of an international conference on African history held at the University of Dar es Salaam in Tanzania in 1965.[2] In an era when African and Caribbean countries were gaining independence and when movements for civil rights in those nations and the United States brought black people to the political forefront and into increased contact with one another, a renewed interest grew in tracing the historical contacts among Africans and people of African descent outside the continent. This was also a time—two decades after World War II and the subsequent creation of the state of Israel—when analyses of the Holocaust and of Jewish history brought attention to the Jewish diaspora and comparisons with other migrations. Expanding studies in African history and culture, including the importance of slavery in the history of Africans abroad, produced an interest in the Jewish diaspora analogy. Step by step, there developed scholarly studies of the African diaspora, university courses on the subject in Africa and in the Americas, and a growing public consciousness of diaspora-wide connections.[3] Continuing struggles for the independence and civil rights of black people (in South Africa, Zimbabwe, and the Portuguese-held territories of Angola, Mozambique, and Guiné-Bissau) encouraged and expanded transatlantic solidarity. One form of such solidarity was the large-scale involvement of Cuban troops in support of the MPLA government of Angola after 1975; another was the campaign for boycotting South African businesses led by Trans-Africa, the U.S.-based black lobby.

At a cultural level, diaspora-wide connections developed in the widespread adoption of Ghanaian Kente cloth, hair styles involving weaving and braiding, and the sharing of musical traditions from Africa, North America, the Caribbean, and South America. By the 1990s, consciousness of the African diaspora had become wide enough that the term "African diaspora" began to be used much more extensively, in academic circles and in black communities. As with other aspects of African diaspora history, adoption of the term "diaspora" took place not only in English, but in Spanish, Portuguese, French, and other languages. Then, once the term "diaspora" gained currency in the study of Africans abroad, scholars began applying it to Chinese and other migrant populations.[4]

I have chosen to organize the geographical framework of this study into three great areas, which I label as the African homeland, the Old World diaspora, and the Atlantic diaspora (see map 1.1). By "African homeland," I mean sub-Saharan Africa, the homeland from which black peoples have voyaged in freedom and slavery. By "Old World diaspora," I mean all the regions of the Eastern Hemisphere in which sub-Saharan Africans have settled: North

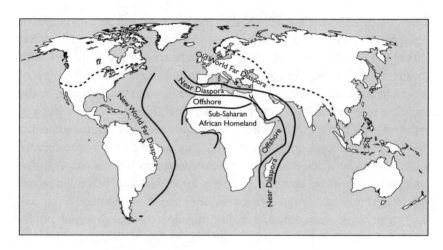

MAP 1.1 Regions of the African Diaspora

Africa, western and southwestern Asia, Europe, South Asia, and the islands of the Indian Ocean. By "Atlantic diaspora," I mean the Americas and also the islands of the Atlantic and the mainland of western Europe. Each of these three regions has its own history, but these histories are tightly connected. For instance, Africans first came to Europe as part of the Old World diaspora, but as the Atlantic slave trade grew, Africans came to Europe especially by way of the Atlantic.

In my opinion, something is gained in this history by giving attention at once to the African continent and to all the regions of black settlement outside the continent. So I propose a formal framework for studying the world of black people in this way: I call it Africa-diaspora studies.[5] This is an approach that traces connections among the various regions of the black world and emphasizes the social dynamics of those connections. In general, the sunburst of African settlement in the diaspora continues to interact with the continent's bright orb. More precisely, this perspective on the history of the African diaspora explores four overlapping types of connections in the history of black people: (1) interactions among black communities at home and abroad, (2) relations with hegemonic powers, (3) relations with non-African communities, and (4) the mixing of black and other communities. These four dynamic dimensions of Africa-diaspora studies, explored across the regions of the black world, add up to a comprehensive yet flexible concept for analyzing the broad historical experience of black people and for setting that experience in a broader social context.

Interactions Within the World of Black People

This initial dimension of analysis addresses the migrations from Africa to the Americas and elsewhere, the survival and development of African culture in the diaspora, cases of return migration to Africa, and the many instances of development and sharing of political and cultural traditions among black peoples. More broadly, this is the study of interplay among Africa, the Atlantic diaspora, and the Old World diaspora. These demographic and cultural connections among black peoples form the core of the history we will trace.

Relations of Black People with Hegemonic Powers

These hegemonic powers, imposing their wills on black people, included slave masters, imperial conquerors, colonial or national societies dominated by propertied elites, government-backed missionaries, and dominant national cultures of the twentieth century. The propertied classes—in the diasporas of the Atlantic and the Old World and, later, in Africa—not only dominated their slaves but mixed socially and sexually with them. For people in slavery, a great deal of their existence was conditioned by the masters who restricted and oppressed them, changing their lives relentlessly. Similarly, people in the African colonies of the twentieth century found their lives pressured and transformed by the colonial powers in general and by individual Europeans. This dynamic brought suffering, resistance, debate, accommodation, and imaginative innovation in response. Resistance to these powers has occupied much of the energies of black people.

Relations of Blacks with Other Nonhegemonic Racial Groups

In the Old World, blacks interacted with people of Arab, Iranian, Turkish, and Indian birth, and with those brought as slaves from the Black Sea region. In the Americas, black communities interacted with Amerindian communities. Later on, black people in the Americas and in Africa interacted with immigrants from India, China, and the Arab world. And in a steadily growing number of instances, black people interacted with white communities under conditions where neither group was a master class—in Europe, for instance. These community interactions engendered new ethnic groups, caused competition for land and for ways to make a living, created political rivalries, and encouraged cultural borrowing and occasional alliances.

Mixing—Biological and Cultural—of Blacks with Other Populations in Every Region of Africa and the Diaspora

These mixes in population and culture are sometimes counted as part of the African tradition: in the United States, for example, mixes of black and white commonly become part of the black community. Sometimes the mix is treated as a category unto itself: the notion of "mestizo," common in Latin America, is often treated as a social order distinct from its white, black, or Amerindian ancestry. And sometimes the mixes leave the black community and join the hegemonic white community, as in the case of the "passing" that has taken place throughout the African diaspora. In the Old World diaspora, including sometimes in Europe, the progeny of blacks and others tended to be treated as part of the dominant community. "Mixes," it should be remembered, can be of several sorts: residential mixing, family formation across racial lines (voluntarily and involuntarily), and eclectic sharing of cuisine, dress, music, and family practices.

The point of this history of the African diaspora is to sustain a story of all four dimensions: the lives of black communities at home and abroad, their relations with hegemonic powers (both under the hierarchy of slavery and in the unequal circumstances of postemancipation society), their relations with communities of other racial designations, and the various types of mixing of black and other communities. The narrative shifts among these issues and pauses occasionally for an analysis of each era's major interpretive questions. Through narratives of social situations but also through cultural representations of life's crises and disasters, this volume balances the differences and the linkages among these four dimensions of the unfolding narrative of the African diaspora. The African continent appears not only as ancestral homeland but as a region developing and participating in global processes at every stage. The exploitive actions of slave masters and corporate hierarchies appear as a major force in history, but so do the linkages among black communities. The tale of an embattled but highly accomplished African-American community in the United States unfolds throughout the narrative, but so do the experiences of black communities in Brazil, Britain, and India. The African heritage shows itself not only able to retain old traditions but also to innovate and incorporate new practices through mixing, intermarriage, and cultural exchange of blacks with whites, Native Americans, Arabs, and South Asians.

My interpretation, organized around these four priorities, differs from other well-known interpretations of the African diaspora and its past. The difference comes partly because of interpretive disagreements I have with other authors, but mostly because this book is set at a wider scale than previous works. One such major interpretation is *Afrocentricity*, by Molefi Kete Asante. His work, which gained wide attention with its second, expanded edition in 1988, linked today's African-American population to its African heritage.[6] Dr. Asante put forth "Afrocentricity" as a philosophy and program for social change, and he connected it in particular to traditions of ancient Egypt and to West African traditions of the nineteenth century. His interpretation did not say much about slavery and emancipation in Africa and overseas, and it made only brief reference to the African diaspora in Europe, Latin America, or the Indian Ocean. The Afrocentricity approach focused on building pride in African-American communities but stopped short of analyzing interaction and transformation. Asante's emphasis was therefore more on race than on community, more on heritage than on exchange, and more on unity than on variety.

Another major interpretation focuses on "the Black Atlantic," a term that developed in the 1990s to describe widespread connections among black people. This phrase, popularized by the black British sociologist Paul Gilroy in his 1993 book of the same name, gained wide attention as a descriptor of literary culture.[7] The difference is one of emphasis, but it is an important difference. The "African diaspora" refers initially to the world of black people. The Black Atlantic, in contrast, focuses primarily on the interaction of black people and white people in the North Atlantic. It emphasizes blacks as a minority and often a subject population in an Atlantic world dominated by Europeans. Within that framework, it argues that black people created a "counterculture of modernity," a set of cultural contributions that expressed their particular response to the challenges of modernity and had a substantial creative effect on "Western culture" as a whole. From a time perspective, analysis within the Black Atlantic focus is restricted to postemancipation society, while the African-diaspora focus employed here includes not only the times since emancipation but also the previous era of Atlantic slavery, and even the times before the large-scale enslavement of Africans. The perspectives of Black Atlantic and African diaspora thus overlap substantially, but they also retain distinctions so significant that they should not be confused with each other. (In fact, both the terms "African diaspora" and "Black

Atlantic" have been given somewhat different meanings by other authors, so the reader should review the meaning of these terms in each text.)

In *The Black Atlantic*, Gilroy fiercely critiqued "essentialists," his term for those who affirmed that the black past consisted of unchanging African roots. He rejected Afrocentric myths paralleling "orientalism"—essentialized European views of the Middle East—which had previously come under attack by the Palestinian-born writer Edward Said.[8] Gilroy's critique clearly extended to the writings of Asante, who pictured an autonomous black American community and traced it to Africa, though not in great detail. Gilroy then argued that this essentialist view of black identity and culture remained locked in debate with a contrasting "antiessentialism." He explained antiessentialism as a sort of pluralism that deconstructs blackness yet falls short in explaining the appeal of black popular culture, and he illustrated this outlook with the writings of novelist Richard Wright. Gilroy offered, as his own position, an "anti-anti-essentialism" emphasizing that "racialized subjectivity" results from the exercise of power in history.[9] In principle, Gilroy affirms a historical rather than an essentialist or pluralist approach to the construction of black culture. In practice, in declining to analyze the days before emancipation, Gilroy implicitly treats the African past as lacking in value. On the other hand, simply to criticize Gilroy for his short time frame and North Atlantic focus does not in itself provide a dynamic interpretation of the past of black peoples.

In a study of "the making of the Atlantic world," a third author, John Thornton, chose to emphasize the agency of African elites, tracing how they made their way in the new Atlantic world by selling into slavery the subordinates they controlled.[10] This interpretation, however, left the African masses essentially without agency, at least until they reached the Americas.

Each of these interpretations provides reassurance for those seeking to locate an active and creative role for black people in the past. In all, however, Africa's place in the developing diaspora is vague and general rather than specific and current: Gilroy identifies foundational work by black creative figures in an emerging transnational culture of postemancipation days; Thornton attributes agency to slave-marketing African political elites in the early years of transatlantic enslavement; Asante portrays African-American populations as acting out the patterns of their deep African heritage. These interpretations address large areas of the past, yet each author worked within boundaries that exclude from discussion important experiences of black people of Africa and the diaspora. I argue that it is not necessary to leave out the other parts of the story. Considering the whole of Africa and the diaspora at once requires extra effort, but it is feasible and can bring a clearer view of this long and broad historical path. As my interpretation, with its vision of Africa-diaspora studies, takes its place alongside others, I hope readers will recall two aspects of my argument: (1) the development of localized regions and social groups in interaction with one another, and (2) the continuing centrality of the African continent and its societies, along with the sunburst of its migrants, in the affairs of the world as a whole.

"Connection" is used as a technical term in this volume to ensure that readers note the variety and complexity of historical interactions. The African diaspora sustained itself and renewed itself as a broad community of shared identity through connections among individuals and local communities. Africa and the African diaspora provide a geographic and social space within which numerous elements and personalities have interacted, serving to unite but also to transform the patterns of the whole. Too often, simplified analyses have identified one-way movements from Africa to the Americas (as enslaved and displaced Africans brought their culture and labor power to the Americas), one-way domination of black people by slave masters or colonial governors, or one-way influences of modern American black cultural leaders on Africa. Instead, I hope that an elaborated notion of connections will make it easier to identify the many types of contacts among regions, people, or situations.[11] These can be one-way or two-way connections between any pair of situations, and these connections become more complex as one considers more situations. In the history of Africa and the African diaspora, the great distances and the restrictions of enslavement and colonial rule meant that many contacts were inhibited. In that same history, as we will see, contacts among dispersed people of African ancestry were also renewed in remarkable ways.

The transatlantic slave trade, linking the situations of West Africa and the Caribbean, can be interpreted as a one-way or a two-way connection. As a one-way connection, one can interpret the slave trade as the influence of West African slaves on the Caribbean (the contribution of their labor and the effects of their culture), combined with the assumption (probably implicit) that Africa experienced no change as a result of slave trade. Viewed as a two-way connection, the links between the two situations are more complex. The slave trade brought a great number of captive settlers to the Caribbean. These involuntary settlers interacted with Amerindians and Europeans and developed new cultures based on their old ones. The simple fact of the departure of slaves changed the population and society in Africa. Then the foods of the Caribbean—including peanuts, maize, and manioc—spread to West Africa. West African cooking styles continued to come to the Caribbean, and they now included ingredients of Caribbean origin. Notions of racial hierarchy, developed in the Caribbean out of the population mix, spread to Africa. Ultimately, the two regions each became more cosmopolitan and more hierarchical through their connection. This approach reveals a historical complexity that is very different from the notion of a one-way connection or "the impact of West Africa on the Caribbean."

Included in the nuances of the two-way example above are what may be called a *departure effect*, where life in West Africa changed simply because of the loss of people to enslavement, and *interactions*, such as the change in African cuisine once peanuts and manioc arrived and the change in Caribbean cuisine once African techniques of stews and marinades arrived. In addition, one may contrast *parallels* and *divergences* in outcomes once situations are connected. For instance, the slave trade brought expansion of slavery in both the Americas and Africa, a *parallel* development. But since more males than females went to the Americas in captivity, there arose a shortage of women in the Americas, while Africa was left with a shortage of men. In this sense, the connection of slave trade brought a *divergence* between Africa and the Americas.

As I noted earlier, this interpretation of the African diaspora relies on overlapping emphases in the history of black people: interactions among black communities at home and abroad, their relations with hegemonic powers, their relations with non-African communities, and the social and cultural mixing of black and other communities. The logic and terminology of connections provides a framework for tracing the dynamics linking these historical groups and their situations. For instance, the interconnections among social situations are known by such terms as "encounter," "hybridity," "creolization," "fusion," "borrowing," "syncretism," "acculturation," "survival," and "resistance." These terms, though they overlap, are not synonyms: the shadings of meaning separating these terms for interaction are sometimes important. Further, it is sometimes helpful to distinguish the dynamics of connections *within* the black community (the connections among subgroups of the diaspora by region, language, or religion) from connections *without* the community (dealing with hegemonic powers, slavers, or co-workers of a different racial attribution) and from connections combining these two, such as those of families spanning racial and ethnic lines. For instance, as free communities of former slaves formed in the nineteenth century on the coasts of Liberia and Sierra Leone, these communities interacted with free black people in the United States and the Caribbean. At the same time, British colonial power and the white-dominated United States limited the options within which these transatlantic black contacts and choices could be acted out, restricting their political and educational options and their freedom of movement across the seas. The logic of connections can help keep track of the full range of the dynamics of the African diaspora.

Race

This story of black people in the modern world acknowledges but does not advocate the concept of "race." That is, my narrative accepts as historical reality that the peoples known as black, Negro, Ethiopian, African, Hamite, or colored (or categorized by any other such terms) have been grouped together under such designations and have, overall, accepted that labeling. At the same time, the narrative emphasizes that racial categorization is socially constructed and usually prejudicial. The changing interpretations of "race" thus become part of the story of the African diaspora.

Almost a century ago, scholar and activist W. E. B. Du Bois published *The Negro* (1915). At that time, he faced a dilemma that remains unresolved. How does one describe the shared experience of black people without accepting the essentializing and invidious concept of "race"?

> There have been repeated efforts to discover, by measurements of various kinds, further and more decisive differences that would serve as really scientific determinants of race. Gradually these efforts have been abandoned. Today we realize that there are no hard and fast racial types among men. Race is a dynamic and not a static conception, and the typical races are continually changing and developing, amalgamating and differentiating. In this little book, then, we are studying the history of the darker part of the human family, which is separated from the rest of mankind by no absolute physical line but which nevertheless forms, as a mass, a social group distinct in history, appearance, and, to some extent, in spiritual gift.[12]

Despite the many changes since Du Bois wrote, the debates persist. Is racism declining? Is it growing? Is it taking new shapes? Formal prohibitions of racial discrimination became widespread as the twenty-first century opened, but racial inequalities still characterize income, education, housing, health, and political participation. In a crucial scientific development, the biological discoveries of the last two decades have confirmed what Du Bois argued: race does not exist as a coherent reality for humans. Yet for this book, which traces centuries of social experience, I assert—as did Du Bois—the need to write of the shared historical experience of black people.

The black peoples surveyed in this book account for a substantial portion of all humanity. With modern censuses, we know that the African-descended population of Africa, the Americas, and other regions makes up one-sixth of today's world population. The African diaspora in the Americas includes 150 million people; the Old World diaspora of Eurasia and North Africa totals nearly fifty million people; and about eight hundred million black people live today in sub-Saharan Africa. Altogether, nearly a billion people can trace their ancestry in the last few centuries to Africa's black population. By comparing global birth and death rates over time, we can be certain that black people once made up an even a larger proportion of the human population—perhaps one-fifth of the human population at the beginning of the seventeenth century and probably a somewhat greater proportion before then.[13]

Overall, I present the history of black people as a history of *community* rather than *race*. The many communities of Africa and of black people throughout the world exemplify the human condition. Community interaction has shaped the historical African diaspora more than the common ancestry and inherent unity of black people. Some characteristics of and traditions in black communities go back so far and down so deep that they can appear to be essential, even racial, traits. Such characteristics and traditions include family structure, elements of philosophy, musical practices, and methods of food preparation. At the same time, the boundaries of the black world set by characteristics and traditions have been permeable—many people have joined the "black race" and many have left it over time. Ideas and practices, as well as individuals, have commonly crossed the "frontiers" in both directions.

Definitions of Racial Difference

So what is "race"? That is, how is it socially constructed? The idea of "race" is the belief that each group of people has some *essence* that makes it different from other groups. In our own time, people usually experience "race" through defining groups that "look different" from one another. That is, we commonly use *color* to identify racial difference. But over time, people have used at least four overlapping definitions of race—four different characterizations of essential differences among groups. The first three definitions focus on superficial differences in *phenotype* (that is, physical characteristics, especially skin color), in *lineage* (for instance, the argument that "purity of blood" defines racial lines), and in *culture* (particularly religious affiliation but also dress). Those who identify Jews as a separate race typically focus on lineage or religion; those identifying black people as a separate race focus on phenotypical differences in color and hair type. Such identifications of superficial racial differences by phenotype, lineage, and culture have probably reinforced one another for thousands of years. The fourth definition of race—the assumption of *biological differences* among human subspecies—emerged and joined the others beginning in the eighteenth century, when the successes in scientific classification of animals and plants suggested to some that the human species could be divided into subspecies. Later, as scientific study progressed, these purported internal biological differences came to be labeled as *genetic* variance.

All four of these visions of "race" rely on a fundamental logic that emerges from human psychology: categorizing people into "us" and "others." The ability to categorize the world around us is perhaps the greatest strength in human thinking: it enabled our ancestors to make distinctions that gradually built our complex society. Yet categorization requires judgment. For some purposes, human psychology tends to exaggerate the unity *within* and also exaggerate the differences *between* categories such as family, ethnicity, religion, or race. The assumption of "otherness"—affirming the unity of one's own group and assuming that "they" are all alike within their groups—underlies the logic of racism. For this reason, it seems that practices of some form of racism have long existed. In addition to the *practice* of racial discrimination, theories and *concepts* of race have arisen from time to time—as with Christians and Muslims demonizing each other, with medieval Iberian insistence on *limpieza de sangre* as a blood purity among Christians to which Jews could never aspire, and later with categories identifying people from each continent by color. Biological racism, in which color and phenotype were seen as reflections of fundamental biological differences, became the most fully developed concept of "otherness," one that reigned from the late eighteenth through the twentieth centuries.

Racial Hierarchies

The categorizations of humans into the groups described above focused on racial *differences*. In addition, people have often ranked the groups they identify into a racial *hierarchy*. With this reasoning, people go beyond assuming a *racial essence* for each group (dividing the world into "us" and "the other") and take the further step of *ranking* racial groups. This hierarchical ranking of groups is of crucial importance, yet it is subtle and sometimes difficult to demonstrate. For instance, historian Frank Snowden studied Greek and Roman representations of black people extensively and concluded that blacks were clearly identified but did not suffer discrimination in those societies. (Not all scholars have been convinced by his argument.)[14] On the other hand, white plantation owners and leading anthropologists of the nineteenth century definitely placed "racial" differences in a hierarchy, putting themselves at the top.

Of the four main types of racial categorization, one—biological racism—has now undergone a definitive test. Racial theorists argued that the superficial aspects of race provided the key to far deeper differences. In their view, biological differences *between* populations, such as between black and white, were greater than the differences *within* populations of either whites or blacks. For the genetic composition of humans, scientific analysis has now shown the reverse: genetic variations *within* populations—black or white, local communities or communities defined almost any other way—are substantially greater than the genetic variations *between* populations.[15] I argue that this result can be generalized. Not only in genetics but in physical characteristics, culture, and lineage, the differences *between* "races" (or any other population) are dependably smaller than the wide range of individual variation *within* any population. The assumption of "race"—of the unity and coherence of subgroups in the human population—is fundamentally flawed. But that has not stopped many humans from making the assumption of "race" in the past, and it may not stop people in the future.

Thus, "race" exists not in nature but in the choices of individuals and groups. As a result, "race" has a history, like everything else in human society. Some social processes reproduce the meaning of "race," while others transform it. All through the history of human interaction, people labeled and discriminated among one another based on visible differences in color, facial features, dress, language, religious practice, and other customs. The need to define the "other" in this manner recurs again and again.

Changing Definitions of "Race"

In generation after generation, changing social situations brought new meanings and new terminologies to what we now call "race." No new era could be completely new, however, because the previous conflicts and attitudes survived, sometimes in altered forms, into succeeding periods. The enslavement of Africans in the ancient and medieval Mediterranean provided an example of racial and social discrimination, though black people were surely a minority of the world's slaves for most of that time. In medieval times, the notion of "blood" or "bloodline" suggested that inheritance of visible and invisible characteristics sets a person's destiny, and in medieval Iberia the notion of "purity of blood" became a formal concept. In this case, genealogy, rather than appearance, provided a destiny one could not escape.[16] The readiness of Portuguese voyagers of the fifteenth century to enslave Africans was an extension of this medieval logic of distinct bloodlines as much as it was a response to skin color.

By the eighteenth century, slavery in the Americas had grown to the extent that Africans became the majority of the world's slaves. In this slave society, "race" came to mean more than ever. The biological description of race became the most powerful justification of fundamental differences among races ever to be advanced, giving new strength to every other sort of prejudice. This expanded vision of race, first hinted at in the eighteenth century as biological theories became more specific, developed in the nineteenth century into formal and more systematically oppressive interpretations of racial hierarchy: this was "scientific racism." Racial discrimination, somewhat remarkably, accelerated with the steady emancipation of black slaves and reached its peak in the early twentieth century. As that century proceeded, new forms of scientific and popular racism emerged—for instance, in medical experiments on blacks and Jews and in Nazi Germany's mass hysteria. By the end of the twentieth century, however, the continuing advances in genetic studies had fully discredited the notion of deep-seated biological differences among races. These scientific results reinforced the political trends of democratization and decolonization that grew after the end of World War II and further challenged surviving practices of racial discrimination.

Defining Racial Mixes

Defining *racial mixes* is as central to racial discrimination as defining *racial essences*. By the logic of separate racial stocks, those labeled as "mixed" are somehow seen as deviant from an ideal of racial purity. If we accept Caucasian, African, and Mongol races as pure stocks of ancestral types, then biological mixing must have created impure combinations. People developed terminologies over time to label each "pure" racial type and to define an elaborate list of mixes: mulatto, mestizo, colored, and many more. The logic of racial mixes is slippery in several ways. For instance, the doctrine of racial segregation confuses biology and culture by claiming that social mixing of different biological types might bring cultural impurity. In biological reality, each of us has drawn randomly on the genes of our two parents, and each parent drew similarly on two ancestors. As a result, even in small communities, we are all mixes resulting from myriads of ancestors. If the notion of racial "purity" has often gained its advocates, the limits of this logic arise with the dangers of inbreeding. Nevertheless, as Du Bois found, we must accommodate the notion of racial mixes, as well as that of racial essences, in order to write a history of human interactions. So I will use such terms as "black," "brown," "mulatto," "mestizo," and "people of color" as they appear in the sources. The term "mixed race" may even appear from time to time in this book, though I find it especially worrisome because it reintroduces explicitly the concepts of purity and impurity in race.

On the other hand, while racial hierarchy has been central to the history of recent centuries, humans tend not to be as orderly or conformist as their leaders might wish. Those who use racist labels sometimes act in practice without regard to color, just as those who condemn racist language remain capable of prejudicial actions. Many people of all races, in their practical social behavior during the last several centuries, ignored or actively disbelieved the social prejudices and scientific arguments for racial hierarchy. Even in societies permeated by racial hierarchies enforced by cruel retaliation, individuals have ignored or reached across the racial divide, motivated by recognition of another's talent, by interest in another perspective, by sexual attraction, or by a simple response to common humanity.

Economy and Family

The two themes of economy and family are introduced together here. While they differ, they are deeply interdependent. Both have changed greatly over the centuries, but in different ways. Economic life—very much in the public sphere—has changed through commercial and capitalist expansion, industrial revolution, urbanization, technical change, and waves of globalization. Family life, mostly in the private sphere of existence, has nurtured old traditions that survive despite changes in economic organization. But family too has changed under the pressure of migration, enslavement, emancipation, and urbanization.

Economic Transformations

The changes in black economic life, though enormous, must not be exaggerated. More than six centuries ago, African societies had already developed sophisticated systems of agriculture, animal husbandry, and artisanal work. Their local and long-distance trade linked most areas of the continent, and their currencies of gold, copper, iron, shells, and cloth facilitated the transactions. Their artisans worked in textiles, metal, wood, leather, ceramics, earth, and stone; they constructed public buildings, watercraft, and elegant jewelry. Africans exchanged ideas and innovations in all directions, so that improvements discovered in one part of the continent were sure to spread to other areas, despite the distances. On the other hand, whenever wealth became concentrated in the Mediterranean and Indian Ocean regions, demand rose for African luxury goods and slaves.

With the opening of Atlantic commerce, the African gold trade expanded, followed by the slave trade. Western Africa's involvement in the global economy now became as deep as that of northern and eastern Africa. But for all parts of Africa, enslavement was to become a growing part of economic life.

Black people in the Old World (including those in Europe) worked especially in domestic service but also in transportation, both as boatmen and teamsters. Blacks also became prominent at the courts of Old World rulers as soldiers, musicians, and domestics. In the Americas, African slaves were put to work on mines for silver, gold, and emeralds, and on plantations for sugar, wheat, indigo, tobacco, and later for cotton and coffee. Other Africans were put to work in personal service, military service, and in artisanal and transport work.

In the nineteenth century, the two great processes of industrialization and emancipation transformed life in the African diaspora. Industrialization brought railroads, steamships, telegraphs, electric power, automobiles, radio, air transport, and new types of work. The end of slavery usually came in two steps: the abolition of the overseas slave trade and then the emancipation of slaves. In the decades between these steps, slavery continued, but in a changed fashion. The system of slavery without slave trade spread in a wave across the Americas, the Old World diaspora, and into the African homeland. Even in the Ottoman Empire, when the slave trade was outlawed in 1857, slave owners had to take better care of their slaves because of the difficulty of replacing them. As slaves but especially as free people, blacks of the diaspora moved deeply into industrial life.

Nineteenth-century economic change in Africa was at least as great as in the diaspora. The previous system of female slavery was replaced by one in which male and female slaves were held in slave villages at a distance from their owners. The growing world trade of the nineteenth century provided work for many. Agricultural exports from Africa, especially palm oil, palm kernels, peanuts, cloves, and later cocoa, grew at remarkable rates. Perhaps the most dramatic change for Africa was the sudden and complete conquest of the continent by several European powers, from about 1885 to 1900. The conquerors abolished the slave trade almost everywhere on the continent but rarely emancipated the slaves—so the African era of slavery without slave trade ran from about 1900 to 1930.

Only after World War II, as political movements arose and claimed independence, did urbanization, widespread literacy, and improved health care come to Africa. Africans hurried to take up urban life, as blacks of the diaspora had done more than a half century earlier. In country after country, black populations became dominantly urban. Professional classes expanded, and both in homeland and diaspora, blacks with higher education joined the top levels of business, medical, and scientific life.

For continent and diaspora, therefore, it is wise to keep in mind the many stages and levels of the economic systems in which black people have participated.

Families Under Pressure

Families are deeply rooted, regionally specific institutions, going back to earliest times—they are not easily remade by new technology or social fads. For patrilineal families, especially in West Africa and East Africa, the founding father was the key ancestor. For matrilineal families, especially in Central Africa and southeastern Africa, the founding mother was the key figure. Age-grade organizations, especially in East Africa and northeastern Africa, elected leaders of all the males or females who were close to one another in age. The full system of family life included traditions of birth, initiation, marriage, burial, and inheritance, plus rules for governance and adoption.

In the era of large-scale slave trade, African families came under several sorts of pressure, beginning with the grief over their losses. The export of a preponderance of males from West Africa and Central Africa meant that the continent was left with numerous captive females. These women became servants and concubines for their owners. As a result, African marriage systems were undermined and slavery became a growing part of family. Children of these relationships generally belonged to the owner, and the slave mother had no rights over them. In fact, she had no family, though she was held within a family.

In the Old World diaspora, most migrants were female, and many had children with their masters. In the Atlantic, most migrants were male—women were in short supply, and masters took some of them. Distance from home, the example of non-African family patterns, and uneven sex ratios each had their influence. Yet black women and men found each other and found ways to reaffirm or reinvent patterns of family life drawn from their African origins.

When there was a biological mix in the children—usually meaning a black mother and an Arab, Malagasy, European, or South Asian father—the children might become socially part of the black community (especially in the Americas, where that most often meant remaining in slavery). Or they might become part of the father's community—a common practice in the Old World, with striking results in such cases as the Moroccan king al-Mansur, the Duke Alessandro de Medici, and the Renaissance Spanish poet Juan Latino. Or they might become a distinct community, known as mulatto or people of color, as in the French Caribbean colonies. The complexities of biological and social mixes increased as the generations passed.

The religious affiliation of diaspora blacks, slave and free, influenced their family life. In most of the Old World diaspora, blacks were incorporated into the Islamic community. Similarly, in Europe, blacks were generally brought into Christian churches. In the Atlantic world, though only at the end of the eighteenth century, large numbers of blacks took up active participation in Christianity, both Protestant and Catholic. In almost every case, however, the principles and practices of African religious beliefs retained their significance.

In Africa, similar changes in religion and family structure came, but at a slower pace. Slavery did not really disappear until the 1930s, and the lack of full legal emancipation meant that families of slave descent may still suffer social discrimination. Rapid conversion to Christianity and Islam brought new social conventions and social practices to most Africans.

Another great change in black family life has come with formal education. First in the diaspora and then on the continent, black families have struggled and sacrificed to obtain education for their children, believing it a key to social advancement. The results, especially in the nineteenth and twentieth centuries, were extraordinary. At the same time, sending children to school meant giving up time with them and the opportunity to mold their skills and values. Particularly in Africa, education often meant that the children would join a new language community. Formal education has brought great benefits, but it leaves new challenges to families wishing to preserve their traditions.

The pressures on diaspora families were different from those in Africa, so that some family practices in homeland and diaspora diverged. Yet other characteristics of family life appear throughout the black world.

Culture

As indicated by the subtitle, "a history through culture," the theme of culture receives a particular sort of attention in this book. Of the five main themes, this one is privileged in that it does the most to help to depict the voices and outlooks of the black people who are our subject. In recent times, black voices have expressed themselves in a flood of creativity through the written word of poetry, novels, and essays, and through vocalized words in music, poetry, and oratory. For earlier times, we have lost most of the words spoken and written by black people, but we have many other records of their self-expression. People have represented the world and their responses to it not only through the spoken and written word but through visual representations, material culture, understandings of the spiritual world, social values, and knowledge of many other sorts. Taken together at the scale of whole societies, these cultural expressions add up to "macrocultural" contours of the civilizations of black people. The same cultural expressions, examined at a more intimate and personal scale, are the "microcultural" dimensions of expressive, material, societal, and reflective culture. This history through culture, rather than relying simply on the historian as narrator, will seek out the commentary of black people on their lives, as expressed in verbal and nonverbal media, at the levels of whole societies and individuals.

The "Macroculture" of Civilization

The idea of "African culture" or "black culture" is labeled with what can be called a "macrocultural" term. That is, "African culture" assumes there is an overall set of practices and identities shared by people of Africa and, perhaps, the African diaspora. In this sense, "culture" is parallel to "civilization," so that "African culture" can be compared and contrasted with Western culture, Islamic culture, Indian culture, Chinese culture, and so forth. Such terms are widely used, but they are problematic because they refer to vague generalities more than to specifics, and they overlap extensively. Thus Trinidad and South Africa can each be labeled African, Western, Islamic, Indian, and Chinese in their culture all at once, even though the two countries are quite distinct from each other. Macrocultural discussions, therefore, tend to be about cultural reputations rather than about actual cultural practices. We cannot escape such discussions, but they make progress only when they get more specific.

For instance, while this volume discusses the changing cultural reputations of black people, it gives more attention to reviewing their practical cultural contributions. In this regard, it draws attention to the fact that at the very moment black people were most denigrated in global cultural comparisons, people in Africa and the diaspora were developing important cultural innovations in music, dance, and visual art. These innovations enriched black communities and then spread to other communities: for example, ragtime pianists in the United States, most famously Scott Joplin, dominated sheet-music sales and then music-roll sales for the newly invented player pianos. And while many whites dismissed the possibility of black creativity, a few attended to and learned from the voices or images from the creative repertoire of black communities: at the opening of the twentieth century, African sculpture inspired Spanish artist Pablo Picasso's contribution to the new genre of cubism in painting, German ethnologist Leo Frobenius published the first three volumes of his study of African culture history, and the British Museum gathered a huge collection of sculpture from the newly conquered kingdom of Benin. As the twentieth century progressed, black people continued to make significant contributions in philosophy, education, government, literature, and film. Black culture, overall, has changed in fascinating ways with time.

The "Microculture" of Cultural Production and Representation

The coming chapters note the difference between elite culture and popular culture, distinguishing those who performed for kings and generals from those who performed for village communities. Elite and popular culture, though they shared traits when they came from the same society, emphasized different values and styles. With time, changing technology and political values gave steadily greater scope to popular culture. Larger theaters, expanded print runs, phonographs, motion pictures, radio, audiotapes, television, videotapes, and the Internet have bridged the old gap between elite and popular spheres. Black popular culture, amplified through this succession of media, conveys artful sounds and images. It also conveys profound social meanings.

To explore the details of human creativity, we must break down the general term "culture" into its various microcultural aspects. We need to explore the details of how people have represented their outlooks and experiences. Here is a simple terminology to help classify the details. *Expressive culture* includes visual art, music, literature, and other interpretations of feelings—this is the category most easily understood as artistic. The *material culture* of the African diaspora consists of such physical manifestations of creative energy as dress, architecture, tools, and cuisine. *Reflective culture* encompasses philosophy, knowledge, and belief. *Societal culture* is the creation and modeling of family patterns, political culture, and rituals.

These terms will reappear when we discuss cultural representations of major issues and events in the history of Africa and the African diaspora. For instance, the drums of West Africa and Central Africa, while they serve as instruments for music, a form of expressive culture, are themselves products of *material culture*. The wide distribution and shared characteristics of drums shows they originated in the distant past. They provide a central element in the region's cultural repertoire. The effectiveness of drums in evoking feeling and meaning has also resulted in their being used for many purposes, some of them contradictory. These drums spread material culture to the Americas and to the world as part of the African diaspora, bringing the expressive culture of their music with them.

Storytelling—for audiences of all ages—is a main form of African *expressive culture*. Among the best-known series of stories is the Akan-language tales of Anansi, the trickster spider who regularly outwitted those more powerful than he. Especially in Jamaica, enslaved settlers from the Gold Coast revised the Anansi stories to make them appropriate for servants seeking to outwit masters. With each new generation, these tales became more ingrained in the Jamaican national culture.

For *reflective culture* in the African diaspora, two contradictory but complementary philosophies developed in the mid-twentieth century, as black people pressed ever more forcefully to gain citizenship rights. One was the philosophy of revolutionary nationalism articulated by Martinique-born Frantz Fanon, as a result of his participation in the Algerian war of national liberation during the 1950s. Fanon found violence to be an inevitable and indeed beneficial aspect of breaking the hold of colonial masters. The other, a philosophy of nonviolent resistance to racial segregation in the United States, emerged at the same time from the speeches of Martin Luther King Jr., who believed that nonviolent resistance could ultimately force authorities to give up their policies of oppression. The two sets of ideas influenced many events in society as well as each other.[17]

Societal culture consists of roles, traditions, and modeling practices that maintain the coherence of societies. Of the many roles fulfilled in African societies, certain of them have been represented with particular attention: prominent among them are the roles of *mother*, *sage*, *king*, and *earth*. The role of motherhood, a widely celebrated aspect of societal culture of West Africa and Central Africa, is illustrated in figure 1.1, which depicts a nineteenth-century sculpture from the Afo-speaking region of Nigeria. The woman, nursing one child and carrying another on her back, conveys strength, love, and competence. The sage served as the seeker and dispenser of various sorts of knowledge: the ancestor with his or her knowledge of the family's experience, the blacksmith with the mysterious knowledge of iron, and the priests and diviners with their knowledge of the supernatural.

FIGURE 1.1 Motherhood

Wooden sculpture, seventy centimeters in height. Created in the nineteenth century by an artist of the Afo people of the Benue Valley, Nigeria. Note the second child on the back of the mother and the adult breasts of the nursing child on the mother's lap.

Source: Courtesy of Horniman Museum, London.

The king, leader of the community, protected its welfare and often provided its justice. The earth, guardian of fertility and renewal, was often seen as a female god.

In the diaspora, these roles became more complex, since the society of black people was usually encompassed by a larger, hegemonic society. The roles and representations of black society—mother, sage, king, and earth—persisted, though they were transformed by the diaspora situation.[18] But the hegemonic society imposed its own social roles on diaspora blacks during slavery and, after emancipation, on blacks as a subordinate racial group. These imposed social roles, reflecting economic production and cultural dominance, included the *performer, soldier, personal servant*, and *laborer*.

From early times, Africans in the diaspora were sought as performers: musicians, dancers, and poets. The Roman-era sculpture shown in figure 1.2, found in central France, shows an appreciation of a young artist: it is described as representing a street singer. Partly this was a response to their

FIGURE 1.2 Performer (c. 200 BCE)

Bronze statuette of Hellenistic style, retrieved in southern France and dated approximately 200 BCE, thought to be a street singer.

Source: Photo courtesy of Image of the Black in Western Art Research and Photo Archives at Harvard University.

distinctive appearance, and partly it was appreciation for the skills in dance and music sustained in African societies. In any case, these performers served to flatter their masters. In a second role, many African males of the Old World diaspora were recruited as soldiers, in freedom or slavery. They drilled and fought together for their generals and rulers. Military service, though dangerous, was a path to social mobility and sometimes real leadership. (Interestingly, military figures are rare in the iconography of the African homeland, at least until the eighteenth and nineteenth centuries, when warfare expanded so sharply.)[19] A third diaspora role often depicted is that of the personal servant: male and female (and often children), they acted as attendants for their owners. A far greater number of diaspora Africans, male and female, served as humble laborers in the fields, as artisans, and in the lowest of tasks.

In the portrayal of blacks by the dominant elites of diaspora societies or colonial Africa, one frequently finds representations of performers, soldiers, servants, and laborers. In contrast, the cultural production of black artists in both homeland and diaspora gives more attention to the roles of mother, sage, and king. As the illustrations in these pages will indicate, the representations of black society from within and from outside its limits have differed in their emphasis, though the two perspectives have also mixed and interacted.

These categories of material, expressive, reflective, and societal culture, while they indicate the range of human creative activity, are not entirely satisfactory, because so many human creations cross their borders. For example, clothing is part of material culture, but style of dress is an expression of identity. The varying patterns of dress provide wonderful examples of individual expression but are also examples of group solidarities. For dress and other aspects of culture, we would do well to analyze them categorically while also looking at them from an eclectic, impressionistic perspective. As another example of how cultural and social categories interact, with the end of slavery blacks were able to take control of their role as subordinated performers, which led to a burst of creativity throughout the black world. Overall, if we as observers give particular attention to the different types of cultural creativity in the African diaspora, we will encounter the comments of black people on the crises, achievements, and daily satisfactions in their lives.

Struggles

In sum, this history of connections across the African diaspora unfolds as the portrayal of race, economy, and family. It becomes "a history through culture" when the stories in these themes are told through the cultural representations of the black people who lived the history. The chapters to come divide this long history into five periods, each dominated by a diaspora-wide social struggle.

The introduction to the tale, focusing on the period from 1400 to 1600, unfolds as African societies developed in interaction with each other and with people from beyond the continent: they faced the benefits and problems of increasing social hierarchy. Then from about 1600, the long-distance slave trade, a long-existing but previously subordinate factor in African life, expanded rapidly. Slavery then became the principal determinant of the place of black people in the world. With slavery and empire, various forces based beyond African societies caused substantial oppression and change. In response, black people of both continent and diaspora carried on a series of social struggles that have continued evolving up to the present day. This dynamic of social struggles resonates across the aspects of life encompassed in the four priorities of Africa-diaspora studies. The forces of oppression and transformation against which black people struggled (and with which some still struggle) included slavery and empire; racial categorization and discriminatory beliefs in racial hierarchy; the global influence of industrialization in manufacturing, agriculture, and mining; and the imperial conquest of Africa by European powers, which placed people of the African homeland under a racialized and oppressive rule similar to that which had governed blacks of the diaspora throughout the history of the Atlantic slave trade.

Influential as these forces of dominance and oppression may have been, they are relegated to the secondary areas of this historical stage. At center stage are the campaigns of black peoples to counter this succession of obstacles and the innovations they created through their struggle to advance in connection with other black communities. Of course, black communities themselves were divided by class, color, culture, ethnicity, wealth, and political power, with alliances and divisions that added to the complexity of their collective social struggle. The tale in this book is told, in large part, through the cultural representations of life and its struggles. Not only did black people go through the experiences of life and death, slavery and freedom, but they created representations of those experiences in song and literature, in family practices, in dress, and in their spiritual life. By focusing on the cultural expression of black people over the last five centuries, we can attempt to hear their voices and share their feelings. This focus on popular cultural expression enables us to emphasize a consistent thread over the large geography and hundreds of years that form the history of the African diaspora.

The story unfolds in a chronological organization. I have proposed boundaries for the five main periods of this narrative in an attempt to identify significant turning points for the African continent and for peoples of the diaspora. Within each period, the narrative explores major developments for Africa, the diaspora, and the subregions of each; it traces the themes of race, economy, culture, family, and, especially, connections among regions and themes. The chronological approach makes it easier to argue for the development and impact of historical patterns—sometimes a new pattern would remain in place permanently, while other patterns brought further change in later times. Wherever possible, I present the story of change, continuity, and connection in the African diaspora through social struggles and their representation in the various forms of popular culture.

Chapter 2 traces the processes of *forging connections* among Africans at home and abroad from early times, and it then explores the dilemmas of *rethinking hierarchies* in the years from 1400 to 1600. It portrays the development of Africa—the connections of ideas and experiences among different regions and groups that led to epic poetry honoring African kings and polyrhythmic music sustaining families and villages. The chapter emphasizes the migrations of Africans to Europe, Asia, and different parts of Africa, as well as the migrations from Asia and Europe into Africa. It also addresses the continuation of these cultural and migratory traditions in the early encounters of Europeans and Africans on the coasts of Africa. But from about 1400, changes within the continent combined with influences from outside to expand African hierarchies and create new tensions. The opening of contacts across the Atlantic led eventually from discovery to oppression. The Spanish domination of the Americas fostered development of a new world economy in which silver, sugar, gold, and tobacco traded across great distances. The Indian Ocean shores reoriented their economies to participate in these new dimensions of world trade. By 1600, Africa's part in the emerging worldwide economy was shifting from exporting gold to providing labor. As a result, the existence of Africa and the growing African diaspora became centered on struggles over slavery and its consequences.

Chapter 3 chronicles the *struggle for survival* in Africa and the diaspora from 1600 to 1800. Enslavement expanded in Africa throughout these two centuries and contorted, as a result, the societies from which the captives came. The enslaved peoples, sent into region after region of the Americas, relied on their cultural and religious traditions to survive and to serve their captors. The burgeoning global economy led to expanded enslavement of Africans along the shores of the Mediterranean Sea and the Indian Ocean and within Africa. Many souls were lost, but African societies and the new societies of Africans in the Old World diaspora and the Americas survived. By 1800, the rise of an Atlantic antislavery movement and the success of the Haitian Revolution had put the global system of slavery into crisis.

Chapter 4 presents the nineteenth century as a *struggle for emancipation*. Those in slavery fought for their freedom, sometimes with allies of all colors among those already free, and they developed powerful rhetoric and soulful music to sustain their campaigns. At the same time, enslavement continued and slavery expanded in some parts of Africa and elsewhere in the Old World. In 1900, millions remained in captivity in Africa. Those freed from slavery subsequently experienced constraints on their legal rights to property and social equality. They also faced a decision between assimilating into dominant cultures and developing new forms of music, dress, and literature. Further challenges to black communities came from the widespread migration of competing white and Asian workers, the expansion of European empires, the elaboration and dissemination of pseudoscientific theories of racial hierarchy, and the spread of racial segregation. This complex struggle for emancipation represents a crucial chapter in human history and a turning point in defining "modernity."

Chapter 5 addresses the *struggle for citizenship* from 1900 to 1960. As black people gained their legal freedom, they still faced a long struggle for recognition of their citizenship. In Africa, people found themselves under European colonial rule with second-class citizenship at best. Africans on the continent, both in slavery and freedom, found governments and missionaries outlawing their traditions. In the Old World diaspora, blacks remained under imperial domination. In Latin America, blacks avoided segregation but suffered neglect of their needs and identity. Despite this repression, in this same era blacks of all social classes throughout the diaspora produced works of music, dance, and literature befitting a life increasingly based in expanding cities. The recognition of independence for most African countries and some Caribbean nations by 1960 and the affirmation of civil rights in the United States brought the struggle for citizenship a remarkable set of victories.

Chapter 6 traces the years from 1960 to 2000 in terms of the *struggle for equality* for black people in the Americas, in Africa, and elsewhere in the Old World. This was a struggle for equality in education, earning power, and political representation within national societies and for equality on a transnational and global level. Greater political power brought new contacts and cultural exchange among black peoples, and emerging black heroes in the arts and sports were celebrated both by blacks and the world at large. Migrations from the Caribbean to Europe signaled a rush of migrants from rural to urban areas throughout the black world. African-descended people of South Asia and western Asia became more conscious of the diaspora. Racism was increasingly decried in social and scientific circles, and more black people rose to wealth and social prominence. Still, the overall relative wealth of blacks continued to decline, a circumstance worsened by medical inequalities that became painfully obvious when the HIV/AIDS epidemic raged across southern and Central Africa and the Americas.

The brief epilogue poses several very important questions pertaining to the future of the African diaspora. In a book that mostly emphasizes the importance of looking back to see where people have come from, this book's conclusion reminds us that black people at every stage have been looking forward and working to create a future. The history of the African diaspora suggests certainties and interesting possibilities for the future identity of black people and the future of racism in society.

I chose the chronological approach presented here, most generally, to make the case for the common struggles and repeated interactions of people across the black world, rather than to encase each region in a separate chapter focusing on its uniqueness. Sections concentrating on Africa, the Caribbean, or the United States would tend to convey the impression that each regional history developed in isolation from the others, and the order of those chapters would tend to set a hierarchy among the regions. The advantage of my chronological organization is that it emphasizes the similarities and links among regions of the black world: the reader may be surprised to see the number of parallels among regions of the African diaspora within each time period. But chapters separating one period from another also have their disadvantage: they may suggest that each century of the history was cut off from others. To respond to this issue and address major questions of continuity and change over time, I have sought to trace five main themes by returning to them chapter after chapter: (1) the overall nature of connection and interaction for Africa and the diaspora, (2) the changing discourse on race, (3) the changing economic structures within which people worked, (4) patterns of family life, and (5) the evolution of forms of popular culture.

Through the chronological organization of the book, I offer an encompassing narrative for the African diaspora as a whole. Of course there are more localized narratives that have their place. For each African nation, there is a tale of the heritage from early times, survival under colonial rule, and the creation of modern national identity. In the Americas, Caribbean narratives, narratives of black people in North America, and Afro-Latin American narratives each retain specific angles on the experience of the Middle Passage, slavery, emancipation, and creation of modern black communities. Similarly, the tales of the African diaspora in the Indian Ocean, in western Asia, North Africa, and in Europe have their specificity. And aside from regional narratives, there are thematic narratives emphasizing pan-African political identity, narratives of conversion to Christianity or to Islam, and stories of cultural transformation or reaffirmation.

My purpose in this volume is to present a narrative that envelops the localized tales of black communities and emphasizes the overall contours and shared patterns in the experience of black people over the past six centuries. It appears to me as a distinctive narrative of the struggle and achievement of black people as they played their part in creating the modern world. This look at the common heritage of black people—linking Africa, the Americas, and elsewhere—yields a perspective and a set of insights valuable for the history of every black community within the African diaspora. By the same token, this six-century view of the African diaspora provides historical lessons of equal significance for the many other communities with whom black people have been in contact.

Out of the continent on which humanity first emerged have come repeated bursts of migrants. In Africa and in the diaspora surrounding it, people have moved, settled, warred, and mixed in various patterns. First, it was settlers moving to lands empty of humanity and gradually building up populations in each region. In the time within the past forty thousand years, minor genetic changes among settlers in the various regions created superficial but functional changes in physical exterior that came to be labeled— much later—as "race."

Even as the great early civilizations emerged on each of the continents, Africa remained a region of innovation and interaction and a source of new migrants. The world was now more thickly settled, but labor was always in demand. Diaspora took new forms: movement by conquest, movements of preachers and traders. As rulers arose and gained wealth and power, they demanded laborers. With labor in short supply and transportation costly, the use of capture and enslavement as a solution grew.

Five centuries ago, bold sailors reconnected the Americas to the rest of the world. In another century, European rulers in the Americas set up a great demand for labor. They seized the previous system of migration, which had long brought small numbers of slaves to Eurasian centers of wealth, and turned it into an unprecedented flow of captives from western Africa to the eastern American shores. For the sixteenth through the nineteenth centuries, the expanded system of slavery—and its accompanying practice of racial discrimination—transformed not only the Americas but also most of Africa, the shores of the Indian Ocean, and much of Europe and western Asia. During all of that time but especially in the nineteenth century, a great struggle for emancipation gradually reduced slavery back to its earlier, marginal level. Even with the emancipation of slaves, the history of slavery and racial oppression continued to haunt Africa, the diaspora, and the world, and it mixed with the trends of industrialism, nationalism, and militarism. The migrations continue for Africans and people of African descent, and so do the interactions of communities throughout continent and diaspora. The story of these amazing, transforming events and experiences begins in the next chapter.

Suggested Readings

Diaspora

The two principal writings of W. E. B. Du Bois on the full extent of the African diaspora are *The Negro* (New York: Henry Holt, 1915) and *The World and Africa* (New York: The Viking Press, 1946). Du Bois relied significantly on the well-informed but racially prejudiced H. H. Johnston, *The Negro in the New World* (London: Methuen & Co., 1910) and *A History of the Colonization of Africa by Alien Races* (Cambridge: Cambridge University Press, 1905). Du Bois's vision of an African encyclopedia is carried out in one form in Kwame Anthony Appiah and Henry Louis Gates Jr., eds., *Africana: The Encyclopedia of the African and African-American Experience* (New York: Basic Books, 1999); and in another form under Saburi O. Biobaku, director, *The Encyclopedia Africana Project* (available online at http://www.endarkenment.com/eap/). The most influential early works using the term "African diaspora" are Martin L. Kilson and Robert I. Rotberg, eds., *The African Diaspora: Interpretive Essays* (Cambridge, Mass: Harvard University Press, 1976); and Joseph E. Harris, ed., *Global Dimensions of the African Diaspora* (Washington, D.C.: Howard University Press, 1982). See also Graham W. Irwin, *Africans Abroad: A Documentary History of the Black Diaspora in Asia, Latin America, and the Caribbean During the Age of Slavery* (New York: Columbia University Press, 1977).

For a recent and concise but important survey of the African diaspora, see Michael Gomez, *Reversing Sail: A History of the African Diaspora* (Cambridge: Cambridge University Press, 2004); see also Michael Gomez, ed., *Diasporic Africa: A Reader* (New York: New York University Press, 2005). An earlier survey by Michael L. Conniff and Thomas J. Davis, *Africans in the Americas: A History of the Black Diaspora* (New York: St. Martin's Press, 1994) is informative but heavily political. Ronald Segal's two surveys, *The Black Diaspora: Five Centuries of the Black Experience Outside Africa* (New York: Farrar, Straus and Giroux, 1995) and *Islam's Black Slaves: The Other Black Diaspora* (New York: Farrar, Straus and Giroux, 2001) are less dependable. In an earlier work, Vincent Bakpetu Thompson provided an introduction to the Atlantic diaspora: Thompson, *The Making of the African Diaspora in the Americas, 1441–1900* (New York: Longman, 1987), and a revised edition, *Africans of the Diaspora: The Evolution of African Consciousness and Leadership in the Americas* (Trenton, N.J.: Africa World Press, 1999). Edward A. Alpers is now completing a survey of the African diaspora in the Indian Ocean, and other works are in preparation.

For works on concepts overlapping that of the African diaspora, see Molefi Kete Asante, *Afrocentricity*, new rev. ed. (Trenton, N.J.: Africa World Press,

1988); Asante, *The Afrocentric Idea* (Philadelphia: Temple University Press, 1998); Paul Gilroy, *The History of Africa: The Quest for Eternal Harmony* (London: Routledge, 2007); Paul Gilroy, *The Black Atlantic: Modernity and Double Consciousness* (Cambridge, Mass.: Harvard University Press, 1993); Paul Gilroy, *Against Race: Imagining Political Culture Beyond the Color Line* (Cambridge, Mass.: The Belknap Press of Harvard University Press, 2000); and John K. Thornton, *Africa and Africans in the Making of the Atlantic World, 1400–1680* (New York: Cambridge University Press, 1992). For the founding work in a large literature on the volume of transatlantic slave trade, see Philip D. Curtin, *The Atlantic Slave Trade: A Census* (Madison: University of Wisconsin Press, 1969).

Race

The historical and sociological literature on race is immense and complex. Three useful primers are George M. Fredrickson, *Racism: A Short History* (Princeton, N.J.: Princeton University Press, 2003); Michael Banton, *Racial Consciousness* (London: Longman, 1988); and Kevin Reilly, Stephen Kaufman, and Angela Bodino, eds., *Racism: A Global Reader* (Armonk, N.Y.: M. E. Sharpe, 2003). On the recent scientific advances on human evolution and the remarkable biological similarity of all humans, see Luigi Luca Cavalli-Sforza, *Genes, Peoples, and Languages* (Berkeley: University of California Press, 2001); and Christopher Stringer and Robin McKie, *African Exodus: The Origins of Modern Humanity* (New York: Henry Holt, 1997). On conceptions of race in the ancient Mediterranean, see Frank M. Snowden, *Before Color Prejudice: The Ancient View of Blacks* (Cambridge, Mass.: Harvard University Press, 1983); and Benjamin Isaac, *The Invention of Racism in Classical Antiquity* (Princeton, N.J.: Princeton University Press, 2004). For debates on race in the nineteenth and twentieth centuries, see George Reid Andrews, *Afro-Latin America, 1800–2000* (New York: Oxford University Press, 2004); Peter Wade, *Race and Ethnicity in Latin America* (Chicago: Pluto Press, 1997); Neil MacMaster, *Racism in Europe, 1870–2000* (New York: Palgrave, 2001); Edward Said, *Orientalism* (New York: Pantheon, 1978); and Paul R. Spickard, *Mixed Blood: Intermarriage and Ethnic Identity in Twentieth-century America* (Madison: University of Wisconsin Press, 1991).

Economy and Family

For a study of the place of Africans in the early stages of the industrial revolution, see Joseph E. Inikori, *Africans and the Industrial Revolution in England: A Study in International Trade and Economic Development* (Cambridge: Cambridge University Press, 2002). The classic early statement of this issue is Eric Williams, *Capitalism and Slavery* (Chapel Hill: University of North Carolina Press, 1944). Writings on the economic lives of black people in the nineteenth and twentieth century have been limited to national rather than pan-African perspectives.

For pioneering studies on black families in North America, see E. Franklin Frazier, *The Negro Family in the United States* (Chicago: University of Chicago Press, 1939); and Herbert G. Gutman, *The Black Family in Slavery and Freedom, 1750–1925* (New York: Vintage, 1977). For African families, leading colonial-era studies in British social anthropology are summarized in A. R. Radcliffe-Brown and D. Forde, eds., *African Systems of Kinship and Marriage* (London: Oxford University Press, 1950). Anthropologist Leo Kuper presents a forceful critique of social anthropology in *The Invention of Primitive Society: Transformations of an Illusion* (London: Routledge, 1988). For a study of urban African family history, see Kristin Mann, *Marrying Well: Marriage, Status, and Social Change Among the Educated Elite in Colonial Lagos* (Cambridge: Cambridge University Press, 1985).

Culture

Contending positions in explaining the dynamics of cultural change in the African diaspora have been set forth in Frazier, *The Negro Family in the United States*; Melville J. Herskovits, *The Myth of the Negro Past* (New York: Harper & Brothers, 1941); and Sidney Mintz and Richard Price, *The Birth of African-American Culture: An Anthropological Perspective* (Boston: Beacon Press, 1992). For an approach in art history that gives more attention to survival than creolization, see Robert Farris Thompson, *Flash of the Spirit: African and Afro-American Art and Philosophy* (New York: Random House, 1983). For a range of cultural studies on the African diaspora, see Isidore Okpewho, Carole Boyce Davies, and Ali A. Mazrui, eds., *The African Diaspora: African Origins and New World Identities* (Bloomington: Indiana University Press, 1999); and Kristin Mann and Edna G. Bay, eds., *Rethinking the African Diaspora: The Making of a Black Atlantic World in the Bight of Benin and Brazil* (London: Frank Cass, 2001).

Struggles

The notion of "social struggles," as used in the organization of this book, draws on the notions of historical agency and social movements, each of which has been developed in a substantial literature. A key development of the understanding of agency (or self-affirmation) is presented in E. P. Thompson, *The Making of the English Working Class* (New York: Vintage, 1963); the analysis of social movements is reviewed in Charles Tilly, *Social Movements, 1768–2004* (Boulder, Colo.: Paradigm Publishers, 2004). On emancipation as a global social movement, see Leo Spitzer, *Lives in Between: The Experience of Marginality in a Century of Emancipation* (New York: Hill and Wang, 1999). On the continuing debate over modernity in black communities, see David Marriott, *Haunted Life: Visual Culture and Black Modernity* (New Brunswick, N.J.: Rutgers University Press, 2007).

≡ 2 ≡

Connections to 1600

Musa, the *mansa* (emperor) of Mali, left his capital of Niani in 1324 (the year 724 of the Islamic calendar) in the company of a great entourage. He set out for the northern boundaries of his realm and then across the Sahara in a two-month crossing. Once across the desert, Musa, his entourage, and the other pilgrims from the savanna country joined with the pilgrims from the Maghrib, or "West" of North Africa. All were headed for Mecca to complete their duties of pilgrimage, the *hajj* to the most sacred places of their Islamic faith. The emperor's own name of Musa (Moses) reflected the historic depth of his religious tradition. Mansa Musa's pilgrimage expedition was perhaps the largest to that date from West Africa, but every year for centuries Islamic believers from that region and other parts of the continent had made the journey to Mecca.

As the Malian and Maghribi pilgrims moved parallel to the Mediterranean shoreline toward Cairo, they sent advance teams to that great city to prepare accommodations. The pilgrims emerged from the desert near the Egyptian pyramids and sent word to notify the Mamluk sultan who governed in Cairo. Musa had brought perhaps a hundred camel loads of gold dust for gifts and purchases. According to reports, his expenditures were so extravagant that the value of the *dirham*, the Egyptian currency, declined.

After leaving Cairo, the Malian expedition crossed the Sinai Desert to the Arabian Peninsula and then traveled south to Medina and Mecca, now as part of the much larger annual caravan of pilgrims moving south from Damascus. The Malians were part of the cosmopolitan mixture of Muslims that came from as far east as China and Southeast Asia. In Mecca, the emperor Musa joined everyone else in walking seven times around the Kaba to honor God, the early prophet Abraham, and the final prophet Muhammad. And in the five times each day they were called to prayer, the Malians doubtless also reflected on an earlier member of the African diaspora: Bilal ibn Rabah, the slave son of an Ethiopian-born mother. Bilal became a companion of Muhammad and an early convert to Islam despite the punishments from his master. He was the first muezzin, or prayer caller, noted for his strong, beautiful voice, and he set the muezzin traditions that continue, with some modifications, to this day.

Owing to exceptional cold in Mecca, Mansa Musa's entourage lost many camels and had to buy more for the return. On the way back, they lost contact with the main caravan and wandered in the desert for some time before reaching the Sinai Peninsula. Back in Cairo, the emperor now had to borrow fifty thousand dirhams from leading merchants to finance his trip home. (One trader's son accompanied the emperor to Mali and there arranged for partial repayment of the loan.) On the way back, Mansa Musa attracted a leading Andalusian poet and architect, al-Tuwayjin, as a companion. Once in Mali, al-Tuwayjin built a domed and plastered building in the Andalusian style.

Black Voyagers in Africa and Eurasia Before 1400

What paths did African societies follow in the times before the slave trade expanded? What choices did African families face? What experiences awaited the Africans who left their homeland—slave or free, destined for the Old World or the New? This chapter, starting with an emphasis on the long pattern of African migration, describes the land and human geography where Africans lived and traveled. It documents the web of connections reaching across the African continent and explores the dilemmas of expanding hierarchy in African life—including slavery.

Mansa Musa in the 1320s and, seven centuries earlier, the mother of Bilal ibn Rabah, followed paths across Africa and out of the continent that many had trod before them. Sub-Saharan Africans traveled beyond the continent as individuals and government representatives. For example, the Kingdom of Kush, which existed for many centuries in the Nile Valley, had conquered and ruled Egypt for half a century (712–664 BCE). After Alexander and then the Romans gained control of Egypt, Kush maintained trade and diplomatic relations with those Mediterranean powers.

In the times of the Hellenistic and Roman states, Greek merchants sailed the Red Sea to the East African coast and to India. Meanwhile, Semitic-speaking migrants came from southern Arabia to Ethiopia and Eritrea in the first millennium BCE and eventually founded Aksum, a highland capital in Ethiopia that became the seat of a great kingdom. In the fourth century CE, the Aksum empire conquered Meroe, the Kush capital in what is now Sudan, and went on to reach its greatest extent over the next three centuries, ruling much of Yemen, most of Ethiopia and Eritrea, and much of the middle Nile Valley. Aksum traded actively with India, Persia, Egypt, and other African regions. The kingdom's port of Adulis was a place through which elephants, gold, perfumes, and animal skins were exported into the wider world of maritime trade.

It was through these trading contacts that Christianity grew in Aksum. The bishop, or *abuna*, of the Aksumite church was appointed by the archbishop of Alexandria, who headed the Monophysite church, one of the major branches of Christianity in that day. The Aksumite church maintained a house of worship and a monastery in Jerusalem. Christianity gained a foothold in Ethiopia at much the same time as in the Black Sea region of Georgia, and the Georgian Christians also kept a monastery in Jerusalem. Through this link, the two churches maintained regular and cordial relations.

Travel in the arid, northern portions of Africa improved with the arrival of horses and camels. On land, Saharan travel expanded with the help of horse-drawn carts during Phoenician times, the second millennium BCE, but that practice declined when the desert became too dry to sustain the horses. Domesticated camels arrived in North Africa from Arabia in the time when the Greeks and Carthaginians dominated the Mediterranean, as early as 500 BCE. Some of the Maghrib Berbers then became specialists in raising camels, moving steadily into the Sahara Desert and inhabiting an area that had become almost uninhabited as the Sahara desiccated. At much the same time, camel herding spread from South Arabia to Somalia. Thanks especially to a reliance on horses and camels, the Arabs who traveled to Africa with Islam's expansion became the largest group of Eurasian immigrants, succeeding the Phoenicians, Greeks, Romans, Yemenis, and even the Germanic-speaking Vandals who came before them.

The oceans also brought a variety of peoples and practices to Africa. Mariners from Indonesia arrived on the coast of East Africa some two thousand years ago, bringing outrigger canoes, xylophones, Asian yams, and a penchant for building stilt houses. These visitors also settled on the island of Madagascar, where they became the dominant population. Since Greek merchants were sailing the African coasts at the same time, one can surmise that their crews and passengers also included adventurers and settlers who stayed in Africa. In later centuries, mariners from Oman, Persia, and Gujarat settled on the coast of East Africa, and the influence of their Persian and Arabic languages on the Swahili of the coast is evident.

The contacts and migrations linking Africa and Eurasia became particularly apparent in the two centuries from 1050 to 1250—and they reveal the racial characterizations of that age. In those two centuries, alternating times of war and peace locked Christians and Muslims in intense contact all along the Mediterranean Sea and the Red Sea, the waters separating the two great continents (Africa and Eurasia) of the Old World. In the Iberian peninsula, Christian knights advancing from the north in hopes of what they called "reconquest" met defeat first by the Almoravids and then by the Almohads, two Berber dynasties based in Morocco that ruled the western Mediterranean with armies that included many black warriors. In Palestine, Catholic armies called together by the pope in Rome invaded and created Christian principalities that survived until their defeat by the Ayyubid leader Saladin and later by the Mamluks, both based in Egypt. In Ethiopia, the Christian Zagwe dynasty rose to power, constructing its famous rock-hewn churches in the late twelfth century and forming a redoubt against Islamic advance. The church of St. George at Lalibela (figure 2.1) is the most famous of these.

FIGURE 2.1 The Church of St. George at Lalibela, Ethiopia

Completed c. 1200 under the reign of King Lalibela of Ethiopia. The church is the best known of the twelve churches carved out of solid rock at a time of renaissance of Christian religion and the Ethiopian state.

Source: Photo courtesy of UNESCO.

People of the twelfth and thirteenth centuries did not know the term "race," yet they categorized one another by culture, lineage, and phenotype. In the wars and the enslavement that accompanied them, religion was as important as phenotype in determining race. For Christians, the term "Moor" in the west referred to Muslims and people with roots in the African continent, whether north or south of the desert. The term "Saracen" in the eastern Mediterranean referred to Muslims, whatever their color. In response, Muslims referred to "Franks," meaning Christians of whatever physical characteristics. The ongoing ebb and flow of capture, enslavement, and conversion moved warriors long distances in the service of many commanders. For example, when a third wave of Crusaders arrived in Palestine in the 1180s, Saladin made a preemptive military strike against the Christian Nubian kingdom on the middle Nile. He then sent his brother to seize Yemen, protecting it against any attack from Christian Ethiopia.

The wars between Christians and Muslims died down in the thirteenth century without much definitive resolution, but they did help increase the number of contacts between Africa and Eurasia, in particular diplomatic contacts. The Ethiopians, for example, occasionally sent missions to other parts of the Christian world, which had some significant effects. In 1441, two priests traveled from Jerusalem on an Ethiopian mission to the Catholic Council of Florence. The mission created great interest at the council, where delegates tended to label the king of Ethiopia as "Prester John." Rumors about Prester John, a mythical Christian priest and king of a wealthy empire somewhere in Asia or Africa, had circulated for centuries in Europe. Meanwhile, fifteenth-century Catholic priests were following the paths of Italian merchants into the Indian Ocean region. Islamic diplomatic contacts are illustrated, for instance, by the travels of the fourteenth-century jurist, Ibn Battuta, from his home in Morocco to the Indian Ocean, Central Asia, China, and Mali.

The expanding contacts also encompassed the continuing flow of Africans to the Persian Gulf and South Asia. At the other end of this trade route, in India, immigrants from Africa were often identified as "Habshis," referring to people from the Horn of Africa (modern-day Somalia, Ethiopia, Eritrea, and Djibouti), and "Siddis," referring to people from East Africa south of the Horn.[1] The chronicles of Indian history identify occasional Africans in leadership positions in Delhi (in the center), Gujarat (in the west), and Bengal (in the east). These migrants came as slaves and free people, and some gained substantial recognition and influence. For example, the Habshi Jalal al-Din Yaqut became a courtier in the Islamic kingdom of Delhi and a favorite of its ruler Queen Radiyya (r. 1236–1240). Over two centuries later, the Habshi palace guard commander in Bengal assassinated the sultan and took power in 1486 under the title Barbak Shah. His three successors on the Bengal throne were also Habshis.

Just as migrations to and from Africa put Africa in contact with other world regions, so also did migrations within Africa put African regions in contact with one another. Individual and group migrations were of many different sorts. A major group migration of medieval times was that of Nilotic-speaking people from the middle Nile Valley, who moved upstream to the area of the African great lakes between the tenth and fourteenth centuries CE. It seems that, compared to the groups they encountered, the age-grade organizations of these migrants helped them maintain their strength. Once in the highland areas of the lakes, they established kingdoms dominating the region's Bantu-speaking populations. The enclosures at Bigo bya Mugyenyi, great earthworks in northern Uganda built beginning in the fourteenth century, are remnants of the kingdoms created by these migrants.

Further south, in the upper Congo Valley, an individual migration came to have great significance. Chibinda Ilunga, an adventurous son of a Luba king who had no chance to succeed to the throne of his father, left his homeland sometime before 1600 and went southwest to the territory of the Lunda. There he met and married Rweej, a queen who had succeeded her brother as ruler of a kingdom. Chibinda Ilunga became king, and the retainers he brought with him helped establish the institutions of Luba-style kingship in what expanded to become the Lunda Empire, the preeminent power of the grasslands south of the equatorial forest. In the ideology of this new empire, the succeeding king took on not only the role but the actual person of his predecessor.

Yet another way to trace travel and communication across African lands is to follow the movement of material culture from one region to another along what I propose to call the *African Web*. This network of pathways and waterways linked African communities to neighboring lands throughout the continent. If villages were often autonomous, they were almost never isolated. Africa had a few main roads—from the Niger bend to Morocco, from the Ethiopian highlands to the Red Sea, and along the great navigable reaches of the middle Niger and middle Congo. But the continent had many more local pathways that linked each neighborhood to the next.

Many material-culture items percolated through the African Web. Musical instruments, for instance, were carried great distances, changing in form and social function as they moved. Thus the *mbira* was developed in Zimbabwe but spread all over the continent. The mbira is a flat piece of wood with metal keys attached to it. The musician plucks the keys by thumb and creates a melodic tune that can be amplified with resonators made of gourds. Mbira keys are made of iron, thus making it clear that mbiras in their present form were made perhaps no more than about two thousand years ago. (In Zimbabwe, children play mbiras with bamboo keys, suggesting that a bamboo version may have preceded the metallic mbira.) Over the centuries, the mbira migrated all the way across the African continent to Mali and Senegal.

Another musical migration centered on xylophones (also known as marimbas). Xylophones were first developed in Southeast Asia, and it appears that Southeast Asian mariners visiting the East African coast roughly two thousand years ago introduced the instruments to the region. Their canoes and houses stayed at the coast, but the accompanying xylophones, bananas, and yams passed from group to group of Africans. Probably as long ago as 1200 CE, xylophones had worked their way across the African savanna to Mali, where they became the instruments of kings. Yams and bananas stayed within well-watered, forested areas, but they too migrated to West Africa and throughout Central Africa. Another musical migration involved iron bells formed of two flat sheets bent and welded together. These bells had ritual significance for monarchs in the lower Niger regions of Benin and the Yoruba kingdoms, where they were first developed, and it was as royal bells that they spread over a large portion of Africa. They moved only slightly west of their homeland but traveled a great distance south and east, all the way to Zambia. Jan Vansina estimated that these bells were first developed about 450 CE and that they had reached Zambia by 1500.

Yet another African material-culture connection can be found in copper production and consumption. The rich copper deposits of Central Africa, at the headwaters of the Zambezi and the Congo, led to the production of copper ingots that circulated throughout the region. For West Africa, including the lower Niger and Cameroon, the demand for copper created a substantial trans-Saharan trade. The copper was exchanged for gold and then distributed throughout the sub-Saharan region.[2]

In sum, these examples show the multidirectional paths of communication across Africa. The three musical instruments just discussed moved from south to northwest, from east to west, and from north to southeast. Similarly, one can trace the movement of iron technology from the center of Africa and the Mediterranean throughout the continent; the tending of cattle and goats from northeastern Africa to the continent's southern and western extremities; and the movement of Asian yams, bananas, and xylophones from the Indian Ocean coast to Central and West Africa. All in all, Africans have shown themselves to be as receptive to travel and travelers as other humans. Africans have moved across their home continent and to adjoining continents by land and sea and hosted those coming from various regions of Asia and Europe to Africa. The movement of people, goods, and ideas across the African mainland was not restricted to a few great highways marked by cities and marketplaces. Thus, the African pattern is quite different from the trans-Asian Silk Road, with its main paths and waystations.[3] In Africa, people and their cultures moved across boundaries and barriers along every available trail. Innovations spread in all directions, sometimes rapidly and at other times in a more leisurely village-by-village progression. This African Web functioned (and continues to function) as an effective mechanism for disseminating material goods, cultural innovations, and information. As a result, since very early times, the African Web has linked the whole of the Eastern Hemisphere—Africa, Eurasia, and the neighboring islands—with a multidirectional network that promotes and facilitates the movement (albeit slow at times) of material goods, people, and ideas from place to place.

Africans at Home, up to 1400

While the passages above have emphasized the movements of Africans, it must be acknowledged that most people stayed close to home. African settlement patterns have been very stable. Permanent communities began to emerge some thirteen thousand years ago and gradually spread throughout the continent to all arable regions. From that time forward, Africans have been settled peoples in much larger numbers than they have been nomads. We turn now to a review of African regions and their inhabitants. Each region had its own name; only with time did it become possible to refer to the continent as a whole, once its size was understood. The term "Africa" was applied by the Romans to the area now known as Tunisia. They apparently borrowed it from the Phoenician term "Afryqah," meaning "colony." The Arabic term "Ifriqiya" indicated the same region. Gradually the term "Africa" spread, in various languages, to encompass the whole continent. Other regional terms, such as the Roman term "Mauretania" and the Greek term "Ethiopia"—as well as the Berber term "Guinea" and "Nobatia," which became "Nubia"— were sometimes applied to larger areas, but Europeans coming from the Atlantic were ultimately able to name the continent.

Geography

During the past century, a rather standard terminology, used throughout this book, has arisen for labeling the regions of the African continent. "North Africa" or "northern Africa" includes the area from the Sahara Desert to the Mediterranean. "West Africa" includes the region from the southern part of the Sahara to the Atlantic coast, from Senegal in the west to the eastern borders of Nigeria and Niger. "Central Africa" or "West Central Africa" includes the region bordering the Atlantic from Cameroon south through Angola, and goes east to the mountains at the eastern edge of Congo and north to the desert edge of Chad. "Southern Africa" includes modern Namibia, Zimbabwe, Mozambique, and the countries to the south. "Eastern Africa" includes the region from Mozambique north to Sudan—or it may be divided into "East Africa," from Mozambique to Kenya, and the more northerly "Horn" of Africa, plus the Nile Valley.

West Africa and Central Africa had the greatest interaction with the Americas through the Atlantic slave trade. But every region of Africa had some connection to the Atlantic slave trade, and the African diaspora in broad terms included people from every region moving either to their east and north (to the Indian Ocean, Asia, and the Mediterranean) or westward across the Atlantic.

The ecological regions of Africa cut across the conventional regions just described, as shown in map 2.1. Most Africans have always lived on the grasslands known as "savanna" that stretch in an immense semicircle from the Senegal Valley east to the Red Sea, south along the East African coast, and west to meet the Atlantic again at the southern fringe of the Congo River valley. The eastern portions of these grasslands between modern Ethiopia and South Africa—some at high elevations and some in lowlands—were the regions where the earliest hominids developed millions of years ago, and it was in these same regions that our own species of *Homo sapiens* emerged some two hundred thousand years ago. It consistently has been a hospitable environment for humanity. Nearly encompassed by Africa's semicircle of grassland lies a long band of dense forest. The forest skips along the West African coast from modern Guinea to Nigeria, and it broadens to include the area on both sides of the equator all the way to the highlands at the eastern frontiers of the Central African Republic and Congo-Kinshasa.[4] The forest too has supported populations, some dense and some sparse, back to very early times.

The waters surrounding Africa separate it from and link it to other regions. The eastern coast of Africa has been connected to Asia by sea lanes

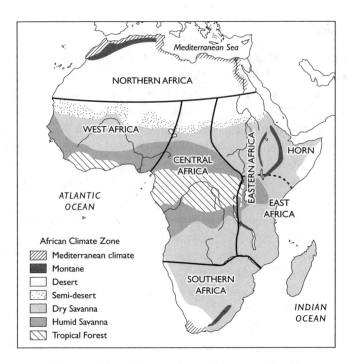

Africa's Mediterranean coast, simi-
larly, has been linked to Europe and Asia for thousands of years. The Atlantic

MAP 2.1 Africa, Showing Regions, Rivers, and Ecology

for thousands of years. From Madagascar and Mozambique in the south to
the Red Sea in the north, East African coastal populations have been in contact with one another and with the societies of Arabia, the Mediterranean,
Persia, India, and sometimes Indonesia. Africa's Mediterranean coast, similarly, has been linked to Europe and Asia for thousands of years. The Atlantic
coast of Africa stretches six thousand kilometers between the deserts of the
Sahara and the Namib. People have fished, voyaged, and produced salt along
it for thousands of years. But with no close connections to other lands, the
Atlantic coast experienced little development. In contrast, the East African
coast, which runs nearly three thousand kilometers from the mouth of the
Zambezi to the tip of the Horn at Cape Guardafui and another two thousand
kilometers up the Red Sea to Sinai, has been frequented regularly by local
and long-distance shipping since the times of ancient Egyptians, who knew
Ethiopia as "the land of Punt." Boat builders on the Atlantic coast did not
construct large sailing vessels like those of East African coastal dwellers, and
Atlantic coastal towns remained small compared to those of the Mediterranean and the Indian Ocean coast. The arrival of European vessels in the
fifteenth century changed all that.

The desert, finally, occupies a huge belt across the northern third of Africa, broken only by the Nile River and tenuous (though regularly traveled) caravan routes connecting North Africa to the savanna regions of West, Central, and East Africa. In addition to the Sahara, Africa's two other desert regions are the desert spanning Somalia and northern Kenya, adjoining the Indian Ocean, and the Namib Desert of Namibia, adjoining a long stretch of the Atlantic.[5]

Africa, the original homeland of human beings, has always been a relatively densely populated continent. The continent's population of eight hundred million today exceeds that of Europe and also exceeds the total population of the Americas. The present African population is eight times the hundred million persons commonly cited as having inhabited the continent in 1600, and recent research suggests that the African population at that time was actually somewhat larger. In any case, in 1600, the population concentrations in West, East, North, and Central Africa were each relatively dense on a world scale.

Language

Africa's population was as diverse in language as in location. Language communities are also historical communities, so that language often—though not always—correlates significantly with major aspects of culture. The distribution of African language groups (see map 2.2) shows that the peoples who speak the major modern languages have been in place for thousands of years. The four great language groups (or phyla) indicate the depth of African historical and cultural traditions, since languages and historical populations are significantly associated with each other. The language distributions thus provide a clear illustration of some of the major African cultural groupings.

The Nilo-Saharan languages extend between the center and east of the African continent. The largest number of Nilo-Saharan languages, and probably their ancestral homeland, can be found in the middle Nile Valley of modern Sudan. But major Nilo-Saharan languages are spoken in areas more than a thousand kilometers in various directions from this nexus: Songhay in the middle Niger Valley, Nubian in the Nile Valley in the desert region, Kanuri in the desert and desert edge in Chad, Eastern Sahelian languages in Chad and Sudan, Nilotic languages in the upper Nile Valley and, south to the equator, Luo and Maasai in Kenya and Tanzania.

Niger-Congo languages are spoken over roughly half of Africa's surface. These languages originated in and then spread from the West African savan-

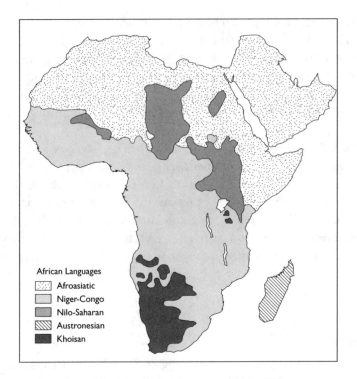

MAP 2.2 African Language Groups and Major Subgroups

nas.[6] The greatest diversity of Niger-Congo languages is still in West Africa: the main Niger-Congo languages there include Wolof, Maninka, Fulbe, Twi, Dogon, More, Gbe, Yoruba, and Igbo. The Bantu languages of Central, East, and southern Africa reflect the steady expansion of settlers whose ancestors began in southeastern Nigeria perhaps five thousand years ago. Among the major Bantu languages of today are Lingala in Central Africa, Swahili in East Africa, and Xhosa in South Africa.

Afroasiatic languages have their greatest variety at the frontier of Ethiopia and Sudan, where the ancestral languages of this group were first spoken. But speakers of these languages spread to other areas long ago. One group moved eastward to the Indian Ocean and then northward along the Red Sea and southward into what is today's Kenya and Tanzania—these are the Cushitic languages and include Somali and Galla. Later, a group moved west across the savanna to the area around Lake Chad—these people speak the Chadic languages, including the widely used Hausa. Still later, a group spread down the Nile Valley to the Mediterranean coast and then split into three subgroups. Those who stayed in the Nile Valley developed the language and society of ancient Egypt. Those who moved west gave birth to the Berber languages of the Maghrib and Sahara. Those who moved east to southwestern Asia gave birth to the Semitic languages. Of the Semitic languages, Ge'ez and Amharic developed later in Ethiopia as a result of migrations from south Arabia. Still later, Arabic spread widely into northern Africa, along with the Islamic religion.

Finally the Khoisan languages—historically very important in eastern and southern Africa—are now spoken by a small number of people in southwestern Africa and even smaller numbers in East Africa.[7]

Material Culture

Food practices, along with other customs and material aspects of African societies, correlate significantly with the large language groups just described. The association of food patterns and language groups implies that these are historical communities of great depth, though the common heritage has been developed in quite different ways by the peoples sharing each linguistic background. Every region of Africa created a characteristic diet, modifying the menu from time to time as innovations became available. Among Niger-Congo speakers, rice became a major crop for the western portion of West Africa, and yams became the principal crop in well-watered eastern portions of West Africa. Central Africans relied on yams and, once they became available, bananas. In the eastern portions of the great semi-circle of African savannas populated by Nilo-Saharan and Afroasiatic speakers, varying types of millet and sometimes sorghum provided the principal grain. Ethiopia's distinctive highlands enabled millet and wheat to be supplemented with teff and enset. North Africans relied principally on wheat. Various sorts of beans were grown throughout Africa, fruits were gathered in each region, and domestic animals were cared for: cattle in the savannas, camels in the deserts, horses for the elite in the continent's northern half, and sheep and goats everywhere.

Another aspect of material culture, iron technology, eventually provided a unifying element in African society. Iron is now thought to have developed independently in perhaps two different African regions—the Niger Bend and the Nile-Congo watershed—somewhat before 1000 BCE. The use of iron spread rapidly through West Africa and just as quickly through East Africa and southern Africa. (Iron technology first developed in Anatolia by 1200 BCE, but it spread slowly for several centuries.) Because of the high heat achieved in African furnaces, the technical quality of African iron, measured in terms of its purity and hardness, consistently rated high. But while the quality of African iron was excellent, the quantity of iron obtainable to African consumers was limited by two factors. First, few of the iron deposits available were of the relatively high ferrous concentration that made them easy to exploit with preindustrial mining technology. Low-grade iron deposits, such as those of Mauritania, have proven profitable in today's industrial era, but they were not economically feasible in earlier times. Second, iron smelting required massive amounts of wood for the furnaces. The relative scarcity of wood in areas of major African populations made it difficult to sustain large-scale iron production over long periods. Thus for the middle Nile Valley center of Meroe in the Kingdom of Kush, large-scale iron production took place two thousand years ago, but the shortage of firewood eventually brought an end to its prominence in this region. Similarly, for the area of Futa Jallon in modern Guinea, large-scale iron production in the tenth through twelfth centuries CE cleared the region's forests and led to an eventual collapse in iron output.

Iron made new weapons and new armor for warfare possible. The sword-wielding smiths of the savanna provided the essential force, along with the cavalry, behind the creation of the empire of Mali in the thirteenth-century wars of Sundiata Keita. (The griots, or praise-singers, celebrated Sundiata's conquests as comparable to those of Alexander the Great.) The development of iron tools for agriculture, construction, and artwork was more important than weaponry, because the former brought essential advances to African life. Iron needles enhanced textile production, knives eased many household tasks, and iron fishhooks and arrowheads increased the efficiency of fishing and hunting. Iron hoes simplified farming and expanded African agricultural production. Consequently, blacksmiths usually held honored positions often associated with mystery and spiritual power. Miners were also very important, but they rarely gained the prestige of blacksmiths. In later times, when European merchants were able to bring iron bars to trade, Africans bought them readily, thus expanding the blacksmith trade while reducing the work of miners.

Expressive Culture

The advance of woodworking tools—iron axes, knives, and adzes—modified the material world through boat building and home construction. These same tools contributed to interpretive expression when used to carve masks and other sculptures representing the world. The woodcarvings of Africa, especially those from Niger-Congo speakers of West and Central Africa, benefited from the development of iron tools. The basic ideas of wood sculpture carried across into other media, and sometimes it was the latter that survived. The terra-cotta sculptures from Nok in central Nigeria, created from one to three thousand years ago, show clear relationships to the brass sculpture of Ife and Benin done over five hundred years ago, and more recent wood sculpture from the same region shows a clear continuity with those brass figures.

Another remarkable expressive-culture tradition that characterizes the Niger-Congo–speaking peoples is polyrhythmic drumming, in which a unit or measure is played in different rhythms by different hands or percussionists: a common unit of twelve beats can be played in several ways at once, creating a complex but compelling overall structure and making many distinct compositions possible. The wide distribution of polyrhythmic drumming suggests the basic tradition goes back many thousands of years, though all players continue to modify the rhythms, performance styles, and cultural associations. (This rhythmic base need not lack for melody: voices, flutes, and other instruments add the melodic component.)

A related aspect of Niger-Congo drumming is that of "talking drums." This term can refer to drums used to send signals and messages from one area to another. It can also denote a more distinctive use: drums that "speak." Most of the Niger-Congo languages are tonal—with rising and falling inflections forming essential parts of the sound and meaning of each word. Drums can imitate these intonations and thus "call out" names and "tell" stories to and about those in the audience.

Drums of widely varying types but underlying similarity are used from Senegal to the coast of the Indian Ocean. The drums of West and Central Africa come in many sizes and shapes, carved out of logs in forms that are cylindrical, barrel-shaped, with a narrowed waist, or with one or more feet. The drumheads have been made of goatskin and other skins—sometimes the sex of the animal is important to the drum's nature. Drumheads are attached by nails, pegs, or laces, and tuned in various ways. Musicians usually played drums in groups, with selected drums for specific occasions. While the specificity of local traditions in drumming is impressive, even more impressive is the depth of shared and parallel drumming traditions across the whole wooded region. Bantu speakers have a single generic term for drums across the huge area they occupy: "ngoma." The ubiquity of this term indicates that Bantu-speaking migrants had drums four or five thousand years ago. Since the Niger-Congo languages are far more ancient than their Bantu subgroup, it is likely that drums go much further back, as does the tradition of modifying drums and rhythms.

Drums and the music they convey became powerful symbols in the lives and experience of Africans. Certain drums became symbols of royalty: large, deep-toned drums in particular. A number of kingdoms in the East African highlands used the term "ngoma" to mean "kingdom" as well as drum. But if the kings took control of some drums, they could not halt their use in family and village ceremonies and celebrations. New ideas about drums, like their use as symbols for kingdoms, spread over portions of the African continent. Sometimes individual ethnic groups had particular names and functions for drums, but most often the instruments and the way they were used spread across ethnic boundaries to neighboring groups.[8]

Another important element of African expressive culture involves the way people adorned their bodies. As in all cultures, African choices in dress and physical decoration "make a statement." The rock paintings of southern Africa—remarkable in their number, precision, and beauty—show the lives of stone-age people over two thousand years ago. In those days people wore little clothing—a short apron, skirt, or loincloth. But they also put on fancy headdresses, decorated their skin with paint, tattoos, and the marks of scarification, and adorned themselves with elaborate beads, bracelets, earrings, and tassels of feathers or fur. As southern Africa entered the Iron Age, people seemed to have had less time for or interest in body painting, and burials from that time show fewer body decorations.

Dress was sometimes a substitute for and sometimes a complement to body decoration. Prior to 1400, cotton provided the fiber for textiles in the northern half of Africa. Clothes made from raffia fiber drawn from selected palm trees were prominent in Central Africa. Across Africa's equatorial belt, barkcloth, made by pounding certain sorts of bark into a thin, supple covering, was the material for garments. Textiles were decorated with multicolored weaving, dyes, embroidery, and painting. Children commonly went with very little clothing until puberty; adults wore some clothes for modesty and more elaborate attire for special occasions such as funerals. Those of high rank wore distinctive ceremonial garments.[9] People who lived in the Saharan and Somali deserts needed protection from the sun in daytime and the cold at night; those who lived in mountainous areas needed additional layers to stay warm.

Societal Culture

African family life varied as widely as the continent's ecology, but some common points can still be advanced. Marriage generally anchored an alliance among families as well as between couples. Payment of a bride price or some other exchange of wealth or labor between families cemented the relationship. Women were strongly encouraged to marry, so they tended to do so young; widows were encouraged to remarry, sometimes to a brother of the deceased husband. Family organizations varied: some were patrilineages (tracing descent through the male line), some matrilineages (tracing descent through the female line), and some bilateral (tracing both sides). Matrilineal inheritance dominated in south-central Africa, among the Akan of West Africa, and in other cases such as the Berber-speaking Tuareg of the Sahara and the Nubians of the Nile Valley. Polygyny was legal in most African societies, but it was usually only powerful senior men who had more than one wife. The specifics of family life varied according to profession—farmers, herders, and artisans, for example—and according to the local ecology. Each society developed rules for housing children, married couples, and the elderly, as well as procedures for instructing and initiating youths into adulthood.

Reflective Culture

The spiritual traditions of African peoples have often been revised to account for recent events and new revelations, but they still can be traced back to their origins in very early times. The histories of words can reveal the histories of meanings. Christopher Ehret, working especially with evidence from language, has suggested that each of the four African linguistic phyla reflects ancient beliefs.[10] These beliefs regarding the nature of spiritual life and the problem of good and evil have been passed down over thousands of years. For people speaking Afroasiatic languages, two very common traditions are belief in a clan deity who watches over people within that community and rituals performed to cast out devils that have "possessed" individuals. Nilo-Saharan speakers often see the world as governed by an abstract animating force rather than a specific god. Occasionally, that force becomes disembodied and dangerous and requires rituals to calm it. Those speaking Niger-Congo languages have had pervasive beliefs in ancestral and natural spirits but also in the possibility of humans being possessed or turning into witches and sorcerers. To deal with problems from any of these beings, specialized doctor-diviners perform ceremonies to cure the afflicted or to identify and remove witches.

Africa up to 1400 functioned as a great, deeply varied continental system with connections between neighboring regions, forming an African Web. There was no uniformity in African life from region to region, nor did African villages and regions exist in isolation from one another. We have seen food crops, musical innovations, and political forms pass along their own pathways through the African Web. In much the same way, the slave trade and slavery gradually expanded to much of the continent.

Africans Rethink Their Hierarchies, 1400–1600

Africa's long history encompassed changes, evolutions, and reversals in every area of human activity. The pace of African change accelerated, however, in the period from 1400 to 1600. Partly these changes resulted from external influences, as Christians crept along the coasts of the continent and as interior regions expanded links with the Islamic heartland. In at least an equal degree, the accelerating changes in African societies resulted from domestic processes. Many of these changes, accumulating from domestic and external impulses, raised the question of hierarchy. Would African life become more hierarchical? Certainly, African societies were becoming more complex and more cosmopolitan, with greater pressures for differentiation. Would the growing number of social roles mean that some became dominant while others became subservient?

The question of hierarchy and social distinction is central to the interpretation of Africa's place in the world's societies. African social orders ranged from small communities to large kingdoms and were held together by a balance of egalitarian society and dominion. The work performed was allocated by sex, age, and ethnic group. Big men and kings had power within societies and control over individual destinies but also found the need to accommodate the desires of relatives, the decisions of councils of elders, and the demands of ritual procedures. The egalitarian social order was not perfect either: women and children who lost the protection of families through disease, famine, or warfare fell between the cracks and were subject to exploitation. The differences between common people and the elite showed up in many areas of material, expressive, and societal culture. Questions of hierarchy had arisen before in various parts of Africa, but the prevailing outlook had emphasized finding ways to allow additional complexity yet minimize hierarchy, in contrast to the greater prevalence of hierarchy in the organization and ideology of the societies of Eurasia. This section explores the African debates and changes in social hierarchy from 1400 to 1600—including the ultimate issue in hierarchy, the place of slavery in Africa.

Monarchy

By 1400, it appears, most Africans lived in societies with kings, though most of the kingdoms were small and localized. Many of the existing major kingdoms expanded in the following two centuries: Jolof in modern Senegal, the Mossi kingdoms in modern Burkina Faso, Benin in modern Nigeria, and Kilwa on the coast of modern Tanzania. The Ethiopian kingdom sustained itself; Mali weakened and was soon to be shouldered aside by rising Songhay. Kanem, on the eastern shores of Lake Chad—already known to Arab geographers in the ninth century—declined from its thirteenth-century peak. Pressured by attackers from the east, the monarchy and its supporters moved just before 1400 to the western side of Lake Chad and founded the kingdom of Kanem-Bornu.

Substantial new kingdoms formed in the fifteenth century. Kingdoms of Akan peoples emerged in modern Ghana; Gbe-speaking elites spread out from the Mono River town of Tado to establish kingdoms in modern Togo and Benin Republic. The kingdom of Kongo in the lower Congo River valley took form shortly before 1400 and rapidly became a large and well-structured state. Along the Indian Ocean coast, smaller Swahili-speaking sultanates expanded in alliance or in competition with Kilwa. In the highlands of East Africa, Nilotic-speaking immigrants known as BaChwezi formed the kingdom of Bunyoro and went on to create such kingdoms as Ankole, Burundi, and Rwanda.

The creation of new kingdoms continued in the fifteenth century. Mande migrants to modern Sierra Leone formed kingdoms. In the middle Nile valley arose the Funj state, supported by a mix of local groups and Arabic-speaking settlers from the north—it displaced the Christian kingdom of Alwa. In the inland southern savanna of the Congo Valley emerged the Kuba kingdom and the Lunda Empire. A set of Maravi kingdoms developed along the Shire River of modern Mozambique. Of course, the new kingdoms did not arise all at once and were certainly not created by a single group of founders. Yet the expanded scale of African monarchy in the fifteenth century is remarkable. Another layer of authority was expanding across the continent.

In a few cases, political change centered on external intervention. Immigrant groups were important in the Funj, Chwezi, and Lunda kingdoms, but in at least some cases the immigrant leaders won power through prestige rather than military might. Portuguese involvement—in Jolof in West Africa, Kongo in Central Africa, and in Mwenemutapa and Maravi in East Africa—weakened those states. The Ottoman Empire gave support to Adal on the Horn, which was fighting Ethiopia and its Portuguese allies. The most extraordinary instance of external intervention involved the collapse of Songhay, and we will return to it at the end of this chapter.

War accompanied statecraft. The expansion of great kingdoms went hand in hand, almost necessarily, with major military campaigns. Large armies of archers, spear carriers, and cavalry arose from time to time in the northern savanna, and the sieges of walled cities sealed the fates of many on each site. The military exploits of Sosso, Mali, Songhay, Kanem, and Borno are known in some detail, as are the wars of Christians and Muslims on the Horn in the fifteenth and sixteenth centuries. But military campaigns did not have to be fought by kingdoms. The oral traditions of the equatorial forest tell of the protracted war of Bolongo Itoko, a fourteenth-century struggle in which lancers advancing from the north were ultimately halted, near the westward bend in the Congo River, by archers and swordsmen from the south. The Jaga of west-central Africa from 1569 and the Zimba of East Africa from 1590 were improvised groups fielding mobile armies that conquered all in their way for a time—both were arguably reactions against expanded slave trade.

A common term that developed in many African languages was the equivalent of "big man"—an individual who had accumulated land, wealth, family, and recognition of his power or wisdom within his household or village. Such distinction had to be earned during the individual's lifetime rather than passing automatically from father to son. Jan Vansina, in his studies of the long-term history of the equatorial forest, has emphasized the recurring significance of big men in advancing new ideas in religion, social organization, and economic life.[11] Women in the same societies gained power in their own ways. Recent scholarship has identified parallel positions of leadership that a senior woman could gain through her children and through her control of household, family, and commercial activities. Such a "big mama" also had to win her eminence individually rather than inherit it.

Autonomous African societies found ways to govern without kings. While all African societies had clear conceptions of leadership and clearly identified leaders, not all Africans allowed the formation of distinctive elite groups with clear cultural attributes. Societies used alternative forms of leadership, such as secret societies, age grades, and the occasional emergence of prophets or military leaders to meet emergencies; family governance took care of life between crises. Yet these societies too felt the pressure to expand hierarchy.

Elite Culture

African hierarchies expanded not simply in the authority of monarchs and big men but also in the cultural representation of their leadership. Yet the works of African elite culture before 1600 appear to have been created with the logic of service to the community rather than as reminders of power imposed on obedient subjects. Take the monumental architecture of Great Zimbabwe produced by the Shona societies, for example.[12] These great stone monuments on the highlands of modern Zimbabwe are best seen as a ritual center rather than a palace. From the ninth century, Shona farming communities of increasing density began to mine and purify gold in the dry season. Their sales of gold and copper drew them into long-distance trade. In about 1000 CE, these communities began building stone walls to turn their houses into linked homesteads, and they expanded their stone carving. Social elites emerged to facilitate this organizing process, providing leadership through centers of worship rather than centers of domination. Larger stone works developed, and finally in the fourteenth century the monuments at Great Zimbabwe were built. The leaders of Zimbabwe attracted the most skillful artists and had them create unique examples of sculpture and architecture that stand out even today.

Similarly, the churches of Ethiopia and the mosques of the Swahili coast and the West African savanna can be seen as monuments to community as well as to state power. On the other hand, the great mud walls surrounding the Hausa cities of modern northern Nigeria were clear indications that military power was necessary to protect the bustling commerce of Kano, Katsina, Kebbe, and their neighboring cities.

Among the greatest achievements of African elites were the bronze and ivory sculptures of two neighboring kingdoms: the Yoruba-speaking kingdom of Ife and the Bini kingdom of Benin, both in southern Nigeria. The Ife bronzes of the fourteenth century were cast exquisitely using the lost-wax method, in which wax models form the basis for metallic casting. These works presented idealized but individual portraits of kings and queens. The example shown in figure 2.2 conveys a warm sense of respect and collaboration between the two aristocrats portrayed, rather than rulers who dominated by military might. The kingdom of Benin, which was founded with a crown brought from Ife, maintained a somewhat different, more authority-centered tradition of bronze and ivory sculpture into the nineteenth century. Benin and Ife were also surrounded by walls, a reminder that warfare was a danger, but the city walls overlapped with those surrounding family compounds, so that the kingdom could be represented as a great family.[13]

The surrounding Yoruba-speaking kingdoms of modern Nigeria, Benin Republic, and Togo reveal a clear example of the range in size and complexity of states and the associated variety in elite and community culture.[14] One of the beaded crowns from Ife went to Oyo (founded c. 1600), which became an empire sustained by a powerful cavalry. An elite class developed there, as it had in the founding kingdom of Ife. The monarchs in smaller Yoruba kingdoms such as Ketu and Dasha in modern Benin Republic and Itsha in modern Togo wore similar crowns, but no elite class developed in these small

FIGURE 2.2 Ife Royal Couple

Bronze sculpture created by lost-wax method. The Oni of Ife, at right, with his queen. Recovered in archaeological digs at the edge of the royal town of Ife, this sculpture is dated to the fourteenth century.

Source: Courtesy of Ife Museum.

states. The Yoruba tradition of sculpture in wood and other media reflects this difference: court artists tailored the sculpture of Ife and Oyo to praise individual rulers and the power of the state; the sculpture of common people used similar artistic conventions but portrayed everyday life rather than the glorification of rulers. For instance, the widely known Gelede masks, produced especially in Ketu, pay tribute to the special powers of senior women through elaborate, often humorous images atop the masks. The audience was the crowds at dance ceremonies rather than the elites.

Two Central African examples of smaller kingdoms with complex forms of leadership stand out in terms of expressive culture. The Kuba kingdom of the Kasai Valley, founded about 1625, created an elaborate hierarchy of titles and an intensive artisanal tradition. Wooden statues of individual kings preserved the memory of their unique characteristics, royal weavers created raffia fabrics of great intricacy, and blacksmiths created beautifully decorated knives. The Mangbetu kingdoms of the northeastern Congo basin created wooden palaces with high domes and huge interior spaces where burnished copper dazzled those who came before the king.[15]

Thus, in cultural representation as in political regimes, the question of hierarchy was under discussion in the Africa of the fifteenth and sixteenth centuries. There were clear advances of hierarchical forms and values. Still, these changes were linked to a larger vision of community, albeit communities in which everyone knew their place.

Orders of Knowledge

In questions of spiritual and other knowledge, similar questions came to the fore. In the bitter struggle at Bolongo Itoko in the Congo Valley, the reliance on *nkumu* spirits, as well as on matrilineal family organization, enabled the defenders to hold off the lance-bearing armies from the north. The Yoruba practice of divination, directed by the god Ifa, showed itself to be valuable and was adopted by people in societies to the west.

Christian and Muslim missionaries preached in Africa, claiming to have a higher and more cosmopolitan knowledge of the spiritual realm. These revealed religions, each with a holy text and a set of formal institutions, brought a more structured approach to spiritual understanding. Yet for Islam, the basic religious principles—the profession of faith, the Qur'an, and prayer—spread more extensively than Islamic law or the cultural practices of the Middle East. The most popular form of Islam was Sufism, the mystical practice in which believers were able to achieve individual contact with God through appropriate rituals. Further, as René Bravmann has emphasized, the steady expansion of Islam in West Africa did not end previous sculpture traditions nor foster neglect of ancestors or nature spirits.[16] Similarly, Monophysite Christianity in Ethiopia and Catholic Christianity in West and Central Africa accepted the possibility of new revelations and accommodated clan and nature spirits. In sum, Christianity and Islam brought only a limited advance in African hierarchy.

The elite practice of religion stands out most clearly among the Timbuktu intellectuals. From the thirteenth century and perhaps earlier, this desert-edge community hosted a remarkable number of Islamic scholars. Learned men filled their houses with manuscripts, and young men came from great distances to study with these specialists in Islamic law and theology. Yet the *ulama* (scholars) of Timbuktu also sustained ties to common people by serving as dispensers of justice.[17]

Closely related to the military and social power of kings was the praise of their exploits. The most famous African tale of praise is the epic of Sundiata, which traces his childhood, his rise to power, and his rule in Mali in the thirteenth century. The epic of Askia Muhammad in sixteenth-century Songhay has been recorded with equal care.[18] The pattern was ubiquitous: the savanna griots, masters of words and music, composed tales honoring many other rulers. These tales served as extended praise songs for the king, but they also served as lessons on moral behavior and models for citizenship to all who heard them sung or saw them enacted over the years. Over time, however, the question emerged of whether the griot was to serve the ruler or the society as a whole.

Occupational groups, each with their specialized knowledge, could sometimes be listed in a hierarchy. Blacksmiths, whose occupation was distinctive everywhere, were formally organized into an endogamous caste in the West African savanna, as were other craft groups. There as well, griots were a caste, as were warriors and merchants, and the castes could be labeled as lower and higher. But people of the region also treated occupational groups as ethnicities rather than castes—as in Fulbe herders and Jula merchants—thus avoiding placing them in a hierarchy.

Knowledge of the ancestors and their desires was an important qualification for family leadership. Patrilineal and matrilineal rules enabled people to be classified clearly as members of one family or another. In this situation, the chief and council of elders in a family were potentially very powerful. They interpreted the rules for adoption; they could expel family members who misbehaved. They could send children to other families for apprenticeship or as pawns, that is, as security for the loan of land or wealth. In the coming era of slave trade, this sort of hierarchy within families could be exploited.

Slavery

How much slavery was there in Africa before 1600? This politically charged question has been debated often but has not yet been sufficiently documented. When it is set in the context of social hierarchy, however, the place of slavery in premodern Africa becomes clearer.

Historian John Thornton has gained wide attention, in recent years, for his hypothesis that Africa brimmed with slaves in times before the neophyte Atlantic trade burgeoned into dominance: "Slavery was widespread in Africa, and its growth and development were largely independent of the Atlantic trade. . . . The Atlantic slave trade was the outgrowth of this internal slavery."[19] Thornton argued that early Portuguese purchasers were almost always able to find sellers of captives, and therefore that Africa was full of slaves. He chose to explain the ready availability of captives by arguing that African law forbade ownership of land but allowed ownership of persons. As he contended, "We have good reason to believe that Africa did not have small property, that is, plots of land owned by cultivators or let out to rent by petty landlords, just as it did not have great property." And later, "It is precisely here, however, that slavery is so important in Africa, and why it played such a large role there. If Africans did not have private ownership of one factor of production (land), they could still own another, labor."[20]

Thornton asserted his hypothesis concisely rather than developing it in detail. That many readers have been convinced by Thornton's initial argument confirms his persuasiveness, but verification of the hypothesis requires detailed, consistent analysis. Here are three reasons for doubting his claims: subordinates were not the same as slaves, ownership of African land was established by tradition rather than by formal contracts, and the later centuries of expanding slave trade contradict the notion that African slavery was fully developed before 1500.[21]

More generally, Thornton's supply-side hypothesis falls into a pattern known as "orientalism," in which writers have contrasted western Europe to an essentialized, timeless Orient.[22] To explain the growth of slave trade through a proclivity of African leaders to sell people—and a legal system encouraging them in that direction—is to explain through definitions. Ironically, Thornton is well known, in most of his work, for emphasizing careful documentation with primary sources and identifying local differentiation in Africa. In this case, in contrast, he proposed two uniform generalizations for all of West and Central Africa.

While there is more research to be done on the place of slavery in the changing social systems of Africa from the fifteenth to seventeenth centuries, some established points can help guide that research. First, the limits of African social hierarchy have been discussed in the previous pages. Second, for a population of over twenty million persons along the coast of West Africa and in Central Africa, from a few hundred to as many as five thousand persons (or up to 0.025 percent of the population) were purchased or seized each year by Europeans in the fifteenth and sixteenth centuries. From this small beginning, Atlantic slave exports rose to average seventy thousand per year in the late eighteenth century, nearly fifteen times more. Third, not all regions of the African coast were involved in early slave trade. In the fifteenth century, the Portuguese had a virtual monopoly on African trade, and they purchased most of their slaves in Senegambia, Upper Guinea, the Kongo Kingdom, and Angola.

Fourth, dominant classes can only hold large slave populations for a good reason. The principal reasons have been to produce goods and services either for the slaveowning class or for sale on the market. Few African societies met these criteria. Songhay was an exception: from the fifteenth century, the Songhay monarchy captured and domiciled thousands of slaves, who supplied goods for the palace and also produced grains sold into the savanna market. In addition, Songhay merchants sold captives into the Mediterranean market. The great monarchies of Benin, Kongo, and Kilwa also supported sizeable slave populations, and the gold-producing areas of Gold Coast and perhaps Mwenemutapa gained enough commercial wealth to buy and use slaves. But aside from such centers of commercial and political power, it required too much effort to capture and control slave populations for the modest rewards brought by their exploitation.

For the period up to 1600, even with the visits of Portuguese merchants in the west and the purchases by Arab merchants in the north, the slave trade had not become a dominant influence on African society. Some of the important changes of that era resulted not from slavery in particular but more generally from new connections in maritime and land-based trade. These included expansions in West African exports of gold, pepper, and gum Arabic; imports of such commodities as cowries, metals, and textiles; and expanded trade among West African ports.

In the medieval Europe of Viking raiders and merchants, enslavement shot up for some centuries and then declined, leaving behind societies where slavery again became rare. One could imagine that such might have become the experience of Africa. But African slave trade did grow. After 1600 it became a unique, large-scale, oppressive system. Prior to that, some had made efforts to stop the slave trade. The Kingdom of Benin, for example, halted slave exports in the 1520s (but reversed the decision two centuries later). Rebel leaders in Senegambia and the kings of Kongo sought to stop the flow of captives to coastal markets and simply failed. The initial patterns of slave trade, as they had developed along the coasts of West and Central Africa by 1600, would grow and expand in the years after. The quantity of captives exported from West Africa accelerated, almost tripling from 1450 to 1650, and most of the increase came from regions braced by Atlantic sea breezes. The expansion of enslavement generated improved techniques for seizing captives, fostered armed raids and kidnapping, and expanded judicial enslavement. Individual regions underwent cycles of expansion and contraction in slave trade. In the peak export years, men came to be in short supply, and populations declined. Walter Rodney has argued, for the Upper Guinea region, that the first century of contact with the Portuguese resulted in an expansion of slavery where it had not previously been prevalent. John Thornton has shown, also for Upper Guinea, the social change brought about by the shortage of men. The developments up to 1600 in Senegambia, Upper Guinea, Songhay, Gold Coast, and Benin foreshadowed the elements of the larger system that emerged later.

Africans expanded the hierarchies in their societies and cultures, but with respect to other cultures around the globe, African societies of the fifteenth century remained remarkably egalitarian. The advances in hierarchy might lead to civilizational brilliance—beautiful buildings, sculptures, or poetry— or they might lead to endless battles for dominance. Many African societies recognized forms of slavery, and the institution expanded in some regions. Yet African reluctance to embrace hierarchy, in many areas of life, makes it illogical to believe that widespread enslavement was automatic in Africa. As it happened, the progressive expansion of slave trade brought types of hierarchy that would eventually be disastrous—it created hierarchy by separating master from slave, yet it was a leveling force in that anyone was vulnerable to capture. This expansion of slavery arose not from the inherent qualities of African society but from the nature of the interactions with outsiders.

Migrations to Old World Destinations, 1400–1600

This section combines with the segment that follows to portray the gradual development of two great arenas of the African diaspora, each related in a specific way to the homeland of sub-Saharan Africa. The Old World diaspora has the longest history and the greatest variety in its localities and populations (see map 2.3). Its existence relied on the continuation of a long migration tradition that established communities of black people outside of sub-Saharan Africa long before. The Atlantic diaspora, in contrast, depended on the opening of new routes and the formation of new patterns. The Atlantic diaspora centers on the Americas but also includes African settlement in Europe through the Atlantic crossing. The antecedents of the Atlantic diaspora can be traced back to the first Portuguese voyages south of the Sahara, but only after 1550 did it come to be clearly distinct from the Old World diaspora. This section addresses the Old World diaspora from 1400 to 1600, and the next traces the Atlantic diaspora from 1492 to 1600.

Contacts among the Old World regions expanded in waves. The Mongol states of the thirteenth and fourteenth centuries created greater links overland, while the fifteenth century saw a growth in oceanic connections. In this time before slave trade grew to dominate Africa's interregional ties, the movements between Africa, Asia, and Europe formed a somewhat typical expansion of interaction among societies. In the fifteenth century and before, many more Africans traversed the Indian Ocean than the Atlantic. Ports along the Swahili coast were in regular contact with South Arabia,

MAP 2.3 The Old World Diaspora to 1600. Dots on this map indicate places in the Old World diaspora mentioned in chapter 2.

India, and Madagascar. Ships sailed the Red Sea and then along the Gulf of Aden on their way to India. Italian merchants mixed with merchants from Africa, Arabia, Iran, and India in the large-scale and remarkably peaceful commerce of the Indian Ocean. A mighty fleet of large Chinese vessels came to the western Indian Ocean in 1415. Smaller vessels carried goods by stages from Africa as far as China (including two giraffes for the Ming emperor) and transported European coins and Chinese porcelain as far south as Kilwa in modern Tanzania and Sofala in Mozambique.

Geography

From an African standpoint, one may think of concentric circles of Old World regions increasingly distant from sub-Saharan Africa, all of them serving as destinations for larger or smaller numbers of African migrants (see map 1.1). At the center of these ripples of migratory movement lay the sub-Saharan African homeland, stretching from the Senegal Valley in the west to Cape Horn in the east and to the Cape of Good Hope in the south.

The first concentric circle of regions may be labeled "offshore"—a semi-circle of lands and waters directly adjoining the populous lands of sub-Saharan Africa. The Sahara desert and its oases have been described metaphorically as a sea of sand; thus, the edge of the African grasslands became known as the Sahel ("coast," in Arabic). East of the desert lay the Red Sea, and southeast of it lay the western Indian Ocean, with islands that could be considered oases. Most people of the Sahara and Red Sea regions spoke Afroasiatic languages related to the Afroasiatic languages both south and north of them. The metaphor of coast appears again in East Africa, where the Swahili language and people took their name from the same Arabic term for "coast." Included in this offshore region are islands and oases such as Zanzibar, Pemba, and the Comoros in East Africa, and Socotra off the Horn. (In later times, when the Atlantic was opened to regular travel, the Canaries, Cape Verde Islands, São Tomé, and Fernando Po became significant offshore points.) Each region of this first circle separated and connected Africa with the populous regions beyond. All involved difficult crossings yet provided havens for travelers. Sometimes, as with Saharan oases and the Comoro Islands, they became dense, if isolated, agricultural settlements and refreshment stations for those on long voyages.

The Middle Passage of the Old World consisted of the journey across the sands and waters of this "offshore" zone. The Old World Middle Passage shared with the Atlantic crossing the characteristic of being the longest and most arduous stage of the journey into slavery.[23] Africans crossed these lanes in ships and caravans and settled as slaves—but also as free persons—on the islands and at the oases along the way. Each offshore region had a unique character that influenced the movement of African travelers into and across it.

The Sahara desert supported major grasslands until temperatures rose and its vegetation declined, somewhere between four and six thousand years ago. At that time, people gradually moved away in all directions. Since then, the land is mostly barren, stony terrain and great sand dunes. Mountains rise here and there, attracting rain, which makes them more habitable, and oases appear at low altitudes, where underground waters bubble to the surface. Temperatures peak from June through September and drop to freezing at night from December through February. Winds blow across the region for much of the year, especially from the northeast.

The Red Sea, stretching from Suez and Aqaba in the north to the Bab al-Mandab in the south, is only three hundred kilometers across at its widest and less than thirty kilometers at the Bab al-Mandab, the southern gateway into the Arabian Sea and the western Indian Ocean. While many ships crossed the Red Sea and traveled its length, the trip was not easy for sailing vessels. Winds were sudden and erratic, and in the southern Red Sea they brought dust storms. The rocky islands were scarcely inhabited. Only a few good ports dotted the coastline: Suez in the north; Sawakin and Jidda, facing each other from Arabia and Sudan halfway down the sea; and at the southern end, Massawa on the African side and Mokha in Yemen. As camel transit improved, many merchants preferred to ship goods by land along the coast of the Red Sea. As a result, Mecca, halfway along the route, became a major commercial town. Because the sea voyage from Africa to Arabia was short, mortality was lower on this route than on any others of the Old World Middle Passage.

The Indian Ocean, its seas calm compared to the stormy Atlantic and Pacific, linked sharply different societies into a single commercial network. Its shores, from west to east, include East Africa, South Arabia, the Persian Gulf, western India, eastern India along the Bay of Bengal, and Indonesia. The *monsoons*—winds generated by the seasonal temperature changes of the Eurasian land mass—set the timing and direction of travel. In the western Indian Ocean, the winds blow from the northeast from December to April and from the southwest from June to October. Dangerous tropical cyclones arise in the periods between monsoons in the northern Indian Ocean. The African coasts of the Indian Ocean are narrow bands of lush growth, populated especially by coconut palms, but with arid lands immediately behind them and occasional roads to more populous zones further inland. The social life for this coastline required a complex interplay among oasis farmers, herd tenders, and people at the water's edge.

The westernmost islands of the Indian Ocean served as oases in this offshore region. Zanzibar, Pemba, and Mafia, within sight of the East African mainland, are centers of Swahili culture. The Comoro Islands, long governed by Islamic sultanates, have served as ports and oases linking East Africa to more distant islands; Socotra, further north, played a similar role for Yemen. (Larger and more remote islands of the Indian Ocean are best classified in more distant concentric circles of the African diaspora.)

A second and slightly more distant "ring" of the Old World diaspora may be called the "near diaspora." It consists of North Africa and the Arabian peninsula—the regions just across the waters or sands from sub-Saharan Africa—along with the big island of Madagascar. These populous lands form a distinctive segment of the African diaspora because they have so intensely interacted with the African homeland. Most of the lands of North Africa and Arabia were arid, so pastoral populations herding cattle, goats, sheep, camels, horses, and donkeys were central to the economies. These populations settled mostly around desert oases, on farmland along rivers or in the higher, wetter mountains, and in towns along the Mediterranean Sea, the Red Sea, the Gulf of Aden, and the Persian Gulf. The interactions between sub-Saharan Africa and the near diaspora of North Africa and Arabia saw the largest numbers of migrants going in each direction, the deepest cultural exchange, and the most complex mixture of free people and slaves. The Berber languages of the Maghrib and the Semitic languages of North Africa and Arabia form part of the Afroasiatic phylum, which first arose in the middle Nile Valley. These regions have been sometimes marginal to world history but central at others—in particular, Egypt in ancient times, Arabia during Muhammad's lifetime, and the Maghrib in the era of the Almoravids and the Almohads. These regions of the near diaspora have often been downplayed in studies of the African diaspora, but they should be highlighted because of their consistent interaction with sub-Saharan Africa.[24]

Madagascar too lies in the circle of the near diaspora. The island, with forests in the east, open grasslands in the west, and fertile highlands in the center, is five hundred kilometers off the coast of Mozambique. Its principal settlement began roughly two thousand years ago, when Austronesian-speaking mariners moved south along the East African coast, where they had earlier settled and intermarried with the local Bantu-speaking population. Regular maritime contact between Madagascar and the continent, most often with stops in the Comoro Islands, ensured that migrants moved regularly between island and mainland. Whether these movements involved enslavement before 1500 is not known. After 1500, the migrants were free persons and slaves. Malagasy, the language of Madagascar, is closely related to the Malayo-Polynesian languages of Borneo, from where its early settlers originated. Otherwise, Madagascar is in many ways analogous to North Africa and Arabia, in that the steady input of sub-Saharan African migrants forms an essential aspect of its regional character.

The third set of lands beyond sub-Saharan Africa, the "far diaspora," stretch in a great semicircle from western Europe to the tip of South Asia. It includes the European mainland; the Black Sea and its surrounding regions (the Slavic areas to the north, the Caucasus to the northeast, and Anatolia to the south); the Fertile Crescent of Syria, Palestine, and Iraq; the Persian Gulf and the Iranian plateau; the great expanse of South Asia (a territory as large as Europe); and the more distant islands of the Indian Ocean. All of these were populous zones, and over the centuries they served as magnets, drawing Africans in freedom and slavery. Most people across this expanse spoke Indo-European languages—from Europe through Iran to India—a key to their ancient common heritage. Smaller numbers of people speaking

Semitic, Turkish, and Dravidian languages reflected migrations in early and recent times. In addition, several groups of Indian Ocean islands, distant from the African coast, compose the final element of the far diaspora. The Seychelles, due east of the Swahili coast, could serve as stopping points in transoceanic slave trade. The Maldives, southwest of India, long played a special role as the principal source of the cowrie shells used as money and for decoration all around the Indian Ocean and as far away as western Africa. The Mascarene Islands (Mauritius, Réunion, and several smaller islands) lie far out in the ocean, a thousand kilometers due east of Madagascar—they were long known but remained uninhabited until the seventeenth century.

A fourth circle of lands encompass the distant areas of Eurasia: the far northern fringe of Europe, the Central Asian regions beyond the Caspian and Aral seas, and the lands of Southeast Asia and East Asia. Here African visitors were infrequent but never absent. While Africans did travel to these regions—for instance, as slaves sold to Chinese merchants, as sailors on Portuguese ships to Japan, and as warriors sent to Dutch territories in Southeast Asia—I will leave their stories for others to recount.

Old World Encounters

Just as Africa experienced growth and development in the fifteenth century, so did the Eurasian continent return to growth following the travails of the Mongol conquests of the thirteenth century and the Black Plague in the mid-fourteenth century. What follows is a political and commercial narrative of the changing links across the Eastern Hemisphere in the fifteenth century, showing the place of African migrants, free and slave, in each of the concentric circles of the Old World diaspora.

From 1370 to 1405, the most powerful individual in Eurasia was Timur or Tamerlane, the brilliant military leader whose armies, based in the Central Asian city of Samarkand, defeated opponents in Russia, Turkey, Iran, and India, and even threatened China. After Timur's death, the Chinese empire sent fleets to the western Indian Ocean in part to contest his legacy. Throughout the fifteenth century, Central Asian princes of Turkish ethnicity, claiming descent from Timur and Genghis Khan, led armies throughout the region. Central Asia was the power center of the era; Europe, India, and Africa were at the margins.

Yet in this era, black men and women continued to move into the far diaspora of Europe, the Middle East, and India, as is indicated in the artwork of the time. For example, in about 1250, the Hohenstaufen ruler of the Saxon town of Magdeburg in northern Germany installed a remarkable sandstone

FIGURE 2.3 St. Maurice

St. Maurice of Thebes, a Christian officer of the Roman army, was a patron saint of the Holy Roman Empire from the tenth century onward. He was represented as a black man in this statue of 1240 in the cathedral at Magdeburg, Germany, and in many other statues of central and northern Europe for several centuries thereafter.

sculpture of a pious young black man in armor, a sword at his side and banner in hand, in the town's cathedral (figure 2.3). This sculpture portrayed Saint Maurice of Thebes, a Roman soldier posted in central Europe who chose death over renouncing his Christian faith. The cult of Saint Maurice had been propagated by kings and armies for centuries, but it appears that the Hohenstaufen rulers of the Holy Roman Empire sought to associate the empire with heroic black figures. Over three centuries, representations of a black Saint Maurice appeared in churches of Saxony, Bohemia, and around the Baltic Sea. In this same region but less frequently, the biblical Queen of Sheba was represented as a black woman. Monk and scholar John of Hildesham (or Hildesheim), in a widely circulated fourteenth-century book, proposed details on the Magi—the three kings who presented gifts to Jesus in Bethlehem. John identified one of them as Jaspar, a tall, black

Ethiopian. Within a century—first in Germany, then Italy, then throughout Christendom—one of the kings came to be portrayed as African.

While it is hard to know the thinking of those who created the sculptures and paintings of Africans in medieval Europe, the precision and individuality of the renditions makes it clear that the artists worked with black people as models. There were, therefore, both robust and elegant black men in Europe able to serve as models and artists able to portray them with accuracy and sensitivity. Similarly, artistic representations from the Byzantine Empire, its Ottoman successors, the Arab and Iranian states, and India provide clear representations of black people throughout the medieval era. It is doubtless true that many of the Africans who left the continent went abroad as slaves, but they are often represented in painting and sculpture as free persons, so many of these subjects may have been so.

The Ottoman kingdom in Anatolia, though nearly demolished by Timur in 1403, rebounded to become the most durable of the expanding states. Ottoman rulers, as they conquered the city of Constantinople in 1453, chose to cut merchants from Venice and Genoa off from Black Sea ports. The growing Ottoman regime began to purchase and seize slaves from all directions, especially the Caucasus, Poland, and the Balkans, but also from the Nile Valley. Merchants from the Italian cities turned toward Africa to buy slaves to replace those previously brought from the Black Sea regions. As a result, by 1500 communities of African origin had grown at various points in Eurasia. For instance, many gondoliers on fifteenth-century Venetian canals were black. A more long-lived black community was that of Abkhazia, on the eastern shores of the Black Sea. This farming community may have formed in ancient times, but it clearly expanded under Ottoman influence from the late fifteenth century.

African warriors, significant in India from the thirteenth century, grew to greater importance in the fifteenth and sixteenth centuries. They, along with Central Asian Turkish warriors, were the main fighting forces in North India. In both cases, a mix of slave and free warriors filtered into India from a great distance and were organized into major fighting forces associated with Islamic princes. Figure 2.4 shows a representation of black warriors painted in the 1580s at the Mughal court of Delhi, in which they battle with Darab, the mythical grandfather of Alexander the Great. On the west coast of India, one group of African immigrants was identified as Siddis from at least as early as the twelfth century. These settlers, descended from people of the Swahili coast, maintained their community and their seafaring ways. One group of Siddis became skilled in naval warfare and seized control of Janjira Island (just south of modern Mumbai) in the 1480s. They ruled the islands

FIGURE 2.4 Zanjis and Darab

Illustration from Abu Tahir Tarasusi, *Darabname*. In stories told in sixteenth-century India, Darab is taken as the grandfather of Alexander the Great, and the Zanjis, warriors of African ancestry, are his enemies. In the sequence of paintings including this one, the Zanjis ultimately submit to Darab.

and patrolled the seas—often in alliance with the Mughal Empire—until the British expelled them in 1759.

African women of the Old World diaspora were commonly personal servants, and the centrality of this role in the social hierarchy of the diaspora emerges from its visual art. A fascinating example appeared just before Columbus voyaged to America. In early 1492, the distinguished painter Andrea Mantegna created an ink drawing of the biblical Judith and her maidservant with the head of the Assyrian general Holofernes, whom they had slain (figure 2.5). The art historian Paul Kaplan argues that Isabella d'Este, the Marchioness of Mantua (a city near Venice), both commissioned the painting and posed as Judith, while the servant pictured was one of several black maidservants that Isabella went to considerable effort to purchase.[25] The story of Judith was well known and painted occasionally, but Mantegna's was the first with a black maidservant. This work launched a series of such images, painted by other masters over the years, confirming the image of Judith and her black servant as a statement of powerful female agency. Mantegna had long experience with portraying black figures, having included a black king in his *Adoration of the Magi* (c. 1464). Isabella, a second cousin of Queen Isabella of Castile, was well aware of voyages to West Africa but also knew of Italian visits by Ethiopian clergy. The new portrayal of Judith's story thus revealed Ethiopian connections (in the earlier portrayal of black heroic figures such as Saint Maurice) and recent Italian contacts with the western coast of Africa (which probably brought to Isabella d'Este the servant shown with her in the painting).

What do we know of the work, family life, and cultural activities of Africans in the Old World diaspora up to 1600? Women served as domestics and concubines, especially in the near diaspora of North Africa and Arabia. Men went in larger proportions to the far diaspora as laborers and warriors. Most were drawn into the Islamic social order; a small number were converted to Christianity. Some worked as laborers on sugar plantations in Syria and on Mediterranean islands, but these were a minority. Most African migrants found themselves in small communities of blacks, so they were more likely to assimilate to local society than maintain their own traditions. Women commonly had children with their masters, and children conformed to the dominant society. At the same time, marriages of black men and women in the diaspora created second- and third-generation black diaspora communities. Black men who rose to elite positions had children, but low-status male slaves may not have had many offspring. Distinct African ethnic groups rarely got recognition, though the difference between Siddis and Habshis shows some ties to African homelands. In later times, however, we find evidence of

FIGURE 2.5 *Judith and Her Maidservant*, by Andrea Mantegna

Ink on paper, 1491–1492. The image illustrates the biblical Judith and her maidservant after they have decapitated the sleeping Assyrian general Holofernes.

Source: Courtesy of the Galleria degli Uffizi, Florence, Italy.

music, dance, and language of African origin and inspiration throughout the Old World diaspora, suggesting that black communities may have sustained their home culture to a degree greater than what has been recorded in written documents.

From 1512, the Ottomans expanded greatly and become the dominant power in the Arab lands of Syria and Iraq, in southeastern Europe, in North Africa, the Mediterranean, the Red Sea, and (briefly) in the Indian Ocean.

The Ottoman expansion magnified the trade links and eventually the slave trade from the African savanna to the Mediterranean. At much the same time, two more great states arose, each led by migrant Turkish princes: the Safavid Empire of Iran, founded in 1500, and the Mughal Empire of India and Afghanistan, founded in 1526. Also in about 1500, in the middle Nile Valley, the Funj Sultanate arose, replacing the earlier Christian kingdoms with an Islamic regime.

In the atmosphere of these expanding Islamic states, Portuguese mariners entered the Indian Ocean in 1498 and returned regularly thereafter. By 1512, the Portuguese navy had used brutal techniques to establish beachheads at Socotra, Hormuz, Goa, and Melaka—fortified harbors from which they could trade and raid to expand their influence. The Portuguese thus entered the great commercial network of the Indian Ocean. Their all-water route gave them advantages over the Italian merchants who also traded there. The Indian Ocean, long crossed by Indians, Africans, Omanis, Iranians, Greeks, Egyptians, and occasionally Chinese, was now traversed by Ottomans and Portuguese as well.

The Portuguese also encountered the slave trade of the Indian Ocean, though they did not dominate it. Before the Portuguese arrival, the Islamic state of Adal, based in the port city of Zeila on what is today the northwestern coast of Somalia, had begun regular slave raids into the kingdom of Ethiopia, sending large numbers of slaves to the Persian Gulf and India. Ethiopian armies responded, and a half-century of warfare resulted in many captives on each side. In 1527, Ahmad ibn Ibrahim came to power in Adal, and his troops, with muskets supplied by the Ottomans, threatened Ethiopia's existence. That kingdom turned to Portugal, which sent an army in 1541. The Portuguese army was defeated, but Ahmad ibn Ibrahim was killed in 1543 and the sultanate of Adal soon collapsed. With that, warfare on the Horn of Africa declined significantly. Shipments of captives from the Horn to Persia and India gradually diminished, though Habshis in the latter remained significant among warriors and officials. Thus, in contrast to the Atlantic trade, the Indian Ocean basin expressed no wealth-driven expanding demand for new African laborers, or at least not for two more centuries. In the Indian Ocean, the Portuguese were influential but not dominant; slave trade continued in this region but did not grow at the rate it did in the Atlantic.

Africa's Atlantic

To complete this overview of the Old World diaspora, let us go back a century to see how the early Portuguese exploration of the Atlantic eventually linked to this story of the Indian Ocean and the Red Sea (see map 2.4). At the western edge of the Old World, Portuguese voyagers had begun in the fifteenth century to visit Africa along the Atlantic coast, a rarely used route. In doing so, they had to overcome the contrary currents off the northwestern African coast that made the return trip difficult. Eventually, they developed ships that could sail closer to the wind and learned that the airstreams further west were more favorable for heading north. As Portuguese and then other European ships moved along the Atlantic coast of Africa, they brought Africans on board, sometimes as free persons but more often in captivity. Through these voyages, Africans took root on the islands of the Atlantic. Portuguese mariners settled the Azores and Madeira in the early fifteenth century, first growing wheat there. Then they worked their way down the African coast, passing Cape Bojador in 1434, reaching modern Senegal in the 1440s and the Cape Verde Islands in 1456. By 1472, Portuguese vessels had completed the eastward path along the Guinea Coast and had discovered Fernando Po and the uninhabited islands of Principe and São Tomé. Diogo Cão reached the mouth of the Congo in 1482, and Vasco da Gama sailed all the way to India in 1498. Obtaining gold and converting people to Christianity were foremost on the minds of the Portuguese at first, but trade in other goods and the seizure of labor grew in importance.[26]

The Portuguese advance was greatly limited by disastrous death rates. While the cause was not known until the nineteenth century, the symptoms were clear: nausea, high fever, exhaustion, and death. For Europeans and any others who had not been exposed, roughly half would die in their first year of exposure. The "fever," as it was known, was long thought to spring from the climate itself. In fact, the illness was malaria, brought on by *falciparum*, a protozoan fluke that infected the blood and was carried by the *anopheles* mosquito. (The high mortality of children in Africa owed much to malaria.) For those who survived their early infections and were reinfected regularly, malaria would be no more than a periodic fever. But for those first arriving in tropical Africa, malaria took a terrible death toll and greatly hindered efforts to trade, settle, or conquer.

The first Portuguese slave trade involved transporting captives to Portugal and, secondarily, to the Atlantic islands (see map 2.4).[27] This trade, lasting from 1450 until it shrank sharply by 1550, brought West African slaves to work in wheat production in Portugal and the islands. Slaves from the Upper Guinea coast were most numerous in Cape Verde; slaves from Senegambia were most numerous in Portugal. An estimated average of six hundred persons per year were taken from the West African coast between 1450 and 1500. In this developing system of commerce and enslavement, a distinctive

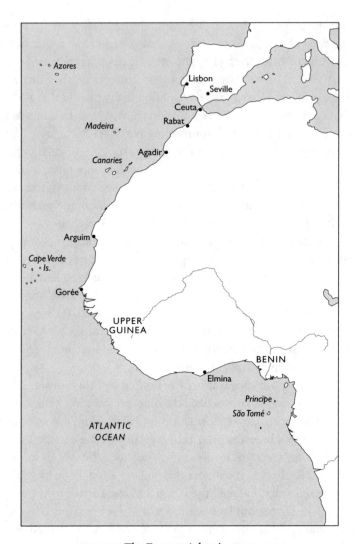

MAP 2.4 The Eastern Atlantic, 1400–1550

population emerged, linking the islands of Cape Verde to the mainland of Senegambia and Upper Guinea. The *lançados*, descended from Portuguese (often Jewish) and African settlers on the islands, came to participate in trade with the African mainland. In the Cape Verde Islands, the beginnings of the Crioulo language emerged—this language merged West African grammar with the Portuguese lexicon, and it linked trading communities along the African coast for centuries.

As the sixteenth century opened, sugar production grew in importance on the Atlantic islands. The role of plantation laborer now took center stage for enslaved Africans. In the Spanish-controlled Canaries, the local population (which had lost the use of boats) was soon overwhelmed in numbers by sub-Saharan African captives who were brought in beginning about 1500 and put to work, mostly on sugar plantations. In 1485, sugar output had already begun on São Tomé using slave labor purchased or seized in and near the kingdom of Kongo. São Tomé's sugar plantations were so fruitful that the island became the world's leading sugar producer through most of the sixteenth century.

In the days before Columbus, the Portuguese focused their attention on five areas of the African coast: Senegambia, Upper Guinea, the Gold Coast, Benin, and Kongo. These remained the principal areas of African contact with the Atlantic until 1575, when the Portuguese seized the town of Luanda and began constructing the colony of Angola.

As Luso-African trade continued to develop, African slaves were brought in increasing numbers to Portugal, and from there they spread in smaller numbers to other regions in Europe. Ivana Elbl has calculated the numbers of Africans taken to Portugal and concludes that the total reached a remarkable two hundred thousand people over the sixteenth century, an average of two thousand per year.[28] The earliest transatlantic slave trade, therefore, involved the movement of captive Africans to the islands of the eastern Atlantic and to Europe. In Portugal, the Africans worked mostly as agricultural laborers. Overall, the earliest Portuguese slave trade increased the African populations on the eastern Atlantic islands and in Europe. The black population of Spain and Portugal reached its peak in the early sixteenth century and then declined. The black population of the Atlantic islands rose to the maximum the land would support and then leveled off.

American Encounters, 1492–1600

News of the existence of the Americas spread rapidly and widely through the Old World. Africans accompanied European voyagers to the Americas almost from the first. They, along with the Spanish and Portuguese, learned of the new territories and the peoples inhabiting them. At least one African seaman is believed to have been in the crew of Columbus's second voyage to the Caribbean. These Africans came to the Americas from Iberia rather than directly from Africa. (The first slave shipment directly from Africa to Hispaniola—the island now containing Haiti and the Dominican Republic—was in 1518.) Africans participated in the initial encounter of peoples of the two worlds, and they played a role in bringing diseases from the Old World that would have a devastating effect on Amerindian populations. These early African migrants to the Americas came as slaves, free people, artisans, soldiers, and adventurers. As early settlers, they fought but also had children with the Taino of the Bahamas and Greater Antilles. They worked on Hispaniola's first sugar plantations, escaped captivity and led early revolts, and did artisanal work in the port towns of Santo Domingo and Havana. From 1519, Africans participated in Cortez's conquest of Mexico. More generally they moved, along with the Spanish, beyond the islands and the coast to the interior of the Americas. Overall, for about the first sixty years after Columbus's first voyage, the Africans who came across the Atlantic were outnumbered by Spanish and Portuguese migrants.

After about 1550, however, for the next three centuries the pendulum swung in the opposite direction. An estimated 150,000 Africans came to Spanish America in the sixteenth century, most after midcentury. For Portuguese America, the numbers were smaller and the Africans came later, even though sugar first reached Brazil in 1536. It was not until the 1580s, after the Portuguese seized Luanda and gained captives from its Angolan wars, that Africans became numerous in Brazil.

Geography

The Americas south of modern Canada form a territory as vast as Africa, roughly thirty million square kilometers. Into these lands would come thousands and ultimately millions of migrants from Africa (see map 2.5). South America and the Caribbean lie directly west of Africa and share much in climate and topography. The Amazon Valley's equatorial forest lies directly west of Central Africa's forest. South of the Amazon forest lies an immense, wooded grassland, known as the *sertão* in Brazil, equal to Africa's southern savanna. Still further south lie the cooler, wooded areas of what is now Uruguay in the Americas, corresponding to Angola in Africa. North of the Amazon Valley, centered on modern Venezuela, are more great wooded grasslands that parallel Africa's northern savanna. One might even argue that the immense ranges of the Sierra Madre and the Andes, on the western side of the Americas, correspond to the Rift Valley and the long mountainous ridge on the eastern side of Africa: in each case, these high altitudes support dense populations.

Of course, the geographic parallels between Africa and the Americas have their limits. The Caribbean Sea does not correspond directly to any portion of Africa (except perhaps the islands off Africa's east coast). Nonetheless, the tropical climate of the Caribbean—on the islands and surrounding mainland—provided an environment rather similar to that of the African

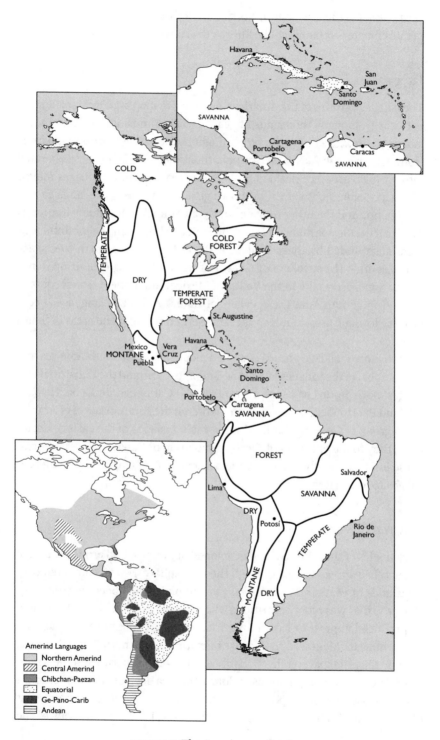

MAP 2.5 The Americas, 1492–1600

Inset (top, Caribbean):
Havana
San Juan
Santo Domingo
SAVANNA
Cartagena
Portobelo
Caracas
SAVANNA

Main map (North and South America):
COLD
TEMPERATE
COLD FOREST
DRY
TEMPERATE FOREST
St. Augustine
Havana
Mexico
Vera Cruz
MONTANE
Puebla
Santo Domingo
Portobelo
Cartagena
SAVANNA
FOREST
Salvador
Lima
SAVANNA
DRY
Potosí
Rio de Janeiro
TEMPERATE
MONTANE
DRY

Amerind Languages
Northern Amerind
Central Amerind
Chibchan-Paezan
Equatorial
Ge-Pano-Carib
Andean

west coast. On the other hand, North America was quite different. The temperate climate was far more like Europe than anything in Africa.

Language

The language groups of the Americas, as shown in map 2.5, reveal settlement patterns from many thousands of years earlier. Almost all the Amerindian languages are related, as they were brought by the earliest settlers who came from Asia through Alaska. With time, their ancestral languages separated into six main groups. Speakers of the Northern Amerind languages moved from the Columbia River valley in two groups, one filling the lands east to the Atlantic and the other moving south of the Rocky Mountains to occupy Mexico's Pacific coast and most of the Gulf of Mexico. In the mountainous areas surrounded by these lowlands—from Utah in the north to Oaxaca in the south—the speakers of Central Amerind languages built up dense populations, especially in the Valley of Mexico. Along the western coast of Central and South America, speakers of Chibchan-Paezan languages occupied the lowland areas. Andean speakers settled the highland areas of South America.

Two more language groups occupied most of eastern South America and the Caribbean: the tongues labeled as Ge-Pano-Carib and the Equatorial languages. Both groups had sent migrants to the Caribbean. In Cuba, Hispaniola, and Puerto Rico, the Spanish encountered the Taino speakers of Arawak (a subgroup of Ge-Pano-Carib). In the smaller islands of the eastern Caribbean, they found speakers of Carib (a subgroup of Equatorial). The Portuguese in Brazil mainly encountered speakers of Tupi languages (a different subgroup of Equatorial).

Material Culture

The peoples of the Americas had developed numerous food crops, and some of them had spread widely through the hemisphere. Maize, cultivated over thousands of years in Mexico's valleys and plains, had become a dependable crop that was highly nutritious when consumed with beans. It came to be produced in most of North America and in parts of South America and the Caribbean. Manioc, a root crop originating in northern South America, became the principal starchy food for eastern South America and the Caribbean. The highland populations of South America developed potatoes and a grain crop, quinoa. Sweet potatoes, domesticated on the northwestern coast of South America, spread through lowland areas. Other food crops of the tropical Americas included tomatoes, peanuts, pineapples, and avocados. Tobacco, hardly a food crop, was domesticated in North America but spread throughout the hemisphere.

The numerous inhabitants of the Caribbean known as the Taino, Arawak, and Carib spoke languages linked to those of South America's eastern mainland. These peoples were skilled in handling boats made from hollowed-out logs and had a rich cuisine based on the numerous fruits, vegetables, and roots first domesticated in what is now Venezuela. Others from these groups had migrated over the millennia throughout the Amazon Valley and across the grasslands of eastern South America.

Amerindian Population

The Americas were remarkably populous in pre-Columbian times. The density of population in the Caribbean, Mexico, and Peru was documented by Spanish officials. More indirectly, documents from Spanish visits and archaeological digs indicate that substantial populations lived in the Mississippi Valley, the eastern woodlands of North America, and the forests and grasslands of South America. Estimates of American populations in 1500 continue to be debated, though they have settled down between a low of forty million and a high of one hundred million for the hemisphere, compared to a population of well over one hundred million for Africa. This suggests that the population size and density of the Americas was comparable to that of Africa in 1500. (Europe's total population was smaller than that of Africa or the Americas in 1500, but it was more densely packed in Europe's smaller area.)

Epidemics struck the Caribbean Amerindian populations from almost the moment Spanish ships and their crews reached the islands. As Old World visitors reached other territories in North, Central, and South America, diseases began to spread. Smallpox was probably the single greatest killer, but measles, typhus, and respiratory diseases also took their toll. While these are often known as "European diseases," they are better labeled as "Old World diseases." Africans were as numerous among New World settlers as Europeans, and it was through them that such tropical diseases as malaria and yellow fever (in addition to those shared throughout the Old World) reached the Americas.[29]

Horrendous stories of successive waves of disease are documented for Mexico, Peru, and portions of the Caribbean, where surviving Spanish officials left records and tales of the devastation. No equivalent records exist for northern South America, Brazil, or North America, where the epidemics apparently ran their course without any chroniclers to preserve stories of their destruction. Records are not as detailed for other regions of the Americas, but it is noteworthy that Hernando De Soto's 1540–1543 expedition in southeastern North America encountered large villages and powerful rulers. Over a century later, when French visitors came to the Mississippi Valley in the late seventeenth century, they found very sparse populations.

The Spanish conquerors—and, somewhat later, the Portuguese—sought work forces to serve their needs. Their principal emphasis was on Amerindian workers: the Spanish commanded labor through a system of recruitment from chiefs under their control; the Portuguese obtained slaves by raiding Amerindian groups. For the Caribbean, stories are often told of the "extinction" of the native population as a result of Spanish brutality and disease. Quite aside from the term's inhuman character, which implies that the Taino and other Caribbean populations were another species that might be extinguished, the tale is not quite true. Though communities of Tainos ceased to exist as separate groupings, many Taino women became wives and concubines of Spanish and African immigrants. It was these women who raised and taught the children, thereby conveying the remnants of Taino language and culture that persist in the Caribbean today.

African Immigrants

As the Amerindian populations of the Americas fell to one-fifth or even one-tenth of what they had been before 1500, the Spanish and Portuguese turned more and more to African laborers. All through the sixteenth century, most of those carried off from Africa in captivity went to the Atlantic islands and Europe. By 1600, however, a majority of African captives were being sent to the Americas. The Spanish, ill equipped to collect slaves directly, began awarding contracts to merchants to supply fixed numbers of African slaves. The contract became known as the *asiento*, and the standard adult male slave became known as a *pieza de India*. Portuguese merchants dominated these asiento contracts from 1580 to 1660. West African captives went in the largest numbers to the urban center of Lima in Peru and to Mexico City and Vera Cruz in Mexico. Urban slaves served especially as artisans and domestics; rural slaves worked as field laborers, artisans, and as miners in the expanding silver mines of the Andes and northern Mexico. As Bowser and Palmer have shown, these slaves came mostly from Senegambia, Upper Guinea, and the Bight of Benin.[30]

Those who went to Peru had a long voyage indeed: from West Africa to Cartagena, then by land and sea across the isthmus of Panama, then by sea to the port of Callao, and finally on land to their destination in Lima or beyond. Enough of them must have survived to work productively after their arrival in the Americas or they would never have been brought. But in these early days of the American slave trade, inexperience with the winds and with putting up adequate provisions meant that delay and starvation, not to mention disease and revolt, occasionally took a heavy toll on the lives of those on board these early slave ships. Figure 2.6 portrays two of the survivors, a black man and woman of Peru, as pious Catholics.

The Portuguese in Brazil, in contrast, lacked mineral discoveries, so agriculture and harvesting (of sandalwood, among other resources) provided the only profitable ways of participating in long-distance trade. The initial Portuguese settlements were most successful in the northeast of Brazil, in areas they named Pernambuco and Bahia. There sugar plantations arose based on the Atlantic-island model (especially São Tomé), which in turn had emulated earlier plantations on Mediterranean islands. The Portuguese commercial connections with the Kingdom of Kongo and, beginning in 1575, their control of the Angolan port of Luanda, provided a growing flow of captives to Brazil. Thus, Africans who crossed the Atlantic in the late sixteenth century went principally to Peru, Mexico, and Hispaniola. Only at the end of the century did they reach northeastern Brazil in large numbers and become more common in "Terra Firme," as the region north of the Amazon, including Venezuela, was then known.

In the Atlantic world—the eastern Atlantic islands, Iberia, the Caribbean, and the American mainland—most slaves were baptized as Catholics and called upon to find their place in an emerging colonial order. Nonetheless, these involuntary African settlers often succeeded in recreating much of their ancestral lifestyle in the Americas. On the home continent, meanwhile, African communities struggled to adjust to their newly widened Atlantic connections. Their responses did not halt the growing demand for slaves and failed to discourage those willing to profit from that trade.

"Charter generations" is a term applied by historian Ira Berlin to describe the lives and experiences of the early African populations of North America, especially in the seventeenth century.[31] These were the Africans who, for this region, first encountered the colonial situation, the native and immigrant populations, and who labored to create families and to achieve social mobility from their positions in slavery. Berlin is effective in using this notion to distinguish this early situation of "slaves in society" from the later "slave society," but he also notes that the "charter generations" of seventeenth-century North America largely repeated the experience of earlier charter generations of the fifteenth century (for the Atlantic islands and Portugal)

FIGURE 2.6 Black Christians of Peru, c. 1600

Guaman Pomo de Ayala, a Catholic priest of indigenous Peruvian birth, included this illustration, labeled as "Black Catholics," in the long description of Peruvian life that he submitted to the King of Spain.

Source: Felipe Guaman Poma de Ayala, *Nueva Corónica y Buen Gobierno* (Paris: Institut d'Ethnologie, 1936), 703.

and the sixteenth century (in the Caribbean, Mexico, Peru, and Brazil). As Berlin suggests, the whole experience of colonization was repeated in each new territory seized by European settlers and merchants: each developing colony underwent a parallel life cycle. Inevitably, however, the experience of the later charter generations was influenced, directly or indirectly, by that of the earlier ones.

An Expanding World

Africans before 1600 experienced a history of connection and change, not just quiet village life. Connections from region to region within Africa resulted in the spread of musical instruments, crops, ideas about spirituality, and of course individual migrants. Similarly, connections beyond the continent led to the exchange of individuals, ideas, and occasionally to African-based conquests of lands in Spain, Arabia, and India. The overall result of this long-term pattern of interaction was an accumulation of technological improvements, expansions in the scale of political structure, developments in religion, and revisions of cultural traditions. The arrival of Europeans along African coasts in the fifteenth century was an extension of previous changes rather than a dramatic shift. Relations with the Portuguese and then with the Spanish across the Atlantic were not greatly different from relations with North Africa through trans-Saharan ties or from those in the Indian Ocean.

These Atlantic voyages expanded the geography of the African diaspora. "Offshore" areas now included the eastern Atlantic Ocean and the Atlantic islands from the Azores to São Tomé, in addition to the Sahara, the Red Sea, and the western Indian Ocean. More importantly, the "far diaspora" now included the Americas as well as Eurasia.

It may be that the discovery of the Americas was a smaller surprise to Africans than to Europeans. That is, the big novelty for Africans was the arrival of new groups of people by sea—Europeans and their caravels. Once Africans became used to the idea of voyages to Portugal, Spain, and the Atlantic islands, it was not hard to imagine that there might be other lands and other groups of people still further away—the Americas. African sailors aboard Portuguese vessels were soon to travel as far as the vessels on which they worked: to India, Japan, the Mediterranean, and the Caribbean. Nevertheless, dealing with European conceptions and living within European empires did begin to change things for Africans. The charter generations of Africans going abroad, mostly in slavery, raised the question of how much to sustain and how much to modify their culture, and they found themselves at an increasing disadvantage in the developing understanding of "race."

Theories were slow to emerge, but practical experience with "race" happened rapidly from 1400 to 1600. Migration brought Europeans and Amerindians to Africa, Europeans and more Africans to Asia, Europeans and Africans to the Americas, and people from every region to Europe. Thus, people from different regions came face to face with differences in phenotype, religious practice, and dress style. Snap judgments and categorizations appeared from the beginning, but overall patterns took a while to develop. For instance, educated Europeans had widely accepted the interpretation, passed down from the Greeks, that the dark skin of Africans came because they were "burned by the sun." But when blacks lived in northern climates for several generations without changing color, some European observers abandoned the environmental explanation and turned to believing that Africans suffered the curse of Ham and were black because of God's displeasure. In this and other ways, every social group developed its understanding and misunderstanding of race during this time of expanded cosmopolitan contacts and new forms of exploitation.

European states were not the only ones to grow in this era of discovery. Of the major global transformations of the sixteenth century, the rise of empires was the easiest to discern. Several great empires appeared. In combination, they controlled a larger portion of the earth's surface and population than ever before. The Ottoman Empire was perhaps most striking in its reach, as it came to dominate the Mediterranean and then the Red Sea. The Ottomans supported Muslim expansion in Ethiopia and Somalia, so when the Portuguese appeared in the Indian Ocean, they found themselves in a struggle with the Turks. In 1698, Ottoman forces expelled the Portuguese from their hold on Mombasa, where the latter had built Fort Jesus in the 1590s.

Other empires include the Safavid and Mughal (both formed in the early sixteenth century), which controlled much of the northern fringes of the Indian Ocean. The Spanish empire came to control lands in Europe and America and islands in the Pacific and Caribbean. The Portuguese empire gained control of small but strategic points of the Atlantic and Indian Ocean basins. The Russian empire began expanding across Siberia. The Ming state, which arose in the fifteenth century, continued to rule much of East Asia. Several of these powers could be considered successors to the preceding Mongol Empire. Nonetheless, the extent of imperial growth in this era was remarkable.

[In Africa, too, great states arose or expanded to control sizeable territories during the sixteenth century: Songhay, Funj, Benin, Kongo, Luba, Lunda, and competing states in Ethiopia. (The Zambezi Valley state of Mwenemu-tapa, in contrast, declined in its first century of connection with the Portuguese.) Did these empires result from the continuation of earlier traditions of development, or did they emerge out of the contingencies of sixteenth-century global connections? Why these empires rose almost all at once remains something of a mystery—a problem for historians to study.

Another major characteristic of the sixteenth-century world was the search for precious metals such as gold and silver. Africa's gold deposits lay in three major areas: in Bambuk and Bure (regions of the upper Senegal Valley), in the Akan-speaking areas of the Gold Coast, and in the highlands south of the Zambezi River. World trade in the sixteenth century led to prosperity for the Gold Coast and to mixed results for Bambuk-Bure. Gold was the major African contribution to world trade until the late seventeenth century, when the export of slaves finally exceeded gold in value.[32] African silver mines, however, never materialized.

The expansion of silver trade around the world provided another clear example of the changes in global patterns. The Spanish rulers of Peru and Mexico came to realize the incredible wealth of the silver deposits in Potosí and in Zacatecas and began organizing their exploitation in the mid-sixteenth century. This required a work force for extracting the ore, transforming it into ingots, and then shipping it to distant places. The initial destination was to Spain and the state, but silver was a commodity with a world market, not simply a metal that could be controlled by an imperial government. Merchants and states throughout Europe bought silver, as did purchasers in Russia, the Ottoman Empire, India, and China. In fact, India and China produced the greatest demand for silver. As a result, the Spanish founded the town of Manila in 1571 and began sending annual galleons across the Pacific, carrying silver to the Philippines for sale to Chinese merchants and purchasing silks and other commodities to bring back to Mexico. Thus, a global circuit of trade came into being, as the silver of Peru and Mexico traveled east across the Atlantic and west across the Pacific to arrive by each route in India and China.[33] Thus, wherever Portuguese visitors landed in Africa, they looked for silver. Africans mined, imported, and used small quantities of silver, but the precious metal did not become a major part of economic life in Africa until the nineteenth century.

Another global transformation of the sixteenth century was wrought by the spread of disease. Illnesses from the Old World—from Africa as well as from Europe—went through the Americas like wildfire, devastating populations, undercutting the social order, and emptying lands. Africans and Europeans were not entirely immune either, and the migrations to their homelands also brought epidemics. Although the evidence is not yet in, smallpox, a major killer in Africa, might have spread significantly in this time of expanding resettlement.

A Turn for the Worse

Songhay, the largest and perhaps the most populous state in all of Africa, lost a crucial battle near Timbuktu in 1591 to an invading army from the Sa'dian kingdom of Morocco. The Songhay archers and horsemen could not prevail against the disciplined musket-bearing infantry of the Sa'dians. The Moroccans seized the capital of Gao on the Niger, and uprisings in Songhay provinces rapidly collapsed the empire. Subsequent kings of Songhay regained control of Gao, but by then it was just a modest kingdom along the Niger. The diminution of Songhay at the end of the sixteenth century reflected a great material weakening of West Africa in the global order and marked a critical turning point that foreshadowed the subordination and oppression of Africans to come in the next three centuries.

The rise and fall of Songhay from 1464 to 1591 is just one part of a tale of interrelated changes linking the Niger Valley to the Atlantic, the Mediterranean, and coastal West Africa. One part of the story is the empire itself. It expanded in spectacular fashion from its Niger Bend homeland to control large areas of savanna, beginning at much the same time as Portuguese mariners started their voyages. Songhay first dominated east-west savanna trade and later controlled the north-south gold trade across the Sahara. Then the founding monarch, Sonni Ali, was displaced by Askia Muhammad, and a dynasty focused more on Islam arose. Its further expansion led to expanded control of gold and salt-producing lands. Songhay also came to rule the slave trade across the desert and subsequently accumulated large slave populations to provision the monarchy. Nevertheless, the empire did not succeed in building a cohesive identity among its multiethnic subjects or an integrated economic structure.

A second part of the tale is the rise of the Atlantic economy led by the Portuguese on the shores of Africa's long Atlantic coast. For almost two centuries, the Christian kingdoms of Iberia had been sending voyagers into the Atlantic. Portugal first dispatched individual vessels to explore the African coast and, in the 1440s, Portuguese ships reached the desert port of Arguin and the savanna shore of Senegal, where they began buying gold and slaves. Then, as their vessels edged along the Guinea coast in the 1470s, the Portuguese began sending well-armed expeditions rather than single ships. In

1482, they built the Elmina fortress to dominate the gold trade. From 1471 to 1505, they seized coastal Moroccan cities. They soon gave up trying to conquer inland areas but carried on trade in local hides and wax. They bought gold, textiles with which to purchase gold, and sugar. Portuguese and Spanish merchants sought sugar wherever they could get it. The Portuguese began producing it on all their Atlantic islands, most successfully on São Tomé beginning in 1485. The Spanish followed suit on the Canary Islands off the Moroccan coast in about 1500. Morocco's southern coast became a significant sugar-exporting area from the 1530s, selling to the Portuguese. When the Portuguese were expelled by the rising Moroccan Sa'dians in the 1540s, the English became major purchasers of sugar in exchange for woolen cloth. Nevertheless, even as the Portuguese began to buy gold and slaves at the western fringes of Songhay and along the Gold Coast, Songhay was able to ignore the Portuguese and expand its political and economic power for a century, in part because of the rising power of the Ottomans.

A third part of the tale is the conflict among newly expanded empires, most impressively Spain, Portugal, and the Ottomans, but with Songhay and Morocco as competitors. The Ottoman Empire conquered Egypt in 1517, gained control of Algeria in the same year, dominated the Red Sea from 1525, took Tripoli in 1546, and began intervening in Morocco from 1545. In Spain, meanwhile, the Castilian monarchy conquered Granada in 1492, made its claim on the Americas in the same year, and under the leadership of Charles I (r. 1516–1556), sought European and global preeminence.

For a brief time in the late sixteenth century, Morocco found itself to be a great power, even among such strong rivals, after its victory in the 1578 Battle of al-Qsar al-Kabir (also known as the War of Three Kings). Abdul-Malik, a claimant to the throne of the newly established Sa'dian dynasty, gained Ottoman support in 1574 and displaced Muhammad al-Mutawakkil in 1576. Al-Mutawakkil went to the Portuguese for help, and the young Portuguese king Sebastião agreed, landing with his army in northern Morocco in 1578. Abdul-Malik's forces won the battle, but all three kings died. Abdul-Malik's brother, Ahmad, succeeded to power. He took the title *al-Mansur* ("the victorious") and managed to remain independent of the Ottomans and Spain. Portugal, lacking an heir, found its throne taken over by Philip II of Spain, and from then until 1640 Portugal had Spanish rulers. Al-Mansur now found himself the leader of a united Morocco, a realm with tax revenue, trade revenue from sugar, gold, and slaves, an alliance with England, and the ability to play the Spanish and Ottoman empires against each other. Using Turkish military strategies in a very diverse army, he built up a formidable force that included an effective musket corps. Claiming to be descended from the prophet, he sought wider recognition as caliph, the spiritual leader of Islam. When the English defeated the Spanish Armada in 1588, Morocco's position seemed all the stronger.

The tale closes with the conquest of Songhay. Ahmad al-Mansur turned to an earlier project of his Sa'dian family: control of the desert salt mines and, through that, control of the Sudan's gold trade. In 1583, he had taken the Saharan oases of Gurara and Tuat, and in 1588, he demanded that Askia Ishaq II of Songhay pay him tax in gold on any salt removed from the Taghaza mines. Ishaq sent an angry response, and in 1590 al-Mansur prepared his invasion. The expedition was led by Spanish captives, and Spanish was the language of command. The desert crossing was difficult and roughly half the Moroccan troops died, perhaps of malaria, on their arrival in the savanna. Their disciplined musketry, however, enabled them to win the initial battle outside Timbuktu. They followed this victory with multiple triumphs in battle with Songhay's main armies, and the defeated empire soon collapsed. Morocco did not try to occupy the whole region, but it held on to Timbuktu and governed it with an occupying force known as the Arma. Distance and distractions in Morocco soon enabled the Arma to gain independence, and it existed for some time as a sovereign regime.

Rapid changes in the world economy confirmed that neither Morocco nor Songhay had a position of strength. Morocco, momentarily wealthy and powerful in the late sixteenth century, destroyed Songhay but could not control its lands or trade. Neither Songhay nor any other African state played a central role in global trade or politics thereafter. Sugar production in Brazil soon drove Morocco and the Canaries from the market. Silver from Peru and Mexico became the principal contribution to holdings in precious metals; gold remained important and profitable but lost its former hold on the market. Gold and slave routes from the West African interior to the coast expanded as those across the Sahara stagnated. A growing system of global trade now encompassed Africa and its labor. For instance, Europeans used Mexican silver to purchase textiles in India. Even cowrie shells, the currency of the Niger Valley that had previously arrived from the Maldives by trans-Saharan caravan after transshipment in Egypt, were now brought to the coast by Portuguese and Dutch ships. These commodities, after passing through Europe, went to West Africa in exchange for slaves, and some of the slaves became mine workers in the Americas. These and other changes opened up the era in which slave trade dominated the Atlantic economy, and West and Central Africa paid the price for that economic growth.

The collapse of Songhay confirmed the lesson taught by the defeat of the Kingdom of Kongo earlier in the century. At that time, the expanded slave trade by Portuguese merchants fostered warfare and defection among provincial rulers and civil war in the kingdom as a whole. Nzinga, queen of Matamba, a kingdom southeast of Kongo, fought the Portuguese in Angola from her accession in 1624 until 1655.[34] Her long, valiant struggle made the failure of African monarchy less abrupt in Central Africa than in West Africa. Overall, however, the portent was the same. The Atlantic economy's growth would do more to consume African societies than to enrich them.

Africa's global connections would now change in character. The close of the fifteenth century ended a long era of gradual but positive development and initiated centuries of struggle for survival. This same era would inaugurate the largest migration in human history and create an African diaspora whose population by 1800 would climb to more than 10 percent of the population of Africa.

Suggested Readings

Black Voyagers in Africa and Eurasia Before 1400

For details on the hajj of Mansa Musa, see Nehemia Levtzion and J. F. P. Hopkins, eds., *Corpus of Early Arabic Sources for West African History* (Princeton, N.J.: Markus Wiener Publishers, 2000). Works on travel in Africa include Stanley Burstein, ed. *Ancient African Civilizations: Kush and Axum* (Princeton, N.J.: Markus Wiener, 1998); Richard Bulliet, *The Camel and the Wheel* (Cambridge, Mass.: Harvard University Press, 1975); and Jan Vansina, *Paths in the Rainforests: Toward a History of Political Tradition in Equatorial Africa* (Madison: University of Wisconsin Press, 1990).

For information on Africans beyond the continent, see T. F. Earle and K. H. P. Lowe, *Black Africans in Renaissance Europe* (Cambridge: Cambridge University Press, 2005); Joseph E. Harris, *The African Presence in Asia: Consequences of the East African Slave Trade* (Evanston, Ill.: Northwestern University Press, 1971); Maghan Keita, *Race and the Writing of History: Riddling the Sphinx* (New York: Oxford University Press, 2000); and V. Y. Mudimbe, *The Idea of Africa* (Bloomington: Indiana University Press, 1994). See also *The Image of the Black in Western Art* (Cambridge, Mass.: Harvard University Press, 1976–1979), vol. 1, *From the Pharaohs to the Fall of the Roman Empire*, by Jean Vercoutter et al.; vol. 2, *From the Early Christian Era to the "Age of Discovery,"* part 1, *From the Demonic Threat to the Incarnation of Sainthood*, by Jean Devisse; part 2, *Africans in the Christian Ordinance of the World* (*Fourteenth to the Sixteenth Century*), by Jean Devisse and Michel Mollat. See also Bernard Lewis, *Race and Slavery in the Middle East: An Historical Inquiry* (New York: Oxford University Press, 1990). For a fine study of a worldwide traveler, see

Ross E. Dunn, *The Adventures of Ibn Battuta: A Muslim Traveler of the Four-teenth Century* (Berkeley: University of California Press, 1989).

Africans at Home, Up to 1400

For a basic review of African historical geography, see Colin McEvedy, *The Penguin Atlas of African History*, rev. ed. (London: Penguin Books, 1995). On the languages of Africa, an excellent introduction is Bernd Heine and Derek Nurse, *African Languages: An Introduction* (Cambridge: Cambridge University Press, 2000).

African Rethink Their Hierarchies, 1400–1600

For social change in Islamic West Africa, see Nehemia Levtzion and Jay Spaulding, eds., *Medieval West Africa: Views from Arab Scholars and Merchants* (Princeton, N.J.: Markus Wiener, 2003); Elias N. Saad, *Social History of Tim-buktu* (Cambridge: Cambridge University Press, 1983); and René A. Brav-mann, *Islam and Tribal Art in West Africa* (Cambridge: Cambridge University Press, 1974). On social change in Zimbabwe, see P. S. Garlake, *Great Zim-babwe* (London: Thames and Hudson, 1973). On social and cultural change in Central Africa, see Eugenia W. Herbert, *Red Gold of Africa: Copper in Pre-colonial History and Culture* (Madison: University of Wisconsin Press, 1984); Georges Balandier, *Daily Life in the Kingdom of Kongo: From the Sixteenth to the Eighteenth Century*, trans. Helen Weaver (New York: Pantheon, 1968); and Jan Vansina, *Kingdoms of the Savanna* (Madison: University of Wiscon-sin Press, 1965). On the art of Ife, see Frank Willett, *Ife in the History of West African Sculpture* (London: Thames and Hudson, 1968). For classic general overviews of art and social change, see Jan Vansina, *Art History in Africa: An Introduction to Method* (New York: Longman, 1984); and Melville J. Herskov-its, *The Human Factor in Changing Africa* (New York: Knopf, 1962). For two important studies of Timbuktu as a center of knowledge, see John O. Hun-wick, *Hidden Treasures of Timbuktu: Rediscovering Africa's Literary Culture* (London: Thames and Hudson, 2008); and Shamil Jeppie and Souleymane Bachir Diagne, eds., *The Meanings of Timbuktu* (Pretoria: Human Sciences Research Council, 2008).

Migrations to Old World Destinations, 1400–1600

For details on sixteenth-century Iberian ventures in the eastern Atlantic, see A. C. de M. Saunders, *A Social History of Black Slaves and Freedmen in Portugal, 1441–1555* (Cambridge: Cambridge University Press, 1982); and Manuel Lobo

Cabrera, *La Esclavitud en las Canarias Orientales en el Siglo XVI (Negros, Moros y Moriscos)* (Gran Canaria: Ediciones de Excmo. Cabildo Insular, 1982). For a wide-ranging narrative of African-European interactions up to 1600, see Stefan Goodwin, *Africa in Europe*, vol. 1, *Antiquity Into the Age of Global Exploration* (Lanham, Md.: Rowman and Littlefield, 2009).

American Encounters, 1492–1600

For an overview of historical geography in the Americas, see A. Curtis Wilgus, *Historical Atlas of Latin America: Political, Geographic, Economic, Cultural* (New York: Cooper Square Publishers, 1967). It is difficult to locate general works on the languages of the Americas; the principal overall survey is Joseph H. Greenberg, *Language in the Americas* (Stanford, Calif.: Stanford University Press, 1987). On Africans in early Spanish settlements, see Frederick P. Bowser, *The African Slave in Colonial Peru, 1524–1650* (Stanford, Calif.: Stanford University Press, 1974); and Colin A. Palmer, *Slaves of the White God: Blacks in Mexico, 1570–1650* (Cambridge, Mass.: Harvard University Press, 1976). For the Americas more generally, see John Thornton, *Africa and Africans in the Making of the Atlantic World, 1400–1680* (New York: Cambridge University Press, 1992); and Ira Berlin, *Many Thousands Gone: The First Two Centuries of Slavery in North America* (Cambridge, Mass.: Harvard University Press, 1998).

An Expanding World

For a multidimensional view of the connection between hemispheres, see Alfred W. Crosby, *The Columbian Exchange: Biological and Cultural Consequences of 1492* (Westport, Conn.: Greenwood Press, 1972). On the global links of the Portuguese empire, see A. J. R. Russell-Wood, *A World on the Move: The Portuguese in Africa, Asia, and America, 1415–1808* (Manchester: Carcanet, 1992). On the expansion of British empire, see David Armitage, *Greater Britain, 1516–1776: Essays in Atlantic History* (Aldershot: Ashgate, 2004).

A Turn for the Worse

On political change in northwestern Africa and the collapse of Songhay, see Jamil M. Abun-nasr, *A History of the Maghrib in the Islamic Period* (Cambridge: Cambridge University Press, 1987); Thomas A. Hale, *Scribe, Griot, and Novelist: Narrative Interpreters of the Songhay Empire* (Gainesville: University of Florida Press, 1990); and Thomas A. Hale, ed., *The Epic of Askia Mohammed* (Bloomington: Indiana University Press, 1996).

⟹ 3 ⟸

Survival, 1600–1800

Pernambuco, the tropical captaincy of Brazil's northeast coast, became a crucial battleground of the seventeenth-century world. The region's *engenhos*, or sugar plantations, which had begun to prosper in the 1580s, relied mainly on slave laborers brought to Recife from Luanda in Angola. Almost immediately, African laborers slipped away from the *engenhos* to set up an independent existence. Some escapees stayed close to the *engenhos* to have access to food and maintain ties to friends. Others moved further away, especially to the southwest and into the interior. There, some eighty kilometers from Recife, they formed settlements that collectively came to be known as Palmares, a name taken from the region's palm trees. What began as a refuge for runaways soon turned into an alternative lifestyle. The settlers created farms, set up households, drew Amerindians into their communities, and raided *engenhos* for food, tools, and recruits, especially women. As early as 1597, Fr. Pero Lopes, the Jesuit provincial of Pernambuco, warned that the fugitives in Palmares might be able to mount a rebellion. He cited the example of São Tomé in 1530, where an uprising of slaves and maroons (runaway slaves) destroyed seventy *engenhos* and briefly drove the Portuguese from the island.

In 1602, the Portuguese sent their first military expedition against Palmares under Bartolomeu Bezerra. On his return, Bezerra announced the complete destruction of the target settlements. His bravado was premature, as the scattered escapees reassembled in Palmares and resumed their raids. Thus developed the largest of the settlements that would be called *quilombos* in Brazil. Elsewhere, escapees came to be known as *cimarrones* in Spanish and, in borrowings of the same term, as "maroons" in English and *marrons* in French. For a time, the Portuguese administration gave up on trying to destroy Palmares. [In 1608, the governor of Pernambuco argued that the sugar plantations could rely on Amerindian slave labor and that no further imports of Africans would be necessary.]

The second great conflict in Pernambuco came with the Dutch invasion. In 1630, a fleet of the Dutch West Indies Company (WIC) landed three thousand troops near Pernambuco. They quickly took the town and then slowly expanded their control over the Portuguese-dominated settlements. The war enabled more slaves to escape to Palmares. As the Dutch gained control of the land and expanded sugar production, they ran short of laborers. But when a WIC fleet seized control of Luanda in 1641, a flood of Angolan captives came to Pernambuco in Dutch ships.

Thus the first serious challenge to Palmares's existence came not from the Portuguese but from Dutch invaders. In 1644 and 1645, they launched two major expeditions against it. They seized a few ex-slaves in small outlying settlements but found the town itself abandoned. Dutch reports describe the long main street, the houses, and the church. As under the Portuguese, the returning Dutch armies announced the destruction of Palmares but their claims were soon shown to be exaggerated.

The Dutch never consolidated their control of Pernambuco. In the Portuguese homeland, a 1640 rebellion against the Spanish overlords succeeded, with the help of England and France, in reestablishing Portuguese independence. Around the same time, Portuguese settlers in Brazil organized an army that fought the Dutch and, by 1648, had regained most of Pernambuco. The same Brazilians—including African and Amerindian warriors who were central to the force—now sailed to Angola, where they linked up with surviving Portuguese and Angolan allies and drove the Dutch from Angola by 1651. Back in Brazil, the Dutch finally capitulated, evacuating Pernambuco in 1654.

After the Dutch expulsion, Palmares enjoyed another period of quiescence. Then from the 1670s the Portuguese made repeated assaults. Using the established technique of flight, the people of Palmares systematically frustrated their attackers. With these mounting assaults, however, the leadership in Palmares passed to a more militant faction: a man named Zumbi became king and military leader and developed a stronger military. The end of the 1680s saw a truce established, as the governor of Pernambuco promised to recognize Palmares. When the Portuguese once again attacked in the early 1690s, Palmares under Zumbi's leadership chose to stand and fight. In a siege lasting over a month, the Portuguese finally shattered the town's defenses. During a follow-up expedition, the Portuguese captured Zumbi, paraded him in the capital, beheaded him, and left his remains on public display.

After that time, *quilombos* continued to form throughout Brazil, but none of them reached the size of Palmares. That community retained its importance in the history and mythology of Brazil for whites, blacks, and Indians. It demonstrated the vigor of African traditions in the Americas and confirmed that a tradition of resistance would exist throughout the era of slavery.

Palmares existed for a century as a set of communities under African governance in Brazil, with a population that reached twenty thousand or more. Had slavery not expanded, this African community might have fit into the mosaic of emerging Brazilian society. But the growth of the sugar trade, the Dutch and Portuguese determination to make commercial profit, and the ability to collect more captives in Africa led events in a different direction. With time, most *quilombos* in Brazil was rooted out and dismantled, which left African migrants to Brazil in a situation where they had to protect and develop their traditions under the watchful eye of well-armed Portuguese masters.

Waves of Enslavement

Why did slavery grow? Part of the answer to this big question lies in the large-scale interactions of the growing world economy. But other aspects of the answer can be appreciated by observing the details on *how* slavery grew. The story of Palmares illustrates the force of growing demand for slave labor but also the countervailing force of resistance to enslavement. Pursuing this approach, the remainder of this chapter explores the experiences of black people in freedom and slavery, in the diaspora and in the home societies of Africa. How did people survive, and what strategies did they create to improve their chances? We address these questions for the Middle Passage and for the changes in life in the Atlantic diaspora, the Old World diaspora, and in the African homeland. After these explorations of economy and family, we inquire into the changing nature of race and identity, and conclude with the Haitian Revolution and its great challenge to slavery. The chapter begins, in this section, with an overview of slave-trading powers and the flows of captives.

From 1600 onward, the global economy underwent a major change, and this transformed Africa along with the rest of the world. As sea lanes and winds came to be known in more detail, as ports and commodity trading were restructured to take advantage of new opportunities, and as governments and armies set new priorities in controlling various sorts of wealth, every region saw its relationships with other parts of the world altered. The Europeans' initial arrival on African coasts after 1450 brought new contacts and experiences to the inhabitants, but it did not cause rapid change. Even during the sixteenth century, the relatively stable life in Africa paralleled that in Europe and contrasted sharply with drastic changes in the Americas. In the seventeenth century, however, the Dutch empire's rise in the Atlantic expanded and redirected the trade in African slaves. While the emergence of the great Brazilian maroon community of Palmares demonstrated the ability of some to escape and resist captivity in the Americas, the practice of slavery would greatly influence much of the world for two centuries. Not surprisingly, the expansion in slavery necessitated a greater struggle for survival among Africans on the continent and in the diaspora.

The ascendance of the Dutch commercial empire signaled a fatal turning point for the place of Africans in the world economy. The Netherlands had been an independent region of northwestern Europe until royal marriage made their grand duke the king of Spain and put the Netherlands under Spanish rule in 1519. But the Netherlands was also a place of active industry and commerce. Partly for religious reasons (the Netherlands was mostly Protestant, while the Spanish monarchy was the most Catholic of states) and partly for commercial ones, the people of the Netherlands became restive under Spanish rule. From 1568, several provinces there declared informal and then formal independence from Spain, and thus began eighty years of war. The result was the division of the Netherlands into the northern portion, which became the Protestant-dominated Dutch Republic, and the southern portion, which remained under Spanish rule (and from 1700, Austrian rule) and stayed mainly Catholic.

Dutch merchants launched two great overseas trading companies. In 1602, they founded the East Indies Company (VOC). Its commanders sent military and trade expeditions to the Indian Ocean, seizing Portuguese trading posts where possible and setting up their own trade centers when they failed to dislodge the Portuguese. This company helped create Dutch outposts in Indonesia, Malaya, India, China, and Japan, and brought a wealth of spices and manufactures from these regions to northern Europe.

In 1621, Dutch merchants created the West Indies Company (WIC). They intended to gain commercial dominance in the Atlantic at a time when Spain and Portugal governed much of the conquered territory in Africa, Brazil, and the rest of the Americas. In 1624, WIC settlers founded a colony in the Hudson and Delaware river valleys of North America. At the same time, the company sent a fleet to capture the main Brazilian town of Salvador in Bahia and a fleet to seize the Angolan capital of Luanda. (One of WIC's greatest coups occurred in 1628, when Admiral Piet Heijn captured the Spanish treasure fleet in Cuba.) Although initially successful, the Dutch eventually lost control of these conquests.

The WIC returned its focus to sugar and slaves in 1630, when it captured Recife on the coast north of Bahia. From there, it gradually extended its rule to all of Pernambuco. Even though the Dutch lost half their battles, by 1641 they had seized Arguin, Goree, and Elmina to dominate West Africa's gold trade; Pernambuco to control Brazil's sugar plantations; and Luanda to dominate Central Africa's slave trade. Also in the 1630s, they seized numerous Caribbean islands, including Curaçao and St. Eustatius, and the mainland territory of Guyana in South America. By 1645, WIC had brought almost thirty thousand captives from Africa to Brazil, half from Angola and half from West Africa.

The Dutch domination of the Atlantic lasted just twenty years—the 1630s and 1640s—yet their conquests and commercial activities transformed the Atlantic world. The Dutch improved the Portuguese models of warfare, slave trade, plantation colonies, and Atlantic commerce. Almost immediately, other European powers—England, France, and Denmark—rushed to adopt the Dutch example. The Portuguese too learned from the Dutch and put that knowledge to work to regroup and drive them out of Brazil and Angola.

Thereafter, the Dutch role in the Atlantic was limited mainly to being merchants rather than rulers of plantations or settlement colonies. After losing Luanda, the Dutch set up a new base at the Cape of Good Hope in 1652. The Cape colony became a rest and replenishment stop for VOC ships on their way to the Indian Ocean, serving much the same function for the Dutch as the island of Mozambique did for the Portuguese. A few years later, in 1664, the English seized the colonies along the Hudson and Delaware rivers, driving the Dutch out of North America. Still, the Dutch held on to important African posts for trade in gold and slaves and to Caribbean ports for slaves, sugar, and provisions.

Most importantly for our story, the Dutch confirmed the slave trade's profitability. They remained active slave traders for more than another century. The big Dutch ships, usually well financed and experiencing fewer captive deaths than their competitors, stopped at Elmina and along the Slave Coast of West Africa, or at the Central African ports of Loango, the mouth of the Congo, and Benguela. They struck deals with African merchants to collect captives and then sold these individuals to anyone who would buy along African or American coasts. By 1660, Curaçao had become the main destination for Dutch cargoes, and the captives went from there primarily to Spanish territories. However, they also were sold to English and French buyers in the eastern Caribbean, who were creating sugar plantations modeled on those of Brazil. Thus began the sugar industry's rapid expansion in the Caribbean and the consequent dramatic growth in demand for African labor.

The English seized the island of Barbados from the Spanish in 1627. They settled it first with English and Irish people (some of them in slavery) and grew foodstuffs and tobacco on small plots. After 1650, however, the encouraging example of Dutch merchants led to a burgeoning sugar industry and the importation of African slaves to work on rapidly expanding land holdings. By 1680, the Barbados population was overwhelmingly African. Just a few years later, the French island of Martinique had a similar experience: white indentured tobacco workers were soon displaced by much larger numbers of black slaves used for sugar production.

The apparently smooth rise and eventual decline in volume of the Atlantic and Old World slave trade (shown in graph 3.1) appropriately represents the overall contours of enslavement and slave transport. But it is a misleading indicator of slave trade in any localized region of Africa or the diaspora. The number of persons exchanged varied sharply from year to year, and the total often rose and fell in waves lasting from ten to forty years.

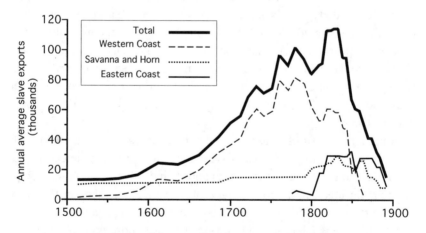

GRAPH 3.1 Volume of Slave Trade, Atlantic and Old World, 1650–1900

Transatlantic captives embarked on the African coast: estimates based on "Transatlantic Slave Trade Database" (http://www.slavevoyages.org). Total of captives dispatched across the Sahara, Red Sea, and Indian Ocean: estimates based on Manning, *Slavery and African Life.*

The history of slave trade in any region thus tended to be a story of massive business for a few years followed by a span of greatly reduced traffic. Perhaps a better way to characterize the ebb and flow would be as steady trade on a large scale that slacked off when the supply of potential captives from Africa was exhausted or the American slave population grew so large that owners feared rebellion and reduced or stopped their importation. What follows is a chronology of some of the main tides of departures from Africa and arrivals in the Americas.

Waves of African departures and American arrivals did not always correspond neatly: the surge of departures from Ouidah disembarked on the coast from Bahia to Virginia, while the wave of arrivals in Louisiana had embarked from Senegal to Loango. The initial expansion of slave exports from Angola, after the Portuguese establishment at Luanda in 1575, lasted into the early seventeenth century. Then in the early seventeenth century, Angolan slave exports declined while those from Upper Guinea rose. Angolan exports then expanded again in the mid-seventeenth century as those from Upper Guinea declined. From the 1680s, slave exports from the Bight of Benin increased at such a rapid rate, peaking in the 1710s, that the region came to be called the Slave Coast, a name that stuck. The Gold Coast experienced a similar wave of slave exports from the 1680s to the 1720s.

As exports from these regions declined in the 1730s, Upper Guinea slave exports expanded again, as did exports from Senegambia, and exports from the Bight of Biafra now joined the slave trade. Also in the mid-eighteenth century, exports from Angola rose again and the slave volume through Loango (from the northern part of the Congo basin) leaped upward. Late in the eighteenth century, shipments from the Bight of Benin reached another peak, and captives from Mozambique began coming to the Americas in large numbers.

Similar fluctuations characterized the slave trade to the Old World diaspora. Moroccan purchases of West African captives expanded in the era of King Mulay Isma'il (1672–1727) and then declined. Dutch slave shipments from Madagascar to the Cape of Good Hope peaked in the early eighteenth century. French shipments from Mozambique and Madagascar to the Mascarene Islands—Ile Bourbon (now Réunion) and Ile de France (Mauritius)—rose from the 1740s to a peak in the 1780s. Slave deliveries from the middle Nile to Egypt expanded with the Egyptian economy in the late eighteenth century.

Numerous factors influenced the shifts in regional export volumes. Warfare and drought were common boosters of slave trade. Sometimes the resolution of conflicts or the return of rains had the opposite effect. The willingness and ability of African merchants and warlords to collect and deliver captives also changed with time. More fundamentally, the population decline in the areas of intensive enslavement made it impossible to sustain export levels. Prices rose when too few captives were available for buyers. Merchants aboard ships made special efforts to develop new supply sources. They made additional stops along the coast whenever they failed to purchase enough captives at the usual ports. Market pressures worked relentlessly to bring region after region of the African coast into the business of collecting and selling captives. Slave merchants would also return a generation or so later to areas that had been exhausted to benefit from yet another wave of enslavement.

These varying pulses of African captives to an assortment of purchasers spread across the Atlantic and Indian Oceans in a chaotic fashion. When new colonies opened up or when a boom developed for sugar, tobacco, or gold, great numbers of captives were delivered for a few years. Barbados and Martinique experienced such surges in slave imports in the late seventeenth century, as the sugar industry began its Caribbean expansion on those islands. The gold rushes of Minas Gerais in the 1690s and of the Pacific coast of New Granada (modern Colombia and Panama) created demand for large numbers of slave laborers. St. Domingue (the western portion of Hispaniola) and Jamaica in the mid-eighteenth century came to dominate the sugar industries of French and British colonies, respectively, and slave imports to those colonies led the Caribbean trade. Large slave population increases in the British Caribbean islands were accompanied by smaller but significant increases in slave deliveries to North American colonies, where much of the work was devoted to provisioning laborers on the island sugar plantations. In this "century of sugar," the *engenhos* of Bahia also expanded with a burst of new slave imports from West Africa. In the late eighteenth century, the two American destinations for the greatest number of captives—the French colony of St. Domingue and the Brazilian southeast (via Rio de Janeiro)—brought in new workers at a relatively stable rate.

At those times when large numbers of slaves were delivered, captive populations were heavily African: up to 90 percent in the new colonies and as much as 60 percent in the old colonies. In the intervening periods, locally born slaves became more numerous, and a generation after the last slaves disembarked from abroad, the creoles (those born in the colonies) may have reached 70 percent of the population. Thus the slave population of Louisiana was almost 100 percent African as the colony expanded in the 1720s, but it had become 80 percent creole by the 1770s. Then a wave of new imports by Spanish investors brought the creole population there down to 40 percent of the total black population. Many black and brown people became free in certain territories, such as Santo Domingo (modern Dominican Republic) and Venezuela in the late eighteenth century. In those locales, the small number of slave imports and the pace of emancipation meant that perhaps 80 percent of the African-descended population were free people of color, and most of the slaves were creole rather than African.

At about the middle of the seventeenth century, the number of Africans sent each year across the Atlantic in bondage came to equal and then exceed the number sent as slaves across the Sahara to North Africa. Thereafter, the trans-Saharan slave trade continued to account for about ten thousand enslaved Africans each year, while the number crossing the Atlantic kept growing, exceeding twenty-five thousand per year by 1700.

The principal routes of captives delivered from Africa to America changed over the seventeenth and eighteenth centuries. From 1600 to 1650, the largest numbers of captives came to northeastern Brazil, and they came principally from Upper Guinea and Angola. The next largest group of imports arrived in New Granada and Peru, coming in particular from Upper Guinea. From 1650 to 1680, the Caribbean's relatively small black population grew rapidly, with captives brought especially by the Dutch from Senegambia and Congo. Brazilian imports remained high and came mainly from Angola. From 1680 to 1730, the Bight of Benin's slave trade grew dramatically and was followed by expanded slave exports from the Gold Coast. Captives from the Gold Coast, likely to be experienced in gold mining, were prominent among those imported to Minas Gerais and New Granada but went in larger numbers to the French and British Caribbean sugar islands.

Captives from the Bight of Biafra were prominent among those brought to the Chesapeake colonies of Virginia and Maryland as they expanded rapidly from 1730 to 1770. By 1750, every region of the western coast and the Saharan fringe of Africa had been deeply involved in the slave trade, and the seizure of captives had extended from the coastline well into the interior. In the 1790s and just after 1800, British and American purchasers brought the peak numbers of Africans into their respective territories. The fluctuations in the location and intensity of enslavement continued for another century, as the practice of large-scale slave trade spread to the eastern coast and the African interior.

The Atlantic Middle Passage

The Middle Passage across the Atlantic was a dreadful and life-bending experience for each of the millions of persons who endured it. (So too was the experience of those taken across Saharan sands or Indian Ocean waters to slavery in the Old World, discussed in a later section of this chapter.) Each individual's story began well before the fearsome moment of being forced on board ship, with being seized and driven in captivity to the coast and then suffering through the wait for sale and embarkation. The passage itself was so horrible that few were willing to speak of it afterward. Disembarkation after the voyage and sale again, for those who survived to that stage, was still another traumatic experience.

The stories of individuals and shiploads of captives traveling the Atlantic Middle Passage have been alternately told, hidden, dug out, and told again, as the descendants of slaves and free people seek to grasp the impact of this process. Daniel Mannix and Malcolm Cowley, Michael Gomez, James Rawley, James Walvin, and especially Marcus Rediker have effectively portrayed the experience of captives, and Hugh Thomas has detailed the viewpoint of the merchants and ship captains. My approach to the story aims at setting these individual tales of cruelty, oppression, and survival in the context of the whole African diaspora. This section will emphasize the history of the Atlantic Middle Passage as a whole. The Middle Passage process that "swallowed" millions of captives can be seen as a Leviathan. The original Leviathan, the immense sea creature described in the Book of Job as too powerful for mortal man to combat, itself had a life course from its creation to its end. So too did the Middle Passage.

Long ago, the English philosopher Thomas Hobbes appropriated the metaphor of Leviathan to speak of the commonwealth or state, which he saw as an artificial man, created by man but "of greater stature and strength than the natural, for whose protection and defence it was intended." Hobbes saw sovereignty as an artificial soul, magistrates as artificial joints, sedition as sickness, and civil war as death—he used the metaphor of Leviathan to argue that the various elements of the state work together to provide an organic political community, though one in which life was "nasty, brutish, and short."[1] I use the metaphor of Leviathan here in some sense closer to the original Biblical sea monster. This new Leviathan—not a single sea creature but a fleet of seagoing horrors—expanded, grew more efficient and more terrible, and came to an end due to internal weaknesses and attacks from its enemies. That history is sketched out here to remind readers that every aspect of the African diaspora underwent transformation over the course of slave trade: the four centuries of transporting captives changed the ships themselves, the composition and survival rate of the human cargoes, the trade methods, and the treatment of those enslaved. Overall, it is a story of an expansion in scale, of technological improvements, of slavers driven into vicious competition by greed, and of captives tossed on the emotional seas of hope, despair, and the desire for revenge. Ultimately, the slave trade's scale of brutality reached a tipping point where people of all colors joined in outrage to bring it to an end.

The Atlantic slave trade began in the fifteenth century with voyages by small Portuguese ships carrying relatively light cargoes. The larger ships of that early time were caravels with capacities of eighty to 130 tons,[2] but the smaller ships of the *lançados* may have carried greater numbers of the early captives. Mortality rates reported on these early voyages usually remained below 5 percent and rarely exceeded 15 percent for trips from Senegal or Cape Verde to Portugal. On the negative side, the slave merchants' inexperience with carrying cargoes of captives would surely have resulted in high mortality. As experience with the winds and provisioning grew, the rate of captive mortality came down to somewhat lower levels. The shorter voyages from Kongo to São Tomé or from Senegal to Lisbon—one to three weeks rather than the eight weeks of transatlantic crossing—also limited mortality. These early forays along the African coast laid the groundwork for the Middle Passage's later expansion.

The slave trade of the early sixteenth century extended that of the fifteenth century, principally bringing captives to the Atlantic coast islands of Africa and to Lisbon and Seville. Small numbers of African slaves were sent in this period to the Caribbean and the American mainland, but these had already been "seasoned" in Iberia and presumably were sent as passengers rather than captives in chains.

From the 1550s, merchants in Seville began buying and then selling contracts for delivery of specified numbers of Africans directly to the Americas: these *bozales* were to be seasoned, renamed, baptized, sold, transported again, taught to communicate with fellow slaves and new masters, and put to work in their new life. The contracts for their delivery soon took the form of the *asiento*, in which Portuguese ships began delivering slaves to the ports of Santo Domingo, Havana, Vera Cruz, Cartagena, and Porto Bello after collecting cargoes in Africa, especially Upper Guinea. In this same era, the Portuguese slave traders visiting Angola took their cargoes mainly to São Tomé, still the leading center for sugar production. After 1580, however, Portuguese merchants began carrying larger numbers of slaves from Kongo and Angola to northeastern Brazil to supply the expanding sugar industry there. (The wars of the Portuguese, Dutch, Spanish, French, and English involved sending large numbers of troops by ship across wide oceans under conditions not utterly different from the dispatch of slave cargoes.)

By the end of the sixteenth century, the pattern of rise and fall of slave exports from African regions had become manifest, notably in Senegambia and Upper Guinea. The greatest exception to these fluctuations was the Portuguese port of Luanda, created in 1575, which remained the mouth of a siphon that steadily drew captives from throughout the Angolan hinterland for dispatch, mostly to Brazil, until 1850.

Dutch ships, which entered the slave trade in force beginning in 1630, were bigger and thus carried larger cargoes than those of competitors. Their *flutes*, capacious vessels of two hundred or more tons, had been built to carry grain across the North Sea and were found to be well suited to the slave trade: for instance, they yielded relatively low rates of slave mortality. According to statistics collected by Johannes Postma, the mortality rate among Dutch transport captives appears to have declined from 14 to 11 percent in the late seventeenth century.[3]

English and French merchants joined in slaving close on the heels of the Dutch expansion, principally to boost slave populations in their new Caribbean territories but also to sell enslaved workers in Spanish territories. The English Company of Royal Adventurers failed as a slave-trading venture after a few years in the 1670s. Its replacement, the Royal Africa Company, succeeded for a longer time, but its inexperience in its first six years of activity resulted in a mortality rate averaging over 25 percent of the forty thousand captives shipped. Thereafter, the mortality rate on British vessels averaged closer to 15 percent.

The early eighteenth century was also the high point of piracy in the oceanic slave trade. At its peak in 1720, an estimated two thousand pirates manned over thirty pirate ships, well armed and strategically located in the Caribbean, West Africa, and Madagascar. They seized perhaps two thousand vessels over twenty years. A substantial minority of the pirate crews was African or of African ancestry, including escaped slaves and men who were children of unions between white sailors and women from the maritime populations of West Africa and Madagascar. These rebels emphasized an egalitarian lifestyle on land and sea. If they were not abolitionists, they were a threat to the mercantile system that relied on slavery. The British navy finally bent all its efforts to suppressing the pirates, and by 1726 had captured and executed all of the principal pirate leaders.

The eighteenth century was the peak period for the Atlantic slave trade, which rose to its highest point near the end of that time. It is also the best documented period, and the differences from its beginning to end are revealed in some simple statistics. The French slave trade from Nantes, in 1714, included eighteen vessels averaging 166 tons in capacity, for a total of three thousand tons during the year. In 1788, Nantes vessels made thirty-three voyages. These ships averaged 380 tons, totaling over twelve thousand tons during the year, four times the capacity of voyages in 1714. In that same time, the average initial crew size declined slightly from forty-two to thirty-seven men. In other words, labor-force efficiency more than doubled in terms of tonnage per crewman. The deaths among French crewmen declined from twelve per voyage (28 percent of the crew) in 1714 to five per voyage (14 percent of the crew) in 1788.[4]

Ouidah, along with Luanda, was the great port for dispatching captives across the Atlantic. Bonny and Calabar were not far behind in volume, and Loango rose over the course of the century to a point of importance. Jamaica and St. Domingue eventually surpassed Barbados and Martinique as importing regions, while Rio came steadily closer to Bahia as a major destination for slave cargoes. Among the Spanish colonies, the ports of Panama remained the greatest importers of captives, with Buenos Aires and Cartagena not far behind, followed by Havana, Caracas, and Vera Cruz.

The number of captives sent across the Atlantic at the end of the eighteenth century exceeded eighty thousand per year. The total size of the crews that carried them was roughly eight thousand. On French ships, the number of captives loaded per crew member remained relatively constant during the century, rising from seven captives per crew member in 1714 to eight in 1788. The French ships from Nantes delivered forty-nine hundred captives to the Americas, with roughly one thousand dying at sea, and ten thousand captives in 1788, with about seven hundred dying at sea. In that time, the death rate for captives declined from just over 20 percent in 1714 to 8 percent for those voyages recorded in 1788. The average ship tonnage (capacity) per slave increased with time, from 0.6 tons capacity per captive embarked in 1714 to 1.4 tons per captive embarked in 1788.[5] One unsuccessful revolt broke out among the Nantes ships in 1714; in 1788, captives successfully seized two ships and escaped to the African coast. Both the efficiency and the ferocity of slave trade grew with time.

In the Brazilian South Atlantic trade, the space per captive did not increase by much during the century. The Portuguese system of taxation and the procedures at Luanda for releasing ships to sail in a politically determined order had the effect of packing slaves very tightly into the vessels. The voyage to Brazil was relatively short, however, and with dependable winds, captains could afford to crowd captives unmercifully without a corresponding increase in mortality.

The records of the eighteenth century reveal information on the condition of captives held on the African coast as well. Day-by-day figures for shipboard mortality show the mortality rate was highest the first few days on board, which presumably reflects the shock of conditions aboard ship and the unhealthiness of the barracoons where captives were held before embarkation.

For the voyage duration, and often for times before and after, captives were generally kept completely naked, often with their heads shaved. The slave traders argued that it was for their own convenience and for the health of the captives, but the systematic effect was the humiliation of children and adults. The cases where captives were given loincloths represented a significant difference. The nakedness and filth of the passage became an ingrained, painful memory for captives and were the voyages' most demeaning aspects. Still, the bonds formed among "shipmates" during this experience offset the horror somewhat. These and other ties of fictive kinship would be essential for passengers during their lives as slaves.

One need not argue that the Middle Passage became more humane during the eighteenth century, but it is clear it became economically more efficient. It successfully brought captives from deeper in the African continent, used leaner crews and bigger ships, kept a larger portion of captives alive in the crossing, and made shipboard rebellions relatively less frequent. By operating more efficiently, slave merchants were able to exploit Africa on a steadily expanding scale. (As every parasite knows, it is best to weaken rather than kill the host.) The monstrous Leviathan of the Middle Passage began with the patrols along the eastern Atlantic shores of Africa, grew fat on the flesh of the laborers it consumed, and learned to stretch itself across to the Americas. It then expanded until some two hundred vessels sailed the Atlantic each year under the flags of six or more nations, consuming an average of three hundred persons each, extinguishing a portion of them, and disgorging the survivors on shore, from which they would be dragged further, revived, and shackled to the labors of new masters.

Changes Within Africa

Parallel to the struggle for survival among New World slaves, whether carried off from Africa or born into captivity in the Americas, was a somewhat different struggle for survival on the African continent. As of 1600, few Africans were in the "legal condition" of slavery, but many were in relations of dependence upon more powerful persons. These relations, which had long provided individuals and families protection by a more powerful figure, were translated by greed and the prospect of wealth into the power to buy and sell a person. Wars, as they occurred, led to captures, but captives were now likely to be sold rather than ransomed back to their families. European purchasers at the coast were willing to pay more for male than for female captives and acquired more males than females. Thus female captives were more likely to be held in Africa than sent abroad. They became domestics and concubines. In these circumstances, they did not formally marry, and their children were not their own but belonged to their owner or to the father.

West and Central Africa therefore became the site of a great struggle in the seventeenth and eighteenth centuries—and so to a lesser degree did other parts of the continent. The millions carried from the continent in captivity faced the challenge of survival in the starkest of terms. But in almost equal measure, the problem of survival transfixed those who remained in the African homeland. For the additional millions enslaved and held within Africa and who died premature deaths during capture or transportation, it was a matter of personal survival. For the people ripped asunder by war and kidnapping, it was a matter of survival of the family unit. For the communities pursued by warriors, it was a question of decimation for some and, for others, flight and a new lifestyle. Even for the families and communities that prospered through enslavement, it was a question of whether their momentary riches undermined their social values, and also a question of whether their enemies would retaliate and send them off in captivity. For African societies in general, these centuries posed the question of whether the fearsome hierarchy brought by enslavement would destroy their social fabric. On this last point, observers within African societies and visitors from beyond the continent have been impressed with the durability of African societies under slavery's moral and demographic weight. Yet not everything remained the same. In society, as in mechanics, every action brings an equal and opposite reaction: the distorting effects of enslavement on African society are there to be uncovered.

Senegambia had already been through three significant waves of enslavement (in the fifteenth and sixteenth centuries) when the War of the Marabouts broke out in 1659. The Moorish marabout (Islamic holy man) Nasr al-Din led a religious movement to create a state in the Senegal Valley and thereby to halt the region's expanding slave exports. The attackers overthrew the monarchs who had participated in slave exports but, after the death of Nasr al-Din in battle in 1674, their resolve weakened. French support of the dethroned monarchs led to the maraboutic movement's defeat in 1677, and slave exports resumed. Yet a few days' journey to the south, in Niumi along the Gambia River, slave trade was not inconsistent with an elegant lifestyle. There in the 1680s lived a noble woman known to European visitors as "La Belinguere" (this was a Wolof title). She fit the growing tradition of *nharas*, female merchants and landowners who set up relationships with visiting merchants. At least three European men wrote of her, and one left a fulsome description of her cosmopolitan dinner parties and elegant attire.

The Kingdom of Kongo, splintered into contending provinces by the early sixteenth-century slave trade, collapsed almost entirely as a result of the wars and enslavement of the late seventeenth century. The monarchy had been in disputes with the Portuguese and so allied with the Dutch when they seized nearby Luanda in 1641. But when the Brazilian expedition of 1648 drove out the Dutch and reestablished Portuguese rule in Angola, Kongo again faced its old antagonist. The kingdom was eventually drawn into direct conflict with Portugal, leading to disastrous defeat and the death of its king in 1665. Civil wars then ensued until, in 1678, the capital city of São Salvador was destroyed by the victorious army of Pedro III, a claimant to the throne. Only in 1718 was the kingdom formally restored. Great numbers of captives resulted from these wars, with most being sent in chains to the fields and households of Brazil.

In the midst of this social turmoil in Kongo (1704–1706), a remarkable young woman named Dona Beatriz Kimpa Vita recovered from a coma, announced she had been possessed by Saint Anthony's spirit, and called for an end to warfare and enslavement. She further claimed to have received an "improved" revelation of Christianity where Jesus was African. Dona Beatriz gained a great following in a short time, but her notoriety ended when the Capuchin priests from Italy who led the Kongo's Catholic Church declared her a heretic and burned her at the stake.

As the seventeenth century came to its end, the Bight of Benin grew in importance as a center of the slave trade. Dutch, English, and French merchants began trading there from the mid-seventeenth century on. The kingdom of Ardra had long had relations with the Portuguese, but these became more intensive. Spanish missionaries visited the court and wrote a catechism in the Gbe language of the region. This Gbe-language introduction to the principles of Catholic Christianity also came to be used in the Americas: captives entering South America at Cartagena were given the catechism and baptized as part of their formal conversion to Christianity. (From 1667 to 1702, the Dutch held the *asiento* contract and delivered most of the slaves entering Spanish territories.)

A period of almost two decades of serious drought in Angola first raised and then lowered the number of captives supplied by that region. Consequently, Brazilian slave buyers came to the Bight of Benin in large numbers in the 1690s, offering tobacco from Bahia in return for captives. The neighboring kingdom of Savi, smaller in area but very densely populated, also became active in the slave trade, and by the end of the seventeenth century Dutch,

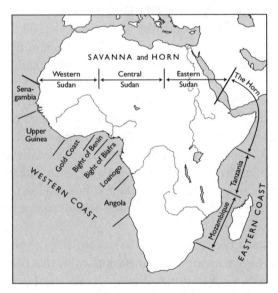

MAP 3.1 Africa, 1600–1800

The top map shows river valleys and major towns of the slave-trade era. The bottom map shows the conventional regions of the coast and desert edge of sub-Saharan Africa for the era of slave trade.

French, English, and Brazilian ships visited the ports of Ouidah (in Savi) and Jakin (in Ardra), purchasing as many as thirty thousand captives each year.

The number of people enslaved in this region was bolstered by wars. While stories abound suggesting that people sent across the Atlantic from the Bight of Benin came from "the interior," the practical evidence points to their coming from the Atlantic shore and its immediate hinterland. African wars continued almost without cease from the 1680s through the 1730s. They began with the attacks of the warlord Foli Bebe from Little Popo on Grand Popo. These assaults led to further wars between Grand Popo and Savi. Warfare intensified at the end of the seventeenth century, as firearms replaced swords, spears, and arrows as the principal weapons. In the 1720s, the kingdom of Dahomey, inland of Ardra, conquered first Ardra and then Savi, establishing control over much of the region. Yet the wars continued: Dahomey had to fight the exiles from Savi and faced raids from the cavalry forces of Oyo, to its northeast. A cycle of firearms and slaves—the sale of captives for firearms used in wars that collected more captives—developed in this part of the African coast, if not in others.

The upheavals caused by the expansion of the slave trade were profound. One of the clearest indications of these changes was the sudden and rapid rise in slave prices. From 1690 to 1730, the prices paid by Europeans on the African coast for captives rose by more than a factor of four. This surely means both that populations available for capture were declining and that profits from the slave trade were increasing for some Africans. Regional populations in the Bight of Benin and the Gold Coast fell sharply in these decades, as evidenced in the descriptions of visiting Europeans and in population simulations. The price increases reflected changes in the practice of the slave trade as well as declining populations. African slave merchants had to pay for food, clothing, and housing of their captives. They also paid for ritual services—for instance, ceremonies conducted to protect against revenge by spirits associated with those captured. In addition, monarchs charged fees and tolls for selling and moving captives.

Merchants measured slave values in money—especially cowrie shells, but also iron bars and crescent-shaped brass *manillas*. Most often, however, slaves were exchanged for a complex package of goods that included textiles, alcoholic beverages, tobacco, household goods, and manufactures such as firearms. The cost of buying these goods in Europe and shipping them to Africa determined the value of each slave. As African slave purchases became more expensive, their selling price in the Americas rose as well. This meant buyers in the Americas needed assurance of profitability from slave acquisitions in order to proceed with these transactions.

Along the Gold Coast, a long era of relative peace came to an end in the late seventeenth century. In the east, in the Volta River Valley, the kingdom of Akwamu expanded to its east and west, its armies of musketmen crushing their rivals. Akwamu began exporting growing numbers of captives to the Danes, who had set up a series of forts on this part of the coast in hopes of getting captives for the plantations they were setting up in the Danish West Indies—the Virgin Islands. In the western part of the Gold Coast, the kingdom of Denkyera expanded rapidly in the late seventeenth century, also relying on musketmen.

The expansion of warfare and enslavement caused a rapid change in the social order of the Gold Coast. In earlier times of gold trade with the Portuguese (Elmina Castle was built in 1482), a prosperous regional economy had developed that centered on small towns, markets, and artisanal production of pottery, metallic work, and textiles. With the expansion of warfare in the late seventeenth century, however, Gold Coast towns declined and populations dispersed into rural areas; apparently this served to reduce the chance of capture.

Coincidentally, it was at the end of the seventeenth century that two major goldfields opened up for exploitation in the Americas. The largest of these was in Minas Gerais, an inland area of southern Brazil. The second was in the coastal river valleys of New Granada. In both cases, the gold was best retrieved by panning for it. Therefore, the Gold Coast miners acquainted with this technique, men but especially women, became particularly valuable for these two regions. As the slave trade expanded in the Gold Coast, Dutch merchants took captives to Curaçao (they went on from there to Cartagena or Porto Bello), and Brazilian merchants took captives to Rio de Janeiro and then inland to Minas Gerais.

The prominence of Akwamu and Denkyera as slave-trading powers was short lived. In the former's case, revolts from within the kingdom caused it to collapse by 1710. For the latter, a new confederation known as Asante defeated and replaced it.

Asante's rise is one of the most striking stories of African state-building. Osei Tutu was a local chieftain fighting to preserve independence from Denkyera, and Anokye was his chief adviser, a man with remarkable magical powers as well as diplomatic skills. Together they assembled an alliance of regional chieftains who wished to oppose Denkyera. As they celebrated their unity, Anokye commanded a stool to descend from the skies, one of the elaborately carved sort representing kingly authority. This one, however, was covered with gold. The assembled chiefs proclaimed their loyalty to Osei Tutu, who took the title of Asantehene. Thus Asante was formed as a confederation of its various states with the Asantehene as the leader. This coalition conquered Denkyera in about 1710, and Asante established its dominion over a large portion of the Akan-speaking area of the Gold Coast.

Asante's expansion and Denkyera's collapse in the west and Akwamu's in the east brought a return of relative peace and a decline in the number of people enslaved along the Gold Coast after 1710. Nevertheless, Asante, through wars and trade, brought growing numbers of captives from interior regions for sale at the coast. In the twentieth century, the Asante state, with its complex government and its displays of gold and elegant garments, became a symbol of modern Ghana's national heritage and a source of pride for black people everywhere. But in the eighteenth century it was a prominent slave-trading power. Even in the nineteenth century, when slave exports halted, Asante continued to purchase and exploit slave labor.

The expansion of slave trade made West and Central Africa a reservoir of labor and skills for the Atlantic economy, and in exchange brought textiles, mostly from India, along with money (cowries, *manillas*, and cloth). Patterns of dress changed accordingly in Africa, and similar textiles went also to the Americas. Through the study of images and textile-trade records, we may hope to reconstruct some of the changing patterns of dress on both sides of the Atlantic in this period. Similarly, we can aspire to trace the movements and changes in musical instruments in this period: the American banjo was invented out of African models, the guitar spread to all areas of the Atlantic, and African drums and drumming moved among the regions of Africa and the Americas. Foods from the Americas—maize, manioc, sweet potatoes, peanuts, pineapples—came to be cultivated widely in Africa, along with tomatoes and tobacco. (Still, the timing and path of adoption for these commodities was not necessarily simple or obvious: recent linguistic research indicates that maize, while it was adopted all over West Africa, traveled mostly on a path that went via the Mediterranean to Egypt and the Nile Valley and then across farmlands to the west until it reached the Atlantic.) African yams, okra, and oil palms came to the Americas. Trade languages based on Portuguese spread along the African coast.

This was a flood time for the Atlantic slave trade, as mines and plantations became organized on a high level. Africans at home and abroad struggled to preserve existing communities and create new ones. African kingdoms in this era, for instance, were created or transformed through slave-trade participation, as with Asante, Dahomey, Segu, Kasanje, and Lunda. The values associated with those kingdoms emphasized hierarchy and the monarch's coercive power rather than ritual prestige and political consensus. For the social strata and ethnic groups seeking to escape conquest and enslavement, the aesthetic values and cultural creations emphasized social egalitarianism, recognizing the spirit world's authority rather than that of the state.

The ups and downs in slave trade led to complicated patterns. From the 1720s to 1730s, slave exports from the Bight of Benin declined while those from the Bight of Biafra expanded, and imports to Jamaica and St. Domingue grew while those to Martinique and Barbados diminished. Africans exiled to the Americas reinvigorated African traditions as they arrived, but they also imported the most recent African developments and arguments, such as the West African missions and wars that brought the expansion of Islam. Most of those sent overseas were male, and the females left behind found themselves enslaved and under the rule of men. As a result, families in Africa changed. The African money supply expanded while the population declined. Demographic pressures made continental African and diaspora families different from each other: a hierarchy of color developed, especially in the Americas, as the category of "mulatto" and then more complex social mixes emerged. In Africa, polygyny expanded as the shortage of males enabled the remaining men to control more women. In the Americas, polygyny declined because of the shortage of women, though some men—especially white slave owners—were able to hold several women in polygynous relationships.

The sale and delivery of so many captives to Europeans at the coast steadily encouraged wealthier Africans to purchase or seize slaves of their own. Female slaves in particular were held in Africa in the seventeenth and eighteenth centuries, as the Atlantic slave trade expanded and more and more males were carried out of Africa. The women who remained became the domestic servants, concubines, and corvée (unpaid) laborers of the expanding class of Africans profiting from slavery. This scenario unfolded repeatedly as the tides of enslavement ebbed and flowed over region after region of West and Central Africa.

The Waalo kingdom of modern Senegal underwent civil wars and saw significant sales of captives during the seventeenth century. As a result, the population declined until the wars halted. In the early eighteenth century, Mamari Kulibali arose as a great warlord among the Mande-speaking peoples that came to be known as Bambara. His warriors seized captives and booty and eventually set up the kingdom of Segu. The male captives were sent to the Atlantic coast for sale, while female captives were either held or sold to merchants who would take them on the long march across the Sahara.

Along the Upper Guinea coast, what historian George Brooks has called "the corruption of African social and cultural patterns" took place. In stratified societies, kings and powerful elites twisted judicial procedures to enslave more people as punishment. At times they conducted raids to capture people within their own states. In unstratified societies, immigrant merchant groups were able to settle, gain acceptance into the community, and build up a trade in slaves.⌉

The process of expanding enslavement damaged every type of existing social order. It also fostered new social institutions and organizations. One of these was a group of female merchants, known as *nharas* in Portuguese and as *signares* in French, who married (under local law or by Catholic priests) European merchants and other visitors. Known for elegance and astuteness, these women traded in slaves and other commodities, linking coastal regions from Senegal to Liberia.

Far to the east, in the hinterland of the major ports of Bonny and Calabar, a network for collecting captives grew steadily through the eighteenth century, gathering in particular young men and women who spoke the Igbo language but also those of the Ibibio tongue and other language groups of the region. In this area, the population was dense but kingdoms were small or nonexistent. Captives were seized by two primary mechanisms: kidnapping and judicial procedures. The kidnapping of young people by small gangs created an aura of insecurity in Igbo country. Yet the practice expanded, condoned not only by the kidnappers but by others of the same region who bought and sold the captives. One particular method of enslaving adults was through the Arochukwu oracle, a prestigious ritual center that rendered judgments in major disputes. Those who lost their cases were commonly "consumed" by the oracle—that is, seized and sent in captivity to what is now the Nigerian coast. The relative smoothness of commercial transactions there, where English and French purchasers dominated, kept the slave trade of the Bight of Biafra expanding even as the region's population declined in the late eighteenth and early nineteenth centuries.

In the equatorial, forested regions of Central Africa, a long-distance slave trade developed in the late eighteenth century. Captives from the hinterland had collected at the port of Loango, in modern Congo-Brazzaville, throughout the eighteenth century, but late in the century captives began appearing from the middle Congo River. Bobangi merchants from far up the river had begun seizing captives and moving them hundreds of kilometers by canoe to Malebo Pool, just above the rapids some three hundred kilometers from the river's mouth. From there these captives were marched overland to Loango (north of the river), Boma (at the river's mouth), or Ambriz (south of the river).

Luanda, however, remained the principal port for dispatching African captives throughout the slave-trade era (only Ouidah, Bonny, and Calabar approached it). Portugal had administered Luanda since 1575, and a combination of direct Portuguese military expeditions, alliances with slave-raiding states such as Kasanje, and the slave gathering of Luso-African merchants brought captives from throughout an expanding region. The slave trade there fluctuated periodically in concert with waves of drought and famine, which increased death rates but also caused more people to be sold into slavery.

In addition to its effect on West and Central Africa, the slave trade affected Africa's eastern and northern regions. Along the coasts of Mozambique and Madagascar, Portuguese, Dutch, and French merchants purchased slaves and sent them variously to Brazil, Cape Province, and the Mascarene Islands. The European demand for captives bolstered the enslavement systems that also sent people from East Africa to the northern shores of the Indian Ocean. Thus Kilwa, which had earlier been a port for gold and ivory trade, now became a slave-trading center, sending those enslaved in the Yao lands near Lake Malawi to Oman on the Arabian Peninsula and to the French Mascarenes.

All across the northern savanna and in the region of the Horn and the Nile Valley, slave trade also expanded in the late eighteenth century. Growing economies in the Persian Gulf, the Hijaz, Egypt, and the Maghrib each brought demand for labor, and slave exports all across the northern band of sub-Saharan Africa appear to have doubled in the late eighteenth century.

One must acknowledge that Africans were able to sustain and rebuild their societies on their home continent remarkably well, given the demographic, material, and moral effects of the steadily expanding trade in captives. Africans survived the slave trade as a group, though millions were lost as individuals. Indeed, the first generation of professional historians of Africa, writing in the era of African independence, chose to emphasize the innovative and recuperative capabilities of African societies and tended to downplay the negative influences of slave trade and the world economy.[7]

But as the details of African societies have come to be more thoroughly analyzed, especially for early modern times, the transformations of African societies through slave trade have become clearer. The more recent studies of African societies include plenty of detail on the inherited conflicts and traditions of societies throughout the continent, but they include equally clear analyses of interaction with Europeans and others from outside the continent. The changes that took place were not simple collapse or a bending to the will of slave merchants: they were complex transformations that drew on African traditions in a global context.

Firearms, for instance, were imported in rather large quantities in the late seventeenth century, and armies along much of the West African coast adopted them. More generally, militarized societies emerged in many areas where the slave trade became intensive. In another pattern, the slave trade commonly involved exchanging people for money, so the use of money both expanded in African societies with the slave trade and came to be associated with theft and exploitation. Religious innovations of this era often had to do with defending a merchant or warrior against the spirits protecting those they had enslaved or sold.]

The expansion of slavery polarized cultural life. The earlier ideologies of kingship emphasized the common interest of the king and his people and how the welfare of the king and the whole population depended on one another. With the growth of enslavement, kings did more to emphasize their arbitrary power and subordinate all others to their wills. Increasingly, common people had to choose between abject submission to rulers and creating an autonomous though sometimes isolated existence. These differences showed up in their representations in sculpture and dress throughout the continent. For rulers, sculptors honored them with individual portraits or with metaphorical statements of their power. Among common people, sculpture gave primary attention to nature spirits and ancestors and thereby to ideas of communal equality and cohesiveness. The same social tensions made themselves felt in music. Kings and warlords commissioned new drums and the creation of new music to celebrate their power; communities threatened with enslavement developed new drums and new music to help sustain their order and protect them from attack. Thus the Niger-Congo traditions of sculpture and drumming, the inheritance of all in West and Central Africa, were used in different and even contradictory ways by those who sought to benefit from enslavement and those who sought to avoid it.

Even at the height of the slave trade, extraordinary creative work continued to be produced in Africa. The iron sword shown in figure 3.1, cast in the workshops of the Kuba kingdom of the Kasai Valley, is one such masterpiece, and the filigree of braided iron wire attached to the slim blade is a unique touch. The sword was brought out from the king's holdings each year for a public ceremony.

Institutions of family and marriage were similarly transformed by the effects of the slave trade. Most significantly, the availability of growing numbers of enslaved females—those who remained after most of the males were sold across the Atlantic—gave privileged men the opportunity to control them as domestics, laborers, and concubines. Formal marriage was restricted to alliances among free families. Among this group, the exchange of bridewealth and other goods and the traditional responsibilities of families linked by marriage continued throughout the slavery era. For many in continental

FIGURE 3.1 Kuba Royal Sword, c. eighteenth century

Iron sword from the Kuba royal treasury, Nsheng, Congo, forty-five centimeters in length, three to four millimeters thick. Collected in 1903, it may have been created in the eighteenth or early nineteenth century.

Source: Courtesy of the William H. Sheppard Collection, Hampton University Museum, Hampton, Virginia; photo by Colleen Kriger.

African societies, however, their lives were torn asunder by the expansion of slavery, which gave men the opportunity to exploit slave women for labor and sex and to control the lives of their children. Women, even in slavery, found ways to counter some of this power, but the eighteenth century in general witnessed a profound subordination of females in West and Central Africa. By the same token, the growth of men's control of women and children through slavery undermined the corporate power of lineages.

Quite a different sort of African cultural change brought by slavery was the change in languages. The development of trade languages along the African coast has been widely noted: Crioulo, the Portuguese-based creole language, maintained its base in Upper Guinea and Cape Verde and had influence beyond that region; pidgin English developed in the Bight of Benin and spread from there. Afrikaans developed at the Cape of Good Hope into a distinctive, creolized language, as Dutch became modified in its interaction with Khoi and with the Austronesian speech of Malay slaves. Portuguese, English, and French also became established speech communities among both Africans and European settlers, in part as Eurafrican children were sent to Europe for education. But perhaps more important numerically were the changes in African languages as large numbers of people were taken in slavery from one language community to another, developing a range of pidgins, creoles, and word borrowings. The Wolof, Twi, and Hausa languages of West Africa underwent such changes, as did the Mbundu language of Central Africa. In addition, there were periodic efforts to reduce African languages to writing, as with the catechisms written in the Kikongo and Gbe languages.

The populations of West and Central African regions declined in size. As the eighteenth century proceeded, region after region found its population shrinking, partly because of the deaths associated with enslavement and the export of males but most fundamentally because young women, even though exported in smaller numbers than men, took with them their capacity to have additional children. These population decreases, occasionally disastrous, as in the Bight of Benin, and sometimes more gradual, as in the Bight of Biafra, left the Atlantic half of Africa with a diminishing populace at exactly the time when populations were growing in all other densely inhabited areas of the world.[8]

The enslavement system seemed so embedded and institutionalized that there was no way to get around it. When rebels overthrew slave raiders and slave owners, their main recourse was to sell their former oppressors into slavery. Scottish observers Archibald Dalzel and Mungo Park, writing at the end of the eighteenth century, concluded that war and slavery were inherent and inevitable in African society. Perhaps this was true from the viewpoint of any individual in Africa. The factor neglected by Dalzel and Park—and perhaps by many of their African contemporaries—was that the system of war and enslavement had developed over more than two centuries from a mix of domestic and external influences and had become ingrained.

Some recent scholars have taken an approach similar to Dalzel and Park in explaining the slave trade and its effects. For instance, David Eltis, a scholar who has done much to quantify the flows of African captives across the Atlantic, nonetheless has argued that the social and economic effect of the slave trade in Africa was minimal. In work with Lawrence Jennings, his analysis of British trade with the western coast of Africa argues that slavery had little influence on African life.[9] A longer-term view of enslavement, however, makes clear the transformations it brought to the continent. African survival skills remained impressive even as the rate of enslavement grew steadily. But the emergence of those survival skills does not mean that African oppression was insignificant or that Africans were insensitive to external forces. Slave trade reduced African populations in the eighteenth and nineteenth centuries and distorted the lives of those who remained alive on the continent, both slave and free.

For all its corrosive effects, slave trade was business and, for the seventeenth and eighteenth centuries, big business. The size of African cities shows the significance of their concentrations of population and wealth on a world scale. In the 1780s, St. Louis in Senegal was as populous as Philadelphia, Elmina as populous as Cartagena, Ouidah as populous as Cap Français, Calabar as populous as Kingston, and Luanda as populous as Rio de Janeiro. With time, however, African cities stagnated while cities on other continents bordering the Atlantic continued to boom.

Another testament to slavery's significance on a worldwide scale can be obtained by comparing the enslaved workforce to that of the emerging system of industrial wage labor. At the end of the eighteenth century, some six million persons of African descent lived in the Americas, with more than four million of them in slavery. Add to these an African population of at least four million in slavery and those in slavery in the Old World diaspora and one sees that this huge slave workforce dwarfed the number of industrial laborers earning wages in Europe and North America, who totaled at most a few hundred thousand at this time.

Metamorphoses in the Atlantic Diaspora

Two great regions were put in close contact with each other through the Atlantic slave trade: the Americas as a whole (but especially the Atlantic coastal regions) and West and Central Africa. These two areas changed in close interaction with one another from the mid-sixteenth to mid-nineteenth centuries. Increases in wealth and population of one generally came at the expense of the other, but there also were a few instances, such as cuisine, where the contacts benefited both regions.

As sugar production expanded in the Caribbean and Brazil, the principal destinations of captives arriving in the Americas were plantations where sugar, tobacco, or indigo was the principal product. These establishments had much work to do in addition to field labor: carpentry and masonry, blacksmithing, sewing and tailoring, handling of horses and carts, handling of boats, cooking, washing, domestic service, hair and other grooming, handling cattle, marketing, and plantation management. The mines required digging, carpentry, masonry, and ore sorting, processing, and transportation. In addition, while large groups on plantations and mines dominated the institution of slavery, many slaves were held individually or in small numbers in households. These shared the full burden and responsibility of running the house and lived in intimate connection with their masters. Their subordination was direct and personal rather than institutional. Slavery was mainly about work—in the Old World and in sub-Saharan Africa, and especially in the Americas. Figure 3.2 shows a sugar plantation of the seventeenth century, though from the perspective of the masters rather than of the slaves. The image nonetheless provides a reminder that—in agriculture, mining, transportation, construction, and household work—it was black slaves and free people of color who played the most central role in construction of colonial economies and, thereby, in the creation of the transatlantic economic system. Work and the work discipline that emerged from successive eco-

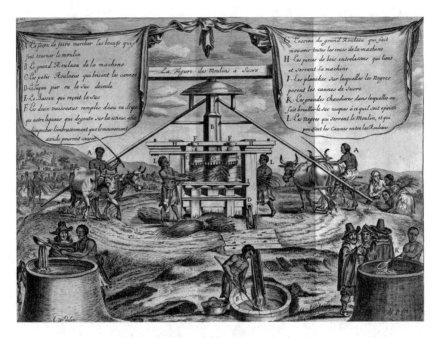

FIGURE 3.2 Caribbean Sugar Plantation, c. 1665

This composite illustration of sugar production in the French Caribbean illustrates a range of the types of work. Most workers are male, but females are shown at right.

Source: From Charles de Rochefort, *Histoire naturelle et morale des Isles Antilles de l'Amérique* (Paris, 1665)

nomic transformations, whether imposed by masters or carried out through self-discipline, developed their characteristics on this enslaved frontier of modernity.

Slave societies developed in each region in their own time: some began in the seventeenth or even the eighteenth century, while others had existed for longer periods. For the Atlantic islands, slavery began in the fifteenth century, so the hierarchy and the complex social mixes of mature slave societies were clearly in evidence there. For Mexico, Peru, and the region known as Terra Firme (the southern coast of the Caribbean, now Venezuela), the system of making black slaves the intermediaries between Spanish rulers and the larger Amerindian population began in the sixteenth century. Slavery in Brazil relied principally on Amerindian captives in the sixteenth and early seventeenth centuries, but growing numbers of captives brought from Africa supplemented them. When the Dutch seized Pernambuco for two decades, it marked a step in the colony's evolution toward greater numbers of African slaves, an experience shared by several Caribbean islands.

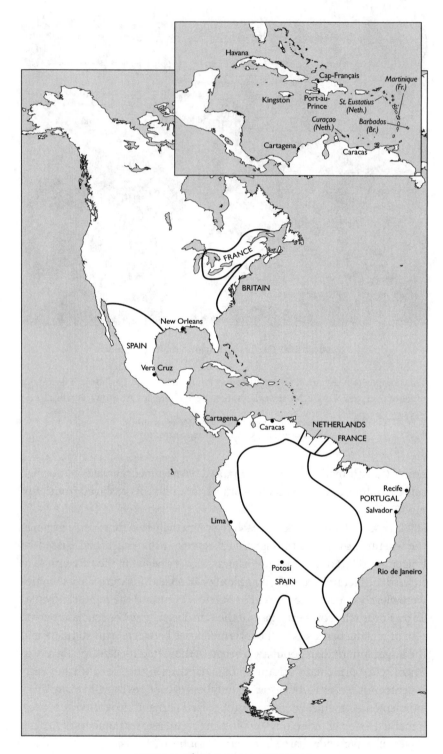

Havana

Cap-Français

Martinique
(Fr.)

Kingston Port-au-
Prince St. Eustatius
(Neth.)

Curaçao
(Neth.) Barbados
(Br.)

Cartagena

Caracas

FRANCE

BRITAIN

SPAIN

New Orleans

Vera Cruz

Cartagena

Caracas NETHERLANDS

FRANCE

Recife

PORTUGAL

Salvador

Lima

Potosí Rio de Janeiro

SPAIN

MAP 3.2 The Americas, 1600–1800

In the mid-seventeenth century, a wave of new colonies came into existence, governed by the powers of northern Europe. Curaçao, Guyana, and New Amsterdam for the Dutch; Barbados and Jamaica for the English, along with Virginia and Carolina; Martinique and Guadeloupe for the French; the Danish West Indies; and the Swedish colony along the Delaware River. Still other colonies began later: the French in St. Domingue at the beginning of the eighteenth century and in Louisiana in the 1720s. Trinidad, barely populated at the time, was opened by the Spanish to French settlers in 1777. In each case, the experience of charter generations newly arrived from Africa or from other American colonies repeated itself. These individuals set the initial patterns of the settlements, under the direction of their white masters and often in interaction with Amerindian populations. After a generation, the initial populations of immigrants came to share the colony with native-born creoles. In the third generation, an increasingly complex mix of different backgrounds emerged, including additional arrivals from Africa, perhaps from different regions than earlier waves. The immigrant populations were mostly young adults. There were hardly any older persons and very few children. The creole population began simply with children, and only after more than half a century might it include significant numbers of the elderly.

Most of those sent across the Atlantic were men and women between the ages of twelve and thirty. Still, significant numbers of young children and older people made the voyage. Death rates were severe at every stage of travel, even after arrival. On the Atlantic voyage, 5 to 25 percent of those who boarded the ships failed to leave them alive. Similar death rates are presumed for the months of capture, travel, and detention in Africa before they embarked. Additional fatalities occurred as slaves traveled from their initial landing point in the Americas—Salvador, Rio, Barbados, Curaçao, Charleston—to their final destination. The latter could be as far from the ocean as Potosí, Minas Gerais, Mexico City, or Kentucky. Not all migrants from Africa were enslaved, however: Rodrigo da Costa Almeida, a Luso-African born in Angola, made his fortune as a slave trader in the Angolan interior, and then moved in 1713 from Luanda across the Atlantic to Bahia, where he established an important family.

The delivery of captive Africans—each forced to take on a new slave identity—soon created a range of new ethnicities in the Americas. The names of African ethnic groups gave way to New World labels: thus the terms Congo and Angola were applied to people from these large and variegated regions: "Bambara" referred to people from the upper Niger Valley, "Coromanti" to those dispatched from the Gold Coast, and "Ardra" or "Arda" for many people sent from the Bight of Benin. These New World terms commonly linked people who spoke similar languages. Indeed, the words "Ibo" and "Yoruba" (or "Nago"), which developed as ethnic terms in the Americas, ultimately gained acceptance in Africa. In this mix of African ethnicities, the "creole" or locally born people of African descent became, in effect, the creole (or Afro-creole) ethnic group of Venezuela, Barbados, or any other territory. Creoles were defined by language as well as birth: they spoke the Portuguese-based (or other) creole language of their territory as a native language. Creoles, however, could also be broken down by color into additional ethnic groups. For instance, in the French colonies, the term *mulâtre* (mulatto) tended to refer to free people with European and African ancestors. This became an ethnic label rather than a phenotypical label: slaves with white ancestors were labeled as "slaves" rather than "mulattos." On the other hand, for the black people who lived out their lives in Europe, usually after birth or a stay in the Americas, it was their status as a minority rather than their specific origins that labeled them. Regardless of color or birth, they tended to be known as "blacks" or "people of color."

Enslaved African women appear, according to some records, to have borne children rather commonly within a year or two of their arrival in a colony. The pattern seems significant, but one is left to speculate as to its meaning. Did the women decide to have children, or was the decision imposed on them by men? Were the fathers black or white, slave or free? One can imagine the children resulted from rape, as the incoming women fell victim to white masters or to black male slaves who had few other areas in which to exercise power. Or one could imagine that the young women arrived in a new region that would be their home, for better or for worse, and decided they would benefit from having someone to love and thus sought an opportunity to bear a child. African captives were ripped away from their families when they began their voyage and had to construct new ones as they lived out their new lives. They also had to replace the society and ritual life of their previous existence.

The number of children born in the Americas to women from Africa was generally smaller than the number of children born to slave women who themselves were born in the Americas. This is partly because the women captured and sent across the Atlantic lost their earlier children to separation or untimely death. But women from Africa were also sometimes unwilling to bring children into the new world of slavery and found ways to abort unwanted pregnancies. New families of American slave society centered principally on the nurturing efforts of the women, whether they were African-born or creoles. Some had male partners for short or long times who joined them in sustaining the family unit. But marriages were rarely formalized among slaves in the Americas.

The women who came to the Americas were almost entirely from the coastal regions of Africa. The ethnicity of female slaves from West Africa was primarily the Wolof in Senegal, the Mande of Sierra Leone, the Akan-speakers of the Gold Coast, the Gbe-speakers and Yoruba-speakers of the Bight of Benin, and the Carabali and Igbo-speakers of the Bight of Biafra. The male slaves of the Americas, in contrast, came from interior groups such as the Bambara, Chamba, and Hausa, in addition to the coastal ethnicities. The explanation of this continuing pattern can be found in the costs and benefits of slavery as seen through African eyes. As African slave holdings expanded along with the overseas slave trade, African buyers consistently preferred female slaves over males. Females performed work that was much in demand—farming and household chores—and they were perhaps more easily controlled than males. As a result, African merchants paid higher prices for females than for males. European purchasers, in contrast, paid higher prices for males than for females, based on their valuations of males and females and their sense of the productivity of men and women on New World plantations. As a result, male captives from the interior were sent to the coast for export, while female captives from the interior were purchased and held within Africa.

Close to the coastline, female slaves were as likely to be sent to the Americas as to be purchased for local exploitation. This pattern is less clear in Central Africa, because of the greater uniformity in language and culture of the region: slaves from Central Africa were usually known simply as "Congo" in the New World, whether they came from the Angolan coast, the interior of Lunda, or the forested valley of the Congo River. Yet if the economics were similar, then it may be that most female captives from Central Africa were from the coastal regions and Kongo in ethnicity. To the degree that mothers and fathers passed distinct traditions to their children in the slave community, one can suggest that slave mothers handed down the customs of the African coastline to their children and that the mores of the African interior were passed on mainly by fathers.

Slave families of Africa and the Americas were mixed in various fashions. Of course men and women of the same African nation or ethnicity tended commonly to set up households, especially for the least-represented ethnicities, to share their language and home culture. But it was also common for fathers and mothers in slave communities to be of different nations and of different religious traditions. Another sort of mixed family was that based on "fictive kinship": the adoption of brothers and sisters, aunts and uncles, following the tradition of closeness among shipmates. In other cases, families were mixed among slave and free, black and white. There certainly were cases where a free white man took an African woman as a full partner who lived in his house and whose children he recognized as his own—with the man perhaps freeing the children and even their mother. More often, however, free white men took lovers among slave women and declined to recognize their children, though they may have provided some support to their offspring. At the extreme were the men who had children with their slaves and later sold their own children. In the Americas, many black men, especially the African born, were left without families except for the fictive "brothers" with whom they worked. In Africa, enslaved women had no family except their masters; the children were theirs to nurture but belonged to their owners.

The eighteenth-century Jamaican planter Thomas Thistlewood recorded in his diary his every act of sex with his principal slave mistress Phibbah and his nearly equal number of sexual subjugations of more than 130 slaves— mostly women he owned—over more than three decades.[10] Thistlewood never recorded the feelings of the women involved in these episodes, but he commonly made small payments to them. Phibbah remained with Thistlewood to the end of his life, living in a manner in some ways similar to that of a free person. His young slave Sally became demoralized under the pressures of slavery, however. She ran away frequently, sometimes after having sex with Thistlewood, and accepted punishments for this and other misdeeds. She even stole food from a woman who had been her shipmate. Thistlewood's diary also recorded events in the life of his first slave, Lincoln, who himself became a patriarch with three wives, though Thistlewood maintained sexual access to Lincoln's two principal wives, Sukey and Abba. Thistlewood controlled all these slaves with threats and violent punishments.

In the first generation or so of a slave community, families consisted simply of parents and children. Only after several generations did they come to include grandparents and great-uncles who could pass on their wisdom and maintain family traditions. Even as slave families began to extend and strengthen, other forces intervened to reduce their size and influence. The masters could sell family members and claim women for themselves. The arrival of new slaves from Africa increased the proportion of young, unconnected individuals.

While Africans arrived in the Americas in slavery, a portion of their descendants and sometimes even the immigrants themselves were able to gain freedom. Women did so in greater numbers than men as their owners and lovers let them go. Owners also sometimes freed their slave children or elderly slaves. Many slaves bought their own liberty. (In Spanish territories, *coartición* gave slaves the legal right to know their purchase price and gain freedom by paying it.) In addition, slaves or free persons purchased the freedom of their parents, children, spouses, or others. Escaped slaves sometimes gained recognition as free people in another region. By 1800, 10 percent of the U.S. black population was free, and somewhat larger portions of blacks were free in the Caribbean (even before the end of slavery in Haiti), in Brazil, and especially in the Spanish mainland territories. Free populations of color often specialized in artisanal work, such as that of coopers, tailors, and seamstresses. In rural areas, they became independent peasant farmers and sometimes slave owners.

Arrival in the Americas meant introduction to a new culture at many levels for each enslaved African. Almost everyone received a new name. Some had the strength of conviction to retain their previous names as well and pass them on to succeeding generations or even impose their use on owners and co-workers. One common compromise was using the given name of the dominant culture and a second name of African identity: Maria Caravali or José Congo. Masters generally provided clothing, but each person had something to say about what to put on each day and how to wear it. The complex story of changing patterns of dress in Africa and the diaspora through the agency of slavery and slave trade is worthy of more careful research. In the Americas, masters and European standards of dress had much to say about how Africans dressed, yet each person retained the habits of their homeland and their individual preferences. In Africa, great quantities of textiles were imported from India and later from Europe in exchange for slaves, and these imports influenced the creation, design, and wearing of garments in Africa. Perhaps a thorough review of images and texts for the Atlantic as a whole will clarify the patterns and the meaning of the developing standards of dress among black people in the early modern world.

A bit more can be said about African musical instruments and their arrival and modification in the Americas. To discuss musical instruments of West and Central Africa, one must begin with drums. The music of these drums and accompanying instruments was associated with every sort of social activity, including birth, death, marriage, initiation, and worship of nature spirits or high gods. A range of drum types was shared across West and Central Africa. They were commonly carved out of logs and sometimes had elaborate figures on the drum body. Drumheads, usually made of goatskin, were held in place by nails, pegs, and laces.

Such instruments had been played for thousands of years, but innovations in drumming spread repeatedly. An interesting question is whether actual drums crossed the Atlantic along with the idea of the drum. One is reminded of the common story of how captive Africans on slave ships were unshackled

FIGURE 3.3 Drum, late seventeenth century

This beautifully carved drum is a relatively small forty-six centimeters in height. The drumhead is held taut by pegs and cords. It was collected in Virginia but was created in Africa (as indicated by the tropical cordia and baphia woods). Drums of similar style are known in several areas of West and Central Africa.

Source: Courtesy of the British Museum.

from time to time, brought on deck, and commanded to dance. But if they were really to dance, why not have them dance as usual, to a drumbeat? And if there is to be a drummer, should it not be someone who can drum with some skill? The beautiful drum shown in figure 3.3 was collected in Virginia; it was likely created in Africa. Perhaps crew members purchased drums and played them, or perhaps the slaves onboard were induced to drum. Such thinking raises the possibility that drums and other musical instruments, along with other elements of African material culture, crossed the Atlantic with some regularity. Drums and drumming are documented throughout the African diaspora: slave owners periodically sought to ban drum playing, most consistently in North America, but the drums and related forms of percussion survived or reappeared almost everywhere in the Americas.

One popular instrument, the mbira, features tuned metal keys plucked with the thumb, often with a gourd attached as a resonator. The instrument developed perhaps two thousand years ago in Zimbabwe, once the adoption of iron-ore smelting allowed metallic keys to replace those made of bamboo. Mbiras came to the Americas and gained importance, especially in Brazil. A related instrument is the xylophone—in fact the term "marimba" came to mean both xylophone and mbira in the Caribbean and Brazil. Xylophones clearly came to the Americas from Africa, but they may have come by other routes as well. The xylophone or marimba took hold in various parts of the Americas and remains part of the African diaspora's musical tradition. A form of marimba was developed separately by the Mayan people of Guatemala, but it was played in a much different way from that of Africans of the diaspora.

Cuisine is one area in which Africa and the Americas gained from the exchange between the two regions. Oil palms, African yams, bananas, plantains, rice, millet, and sorghum came to the Americas from Africa, plus akee, okra, and earth peas. In addition, African methods of cooking became widely influential in the Americas. In the stews, a basic starch (yam, rice, millet, sorghum) was served with a source of protein (such as fish, shellfish, meat, or beans) that was marinated in a sauce that included peppers. The stew was then garnished with greens and served with fruits on the side. The foodstuffs of the Americas provided new ingredients for such stews, both in Africa and in the Americas: new starch (maize, manioc, and sweet potato), new forms of protein (peanuts), new spices (chili peppers), new materials for marinades (tomatoes), and new fruits (pineapples). African fashions of eating, such as the West African tradition of eating from a common bowl and eating with the fingers, survived more unevenly in the Americas.

Africans in the Americas entered a world where Christianity was the religion of the master class. The Catholic powers—Spain, Portugal, and later France—tended to baptize African slaves and treat them formally (if not fully) as part of the Christian community. Some Africans who came to the Americas were indeed Christian—especially those from Central Africa, and a much smaller number from West Africa. White Protestants (the Dutch and English) showed little interest in the souls of their slaves and left them to their own practices. Some slaves were Muslims, and those schooled in the Islamic faith could speak and perhaps read and write Arabic. This group grew in time, in part because of the continuing expansion of Islam in West Africa. Most Africans, however, professed religious traditions specific to their homeland. In the mix of religious practices of the Americas, the black populations were left to develop an eclectic set of spiritual traditions.

Michael Gomez, in a thorough analysis of African cultural contributions to slave life in the American South, gives attention to the growing proportion of the American-born even during the eighteenth century. He acknowledges but counters the argument of Melville Herskovits, who concluded that since blacks and whites in the United States lived in close proximity, black culture was unlikely to survive. The strongest contrary evidence was that of New England, where William D. Pierson showed the liveliness and distinctiveness of the black community, even if it was tiny. In Louisiana, free mulattos and quadroons were the first to baptize their children and often had formal church marriages, following a strategy aimed to preserve and advance their position in free society through dedication to formal social values. North America was unusual among slave-importing regions in that it imported nearly equal numbers of females and males, along with a large proportion of children. This pattern resulted in part from the marginal position of the North American market, whose purchasers took mainly the cheaper slaves, but it also enabled the black population to grow more rapidly. Gomez emphasizes that Muslims were significant among New World slaves from the start and suggests that, because Muslims were often of elite status, they experienced tense relations with those of other religious backgrounds.[11]

While it is possible only in the rarest of cases for individuals in the Americas to trace their ancestry back to Africa, records do exist that clearly indicate the migration patterns, year by year or at least decade by decade, in which people left each region of the African coast and arrived in each region of the Americas. These patterns, if studied with sufficient care, may yet reveal more specific information on the relationship between the black populations of each American region and their African ancestors. Certain examples have already been analyzed in detail: for instance, the sudden increase in Central African imports to Charleston in the 1720s provides background for the Stono rebellion of 1739.[12]

Did African culture survive in the Americas? Scholars have devoted great energies to modeling and interpreting the fate of African culture and the basis of black culture in the Americas. Four basic models are now under debate, and one can be certain that the discussion will continue. One straightforward model is that of dominance: the power of the masters was sufficient to limit slave behavior to the extent that black culture in the Americas owed nothing to Africa and everything to conditions in slave society. A second model, nearly the opposite, is that of survival: Africans found ways, even under oppression and deprivation, to sustain the essence of their cultural heritage, so that black culture in the Americas developed primarily as a continuation of African traditions. A third model is that of syncretism: blacks in the Americas assembled the elements of various African cultures and European cultures into a cultural mosaic that drew eclectically on many ancestries. A fourth model is that of creolization: blacks in the Americas combined elements of African and European traditions with their own ingenuity to create a distinctly new culture. As the debates have continued, scholars have recently turned to combining the basic hypotheses to produce more nuanced interpretations of cultural change in the African diaspora.[13]

Language studies provide one of the many approaches to analyzing the fate of African folkways. In most cases, the speech communities of Africans in the Americas have been distinctive, but the nature of the distinction has varied widely. African languages continued to be spoken in the Americas, especially in the eighteenth century, but also later, as with Yoruba and Kimbundu in nineteenth-century Brazil. Creole languages developed on the model of Crioulo, with its Portuguese lexicon and Atlantic grammar. Creoles with a French lexicon became the principal languages of St. Domingue, Martinique, Guadeloupe, and elsewhere; creoles with an English lexicon became widely spoken in Jamaica and along the Carolina coast. Spanish as spoken in Cuba, Puerto Rico, and the Dominican Republic took on a rhythm and vocabulary that owed much to African inputs. The patterns of change and preservation in language may be different from those for religion, dance, dress, or philosophy. Like the other components of cultures, however, the evolution of language does not lend itself to a simple summary of cultural survival patterns.

Not all Africans in the Americas lived in slavery. Through manumission and escape, significant free populations grew up, notably in Brazil but also in the French colonies of the Caribbean and in Spanish colonies of the mainland and the islands. Many of the free people of color were artisans, living in towns and practicing their trades. In addition, peasant or free farming communities were able to form in Minas Gerais, Venezuela, St. Domingue, Hispaniola, and Suriname. Several scholars have compared the peasant communities of Suriname with those of Africa, and it would be useful to expand these comparisons to see how other New World communities of independent farmers—for instance in New Granada and Minas Gerais—compared with peasants in Africa. The free black communities of the Americas up to 1800, living in a world dominated by slavery, had the opportunity to define their relationships with black slave populations, Amerindian communities, poor white communities, and the white elite. In the legal arena, their options were restricted by "caste laws" created to keep them out of political and religious institutions dominated by whites. Such rules were formalized, especially by the Spanish but also by the Portuguese and French colonial regimes and by legislatures in English colonies. People of color, free and slave, were commonly registered in separate books from whites for baptisms and funerals. Nonetheless, free people commonly sought to remain very close to the church, perhaps rising in prestige as a result. One response to caste-law restrictions was the formation of separate Catholic brotherhoods for the blacks.[14] Similarly, free people developed specializations as artisans and sometimes established profitable farms, purchasing slaves to expand their production. Since military service was very important in the Spanish empire, free people of color often volunteered and sought to rise high in rank in militias and the regular army. As free populations grew in size and diversity, there developed a complex discourse on the precise combination

of color for each individual. For instance, in two censuses of artisanal families of Buenos Aires in the 1790s, a majority of the individuals were given
different racial labels in the second census than in the first. This discourse
enabled families to press suits and protests to officials, complaining about
implementation of the caste laws. In addition to these campaigns of social
mobility, there were examples of discreet "passing," as some of the people of
color gained acceptance as white.

The metamorphoses of black communities in the Americas, though con-
tinuous, maintained visible underpinnings of African society and culture.
The cultural changes were substantial, but there was no way simply to impose
European ways on large populations of African origin. The metamorphoses
in quality of life were paralleled by changes in the quantitative dimension of
life in the Americas. In 1500, the combined population of West and Central
Africa was perhaps fifty million, while that of the Americas in total was fifty
million or more. But by 1600, the American population had fallen to perhaps
ten million, principally but not only from disease, and it hardly increased
during the seventeenth century. During the eighteenth century, the black,
brown, and white population of the Americas grew while that of the western coast of Africa declined, but nineteenth-century African populations
remained closer. For people of African ancestry alone, the diaspora population of the Americas reached some six million in 1800, about 30 percent of
the total populace. The African-descended population of the Americas in
1800 was therefore about one-tenth of the population of West and Central
Africa and about one-twentieth the population of the African continent.

Expansion of the Old World Diaspora

The Old World diaspora—more precisely, the populations of black people in
regions to the north and east of sub-Saharan Africa—had existed for many
centuries as a result of migration and settlement by Africans of free and
slave status. In the seventeenth and early eighteenth centuries, an estimated
ten thousand persons moved annually from sub-Saharan Africa into the Old
World diaspora. Of the captives dispatched each year, the majority crossed
desert or ocean to be settled in the "near diaspora" of North Africa, Arabia,
and (far to the south) Madagascar. A minority of the total went beyond these
regions, across further lands and waters, to the "far diaspora" of Europe, the
Middle East, South Asia, and distant islands of the Indian Ocean. Late in the
eighteenth century, the slave trade to the Old World diaspora grew sharply
and continued expanding well into the nineteenth century.[15]

The Middle Passage of captives destined for the Old World diaspora paralleled the Atlantic crossing in time and mortality. For those crossing to the "near diaspora" of the Old World, death rates were highest on the route to North Africa and somewhat lower on the way to Arabia and Madagascar—the number of fatalities is not known with precision but has been estimated at 15 percent of captives starting the journey. For those making the long trek across the Sahara, the distance could reach two thousand kilometers. The crossing was dangerous and exhausting; on occasions whole caravans lost their lives. For those sent by sea from the Horn and from Mozambique, the voyages across the Red Sea to Arabia and across the Mozambique Strait to Madagascar were safer than the Atlantic, yet the usual problems of shipboard mortality remained ever present.

Captives traveled across the Sahara on foot, while camels carried other trade goods and supplies. Good leadership and timing were critical qualities for the caravan leaders, who were mostly of Tuareg ethnicity in the western desert, Kanuri ethnicity in the central desert, and Arab ethnicity in the east. In all cases, they needed to avoid storms and reach widely spaced sources of food and water. Along the Red Sea and the East African coast, large and small dhows carried captives to their destinations. These flexible and maneuverable craft, with lateen sails and hulls of planks lashed together with cords, were built from lumber wherever it was available. Far to the south, the slave trade to and from Madagascar relied not only on dhows but on outrigger canoes powered by square sails and paddles.

While the largest number of captives probably traveled from sub-Saharan Africa to the near diaspora, the slave trade did operate in both directions: Andalusian women and others from the Mediterranean were sent in captivity to the western savanna, Yemeni captives were sold in Ethiopia, and Malagasy captives were sold on the African mainland, especially as Dutch vessels brought cargoes from Madagascar to the Cape Colony.

Even within the near diaspora, destinations of African captives ranged over a huge area. To begin with, many captives went no further than the Sahara itself. Regular demand for laborers emanated from the desert salt mines of Taghaza and from the more northerly oases, where dates and wheat were grown. North of the desert, the long rule of Mulay Isma'il in Morocco (1672–1727) saw substantial purchases of black captives for the large military force the king maintained. Purchases of captives in Algeria, Tunisia, and Libya, all under Ottoman rule, were steady but modest. Egypt, a major center of population with an elite that required domestic servants, imported large numbers of girls. Along the Red Sea route, significant numbers of captives were delivered to South Arabia and the Hijaz. All these regions thus gathered concentrations of African populations, for which African institutions and ethnic identities could be propagated from generation to generation. Of course, the Arabic language and Islamic religion became dominant in these communities, and many of the women had children with local men. Yet Swahili influenced the speech of Muscat, and East African music added to the culture of Oman. The *gnawa* ritual, relying heavily on drumming and on oral conveyance of key texts, characterized the Islamic practice of black people in Morocco. And the *zar* possession ritual, stemming from the practice of women healers in the Horn and middle Nile Valley, became influential among blacks and others in Egypt, Arabia, and regions beyond.

Movement of African captives to the "far diaspora" of the Old World took place directly and indirectly. The most direct shipments to the far diaspora took cargoes of captives from the Swahili coast by monsoon-propelled dhows to the Persian Gulf and India's western coast. These long oceanic voyages were comparable to the transatlantic slave voyages, lasting several weeks and requiring ample stores of food and water.[16] Similarly, Dutch and then French ships carried captives from Mozambique and Swahili ports to the Mascarenes in response to the coffee boom that began in the 1740s and the sugar upsurge that started in the 1780s. (But slaves also came to Ile Bourbon and Mauritius by stages, with transshipment in the Comoros, Madagascar, or the Seychelles.) Quite a different long-distance voyage was that of captives taken in India and the Indonesian archipelago and delivered in Dutch ships to the Cape Colony during the eighteenth century.

The indirect conveyance of Africans to the far diaspora included captives shipped from Egypt to Anatolia, often in galleys—indeed, many African slaves were put to work as oarsmen. Similar travel in the Mediterranean Sea and Black Sea, and along the Persian Gulf and the long South Asian coast, brought Africans to such destinations as Italy, Corsica, Cyprus, the Caucasus, Ceylon, and Bengal. Further overland travel led Africans to central Europe, Damascus, Baghdad, Isfahan, and Delhi.

The character of slavery in the Old World diaspora differed significantly from slavery in the Americas. In the lands of the Old World diaspora—especially the far diaspora—slavery had existed for thousands of years, and conditions there brought substantial pressure for integrating the Africans biologically and socially into the society around them. In lands adjoining the Mediterranean Sea and Indian Ocean, the enslaved included Africans, Slavs, Circassians, and others, so that slaves of one group could substitute for another if needed. Children of a slave woman and her master were born free, and there were other incentives that led to manumission of slaves at the death of an owner. Africans were commonly dispersed among other peoples and tended to adopt many elements of local culture. In second and later generations, African immigrants were identified in generalized ethnic groups such as Siddis, Habshis, or Kaffirs; others joined local ethnic groups through marriage. Islam became a system for integrating people of most all these origins. In addition, Islam was typically the religion not only of those who purchased the captives at their destination but also of those in sub-Saharan Africa who dispatched them. Nonetheless, as in the Americas, Africans had input into the societies in which they lived. The spirit-possession cult of *zar*, with its emphasis on healing, took root in Iran and India. Black communities arose and sustained themselves in Morocco, Abkhazia, Arabia, Iraq, India, and Ceylon. The Abkhazian community, which had grown through immigration of blacks with the rise of the Ottoman Empire, fell under Russian rule when the Russians gained control of the Caucasus in the early eighteenth century. Ethnicity faded in more distant regions with smaller numbers but was able to reconstitute itself where groups could gather and reproduce, as with Abkhazians and Siddis.

The Ottoman state purchased and relied on large numbers of African slaves, buying young boys and girls and grooming them for service. Most girls became domestics; some went into harems. The boys became pages, soldiers, servants, or laborers. Armies sent by the Ottomans into major battles of the eighteenth century, as in Hungary in 1717, included tens of thousands of African soldiers. An elite group of African slaves consisted of eunuchs, boys who had been castrated before departure from sub-Saharan Africa and had survived the terrible death rate of the operation. Some of the eunuchs rose to great importance, not only as governors of the harems but as counselors of state.[17]

The African diaspora in Europe is of particular interest, as it exhibited characteristics of the Atlantic diaspora and the Old World diaspora but also developed its own specific qualities. An outstanding individual story is that of Abraham Hannibal, born in sub-Saharan Africa, enslaved as a boy, sold and transported to Russia, probably via the Ottoman realm. He became part of the team of black guards in Russia and came to the attention of the emperor Peter the Great. Then he was sent to France to study and became an engineer. As a military engineer, he rose to the rank of general. After a failed first marriage into one elite family, he married into a second. Late in life he took the name of Hannibal, linking himself to the Carthaginian general of two thousand years earlier.[18]

The place of Hannibal in the army and court of imperial Russia reflected a frequent destiny for male African migrants to the Old World. In the retinues of German kings in the seventeenth and eighteenth century, military bands and royal retainers often included Africans because of their skills and their distinctive appearance. In France, the young Joseph Saint-Georges, born into slavery in Guadeloupe but protected and freed by his noble French father, rose to prominence as a champion fencer. Later this multitalented man became a military officer and gained his greatest prominence in the 1770s as a composer and musical director of court music.[19]

For Europe, the patterns of the Old World diaspora and the Atlantic diaspora met and overlapped. In countries of the Atlantic shore—Portugal, Spain, France, England, the Netherlands, Denmark—the black population came mainly across the ocean as an extension of the Atlantic diaspora. In countries of the Mediterranean and central and eastern Europe, the black population came across the Sahara as part of the Old World diaspora. The patterns of life for black people in Europe drew on traditions of both great diasporas.

The African diaspora in Europe developed some distinctive characteristics in the eighteenth century. The access of some African-descended persons to elite education stood out—as in the cases of Joseph Saint-Georges of France and Abraham Hannibal of Russia. These individuals, remarkable for their skill and accomplishments, had their equivalent in the leading black generals, political figures, and artists of Asia and North Africa. In addition, some well-educated black Europeans took the additional step of writing and speaking on issues of slavery and equality—notably Anton Wilhelm Amo, Jacobus Capiteijn, Ottobah Cugoano, and Olaudah Equiano.[20] This last group was small in number but of great importance in establishing the patterns by which people of African ancestry grappled with the intellectual traditions of Europe.

The African diaspora under European control extended to the islands of the Indian Ocean, where European merchants instituted their ideas and practices. The Dutch set up a garrison on Mauritius in 1638, and the French soon followed in nearby Ile Bourbon. The Dutch abandoned Mauritius in 1715, perhaps because of an uprising by slave and maroon communities. In the 1720s, as demand for coffee grew, the French took Mauritius and began building up slave populations on it and Ile Bourbon. The development of these islands closely paralleled that of the Caribbean islands: sugar production expanded in the Indian Ocean at the end of the eighteenth century as it reached its limits in the Caribbean. Dutch merchants bought captives in Madagascar and Mozambique early on, and French merchants replaced the Dutch later in the century. The Makua ethnicity, meaning people from northern Mozambique, became well established on Madagascar and in the Mascarenes; the Malagasy ethnicity also became established in the Mascarenes.

By the eighteenth century, a worldwide system of slave labor had developed, linking the capture, transportation, and exploitation of Africans in the Americas, Africa, and the Old World diaspora. This global network relied principally but not entirely on people of African descent. Others were enslaved in regions surrounding sub-Saharan Africa on three sides. Directly north of sub-Saharan Africa were enslaved Romani, Circassians, Russians, and others of Slavic heritage held in lands bordering on the Black Sea, and also people of Mediterranean lands captured in wars and raids. To the east were captives taken in India, Malaya, Thailand, and the Indonesian archipelago. Far to the west were Amerindians captured in Brazil and North America.

What was it that made slave labor a global system rather than a collection of local practices? One can demonstrate the system's existence in the changes and mutual influences throughout the world, especially the interconnections of global commerce. For instance, supply-and-demand factors encouraged the expansion of the slave trade to the Old World diaspora at the end of the eighteenth century. On the demand side, the eighteenth-century world economy developed a growing need for labor and thus saw an expanded system for using slave labor in domestic service and production for markets. On the supply side, the steady expansion of enslavement raids and retaliations across the African continent brought the slave trade to East Africa, and so larger supplies of captives became available. Dutch and French demand for slaves in the Mascarenes helped fuel the expansion of slave supply along the East African coast, which then made slaves available for delivery to the Persian Gulf. Growing demand for sugar, coffee, pearls, and ivory each boosted demand for slaves in the Indian Ocean. (On the other hand, the Russian substitution of serfdom for slavery early in the eighteenth century reduced slave demand somewhat.) By 1800, the transatlantic slave trade had reached its peak and would gradually decline. The Old World trade, in contrast, had begun to expand rapidly and would continue its growth well into the nineteenth century.

Further evidence for the systemic nature of global slavery, in addition to these economic and demographic links, can be found in the repeating patterns of cultural characteristics—such as the widespread black warrior tradition, the presence and influence of Islam, and the spread of spirit-possession cults—and in the family structures that developed from within a life in slavery.

Identity—Nation, Color, Race

Slave owners presented slavery as a natural phenomenon, one built inherently into the destiny of masters and slaves. In fact, it was nothing of the sort—every aspect of the life of slaves resulted from human decisions in a hierarchical exercise of power. The reorganization of society in all the lands of Africa and the diasporas in the seventeenth and eighteenth centuries demonstrates how humans defined and redefined their social order. In Africa, this process brought legal changes that allowed humans to be seized and held and that redefined marriage in hierarchical terms. In the Americas, the expansion of slavery redefined the rules of society generally: slave identity and subordination became codified, classifications of race and color developed, and the notion of "nation" evolved in its meaning. In most of the Old World diaspora, the shifts in law and social practice were less drastic, since small numbers of Africans had long been enslaved in those regions. Nevertheless, the expansion of slavery and its central role in the world economy also brought new perspectives of race, color, and nation there as well. In Western Europe, the region that governed the Americas, the minimal presence of Africans was defined in hierarchical terms but, as elsewhere in the Old World diaspora, some Africans rose to positions of power and recognition in elite society. In an important development for black people in general, literate Africans in Europe were able to comment on racism and on the place of Africans in the world.

The first point of this section is to show how identities of black people—their views of themselves and their categorization by others—underwent transformation as a result of human decisions and the effect of broader social forces during the seventeenth and eighteenth centuries, yielding a practical system of social and racial hierarchy. The second point is to show how a new European-based, oppressive interpretation of race, color, and nation came into existence at the end of the eighteenth century, rationalizing the existing hierarchy and structuring "race relations" for the nineteenth and twentieth century. The third point of this section is to show that, despite the power of rising concepts of race, color, and nation, humans remained more complex than any hypothesis could capture, and that the lives of individuals and groups evolved in quite different directions than those envisioned by European theorists.

The redefinition of individual lives and socially stratified identities through enslavement becomes manifest in the basic documents of individual existence. Here, for instance, is the baptismal record of a child recorded at the Catholic Church of St. Louis in the city of New Orleans:[21]

> On 27 May 1792 . . . I baptized a black girl of Mr. Lioto, born two years ago, having come from Africa, who was given the name Julia, natural daughter of Felipe and Madalena, unbaptized blacks of said Lioto: godparents Valentin Florez, and Julia, the first a grif slave of Madama Gayard, the second a black of Madama Mermiyon.
>
> Fr. Diego de Canniedo

This concise record is extraordinary, first because it lists the father and mother of a slave child, but especially because it demonstrates one of the rare cases where two parents and their infant daughter managed to survive the transatlantic voyage and stay together once settled in the New World.[22] One can imagine that the parents, given the names Felipe and Madalena on their arrival, were introduced to the customs of Louisiana by people of the slave community there, who were convinced their daughter should be baptized into the Catholic faith. The parents, however, remained true to the religion of their homeland that brought them together.

This same baptismal document, in addition to providing evidence on individual experience, reveals many of the categories imposed on slaves and indeed on all people of the Americas in colonial times. It identified the child Julia as a female, born in Africa, black in color, and a slave (following the condition of her mother). It identified the mother and father as black, of African birth, unmarried, and as slaves owned by Mr. Lioto. The godmother was identified as black and the godfather as "grif" (of reddish hue, meaning the child of black and mulatto parents, or perhaps with Amerindian ancestry); both were slaves. Most people throughout the Atlantic world in the early modern period had such complex identities. The full list of attributes included their name, sex, parents, free or slave status, owner (if slave), color (or race), nation, birthplace, and marital status.

Of these elements of identity, the facts of nature determined only the sex and birthplace of parents and child. Social decisions determined the other categories—name, nation, slave status, marital status, and even color. The actual colors of parents and child were determined biologically, but the labels given to color were socially charged. Even the parentage of this child depended on social choice—most baptisms of slave children suppressed the father's identity. Identity, in short, resulted from a complex accumulation of categories, labeling each person at once as an individual and as a part of several groups. Gender was the most stable and lasting of these categories, but, in the early modern Atlantic world, slavery and race played an especially important role in establishing human identities. These categories of identity established *difference*—as between male and female, Kongo and Maya, or variations in skin color and height. The same categories could also establish *hierarchy*—setting free over slave and white over black. The *differences* among categories were usually determined by social decisions rather than by nature (as between married and unmarried or between one nation and another). The *hierarchies* among categories (men over women, married over unmarried, Portuguese over Kongo) were definitely set by society rather than by any natural order.

Here I seek to trace the changing balance among categories of identity and the degree to which individual *difference* became social *hierarchy*. Simply stated, the differences in people's color and the hierarchy of free over slave remained fairly stable across the centuries, but the process of articulating the logic and social hierarchy of "race" gradually created a substantially different social order. Race came to be defined through color more than (as earlier) through lineage or culture, and after a time color came to be seen as a key to biological subspecies among humans set in a hierarchy.

Maritime travel brought greater intermingling and thus greater complexity to human identity. Portuguese and then other voyagers expanded migration, empire, and enslavement—they created new social orders and a range of new identities. People named themselves, named other individuals and groups, and took on additional names as they moved from one place to another and from one language community to another. In Spanish, the terms *indio* and *mulato* developed out of this experience; in the Wolof language of West Africa, the term *toubab*, for foreigners, now was extended to Europeans; and the Arabic term *kafir* for "unbelievers" was sometimes extended to blacks as a group.

Slavery compounded the complexity of naming. Purchasers renamed their slaves to cut them off from their previous identity and put them in their place. Slavery relied on a fundamental inconsistency in law: when one person seized another by force, others recognized the subordination of the slave as legitimate. A free-born person had a set of social rights, but those rights could be suddenly eliminated by capture for fair reason or foul. Thus slavery involved at least two levels of hierarchy: the master's physical dominance over slaves and the master's legal dominance. The latter came not only because the master interpreted the law that held the slave in captivity but because those newly enslaved were now denied access to the laws that had protected them when they were free. With time, separate bodies of law developed for slaves in the Americas, in Africa, and in the Old World diaspora, which both gave them some protections and ensured their subordination to owners.

Skin color was always central in identity, but its meaning changed with time. The distinctions of skin color often labeled as "white" and "black" existed before the Europeans took to the oceans in force. How did one interpret these differences in color? We have more information on the beliefs of Europeans than of Africans in the early modern period. In a set of ideas inherited from the Greeks, early modern European thinkers believed that dark African skins resulted from prolonged exposure to the sun and light European skins from less exposure. But when Africans had lived in Europe for generations without becoming lighter, Europeans looked for other reasons for skin-color variations. This opened the door to religious rather than environmental explanations: Africans were the progeny of Ham and his son Canaan, cursed by Noah, who had seen him naked, as suggested in Genesis. The Bible did not explicitly state that the curse on Ham and Canaan involved dark skin, but this idea came to be accepted among many Christians and Muslims with steadily increasing certainty up to the nineteenth century.

In varying parts of the African diaspora, different interpretations of color developed. In eighteenth-century Mexico, a ritualized set of images evolved, presented in a series of paintings portraying a father, mother, and their child, to show every combination of color and ethnicity among parents of European, African, and Amerindian ancestry and providing descriptive labels for the parents and child. These *casta* paintings, as they became known, changed over the century—revealing the social life of ordinary people in contrast to the high religious art produced for the elite. These paintings disappeared, however, when Mexico gained its independence from Spain.[23] In Brazil as in Mexico, European, African, and Amerindian ancestry were each significant, but Africans were most numerous—the resulting socioethnic hierarchy distinguished *branco, amarelo, moreno, pardo, preto,* and various other color gradations, each of which came to be recognized as virtually equivalent to ethnic boundaries. In the Caribbean, with its small white elite, large black slave population, and mixtures of color and status, mulattoes and creole blacks tended to be seen as separate ethnicities. In North America, while color difference was of great importance to whites and people of color, the law and opinion of whites determined that all people of African descent would be categorized into a single group known as "colored" or "Negro." In Africa, color was not used to distinguish between slave and free, but color did become an aspect of social hierarchy among those interacting with Europeans.

Nation, another central dimension of identity, changed as much as race did. The term "nation," used in all the languages of colonization from the sixteenth to the eighteenth century, referred initially to what would be called today the "ethnicity" of a person. So it is helpful to keep in mind both terms and both descriptions of social groups: "nation" as it was understood in past times and "ethnicity" as we understand it today. The term "nation" specified the identity defined for groups in terms of their language, region, and cultural background. These "national" identities were often inconsistent—for example, a person could be lumped into a different nation in the New World than in the Old World. More specifically, any German-speaking person in the Americas would be called German, regardless of which of the many German states was his or her homeland. Similarly, people identified as "Igbo" because of their language commonly had never heard the term and had not previously conceived of themselves as part of an Igbo grouping. Nonetheless, these categories of nation identified the many African, Amerindian, and European groups that populated the Americas. Similarly, people in Europe and Africa were also classified by nation. Applying the modern notion of "ethnicity," we can see that ethnic groups formed and changed throughout the African diaspora. Ethnicities developed among slaves, based on specific African origins. Yoruba, Ibo, and Congo ethnicities in the diaspora did not correspond precisely to African ethnicities but were aggregations of related groups. Free people and creole Africans whose parents and grandparents had lived in the Americas were more likely to form ethnicities based on common territory and language. Kreyol-speakers in Haiti ultimately formed a nation, for example, and Jamaicans and Afro-Cubans formed colony-wide identities. In North America, the differences in culture between the plantation society of the South and the urban life of blacks in the North might have allowed the creation of two separate ethnicities. Nevertheless, the connections maintained among free blacks of the North and South ensured a common identity even as their language, religion, and cuisine showed regional differences. In Europe, blacks rarely had the opportunity to form ethnic groups, as many lived in isolation with no family and no assigned or adopted ethnicity. Others were accepted into British or French ethnicity, though most commonly at a low status level.

In Africa, new ethnic groups formed. Escaped slaves and refugees from slave raids in particular created ethnic groups, including the Kisama southeast of Luanda, the Weme east of Dahomey, and the Yangiakury settlement in Sierra Leone. In the Old World diaspora, some African-descended groups were able to form ethnic groups, including the Siddis of India. Those integrated into the Moroccan army, while sharing language and religion with their fellow Moroccans, may reasonably be labeled as an ethnic group in the eighteenth century; their group identity was sustained in particular through practice of the *gnawa* religious sect. It is more difficult to label the ethnicity of women born in Somalia who lived out their lives in Arabia. There as elsewhere, many blacks of the diaspora were women who had children with men from the host society, so their ethnicity becomes difficult to specify.

[*Birthplace*, especially in the Americas where so many were migrants, became a central aspect of identity.]In all the languages of Atlantic colonization (Spanish, Portuguese, English, French, and Dutch), *creole* or its equivalent initially meant—when used as an adjective describing a person—a person born in the colonies rather than in Europe or Africa. On the other hand, when used as an adjective describing a language, *creole* meant a language constructed in the colony out of a mixture of the languages brought in from various directions. By the end of the eighteenth century, *creole*, when used as a noun, had come to refer to white people only, that is, it distinguished the whites born in the region from the newly arrived migrants from the metropole.[24]

The institution of *marriage* and the identification of progeny of unions as the generations passed did much to determine the identity of those in future generations. Who married? Throughout the African diaspora and the global system of forced labor that overlaid it, marriage was rather consistently for free people and not for slaves. Most often, free people married when they set up permanent relations with others from their own social category. These unions created ties not only between the couple but between families as well. Relationships across racial or ethnic lines tended not to be formalized by marriage; relationships where one or both persons was in slavery rarely gained the sanctification of marriage. (To put these differences in formal terms, one may say that *procreation* is the beginning of a new life, *family* is a set of relations among adults and children, and *marriage* is a formal recognition of certain family relations.) Marriage generally involved acquisition and disposition of property and was obviated in cases where property was minimal. In fact, the complexities and limitations of marriage applied not only to the Americas and the Old World diaspora but also to sub-Saharan Africa, where marriage also was generally limited to free people. Marriages of slaves in Africa and the diaspora, however heartfelt and lasting the commitments, had little standing among the leaders of their societies.

The laws of slavery had great local variation, but some general patterns emerge. Children of a slave couple belonged not to the parents but to the owner. Children of a free man and a slave woman belonged to the woman's owner. In some African societies and under Islam in Africa and elsewhere, the father of a child by his slave was to free the mother and child. (The woman, though freed, generally had no family of her own, except her children.)

In every migrant population of the African diaspora and especially in the American colonies, identity and its hierarchies evolved within generations toward greater complexity. The example of Louisiana reveals the evolution of colonial identities from the first encounters to later conflicts and coexistence. In the New Orleans settlement, the founding generation of whites, blacks, and Amerindians, slave and free, came together in 1720. In a few years, the first children to be born were of many of the possible mixes. These second-generation children, born in the 1720s, immediately gained free or slave status, but only gradually, as they grew up, did they begin to be labeled by such terms for mixing as "mulattos" (black and white), *métis* (white and Amerindian), and *zambos* (black and Amerindian). Then in the 1740s, this second generation reached adulthood and began having children, again with numerous mixes. Some of the third-generation children, as they came to maturity in the 1760s, began to be labeled with new terms such as "quadroon"; in yet another generation, the fourth, terms such as "octoroon" emerged.

Further, in those early days of Louisiana, any child labeled as brown had clearly come from a relationship between white and black. At the end of that century, however, a brown child might have been the offspring of two mulattos or any of several other combinations. Furthermore, in the 1720s, Louisiana families consisted almost exclusively of young adults and their children. Only after two or three generations could there also be grandparents and distant cousins. Each colonial society, therefore, underwent a logical evolution from simple categories at the time of formation to much more complex categories after two or three generations. When migration stopped for a time, as it did in Louisiana during the 1750s and 1760s, and then started up later, the process could begin again, as the simple migrant categories of black and white were imposed on a complex society: Gwendolyn Midlo Hall called this "re-Africanization" for Louisiana. Then as before, more complex categories were created through intermarriage.

Identities evolved both within each colony and in the Atlantic-wide system of slavery and freedom. As the number and proportion of slaves grew in the Americas and in Africa, the meanings of categories changed. In the eyes of slave masters, Africans became not just different but inferior—they and their children were born to be slaves. Slave owners sought increasingly to affirm their inherent superiority. Slave rebellion against this hierarchy led to growing brutality on each side—for instance, the development of elaborate punishments and masks, chains, and other restraints for disobedient slaves.

But slaves and masters, blacks and whites (and every other color) lived in close contact, so it was not only hierarchy and hostility that grew. There was love as well as lust, politeness as well as enmity, shared work as well as competition, mutual respect as well as theft and violence. The hierarchy of slave over free and white over black was powerful, but it was limited by many normal human patterns. The growing number of free people of color in the Americas provided a clear indication that racial hierarchy could be undermined.

Slavery and racial hierarchy could only be sustained with an effective ideology, and such an ideology gradually emerged: what today we call racism.[25] The ideology of racism developed three major elements: color, nation, and biology. Each had its own logic, and the combination of the three became a powerful defense for social hierarchy and a rationalization for oppression.

The most crucial element was the last to develop: the argument for biological differences among humans. Once the idea of species of plants and animals gained a foothold, it was a small step to suggesting that human phenotype reveals a deep difference in biological type—in effect, subspecies among humans. In the eighteenth century, the advent of biological classification introduced the notion of species and their relationships and the idea of deep biological differences among regionally based races. Carl Linnaeus, the pathbreaking Swedish biologist who completed the first general classification of biological species, clearly placed humans among other animal species. Ironically, this scientific advance helped pave the way for new notions of racial hierarchy. From the time of his classification of animals in 1758, the family tree—and the hierarchy—of the animal world became evident to leading scholars. While it would be another century before Darwin published his theory of evolution, it became logical to consider the biological hierarchy among humans: Linnaeus himself identified Africans, Asians, and Europeans as human subspecies.[26] Johann Friedrich Blumenbach, an early leader in human physical anthropology, coined the term "Caucasian" in a 1795 book to refer to the physical type earlier writers had called European. The term was widely adopted.

The second element of the new racial ideology was a new meaning for the term "nation." The historical philosopher Johann Gottfried von Herder led in this thinking with his 1784 book on the history of mankind. He treated a "nation" and its associated "people," rather than empires and dynasties, as the basis for politics and history. In developments that were clearest in Europe, the eighteenth and early nineteenth centuries brought a new set of meanings for the terms "nation" and "race." Where "nation" previously meant any ethnic group unified by language and culture, the term came to refer more narrowly to nations accompanied by a recognized, powerful government and borders. By this logic, the Hausa nation was reduced to a Hausa "tribe." At the same time, the term "race," which had been little used, was applied to wider groupings. The confusion in terminology was long lasting: the British spoke of the Irish race and the German race but also of a Mediterranean race and a Caucasian race. Ultimately, however, "race" came to mean distinctions among four to eight broad groupings of regional origin and physical type.

The third element of the racist ideology focused on color. Color had long been the practical basis for racial discrimination, but some writers of the eighteenth century theorized and codified color differences. Edward Long, an English-born planter, published in 1774 a history of Jamaica that used color distinctions to argue that blacks were distinct and systematically inferior to whites.[27] Bryan Edwards, a longtime resident of Jamaica, and Médéric Louis Elie Moreau de Saint-Méry of St. Domingue each wrote widely read descriptions of the Haitian Revolution, focusing on color distinctions. While neither of them mentioned racial hierarchy in such explicit terms as Long, their works fed into the growing ideology.

Thus, while the religious categorization of differences in color continued to be influential, there now developed a basis for identification of races based on natural and biological criteria. This scientific identification of "race" was destined to grow with time. The social hierarchy inherent in slavery began to have a scientific rationalization. In the increasingly secular world, biblical rationalization of the social order began to be supplemented and then replaced with the logic of natural law.

Combining these three sets of categories, the ground was set for the emergence of a theory. Race was redefined through crystallization of a set of concepts—biological race, nation (a term increasingly limited to whites), and ethnicity (through the increasing use of the term "tribe"). Racial discrimination and the institutions of racial hierarchy went on as before. But the developing theory of race provided a new, effective ideological tool for opposing the burgeoning antislavery movement and the growing claims for liberty, equality, and fraternity. In this theory, "race" became set in a biological hierarchy. Color became the best index to race. "Nation" became a set of categories within the white race. Nonwhite races could have tribes but not nations. From this standpoint, for white Europeans, nations and races—now seen as consisting of larger groups than before—were essential and pure in origin and ranked in a hierarchy. For mixes of these nations and races, impurity and further inferiority were expected.

The categories of race, nation, color, slave, and free brought both division and coherence to a hierarchical system of economics and politics spanning the Atlantic and beyond. This capitalist economic system, with steam-driven industry as its emerging core but with slavery as its distant sinews, was labeled "the modern world-system" in an influential 1974 analysis by Immanuel Wallerstein. Africans and African-descended people of the Americas made up a significant minority of the people in this world-system. Wallerstein's analysis put them at the fringes of the system, yet they were still at the center of their own lives.[28] The world-system, with its voracious demand for more labor, its incremental technological efficiency, and its concentration of wealth and capital, transformed African politics and society and remade the Americas. In the seventeenth and eighteenth centuries, it modified African trade and agriculture; expanded sugar, tobacco, and indigo production in the Americas; and constructed the cities and infrastructure of colonization.

The social hierarchy of the Atlantic world had come to appear inescapable, but not everybody believed in it or acted consistently with it. There remained significant differences in how individuals responded to those social structures. Among the masters, there were cruel people who appeared to gain pleasure from vicious treatment of slaves under their control. Others, however, treated people with dignity whatever their social station. Among the slaves were those shamed, disabled, and embittered by their humiliation and others able somehow to hold up their heads and speak to any person as an equal.

The evolution of each colony included the persistence of values of human equality and understanding alongside those of hierarchy and discrimination. Slave wet-nurses suckled and nurtured children of the masters. People of all ranks exchanged greetings, jokes, and proverbs. Sexual attraction crossed all barriers of language, color, status, and even age. People of remarkable brilliance and stupidity emerged at all levels of society. Certainly the social order privileged white over black, owner over slave, male over female, and royalty over commoner. Yet it remained common knowledge that all had come into the world from a mother's womb and that none would live forever. This shared wisdom put limits on the colonial systems of slavery and racial discrimination.

Crisis in Slavery

The system of slavery was vulnerable to attack from several sides. One of the most general threats to slavery was the global economic system of which it formed a part. The expanding industrial order, centered initially in England, relied significantly on earnings from the goods sent to Africa, the trade in African captives transported across the Atlantic and Indian Oceans, and the produce of slave labor in the Americas, the islands, and Africa.[29] Other factors were the growing size of slave populations and the changing forms of labor in factories, plantations, and mines. The coincidence and occasional coordination of various forces coalesced to bring slavery down—not all at once in an apocalyptic confrontation, but slowly, painfully, and incompletely. The immense system of slavery, holding scores of millions of persons in captivity at the end of the eighteenth century, would be forced almost to its knees over the next hundred years.

But already by 1800, the system of Atlantic slavery had reached its peak and met its most fearsome challenge: the massive 1791 uprising of slaves in St. Domingue and their subsequent success in protecting their hard-won freedom. This revolutionary upheaval did not end slavery, but it did end an era: although slavery mutated and survived through the nineteenth and into the twentieth century, the campaign of emancipation that began in Haiti gained strength and, eventually, all but eliminated the exploitation of human captives.

In May 1789, the delegates to the Estates General of France, convened for the first time in over a century by a nervous king, rapidly transformed themselves into a National Assembly that gave voice to claims for citizen rights. All of France felt the rising tide of liberty, equality, fraternity. Within weeks, these calls resonated throughout St. Domingue, France's richest colony. White planters, who dominated the colony's sugar plantations in the north and the west, joined the revolutionary clamor, calling for an end to feudal taxation, commercial regulation, and the central government's arbitrary power. Landowners among the free people of color, predominant in the southern coffee lands, claimed the right of citizenship and representation, supported by their allies in France among the Société des Amis des Noirs. Some of them had fought against the British in the American Revolution. The lawyer Vincent Ogé led a northern group of free people of color in a rebellion early in 1791. They were crushed, and Ogé was executed brutally. Some of the triumphant white leaders, however, began to think of independence for themselves.

In August 1791, the slaves in the north arose. In a secret midnight meeting at Bois Caiman, the leading *houngan* (vodun priest) Boukman Dutty presided over a ceremony where slave leaders pledged to rebel. In a few days, the rebels attacked with extraordinary force. The battles raged fiercely and endlessly. Neither the rebels nor the planters and French troops showed any mercy. At one point in 1792, the black leaders, isolated and having suffered great losses, agreed to capitulate, but the rank-and-file rebels rejected the agreement and the struggle went on. Driving the slaves onward was the opportunity for freedom, much more so than the ongoing discourse on human rights.

The rebellious slaves correctly judged the strength and dedication of their numbers. By being ruthless and willing to sustain many casualties, they widened the divisions among their masters and the imperial powers and exposed the vulnerability of slavery as a system. Rebel leaders, however, were involved in diplomacy as well as war: after a time they moved from dwelling on the basic distinction between slavery and freedom to more nuanced arguments for general human rights and critiques of feudalism.

As the war with the St. Domingue slaves went on, the leaders of the Legislative Assembly in France allied with the free people of color in early 1792, awarding them citizenship. This was a preeminent moment for the free people of color. In 1793, soon after Louis XVI's execution, France was at war with Britain, Spain, and Austria, and the conflict came rapidly to the Caribbean. British and Spanish forces were in St. Domingue by mid-1793. The black armies of the north allied with Spain against France to protect their freedom. French forces, allied with an army in the south led by Rigaud and other free men of color, sought to win over the blacks. Toussaint Louverture was the leader among the blacks who chose the key moment to rally to the French. Toussaint had joined the rebellion in late 1791 and rapidly gained ascendancy because of his skills in discipline, military tactics, and diplomacy.

French officials in the colony abolished slavery in August 1793, and the National Assembly in Paris ratified the decision in January 1794. The war continued for four more years, however. The Spanish withdrew in 1795, but the British held on until 1798. By that time, the slaves seemed to have won their freedom, and free people of color gained the right to full political participation in 1792. Yet conflicts of class and color continued. Toussaint sought to return sugar fields to production to earn revenue and sustain the army, but the ex-slaves showed no interest in sugar work. Toussaint found himself quarreling with French officials, with other black generals, and with Rigaud and mulattos in the south. Coffee production and export continued; sugar production largely halted.

Napoleon Bonaparte, who now controlled France, decided that Toussaint was moving too close to declaring independence. In 1802, Napoleon (with the British navy providing safe passage) sent a huge army to reconquer St. Domingue. The expedition succeeded initially. Toussaint was seized and exiled, and he soon died in a French prison. But within months, the news that slavery would be reestablished brought a great new rebellion that, in combination with yellow fever, destroyed the French army.

Three symbolic acts punctuated this definitive achievement of Haitian freedom. First, in April 1803, Jean-Jacques Dessalines, Toussaint's successor as leader of the national movement, prepared for the crucial battles to come. Dessalines seized a revolutionary French tricolor flag, ripped out its middle white stripe and linked the remaining blue and red stripes in a new flag. This indicated symbolically that the black people of Haiti, rather than the whites of France, had been most loyal to the ideals of liberty, fraternity, and equality. The new flag was formally revealed to the public in the town of Arcahie on May 18, 1803.

Second, as the defeated French were departing in November 1803, the provisional government prepared its declaration of independence. The draft statement, written in formal, legalistic terms, struck many Haitians as too restrained. Its Age of Enlightenment language regarding the rights of man skirted many realities of the bloody, racially divisive conflict. Boisrond Tonnerre, secretary to Dessalines and author of the proclamation of Haitian independence, called out a terse, forceful critique of the declaration that became famous among Haitians. If they were to have a declaration of independence, it would have to meet some conditions:[30]

Il nous faut la peau d'un blanc	We must have the skin of a
pour parchemin	white for parchment
Son crâne pour écritoire	His skull for an inkstand
Son sang pour encre	His blood for ink
Et une baïonette pour plume	And a bayonet for a quill

This statement of "true feelings" drew on the symbolism of West African states, where victorious kings exhibited the skulls of their defeated rivals, but the anger behind it was fueled mostly by Napoleon's campaign to reenslave those who had just won their freedom.

Third, in the months before the declaration of independence, a seemingly spontaneous movement developed that proposed adopting "Haiti" as the new nation's name. This word, taken from the Taino name for the island, crossed a racial boundary to link the new, predominantly black nation to its original Amerindian heritage. On New Year's Day of 1804, Dessalines proclaimed the independent state of Haiti.

In these fifteen years of struggle before St. Domingue became Haiti, the two great rebellions of 1791 and 1803 made the difference between slavery and freedom. The energy and brilliance of Toussaint and other black generals sustained the long campaign. Eventually, the white people were driven out. (Those whites willing to deal with former slaves were always outnumbered by those seeking to reimpose slavery.) The conflicts and contending visions separating black and brown people, revealed from the first, characterized independent Haiti thereafter. The bitterness of the war in St. Domingue on all sides—the loss of life in battle and the massacres in between—makes the revolutions in the United States, France, and the Latin American nations appear as gentlemanly disagreements in comparison.

As the eighteenth century gave way to the nineteenth, new forms of economic organization, catastrophic wars, campaigns of religious conversion, popular demands for democratic rights, and claims for recognition of national sovereignty all shook the planet in various ways. Leaders of social movements demanded equality, yet new inequalities appeared more rapidly than the old ones disappeared. Slavery stood as a pillar of the social systems of the Atlantic, the Old World, and Africa—yet the contradiction of its oppression threatened to destabilize society. By 1804, it had become clear that destroying slavery would be as bloody as the capture of slaves had been. Yet the antislavery campaign persisted and grew, and the Haitian nation survived. This nation, though weakened through isolation as white-led nations shunned it and weakened further by its own divisions, formed a pivot on which antislavery activists could rely. In the nineteenth century, the campaign against slavery would be the principal challenge to the growing inequality of the world.

Suggested Readings

The seventeenth-century struggles that brought expanded enslavement and a rising sugar industry have been analyzed repeatedly, but some early studies retain their relevance. The brilliant maritime historian C. R. Boxer wrote three such volumes: *The Portuguese Seaborne Empire, 1415–1825* (New York: Knopf, 1969); *The Dutch Seaborne Empire, 1600–1800* (New York: Knopf, 1965); and *Salvador de Sá and the Struggle for Brazil and Angola, 1602–1686* (London: University of London, 1952). For a detailed analysis of the Brazilian state of Palmares, see Raymond K. Kent, "Palmares: An African State in Brazil," *Journal of African History* 6 (1965): 161–176; and especially Décio Freitas, *Palmares: A Guerra dos Escravos*, 5th ed. (Rio de Janeiro: Graal, 1990). P. C. Emmer, *The Dutch Slave Trade, 1500–1800*, trans. Chris Emery (New York: Berghahn, 2006), adds new information on Dutch perspectives.

Waves of Enslavement

This section is drawn from a wide range of sources. Two surveys that provide consistent detail on the ups and downs of the slave trade are Patrick Manning, *Slavery and African Life: Occidental, Oriental, and African Slave Trades* (Cambridge: Cambridge University Press, 1990); and David Eltis, *The Rise of African Slavery in the Americas* (Cambridge: Cambridge University Press, 2000).

The Atlantic Middle Passage

For a striking and authoritative study of slave vessels, see Marcus Rediker, *The Slave Ship: A Human History* (New York: Viking Penguin, 2007). On the early English slave trade, see Stephanie Smallwood, *Saltwater Slavery: A Middle Passage from Africa to American Diaspora* (Cambridge, Mass.: Harvard University Press, 2008; for the eighteenth century, see Alexander X. Byrd, *Captives and Voyagers: Black Migrants Across the Eighteenth-Century British Atlantic World* (Baton Rouge: Louisana State University, 2008). Two general overviews of the Atlantic slave trade are James A. Rawley with Stephen Behrendt, *The Atlantic Slave Trade*, 2nd ed. (Lincoln: University of Nebraska Press, 2005), which summarizes the literature; and Hugh Thomas, *The Slave Trade: The Story of the Atlantic Slave Trade, 1440–1870* (New York: Simon & Schuster, 1997), which focuses on the slave merchants. Edited collections on the slave trade include David Northrup, ed., *The Atlantic Slave Trade*, 2nd ed. (Boston: Houghton Mifflin, 2002); and Patrick Manning, ed., *Slave Trades: Globalization of Forced Labour, 1500–1800* (Aldershot: Variorum, 1996).

The quantitative analysis that launched a generation of studies on the details of slave trade is Philip D. Curtin, *The Atlantic Slave Trade: A Census* (Madison: University of Wisconsin Press, 1969). Studies of specific aspects of the slave trade include, on the *asiento* trade: Colin A. Palmer, *Human Cargoes: The British Slave Trade to Spanish America, 1700–1739* (Urbana: University of Illinois Press, 1981); on pirates: Marcus Rediker, *Villains of All Nations: Atlantic Pirates in the Golden Age* (Boston: Beacon Press, 2004); on the history of an individual slaving voyage: Robert W. Harms, *The Diligent: A Voyage Through the Worlds of the Slave Trade* (New York: Basic Books, 2002); on a major slave-trade port: James A. Rawley, *London, Metropolis of the Slave Trade* (Columbia: University of Missouri Press, 2003); and, on Jews in the slave trade: Saul S. Friedman, *Jews and the American Slave Trade* (New Brunswick, N.J.: Transaction, 1998). Three museum catalogs on slave-trade exhibits are Anthony Tibbles, *Transatlantic Slavery: Against Human Dignity* (London: HMSO, 1994); Madeleine Burnside, *Spirits of the Passage: The Transatlantic Slave Trade in the Seventeenth Century* (New York: Simon & Schuster, 1997); and Anonymous, *Captive Passage: The Transatlantic Slave Trade and the Making of the Americas* (Washington, D.C.: Smithsonian Institution Press, 2002).

Changes in Africa

For economic and social life, Donald R. Wright, *The World and a Very Small Place in Africa* (Armonk, N.Y.: M.E. Sharpe, 1997), displays the links between a Gambian region and the world economy. For visual art, Jan Vansina, *Art History in Africa: An Introduction to Method* (London: Longman, 1984), provides clear insights into artistic change in the era of slave trade. Among the many studies on West African changes in the era of slave trade, see especially Boubacar Barry, *Senegambia and the Atlantic Slave Trade* (Cambridge: Cambridge University Press, 1998); René A. Bravmann, *Islam and Tribal Art in West Africa* (New York: Cambridge University Press, 1974); George E. Brooks, *Eurafricans in Western Africa: Commerce, Social Status, Gender, and Religious Observance from the Sixteenth to the Eighteenth Century* (Athens: Ohio University Press, 2003); Edna G. Bay, *Wives of the Leopard: Gender, Politics, and Culture in the Kingdom of Dahomey* (Charlottesville: University Press of Virginia, 1998); Robin Law, *The Slave Coast of West Africa, 1550–1750: The Impact of the Atlantic Slave Trade on an African Society* (Oxford: Clarendon Press, 1991); and Robin Law, *Ouidah: The Social History of a West African Slaving "Port," 1727–1892* (Oxford: James Currey, 2004). An equally strong literature on change in Central Africa includes Georges Balandier, *Daily Life in the Kingdom of Kongo, from the Sixteenth to the Eighteenth Century* (New York: Pantheon, 1968); Jan Vansina, *Kingdoms of the Savanna* (Madison: University of Wisconsin Press, 1966); Joseph C. Miller, *Way of Death: Merchant Capitalism and the Angolan Slave Trade, 1730–1830* (Madison: University of Wisconsin Press, 1988); John K. Thornton, *Kingdom of Kongo, Civil War, and Transition, 1641–1718* (Madison: University of Wisconsin Press, 1983); John K. Thornton, *The Kongolese Saint Anthony: Dona Beatriz Kimpa Vita and the Antonian Movement, 1684–1706* (Cambridge: Cambridge University Press, 1998); and Robert W. Harms, *River of Wealth, River of Sorrow: The Central Zaire Basin in the Era of the Slave and Ivory Trade, 1500–1891* (New Haven, Conn.: Yale University Press, 1981). The nature and extent of African poverty in the era of enslavement is explored in John Iliffe, *The African Poor: A History* (Cambridge: Cambridge University Press, 1987); the negative impact of slave trade on the African population is documented in Patrick Manning and Scott Nickleach, *African Population, 1650–1950: The Eras of Enslavement and Colonial Rule* (forthcoming).

Metamorphoses in the Atlantic Diaspora

General studies addressing social change in the Atlantic diaspora include Philip D. Curtin, *The Rise and Fall of the Plantation Complex: Essays in Atlantic*

History, 2nd ed. (Cambridge: Cambridge University Press, 1998); David Eltis, *The Rise of African Slavery in the Americas* (Cambridge: Cambridge University Press, 2000); and Sidney Mintz, *Sweetness and Power: The Place of Sugar in Modern History* (New York: Penguin, 1986). The best personal account remains that of Equiano, and the edition with the most historical analysis is that of Robert Allison: see Olaudah Equiano, *The Interesting Narrative of the Life of Olaudah Equiano, Written by Himself*, ed. Robert J. Allison (Boston: Bedford Books, 1995). Vincent Carretta's biography advances the case that Equiano was born in South Carolina: Carretta, *Equiano, the African: Biography of a Self-Made Man* (New York: Penguin, 2007). For a detailed exploration of Central Africans in the Americas, see Linda M. Heywood and John K. Thornton, *Central Africans, Atlantic Creoles, and the Foundation of the Americas, 1585–1660* (New York: Cambridge University Press, 2007). For broad studies of cultural issues, see Janheinz Jahn, *Muntu: The New African Culture* (New York: Grove Press, 1961); Jack D. Forbes, *Africans and Native Americans: The Language of Race and the Evolution of Red-Black Peoples*, 2nd ed. (Urbana: University of Illinois Press, 1993); John A. Holm, *Pidgins and Creoles*, 2 vols. (Cambridge: Cambridge University Press, 1988–1989); and Robert Chaudenson, *Creolization of Language and Culture* (London: Routledge, 2001). On the slave trade and the Atlantic economy, see Eric Williams, *Capitalism and Slavery* (Chapel Hill: University of North Carolina Press, 1944); and Joseph E. Inikori, *Africans and the Industrial Revolution in England: A Study in International Trade and Economic Development* (Cambridge: Cambridge University Press, 2002).

On Africans in early Spanish colonization, the two best studies remain Frederick Bowser, *The African Slave in Colonial Peru, 1524–1650* (Stanford, Calif.: Stanford University Press, 1974); and Colin A. Palmer, *Slaves of the White God: Blacks in Mexico, 1570–1650* (Cambridge, Mass.: Harvard University Press, 1976). Major studies on Africans under Portuguese colonization include Luiz Felipe de Alencastro, *O Trado dos Viventes: Formacão do Brasil no Atlântico Sul* (São Paulo: Compañía das Letras, 2000); Stuart B. Schwartz, *Sugar Plantations in the Formation of Brazilian Society: Bahia, 1550–1835* (Cambridge: Cambridge University Press, 1985); Stuart B. Schwartz, *Slaves, Peasants, and Rebels: Reconsidering Brazilian Slavery* (Urbana: University of Illinois Press, 1992); and James H. Sweet, *Recreating Africa: Culture, Kinship, and Religion in the African-Portuguese World, 1441–1770* (Chapel Hill: University of North Carolina Press, 2003). For a clear, continental overview, see Herbert S. Klein and Ben Vinson, *African Slavery in Latin America and the Caribbean*, 2nd ed. (New York: Oxford University Press, 2007).

For the Caribbean, including the Guianas, a detailed first-person account is that of John Gabriel Stedman, *Narrative of a Five Years' Expedition Against the Revolted Negroes of Surinam*, ed. Richard Price and Sally Price (Baltimore, Md.: The Johns Hopkins University Press, 1992). On the Dutch context for the colonization of Surinam, including analysis of the home country, see Allison Blakely, *Blacks in the Dutch World: The Evolution of Racial Imagery in a Modern Society* (Bloomington: Indiana University Press, 1993). On gender in the Caribbean, see Hilary Beckles, *Centering Woman: Gender Discourses in Caribbean Slave Society* (Kingston: Ian Randle, 1999); and David Barry Gaspar and Darlene Clark Hine, *More Than Chattel: Black Women and Slavery in the Americas* (Bloomington: Indiana University Press, 1996). See also David W. Galenson, *Traders, Planters, and Slaves: Market Behavior in Early English America* (Cambridge: Cambridge University Press, 1986); and Maureen Warner-Lewis, *Central Africa in the Caribbean: Transcending Time, Transforming Cultures* (Kingston: University of the West Indies Press, 2003). Trevor Burnard, *Mastery, Tyranny, and Desire: Thomas Thistlewood and His Slaves in the Anglo-Jamaican World* (Chapel Hill: University of North Carolina Press, 2004), provides a telling analysis of the remarkable diaries of a Jamaican planter.

On North American slavery, see Ira Berlin's comprehensive overview, *Many Thousands Gone: The First Two Centuries of Slavery in North America* (Cambridge, Mass.: Harvard University Press, 1998). Peter Wood's study of South Carolina, *Black Majority: Negroes in Colonial South Carolina from 1670 Through the Stono Rebellion* (New York: W. W. Norton, 1974) remains valuable, and a keystone for the long debate on racism remains Winthrop Jordan, *The White Man's Burden: Historical Origins of Racism in the United States* (New York: Oxford University Press, 1974). Recent studies that have added to the understanding of North American slavery include Alan Gallay, *The Indian Slave Trade: The Rise of the English Empire in the American South, 1670–1717* (New Haven, Conn.: Yale University Press, 2002); and Michael Gomez, *Exchanging Our Country Marks: The Transformation of African Identities in the Colonial and Antebellum South* (Chapel Hill: University of North Carolina Press, 1998).

Expansion of the Old World Diaspora

Sugata Bose has written a new overview of the Indian Ocean: *A Hundred Horizons: The Indian Ocean in the Age of Global Empire* (Cambridge, Mass.: Harvard University Press, 2006). For an excellent collection of studies on the Indian

Ocean diaspora, see Shihan de S. Jayasuriya and Richard Pankhurst, eds., *The African Diaspora in the Indian Ocean* (Trenton, N.J.: Africa World Press, 2003); see also Joseph E. Harris, *The African Presence in Asia* (Evanston, Ill.: Northwestern University Press, 1971). On northern Africa, see John Hunwick and Eve Troutt Powell, eds., *The African Diaspora in the Mediterranean Lands of Islam* (Princeton, N.J.: Markus Wiener, 2002); and Jamil Abun-nasr, A *History of the Maghrib in the Islamic Period* (Cambridge: Cambridge University Press, 1987). For the African diaspora in Europe, see Maxim Matutsevich, *Africa in Russia, Russia in Africa: Three Centuries of Encounters* (Trenton, N.J.: Africa World Press, 2006); Stefan Goodwin, *Africa in Europe*, Vol. 2, *Interdependencies, Relocations, and Globalization* (Lanham, Md.: Rowman and Littlefield, 2009); and James Walvin, *Black Ivory: Slavery in the British Empire*, 2nd ed. (Oxford: Blackwell, 2001); and James Walvin, *Making the Black Atlantic: Britain and the African Diaspora* (London: Cassell, 2000). For African perspectives on Europe, see David Northrup, *Africa's Discovery of Europe, 1450–1850* (New York: Oxford University Press, 2002).

Identity—Nation, Color, Race

The intellectual outlooks of blacks in the seventeenth and eighteenth centuries have yet to receive a major interpretive study. But the outlooks of white British and French have each undergone substantial analysis in Philip D. Curtin, *The Image of Africa: British Ideas and Action, 1780–1850* (Madison: University of Wisconsin Press, 1964); and William B. Cohen, *The French Encounter with Africans: White Response to Blacks, 1530–1880* (Bloomington: Indiana University Press, 2003). On the adoption of new identities in North America, see James Sidbury, *Becoming African in America: Race and Nation in the Early Black Atlantic* (New York: Oxford University Press, 2007). For a detailed analysis of Mexican *casta* paintings, see Magali M. Carrera, *Imagining Identity in New Spain: Race, Lineage, and the Colonial Body in Portraiture and* Casta *Paintings* (Austin: University of Texas Press, 2003). On social conflict and racial identity in eighteenth-century Louisiana, see Gwendolyn Midlo Hall, *Africans in Colonial Louisiana: The Development of Afro-Creole Culture in the Eighteenth Century* (Baton Rouge: Louisiana State University Press, 1992). On the social struggles over control of the "creole" label in nineteenth-century Louisiana, see Virginia R. Domínguez, *White by Definition: Social Classification in Creole Louisiana* (New Brunswick, N.J.: Rutgers University Press, 1986). Two collective works provide additional perspectives on changing identities in the African diaspora: Joseph E. Harris, ed. *Global Dimensions of the African Diaspora*, 2nd ed. (Washington, D.C.: Howard University Press, 1993); and Elikia M'Bokolo, ed., *L'Afrique entre l'Europe et l'Amerique*. For a concise introduction to the historical logic of world-systems analysis, see Immanuel Wallerstein, *World-Systems Analysis: An Introduction* (Durham, N.C.: Duke University Press, 2004).

Crisis in Slavery

Recent research on revolutionary Haiti is best presented in David Patrick Geggus, *Haitian Revolutionary Studies* (Bloomington: Indiana University Press, 2002); and David Patrick Geggus, ed., *The Impact of the Haitian Revolution in the Atlantic World* (Columbia: University of South Carolina Press, 2001); see also David Nicholls, *From Dessalines to Duvalier: Race, Colour, and National Independence in Haiti* (London: Macmillan Caribbean, 1996). Michel-Rolph Trouillot makes the case that Europeans found it impossible to conceive of the Haitian rising, thus effectively denying that it had taken place: see his *Silencing the Past: Power and the Production of History* (Boston: Beacon Press, 1995).

⇒ 4 ⇐

Emancipation, 1800–1900

T he nineteenth century in West Africa opened with two major enterprises aimed at improving the human condition. In the central
savanna lands where the Niger flows southeast, the Muslim cleric
Usuman dan Fodio followed his years of preaching and debating with a call
to action. He declared a *jihad*—a holy war to establish a "rightly guided"
regime and to spread the Islamic faith as far as possible. Shehu Usuman, a
leader of the Qadiriyya religious order and of the Fulfulde-speaking Fulani,
had concluded that the Hausa leaders of the cities and states of this populous grassland region between forest and desert were ineffective and impi-
ous in their leadership of the faithful. A learned man and a highly regarded
teacher, the Shehu wrote in Arabic, Hausa, and his native Fulfulde, preaching
of the rightly guided life of Islam. In a long poem in Fulfulde, he wrote of his
admiration of the prophet Muhammad:

> When we have mounted and are setting out to fight for the Sunna,
> It is as if he and I are together, and great is my joy,
> When I sleep for a while I will remember,
> Wait! For I have seen many things throughout my life,
> It is as if I sit and look upon his face.[1]

Through such imagery, the Shehu inspired Muslims, especially among the
Fulani, to prepare to build a pious, religiously governed order. Among other
issues, the Shehu had criticized the leaders of Gobir, Kano, Zaria, and other
states for enslaving Muslims. In response to the confrontation that devel-

oped in 1804 with the Emir of Gobir, the Shehu accepted the title *Sarkin Musulmi* (Commander of the Faithful) offered by his supporters, and the jihad began. After initial victories, the Shehu and Muhammad Bello, his son and the principal military commander, began to give flags to their allies, much as the prophet Muhammad had given flags to his generals, and commanded them to seize control of each kingdom in the name of God. As the military and political leader of the movement, Muhammad Bello coordinated troop actions. War continued until 1810, and out of it emerged a caliphate, a theocratic state governing Muslims over a great expanse, with its capital Sokoto in what is today northwestern Nigeria. Shehu Usuman, as head of state, delegated administrative responsibilities and focused mainly on religious devotion; when he died in 1817, Muhammad Bello succeeded him.

Usuman's jihad did indeed bring on a major transformation, one that reflected earlier Islamic movements that sought to purify religious practice while combating the expansion of the slave trade, including those of Senegal in the seventeenth century and Futa Jallon in the early eighteenth century. But, as in the earlier cases, the results were not so much emancipation as the establishment of a new hierarchy. The caliphate, while giving attention to rescuing Muslims from slavery, carried out continual wars around its frontiers that put many thousands of non-Muslims into slavery. These captives, held in slave villages, were commanded to produce grains and artisanal goods and otherwise serve the needs of their owners and rulers. The wars to create and expand the caliphate led to many captures on both sides, and the number of Hausa, Fulani, and other peoples of the central savanna sent into slavery—both across the Atlantic and across the Sahara—increased to an all-time peak between 1800 and 1830.[2] Still the caliphate sustained its existence for almost a century, and its political and theological outlook became a major force within nineteenth-century discussions on Islamic reform. It also laid important groundwork for Islam's twentieth-century expansion.

At much the same time, another experiment began that, while much smaller in size, had the backing of Britain's imperial might. The colony of Sierra Leone, with its port city and capital of Freetown, became the heart of a community of freed slaves and the center of a series of projects intended to reform African life. In earlier years, the British had enabled black settlers from Nova Scotia, Jamaica, and London to voyage to Freetown and establish the beginnings of such a colony under British government.[3] When the British parliament voted in 1807 to abolish the oceanic slave trade, a decision was made to select Freetown as a place to settle the captives seized on the high seas from now illegal slave ships. From 1808 until the 1850s, the British navy brought thousands of "recaptives," as they became known, to

Sierra Leone. While some of them learned English, most came to speak Krio, a creole language modeled on the early Portuguese-based creole but with a lexicon based on English. Many of the recaptives converted to Christianity, went to school, and entered commerce and the liberal professions. The largest single group of these Sierra Leoneans was of Yoruba ethnicity from modern Nigeria and Benin, as theirs was the West African region that saw the most intense slave trade from the 1820s through the 1840s. In the generations thereafter, Sierra Leoneans migrated to areas all along the coast as merchants, missionaries, and practitioners of other professions.[4]

Slavery and Antislavery

The achievements and ironies of the Sokoto Caliphate and Sierra Leone illustrate both the positive and negative aspects of the complicated see-saw battle over emancipation that dominated the nineteenth century. More than a simple matter of right and wrong, this struggle involved competing efforts that transformed much of the world, especially Africa and the African diaspora.

How was emancipation achieved? What black achievements and cross-racial alliances ended slavery on each of the continents and all the islands? What were the connections between freeing the slaves and the emancipatory campaigns of women, serfs, industrial workers, and oppressed ethnic groups? Why did emancipation take so long? Would there be compensation to ex-slaves for the theft of their lives? What were the aftereffects of enslavement? Were the negative effects of deprivation, poverty, and racism sufficient to neutralize the enthusiasm of their liberated energies and plans for mutual assistance? Why did slavery still grow in the era of emancipation?

This interpretation of the struggle for emancipation proposes to answer these questions by tracing three overlapping social movements that occupied and altered the lives of black people everywhere. The first and most easily recognized was the drive to abolish the slave trade and free the slaves. The second movement, countering the first, fought to defend and even expand slavery. The third was a crusade to create postemancipation societies drawing on the labors and imagination of free and newly freed blacks in the Americas, Africa, and the Old World diaspora. In it, black people struggled to surmount their history of slavery and gain places of dignity and security in a world of industrializing, expanding nations and empires. These three countervailing campaigns brought immense change to Africa and the African diaspora.[5] This remainder of this section introduces the three campaigns briefly, then sets them in the context of global industrialization and the changing demography of the African diaspora. The chapter as a whole explores the three contending struggles in greater depth.

The campaign against slavery was long, bitter, ultimately triumphant, and yet incomplete. It had two distinct aspects that need to be emphasized. The language of the time distinguished these as the *abolition of slave trade* and the *emancipation of slaves*. I rely on this pair of terms to clarify the complex contrasts and overlaps that marked the end of slave trading and slavery. To these, I add the term *destruction of slavery* to encompass abolition and emancipation. (Readers in the United States may note that the term "abolitionism," widely used in the United States after the abolition of the oceanic slave trade in 1808, often refers to what I call "emancipation." To link the two terminologies, it may help to remember that the final and successful stage of the U.S. abolitionist movement came with Abraham Lincoln's Emancipation Proclamation of 1863.)

The defenders of slavery held out energetically. Proslavery activists in the Americas, with European allies, mounted a backlash against the antislavery movement. The oceanic slave trade continued up to 1850 and even beyond in the Atlantic, especially to Brazil and Cuba. Across the Indian Ocean, the Red Sea, and the Sahara, slave exports went on to nearly the end of the 1800s. Within sub-Saharan Africa, even as slave exports declined, enslavement continued at a high rate through most of the century. At the same time, the eighteenth-century African system of mostly female slaves working to provide services directly for their masters changed to a system of slave villages where male and female slaves worked primarily to produce goods for regional and overseas markets.

Where the slave trade was abolished but slavery continued, the changed situation forced a compromise: slavery effectively became "reformed." Without access to young captives, slave owners paid more attention to the birth and care of young slaves. This reformed scheme existed, for instance, in the British Caribbean (1808–1838), the French Caribbean (1815–1848), the United States (1808–1865), Cuba (1851–1886), and Brazil (1851–1888), and also in North Africa and the Arabian peninsula in the late nineteenth and early twentieth centuries and in most African colonies between 1900 and 1930. In this same system, slaves sometimes had to migrate great distances to take up new work. The slave rebellions that eventually came about brought responses ranging from brutal repression to a sympathetic easing of conditions.

The third major campaign focused on creating a tenable postemancipation society for free people of color and former slaves. To understand the significance of a "postemancipation society," one must distinguish between the lives of free people in a slave society and life in a society where none are in slavery. Those already free could labor to construct a society of free black people, yet their energies were drawn relentlessly to the need to end slavery. Once those still in slavery gained freedom, the lives of all black people could be redefined. A fully postemancipation society began to take shape in Haiti from 1804, as it had in the New England states in the 1790s. In Haiti and in British territories after 1838, the United States after 1865, Brazil in 1888, and African territories over a wide range of times, the questions of land, labor, law, political participation, marriage, and family were debated for freed persons and for all blacks. The nineteenth century in the Americas began with roughly three million free people of color and ended with over twenty million; in Africa, the number of free people fell but then recovered. In the Old World diaspora, emancipation took place at widely varying speeds: few European blacks were in slavery in the nineteenth century, while few slaves were freed in Arabia. Between these extremes, slaves gained formal emancipation in the Indian Ocean islands and in much of North Africa; in India and the Middle East, on the other hand, such freedom came slowly.

The three slavery-focused campaigns of the nineteenth century unfolded within the context of a fourth great change: the advent of the Industrial Age. The slave trade contributed new labor for agriculture, mining, and craft and domestic work; plantations began to build and staff their own factories with slaves; black peasants produced commodities sold in worldwide markets, including wheat, cotton, palm oil, peanuts, cocoa, coffee, and bananas; black consumers purchased growing quantities of industrially produced goods such as textiles and iron tools; and the global systems of finance, banking, and insurance rose partly in response to the worldwide slave labor system contributing to industrialization and economic growth. Looking at industrialization in this way emphasizes the interconnected international synergies of economic change rather than focusing on separate national units such as England and makes it possible to see the deep involvement of black people worldwide in the process of industrialization, both in its positive and negative dimensions.[6] The people of Africa and the African diaspora not only contributed to the rise of the industrial economy, but, by the end of the nineteenth century, their lives had become deeply entwined in the industry-linked life and work of rural and urban areas.

The identity and cultural life of black people in Africa and the African diaspora developed and diverged in response to these competing, overlapping movements. As the decline in slave imports made diaspora communities more stable, these black communities faced choices on whether to model themselves on the dominant strata of society or to affirm their own distinctive culture. Thus, diaspora communities in the Americas assimilated by adopting English and other Indo-European languages, but they affirmed their distinctiveness by developing an autonomous culture, as reflected in musical innovations such as spirituals and in the storytelling traditions of Anansi and Uncle Remus.[7] At the same time, black identities had to respond to the developing racial hierarchy in ideology and science, theorized especially in Europe, which sought to place Africans at the bottom of a racial hierarchy in civilization, intelligence, and biological capacity. The varying terms applied to people of African ancestry—including "colored," "Negro," "people of color," and other terms in nineteenth-century English—arose partly within black communities and were partly imposed on them.

The changing demographic patterns of the nineteenth century reflect the social struggles of black people in freedom and slavery. As table 4.1 shows, slavery was almost entirely eliminated in the Atlantic diaspora by 1900 and had declined sharply in Africa and the Old World diaspora. In all three regions, however, the number of people in slavery rose to a peak in midcentury before declining. Table 4.1 provides a basis for revealing comparisons of racial groups and regions of the African diaspora, but the numbers in the table have two major deficiencies. First, they are only approximate in their magnitude, as the historical study of population has still not progressed to the point of providing clear estimates of populations outside Europe and North America. Second, the figures do not account for racial mixing. By labeling people as black, white, Amerindian, North African, and Asian, the table neglects the substantial biological and social mixing in each of these groups. In the Atlantic diaspora, the free and slave populations listed as "black" include many with white and Amerindian ancestry; the populations listed as "white" and "Amerindian," similarly, include significant black ancestries. The same is true for the Old World diaspora, where the populations listed as "black" include European, Arab, and South Asian ancestries, and where those listed under European, Asian, and North African categories sometimes included significant black African lineage. Within these limits, however, the table presents a concise display of the shift in slave and free populations over the nineteenth century along with the advent of large-scale migrations of Europeans and Asians.

As noted, the slave trade continued at a high level to the middle of the nineteenth century—its growth in Africa and the Old World diaspora offset its contraction in the Atlantic—and then declined. Meanwhile, migration from the most populous areas of the world—Europe, South Asia, and East Asia—grew to a level exceeding all previous human resettlements. The development of dependable steamships by the 1850s meant that safe, affordable, and eventually scheduled passenger travel soon linked major ports all over the world. As a result, the migration of free people expanded dramatically. Africans, whether free or slave, suddenly became a small proportion of the world's overseas migrants. The large-scale exodus from Europe began with impoverished Irish fleeing starvation between 1845 and 1849, yet most European migrants came late in the century on steamships and experienced low mortality levels. Africans, in contrast, came early in the century on sailing vessels and suffered higher death rates. Migrants from South Asia and East Asia also came to the Caribbean and to eastern and southern Africa on steamships. Roughly two and a half million African captives traveled to the Americas in the nineteenth century, while over ten million free Europeans came to the Americas, mostly toward the end of the century. Many of the Europeans and Asians returned home after working several years; almost no Africans were able to go back.

The balance of free and slave populations among blacks, as shown in table 4.1, changed dramatically during the nineteenth century in every region. In the Americas, the slave population declined steadily from about 60 percent of the black population in 1800 to almost zero in 1900, though the actual number of slaves in 1860 exceeded that in 1800. In Minas Gerais province of Brazil, for instance, the slave population declined at the end of the eighteenth century as the booms in gold and diamonds died down, but the slave population shot up in the mid-nineteenth century with the coffee boom.[8] In sub-Saharan Africa, the slave population grew from roughly 15 percent of the total black population to about 30 percent in 1860 and then fell after 1880. In the Old World diaspora as a whole, the slave population doubled by the mid-nineteenth century and then decreased. In Europe, in contrast, the small black population included almost no slaves throughout the century.

In the nineteenth century as before, the population of the Atlantic and Old World diasporas expanded, while the African population remained little changed overall and fell in areas of intense slave trading. The number of black people in slavery throughout the world rose from about thirteen million in 1800 to as many as thirty million in 1860 and then declined to some eleven million in 1900. The number of Africans enslaved in the world thus peaked in the middle decades of the nineteenth century, and the total number of persons held in slavery in the nineteenth century—combining Africa, the Americas, and the Old World diaspora—was far greater then than at any other time.

In the Americas, the white populations grew during the nineteenth century from three main causes. Most significant was immigration from Europe.

TABLE 4.1 Slave and Free Populations, 1800–1900 (in millions of persons)

	1800	1860	1900
Africa			
WEST AND CENTRAL AFRICA			
Free blacks	57	48	56
Slave blacks	6	11	5
Total African-descended	63	59	61
EAST AND SOUTHERN AFRICA			
Free blacks	53	46	53
Slave blacks	1	7	4
Total African-descended	54	53	57
White settlers	0	1	1
Asian settlers	0	0	1
Total East and Southern Africa	54	54	59
Atlantic diaspora			
Free blacks	2.5	5	25
Slave blacks	3.7	7	0
Total African-descended	6.2	12	25
Native Amerindians	6	12	24
White settlers	7	25	70
Asian settlers			
Total Americas	19.2	49	119
Old World diaspora			
Free blacks	4	4	8
Slave blacks	2	4	2
Total African-descended	6	8	10
Native Asians	223	236	250
Native North Africans	21	22	27
Native Europeans	160	180	200
Old World settlers	0	1	2
Total Afro-Eurasia	410	447	489
World			
Free blacks	116.5	103	142
Slave blacks	12.7	29	11
Total African-descended	129.2	132	153

Sources: Patrick Manning and Scott Nickleach, *African Population, 1650–1950: The Eras of Enslavement and Colonial Rule* (forthcoming); *Historical Statistics of the United States*; Stanley L. Engerman and B. W. Higman, "Caribbean Population," in *General History of the Caribbean* (London: Palgrave Macmillan, 2007).

Second was natural increase. Third was the "passing" or assimilation into the white population of people of color of African and Amerindian ancestry. Overall, these processes of "whitening" were effective to varying degrees throughout the Americas, reducing the proportion of the African-descended population from one-third of the New World population in 1800 to one-sixth in 1900.

The struggle for freedom was a long, uphill battle. Though the emancipation of slaves and the development of postemancipation society were ultimately the most important trends of the nineteenth century, slavery itself was far from over. The chapter's more detailed discussion of these trends begins with the campaign for the destruction of slavery and then turns in sequence to the expansion and transfiguration of slavery and to the lives of free people in Africa and the African diaspora.

The Pace of Slavery's Destruction

The campaign against slavery relied on the efforts of people all over the world. Most fundamentally interested in the elimination of slavery were those held in slave status and free people whose loved ones lived as slaves. The protests and rebellions of slaves changed in character with time, especially as opposition to slavery in other communities became known. As antislavery movements arose, communities of free black people gave support to them (although less commonly in Africa until late in the nineteenth century). Humanitarian and religious opposition to slavery grew in white communities, first in England and parts of the United States, then elsewhere. In addition, movements of economic opposition to slavery and the slave trade grew among those favoring the expansion of wage labor but also among those fearful of slave uprisings. Ultimately, as these social movements grew in strength, governments declared slave trade and slavery illegal and used their powers to suppress slavery, stage by stage.[9]

The campaign for emancipation—black and white, slave and serf, female and male, on every continent and every island—had successes and failures everywhere. This monumental process in social change, propelled by the massive extent of Atlantic slavery and by the revolutions of the Enlightenment age, continued into the twentieth century with the formal recognition of women's citizenship and the end of slavery in all its forms. When the great movement concluded, the economic inequality among humans had perhaps become wider than ever, but the categorical distinctions in the status of slave and free, male and female were removed in law, and the self-determination of nations was recognized in public pronouncements if not in practice. This massive, transoceanic, multiracial amalgamation of social movements never had a name and never had an overall leadership. Yet it created a curious sort of shared purpose that hinted at a vision of social equality. The most humble activist and the battle-scarred leaders of the underprivileged joined, along with some heads of state and public heroes of the elite, in the broad emancipatory push that, as its principal achievement, eliminated slavery as a recognized state of existence nearly everywhere in the world.

If the overall effort for emancipation lacked organized leadership, many of the localized social movements that composed it had clear leaders and strategies. The British Anti-Slavery Society had consistent leadership for over a half century from its founding in 1787. The society decided to focus first on abolishing the overseas slave trade and then on emancipation. The abolitionist movement of the United States, with its overlapping white and black factions, campaigned for nearly half a century, first for limiting the extent of slavery and then for emancipating slaves. A French antislavery drive, moribund from the time of Napoleon, regained its purpose in 1830 and carried on for twenty years. A Haitian push for emancipation carried on from the 1790s to the early 1820s but faltered thereafter because of the country's isolation. Meanwhile, the slaves in every region, always in small groups and sometimes in large ones, conspired systematically to escape slavery and to end it. The 1835 rebellion led by Hausa slaves and their free allies in Bahia was perhaps the most spectacular of these attempts, but it was only one of many.

The freeing of slaves by legislative or judicial acts ended slave trading to several regions: Portugal in 1761, England in 1772, several New England states in the 1780s, and France in 1794. Thereafter, naval and diplomatic campaigns against the slave trade took place in the North Atlantic from 1808 until 1865, in the South Atlantic from 1830 to 1851, in the Mediterranean and the Indian Ocean from the 1840s to the 1880s, and up to 1915 in parts of the African continent.

Changing circumstances also led to less peaceful responses, such as Nat Turner's rebellion in the United States and the 1835 Hausa rebellion in Salvador. Such uprisings created fear and brought forceful retaliations. The 1831 Nat Turner mutiny in Virginia resulted in the execution of those accused of participating and many others and in a reaffirmation of the hierarchy of slavery. The rebellion in Salvador led to thousands of free blacks being expelled from Brazil—most went to West Africa—and an increasingly severe regime for those who remained in slavery.[10]

The British antislavery campaign, having as early as 1792 gained majority support in the House of Commons for abolishing the slave trade, had to bide its time for almost fifteen years as the European wars ran their course. Then in 1807, William Wilberforce brought the bill for the abolition of slave trade forward again and was able to win approval in the House of Commons and the House of Lords. As of 1808, it was illegal for any British subject to participate in the transoceanic slave trade, and the ban was imposed with considerable effect.

Earlier, in 1794, the French National Assembly had voted to emancipate all slaves under French rule. At the time, this was the greatest legislative statement on emancipation. Yet Napoleon reversed it only eight years after it was enacted, and it thereby fell into insignificance. Instead, the more modest act of the British parliament in 1807, abolishing overseas trade in slaves for British subjects, was the most effective legislative act, since it gave practical support to the growing antislavery movement. Nevertheless, the French act of emancipation in 1794 is worth remembering because it shows that antislavery activity was part of a wider movement of social emancipation sweeping Europe and the world in the late eighteenth and nineteenth centuries. Claims for new rights came from all sides: emancipation of serfs from feudal privilege, the emancipation of Jews from the laws denying them citizenship, claims of women for emancipation from patriarchy, demands of subject nations to end the domination by their conquerors, and campaigns by wage workers for emancipation from their employers' arbitrary terms. The condition of slavery interacted with these other inequities, and the status of slaves served as a metaphor for all other sorts of discrimination.

War raged between Britain and France from 1792 to 1815, and in that time Britain seized most of France's territories in the Caribbean and the Indian Ocean, plus some Dutch and Spanish territories. After the war, the British returned Guadeloupe, Martinique, and Réunion to France but kept Mauritius, the Seychelles, and certain Caribbean islands. Great Britain successfully halted slave trade by its nationals in 1808; the 1808 U.S. prohibition on slave trade was less effective than the British one, as merchants from Rhode Island continued to engage in trading, especially to Cuba. At the war's end in 1815, Britain sought to impose anti–slave trade treaties on all other powers. By 1825, they had pressed the French, Dutch, Swedish, Portuguese, and Spanish to sign agreements limiting or renouncing slave trading. By 1830, slave trading to Brazil had become illegal, though it continued along with the trade to Cuba. The British antislavery squadron began patrolling the Atlantic in 1816, first with three ships and then up to as many as thirty-six in the 1840s. Mixed Commission Courts were set up to try ships taken and accused of carrying slaves. The principal court at Freetown in Sierra Leone sat in judgment on three-fourths of all the ships seized by the British navy; other courts handled captures in Rio de Janeiro, Havana, and Paramaribo in Suriname. Despite the antislavery campaign, the Atlantic slave trade expanded in response to the postwar economic boom from 1815 to 1830.

The British decision in 1834 to emancipate slaves brought greater activity against the slave trade. The expanded antislavery squadron and diplomatic efforts negotiated treaties in the Bight of Biafra that ended slave exports from that region by 1840. With the actual freeing of slaves in British territories in 1838, Britain expanded its antislavery campaign even further, pressing states throughout the Atlantic and Indian Oceans and Mediterranean to end the oceanic slave trade and, to a lesser degree, to emancipate slaves. In the Atlantic, smaller antislavery squadrons were supported by France (which landed some recaptives at Libreville in Gabon, especially in the 1840s), the United States, and Portugal in the 1840s. Additional mixed commission courts were established, and British consuls in every port conducted surveillance for evidence of slave trade.

The British campaign to abolish oceanic slave trade now expanded beyond the Atlantic and into the Indian Ocean and the Mediterranean. In 1838 Britain pressed firmly on the emperor of Iran to sign an anti–slave trade treaty but did not succeed. In the same year, Britain gained control of the port of Aden at the mouth of the Red Sea and, by the end of the 1850s, had expanded its influence to the whole South Arabian coastline. More important to the British was halting the flow of captives into India. The English East India Company, the private company that governed most of India on behalf of the British crown, agreed in 1843 to cease recognizing slavery as a legal institution. This measure did little to free those already in bondage within India but did effectively halt the import of additional slaves. Under similar pressure in the Mediterranean, the Ottoman Empire closed the Istanbul slave market in 1847 and soon began restricting the sale of African, Circassian, and Georgian captives.

At the same time, along the western coast of Africa, the British signed numerous anti–slave trade treaties, forced the kingdom of Dahomey to reduce its slave exports in the 1840s, and occupied the port of Lagos in 1851. In Central Africa, however, Spanish and American merchants gathered cargoes at Loango until 1850, and Portuguese shipments from Luanda to Brazil continued until just after 1850. The Brazilian government agreed in 1850 to enforce the abolition of slave imports. With that, the large-scale shipment of slaves across the Atlantic came to a halt.

In the Mediterranean, British diplomacy continued to press on the Ottoman government until it issued, in 1857, a general prohibition against African slave trade. Halting trade that was now illegal was a slower process in

Ottoman and other lands. French planters in Réunion, for instance, relied on slave labor even after official emancipation. France had taken over trading stations such as the island of Mayotte (in the Comoros) in 1843, shipping slaves and, after 1848, engaging "contract workers" from Mozambique and Madagascar, whose conditions were in fact the same as for the previous slaves. Zanzibar continued as a major center not only for settling slaves, where they were put to work on clove plantations, but for dispatching slaves to Arabia and the Persian Gulf. British pressure on the region resulted in an 1873 treaty with Sultan Barghash ending Zanzibar's oceanic slave trade.

Slave trade persisted, though within narrower limits: the dispatch of captives continued to the end of the nineteenth century across the Sahara to North Africa, across the Red Sea to Arabia, from the east coast of Africa to Madagascar and French islands, and even through the Suez Canal to Anatolia. Nevertheless, the pressure of the emancipation movement, especially through a combination of British pressure and the protests of slaves, opened up critical debates on slavery within Islamic societies of the Mediterranean and Middle East and brought parallel debates within sub-Saharan African societies whether Islamic or not.[11]

This great campaign of suppressing the overseas slave trade, important as it was in cutting slave owners off from their source of new captives, resulted in the emancipation of relatively few slaves. While the abolition of transoceanic slave trade was largely complete in Atlantic in the 1860s and in the Indian Ocean by 1900, the freeing of slaves in every region was a slower process.

The emancipation of slaves required a major change in the legal and social system of each slave-holding territory. The process of emancipation thus depended on the nature of government and on the political strength of the enslaved and their allies. Antislavery movements began early in Europe and North America, as with the end of slavery in New England and Canada by the 1790s. Following the acts of emancipation by some territories in Europe and North America and the revolution in Haiti, the next wave of emancipation was brought by the wars of independence led by Spanish colonies in the Americas from 1810 to 1826.

The independence of Spanish American territories led to slave emancipation more rapidly in some areas than others. In some of these cases, the change happened fairly rapidly: Central America in 1824, Chile in 1825, Mexico in 1829, and Bolivia in 1831 declared all slaves to be free. The Mexican case was incomplete, however, because the northern Mexican territories in Texas included immigrant American settlers who refused to give up their slaves. In 1836, these settlers rebelled, defeated the Mexican army, declared the republic of Texas, and formally reestablished slavery until 1865. (The Texas rebellion had a remarkable parallel in the Cape Province, where the British decision to abolish slavery was sufficient to convince Afrikaner slave owners that they should escape British rule. Beginning in 1834, many migrated with their slaves in the Great Trek to the high plateaus, where they established independent republics.) Elsewhere, emancipation in mainland Latin America was a long, conflict-ridden process. In what became Venezuela, Colombia, Peru, Ecuador, and Argentina, black men joined in the wars of independence with promises of emancipation, then found themselves having to fight again for freedom. Brazil's declaration of independence from Portugal in 1822 led many slaves to believe they too would be freed. They were disappointed, however. The last vestiges of slavery did not end in Brazil until 1888.

The British movement for emancipation, led by Thomas Fowell Buxton, succeeded in 1833 in gaining parliamentary approval for freeing the slaves. This bill followed the British public outcry about the punishment of Jamaicans for attending Baptist rather than Anglican church services and the resulting uprising, known as the Baptist War. Even then, the slaves were not freed but were required to work for their masters as apprentices. Only in 1838, after yet another uprising in Jamaica, were slaves given their full freedom in British colonies. The British emancipatory legislation of 1833 and 1838 applied to all colonies directly under British rule, hence to the West Indies and to the small African territories of Gambia, Sierra Leone, the Gold Coast, Cape Province, and Natal.

But where British rule was indirect rather than direct, the legislation did not apply and slaves were not freed. The most important example of this case was India, which was ruled up to 1857 by the English East India Company. In 1843, the East India Company responded to the antislavery pressure of the British navy with an artful dodge: the company declared that, for the territories under its rule, slavery was no longer a recognized legal status. That meant, in practice, that slave owners could not ask the company to help retrieve runaway slaves since the company did not recognize their enslavement. At the same time, slaves could not sue for their freedom, since the company claimed that slavery did not exist. (Meanwhile, in the 1840s the East India Company had begun to send Indian contract laborers to Mauritius, Trinidad, and Guyana as replacements for freed slaves.) When the British Crown took control of India after the Indian Uprising of 1857, the decision was allowed to stand. With this precedent, when Britain took over immense African territories after 1880, most of them were governed as protectorates rather than as colonies, and the British law freeing all slaves did not apply.

In France, an antislavery movement came to life after 1830, led by Victor Schoelcher, a young member of the French elite who was horrified by slavery when he visited the Caribbean. The movement publicized the abuses of slavery but did not gain much political traction until the July Monarchy of Louis Philippe collapsed suddenly in 1848. With the support of nascent trade unions in France that had common cause with the enslaved workers of the French colonies, Schoelcher was able to convince the new government to make as its first act the unconditional emancipation of slaves in French territory. Imposing this act on the colonial governments in the French Antilles took some months, but the change was made. Included in the emancipation were all the slaves who inhabited French islands of the Indian Ocean as well as St. Louis and other small territories on the coast of Senegal. Furthermore, the emancipation applied to Algeria and required the French to halt slave trade there. But when France seized immense African territories after 1880, it governed them as protectorates rather than as colonies—in a parallel to British policy—so that emancipation was usually not implemented.

In the United States, slavery was challenged by an increasingly powerful antislavery movement that carried out public protests often spearheaded by charismatic leaders such as Frederick Douglass, who was born a slave (on Maryland's eastern shore) but went on to gain freedom and become the most effective orator and writer among black abolitionists in the United States. The freedom movement also involved clandestine liberations of slaves from the South to the relative safety of northern cities or over the border to Canada. Harriet Tubman was the most successful and famous individual activist in this Underground Railroad, making repeated trips from Philadelphia to Maryland's eastern shore, where she was born, to lead groups back into Pennsylvania.

From 1820 to 1860, U.S. politics focused significantly on the struggle between those who wished to abolish slavery and those who wanted to extend it. The proslavery forces won battle after battle, extending the practice into the new states of Kansas and Nebraska and winning a key 1859 Supreme Court case—the Dred Scott decision—that no slave or descendant of a slave could be U.S. citizen. Yet the pressures against slavery continued, and Abraham Lincoln's election as president in 1860 put the antislavery party in national leadership. This led to most of the southern slave states seceding to form the Confederate States of America and to a bloody four-year civil conflict, most of it on Confederate territory. The South's surrender in 1865 allowed Lincoln's 1863 Emancipation Proclamation to be implemented. Also in 1865, the U.S. Constitution was amended to abolish slavery, and in 1868, the Fourteenth Amendment granted citizenship to all persons born in the

FIGURE 4.1 Emancipation

This life-size wood sculpture (190 centimeters in height) was created in the United States in the late nineteenth century by an unknown artist.

Source: Courtesy of the Merseyside Maritime Museum, Liverpool.

United States. The anonymous African-American artist who carved the life-sized sculpture shown in figure 4.1 provided a memorable statement of the moment.

As the American Civil War broke out, Tsar Alexander of Russia issued an 1861 manifesto announcing a stage-by-stage emancipation of millions of serfs. This act, which also included the emancipation of Romani (Gypsy) slaves and civil rights for Jews, confirmed the global reach of the nineteenth-century wave of emancipation. In the Caribbean, the last two powers to abolish slavery were the Dutch and the Spanish. After a long debate in the Netherlands, the Dutch ended slavery in all their colonies in 1865. The end of the U.S. Civil War certainly influenced this timing, but most of the slaves affected by emancipation were in Java and other islands of the Dutch East Indies rather than in the Caribbean. The Spanish, meanwhile, maintained slavery in Puerto Rico until 1873 and in Cuba until 1886. While Puerto Rico remained relatively docile, in Cuba the Spanish faced constant rebellion. In the Ten Years' War (1868–1878), many slaves and free people of color fought for independence, including the general Antonio Maceo. Only after quelling that rebellion did Spain finally agree to free the remaining slaves.

Africa also saw moves toward emancipation as it witnessed the final peak in enslavement. Many Africans gained their freedom through manumission or were born free of slave parents in various African societies. Some well-armed maroon movements even managed to defend their communities against enslavement. One such community was the settlement of Laminyah in what is now Sierra Leone, created under the leadership of Bilali in 1838.[12] Yet at the end of the nineteenth century, Africa still had millions in slavery. Emancipation as part of a great social movement did not happen there; rather, it came about piecemeal when slaves escaped or were freed individually. Aside from the runaways and some free communities, emancipation in Africa did not make significant headway until the late nineteenth and early twentieth centuries and, ironically, came mostly as result of Europe's imperial encroachment on the continent.

European imperial struggles with emancipation addressed the Americas and Africa in overlapping times. Portugal, seeking desperately to hold on to its African territories of Angola, Mozambique, and Guiné, had to declare a general emancipation formally. In Angola especially, the Portuguese had to deal with the infringement of King Leopold II of Belgium and the International African Association, which seized control of the Congo basin in 1885 on the pretext of opening free trade and ending slavery. In fact, the Congo Independent State, governed personally by Leopold from Brussels, used forced labor to such an extent that it was as bad as slavery. In general, the European powers, as they seized African territories from 1880 to 1905, usually did not require slaves to be freed. They halted the capture of new slaves but generally did not end the sales of persons already enslaved. One exception was Madagascar. In 1877, the Merina kingdom there abolished slavery among its private subjects but made the ex-slaves into a government labor reserve, so the slave trade still continued. France extended its protectorates from nearby islands to parts of the big island, then conquered the whole island in a hard-fought campaign in 1895. In the next year, the French conquerors formally emancipated all slaves—a total of five hundred thousand persons, the same number who gained freedom in St. Domingue a century earlier. Most of the freed slaves were of Malagasy ethnicities, but over 10 percent were Makua from the African mainland.[13]

The great empires set the timing of slave emancipation in their colonies according to political considerations of the metropole rather than the colonies. Britain, France, the Netherlands, Spain, and Portugal all fit into this perspective. Here the home governments acted in response to several constituencies, in contrast to self-governing territories such as the United States and Brazil, where slave owners could veto antislavery efforts. (The Ottoman Empire provides a somewhat different case, because there remained large numbers of slaves in the home territory as well as in its colonies.) All the great powers sought to avoid the spread from Haiti of the slave rebellion. There was no serious move toward freeing slaves in the territories of the great empires for almost three decades after Haiti's independence in 1804.

The destruction of slavery—through both abolition and emancipation—was a worldwide process. Historians Eric Williams in the 1940s and Robin Blackburn in the 1980s each wrote brilliant books on the end of slavery in the Americas.[14] The fundamental weakness of their perspectives, however, lay in neglecting events in the Old World, especially the continuing practice of slavery in Africa. In attempting to write the history of emancipation within the limits of the Caribbean or the Americas, they ignored the validity of pronouncements by the black nineteenth-century abolitionists who viewed black people everywhere as enslaved as long as slavery existed. Indeed, only after 1930, when slavery had ceased to be central in Africa, was it possible in practice for black people everywhere to present themselves as free people and citizens.

Slavery's Expansion

The very process of restricting slavery in some regions led to its expansion in other areas; the greater rebelliousness of slaves brought more brutal ways of repressing them. This was the irony of the global slave system. Once the capture and exploitation of slaves had reached the scale of the late eighteenth century—with booming sugar production in the Americas as well as labor needs for mining, other agriculture, transportation, artisanal work, and domestic service stretching over more than half the globe—the emancipation of slaves in one region brought new demands for labor elsewhere. Not only had slavery become a traditional part of the social order, but the world economy, while increasingly capitalist, called for more slave labor.

The broad perspective of the African diaspora makes it possible to track the expansion and defense of slavery throughout the world during the nineteenth century. This summary begins with the expansion of slavery in the old way, through enslavement and slave trade. Then it turns to a new situation—the determined defense of slavery in the numerous cases where the supply of new captives had been cut off but where the slave population grew through natural increase. The expansion of slavery through enslavement took place especially in sub-Saharan Africa but also in the Americas (especially Cuba and Brazil) and the Old World diaspora (in North Africa, the Arabian peninsula, and islands of the Indian Ocean)—see map 4.1 for the geographic location of slave populations in the mid-nineteenth century. In almost all cases, Africa was the source of new slaves, so population decline and displacement were severe throughout the continent even though some regions benefited from abolition and even emancipation. The defense of slavery even in the absence of enslavement—and, in many cases, the demographic growth of slave populations—took place in parts of the Americas up to 1888 and in Africa and the Old World diaspora until as late as the 1930s. This widespread system of "slavery without slave trade" needs to be understood as an important stage in the history of slavery, one in which the conditions and life of slave populations were significantly different from the preceding system of continuing enslavement. A third aspect of this summary of the expansion and defense of slavery is the "reform" of slavery, which resulted especially from campaigns by the slaves to improve their conditions even when they were not able to escape slavery. Each of these three aspects of the continuation of slavery brought its cultural and social impact to the enslaved population.

The nineteenth-century expansion of enslavement in the Americas focused on Cuba and Brazil. These lands of large-scale sugar, coffee, and tobacco production brought in large numbers of African captives (as late as 1851 in Brazil and 1866 in Cuba). Over seven hundred thousand captives disembarked in Cuba during the nineteenth century, more than half coming after 1830. These continuing imports contrasted with Britain and the United States, which brought in a combined total of 250,000 "legal" slaves in the years up to the 1808 abolition of the slave trade and no more than forty thousand "illegal" slave imports afterward. In Brazil, more than 1.7 million Africans were imported in the nineteenth century, seven hundred thousand of them after 1830, going principally to the southeastern regions of São Paulo and Rio. Of the more than three million Africans sent in chains to the Americas after 1800, one-third made the crossing after 1830, and they went over-

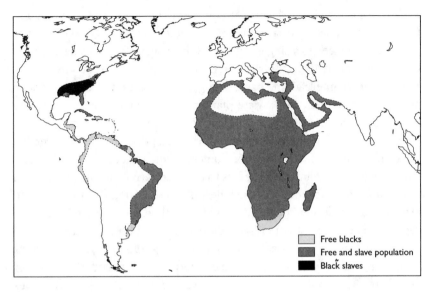

MAP 4.1 Slave Populations of Africa and the Diaspora, c. 1850

whelmingly to Brazil and Cuba. Fifty thousand Africans were also brought to French and even British territories and to Venezuela and Colombia after 1830.[15]

One of the most remarkable cultural consequences of this wave of enslavement was the spread of the Yoruba religion to Brazil, Cuba, and elsewhere in the Americas. Yoruba-speaking captives from regions now located in modern Nigeria and Benin became numerous in the Atlantic trade from the 1780s through the 1840s as a result of protracted warfare in their homeland. The Yoruba pantheon of gods—Shango, the god of thunder and lightning; Ogun, the god of iron; Ifa, the god of divination; Eshu, the divine messenger; and others, all under the governance of the high god, Olorun— had arrived earlier in the Americas, but now it took deep root. The priests, the initiations, the healing, the divination of the future through Ifa, and other practices of this regional religion served black communities both slave and free. With the end of slavery, this religion attended to the spiritual needs of postemancipation communities. It thrives to this day under the names of Candomblé in Brazil and Santería in Cuba and has spread to many parts of the Atlantic diaspora.[16] In the same era, an even larger number of captives arrived in Brazil and Cuba from the Bantu-speaking region of Central Africa. Their heritage—particularly that of the Kongo ethnicity—also survives in the Americas.[17]

On the eastern side of the African continent, the slave trade expanded and then contracted at rapid rates over the nineteenth century. As a result, the region experienced in a single century all the stages of slave trade and slavery that West and Central Africa had experienced over four hundred years. Expanding commercial prospects brought increased purchases of African slaves for settlement in the date plantations of Saharan oases, castrated boys to become eunuchs for the Ottoman elite, construction workers for the expanding cities of Mecca and Jidda, boys to be pearl divers in the Persian Gulf, and young women to become domestics and concubines in urban and rural areas.[18] The volume of imports to the Mediterranean and the Arabian Peninsula from the Horn and the Nile Valley nearly doubled from 1800 to 1870, peaking at fifteen thousand per year, and then declined. In this era, the regions that are now Ethiopia and Sudan were major sources of captives.

For the East African coast in the same period, the volume of slave exports rose from under five thousand per year in 1800 to over twenty thousand per year from 1820 to 1880 and only then decreased. From East Africa, captives went to the expanding clove plantations of Zanzibar and Pemba and in larger numbers to the French-run sugar plantations of Réunion, to plantations in the Merina kingdom of Madagascar, and to the Persian Gulf. From the valley of the Rovuma River south to the valley of the Zambezi, captives were seized from the matrilineal peoples by Yao merchants and the *prazo* regimes of Luso-African landholders. The captives were purchased at the coast by French, Swahili, and Malagasy merchants. Slaves from south of the Zambezi, taken from the patrilineal Shona and Tonga peoples by warriors of the Gaza state, were held mostly within the Gaza kingdom but also sold to French and Malagasy purchasers.[19] This hurried expansion of the slave trade, associated as well with the expanded Indian and European demand for African ivory, resulted in severe dislocation and population decline throughout the areas now known as Tanzania, Mozambique, Malawi, and Madagascar.

The East African wave of enslavement also brought generations of cultural interchange throughout the Indian Ocean basin. Somali and Swahili languages were heard in Muscat, and East African music provided entertainment in Oman. In South Arabia and Iran, *zar* and *tanburah* possession cults, originally from Ethiopia, remained a significant aspect of the healing practices of the poor. For the islands of the western Indian Ocean—the Seychelles, the Mascarenes, and the smaller islands—the principal languages were creoles based on French. Robert Chaudenson's detailed analysis of these languages reveals how they reflect the settlement and innovations of the enslaved settlers.[20] The Comoro Islands, principally Swahili speaking, became overlaid with the Makua and Yao languages of slaves brought from the mainland and with the creole of slaves brought from other islands. Similarly, Makua-speaking communities sustained themselves in Madagascar, and Malagasy, Makua, and other ethnicities and languages persisted throughout the nineteenth century in Réunion.

The narrative of the rise and fall of slavery in eastern Africa and the Indian Ocean is a story of empires, large and small. The Sultanate of Oman, in 1780, went from trade contacts with East Africa to occupation of the islands of Zanzibar and Pemba. The prosperity of these East African possessions became such that in 1840 Sultan Sayyid Said moved his capital to Zanzibar, now the center of clove plantations tended by slave laborers. The Egyptian empire of Muhammad Ali (r. 1803–1848), nominally an Ottoman governor but in fact an independent sovereign, expanded south in 1821 when he invaded and conquered the Nile Valley up to the edge of the highlands and bolstered his army with captives from the Sudan. The imperial growth of Oman and Egypt were thus remarkably parallel to the Moroccan invasion of Songhai in 1591.

Two further imperial movements in the early nineteenth century boosted enslavement and changed the map of southern Africa. The Zulu kingdom, beginning in 1816, conquered most of what is now KwaZulu-Natal. Defeated armies then fled in all directions. Among them, the Gaza state of Soshangane invaded and became a major power in Mozambique south of the Zambezi. At much the same time, the Merina state in the highlands of Madagascar expanded and conquered most of the island. The French empire, which had Indian Ocean possessions since the seventeenth century, increased its commerce in slaves and sugar during the nineteenth century. And the British empire, also present from the seventeenth century, gained global dominance in the nineteenth century and ultimately annexed numerous territories, becoming a leader in forcing the slave trade to end.

Primacy in the expanding Indian Ocean slave trade passed from group to group. In the eighteenth century, French merchants had dominated, taking slaves to Réunion and Mauritius, half from Madagascar, half from Mozambique. Then in the years from 1785 to 1830, Sakalava merchants from the western coast of Madagascar expanded their involvement in the slave trade, dispatching war canoes to the Comoros and Mozambique to capture or purchase slaves. Periodic drought in the region made it easier to get slaves. The British navy seized Mauritius and Réunion from France in 1810 during the Napoleonic wars; Britain kept Mauritius and returned Réunion to France in 1815. As a result, the slave trade to British Mauritius ended in 1810, but French planters on Réunion purchased captives for the rest of the nineteenth century. From 1820, the expanding sugar market brought demand for labor in French Réunion, and slaves arrived there from three directions—

from Madagascar, the Comoros, and Mozambique. The Comoros became a major transfer port for slaves going to Madagascar, Réunion, and to the north. The rising Merina state gained recognition from Britain in 1817 in a move the British thought would limit slave trade. Instead, the Merina conquered most of the island of Madagascar and expanded their slave holdings. The Merina state seized and purchased many slaves for its imperial projects, but the main demand for labor came from the island's burgeoning market economy. Thus, in East Africa and the Indian Ocean—as with the Caribbean islands in the eighteenth century and West African societies of the nineteenth century—the slave trade and a growing market economy reinforced one another.

In sub-Saharan Africa, the institution of slavery would remain in place for the whole century in most regions. Even though most people in Africa were free, enslavement continued through capture in warfare, kidnapping, or other means. As a result, free people could not be entirely confident of their liberty. A great wave of expansion in slave holdings took place in West Africa and to a lesser degree in western Central Africa. As the number of slaves purchased by Europeans declined after 1800 and as British antislavery patrols added difficulty and risk to shipping slaves across the Atlantic, slave prices at the African coast declined. As the mechanisms for seizing additional captives were still in place, the supply of slaves remained high. In response, Africans wealthy enough to buy captives took advantage of declining prices to acquire even more. The number of persons captured in Africa expanded, and the total people held in captivity in West Africa rose even more rapidly in the first half of the nineteenth century.[21]

At the same time, the institutions of slavery changed. Since men were no longer exported in such large numbers, male and female slaves were purchased together and housed in slave villages. Along the West African coast, this transformation fit with expanded demand for agricultural commodities. Peanuts, palm oil, and palm kernels especially, exported in steadily growing quantities, were produced by slaves and by independent peasants. In the savanna, slave villages—for instance in the Sokoto Caliphate emirates of Nupe and Kano—were responsible for producing grains and for weaving and dyeing textiles. One result of the expansion of slave holdings was a series of midcentury slave rebellions, especially the Yoruba slaves of the kingdom of Dahomey, Igbo slaves in the Niger Delta, and slaves of the Efik rulers of Old Calabar. (The images in figure 4.2, each created in the nineteenth century, show the contrasting outlooks brought by the expansion of slavery: the Fon god of war emphasizes hierarchy and dominance; the Hongwe reliquary figure emphasizes respect within a community.) Nevertheless, slaves

FIGURE 4.2 Fon God of War; Hongwe Reliquary Figure

Gu, the god of war of the Fon people of the Dahomey kingdom, is here portrayed in iron with a great sword (lost in travel to an exhibit): it conveys the power and authority of the monarchy. The Hongwe reliquary figure of Gabon, accompanying bones of ancestors, conveys in more abstract terms a concern for the welfare of the community. Centuries of war and enslavement helped separate the contrasting social values conveyed in these two sculptures.

Source: Courtesy of Musée de l'Homme, Paris.

became the majority of the population in several large regions in the late nineteenth century, including the Upper Niger Valley, several regions of the Sokoto Caliphate, and the Upper Congo Valley under the rule of Zanzibari conquerors.

At the end of the nineteenth century in the western Sudan, the number of female slaves appeared to greatly exceed males. The region had become militarized, and it was not uncommon for the men to be slaughtered wholesale by their captors and the women seized and put to work. Claude Meillassoux, Martin Klein, and Richard Roberts have documented the lamentable expansion and periodic brutality of this aspect of slavery.[22]

In the nineteenth century, slavery was definitely not in danger of becoming an antiquated, uneconomic practice. Rather, it became a godsend for ruthless, powerful, innovative people in a hurry to create a rich future for themselves. In the last years of the Atlantic slave trade, slavers used the fastest clipper ships extant to escape the British antislavery patrol. For loading captives on the African coast, they force-marched their cargoes or took them in boats to obscure points on the coast and quickly loaded them on ships. They were paid rapidly with silver dollars rather than by leisurely bargaining over a bundle of imported goods, as they had in earlier times. Among the continuing trades was that in castrated boys sent from the central Sudan across the desert to North Africa, where they served as eunuchs in the harems of the wealthy (see figure 4.3).[23] When the Suez Canal opened in 1869, slaves could be taken on steamships from Massawa through the canal to Istanbul.[24] The captives, when questioned by steamer officers, did as instructed and claimed to be relatives or wards of their owners. And most generally, as the mortality of transoceanic slave trade declined with time, the ages of captives became younger. This system of slavery—profitable yet exploitive and destructive—remained the target of the growing emancipation movement.

Once the acquisition of new slaves by capture and transportation was brought to a halt, the dynamics of slave society changed: this was "slavery without slave trade." It was a stage in slavery ranging from 1808 to 1838 for the British, 1808 to 1865 for the United States, 1851 to 1888 for Brazil, and 1900 to 1930 for much of Africa. Lacking access to new captives, slave owners had to ensure the survival and reproduction of the slaves they owned, as it would now be more difficult to find replacements. The internal trade in slaves continued. People could still be bought and sold even though new slaves could not be brought into the country. Sometimes this was called the difference between the "slave trade" (the enslavement of free people and trade across the oceans) and "slave dealing" (sale within a territory of those already enslaved). One immediate result was that the value and the prices of slave children (as future workers) and of adult females (as potential moth-

FIGURE 4.3 Eunuch (Egypt)

This man was one of the many eunuchs sent from the central Sudan to North Africa.

Source: Richard Millant, *Les Eunuques à travers les ages* (Paris: Vigot Frères, 1908), 210.

ers of slave children) rose relative to the price of male adults. Along with this change, female and child slaves received better treatment and nourishment. But they remained slaves. In the British Caribbean, to ensure that no new captives were brought in, the government conducted an elaborate census of the slave population each year, identifying them by name, owner, birthplace, age, and occupation. These records have since been used by historians—most effectively by B. W. Higman—to study the lives and experience of slave populations.[25] Other sorts of gradual amelioration of slave conditions that stopped short of emancipation also occurred. One was the "free womb" laws, passed in several Latin American nations, that granted, beginning at a certain date, free status to all children born to slave women. Usually, however, these offspring had to wait until they reached the age of majority before they could exercise that right.

The decline of the overseas slave trade did not halt the sale and forced migration of those already in slavery. Slavery in the United States was already distinctive because the black population had begun to reproduce and grow internally from the mid-eighteenth century. U.S. slavery became even more unique as cotton production rose to satisfy the expanding mills of the British Midlands and New England. From 1810 to 1860, roughly a million black people migrated in slavery, sent by their masters from the tobacco lands of the Old South to the cotton lands of the New South. Sometimes the owners moved to new lands, bringing slaves with them. At other times the owners sold the slaves, who traveled by sea or land to new cotton territories in Georgia, Alabama, and Mississippi. As Americans gained control of Louisiana in 1803, Florida in 1819, and Texas thereafter, slaves from the Old South were sent into those areas.

At much the same time, slaves in Brazil experienced a similar migration of almost equal magnitude: slaves from the declining sugar lands of Bahia were sent to the thriving coffee lands in Rio de Janeiro and São Paulo. Some of these migrants had recently arrived from Africa. Between 1820 and 1860, roughly a million slaves moved from northeastern to southeastern Brazil, a distance commonly exceeding a thousand kilometers. For the coffee-growing southeast, the combination of newly arrived Africans and migrants from the northeast brought a total of two million blacks into the region.[26]

The migration and other social changes brought by slavery without slave trade generated substantial effects on slave culture and society. As Michael Gomez has emphasized for the U.S. South, when the proportion of creole slaves increased, a coherent creole culture began to develop. Gomez is not explicit on the next point, but his argument implies that African-American ethnicity developed in the slave community and was adopted by the free blacks.[27] Some of the changes in the expanding, shifting slave populations involved accommodating the habits and beliefs of new owners, and some involved creating new cultural forms. Examples of accommodation are the adoption of the Baptist faith in the United States and of Catholicism in Cuba and Brazil. Such cases of slaves integrating with their current milieu

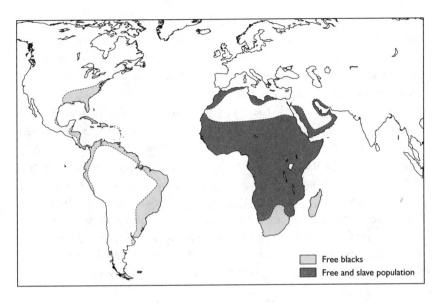

Free blacks
Free and slave population

MAP 4.2 Slave Populations of Africa and the Diaspora, c. 1900

led to triumphal self-praise by the masters, who reaffirmed the righteous-
ness of their paternalism. Some of the new recreational and religious forms
created by slaves in this time include the rumba and Santería in Cuba, spirituals and the ring shout in the United States, and Candomblé and *capoeira*
in Brazil. In much of sub-Saharan Africa and such parts of the Old World
diaspora as Arabia, the slow process of individual manumission and gradual
integration of slaves into their masters' societies continued well past 1900
(see map 4.2).

The cultural innovations that came out of slavery spread and evolved
beyond the originating communities. For example, the aforementioned
Cuban rumba developed in the nineteenth century among the growing slave
population, though it was doubtless an updated version of earlier traditions.
In it one or two dancers moved to music provided by an ensemble of three
drums accompanied by a lead singer and a chorus. Both the basic rhythm
and the phrases in the music followed a regular pattern. A simplified version
with less of the rumba's lascivious movement emerged among free people of
color and became known as the *contradanza habanera*, gaining popularity in
Europe in the 1830s. The Negro spirituals of the nineteenth-century American South originated in the conditions of slavery. Sung *a cappella* by choral
groups with male and female soloists, they drew especially on metaphors
from the Old Testament to criticize slavery, express desires for liberation,

and acknowledge the trials and tribulations of life. Drums were forbidden in most areas of the United States, but the spirituals remained percussive, for instance through handclaps. In postemancipation years, spirituals remained important in the church and social life of rural black populations. At the same time, they became attractive to more affluent communities. The Fisk Jubilee Singers at Fisk University in the post–Civil War era played a large role in formalizing spirituals for concert performance. These songs gained in popularity as they became known to whites and were transcribed. In nineteenth-century Brazil, the martial-arts form *capoeira* emerged, mixing dance, music, and combat in a fashion that could be presented as a show or a real contest. The religious innovations mentioned earlier—Santería, ring shout, and Candomblé—principally served the slave communities. Nonetheless, for Santería and Candomblé, the ability of their adepts to serve as diviners and healers drew numbers of people from outside the world of black people. The ring shout, in contrast, attracted little external interest or involvement.

Ambitions of Free Blacks

Free people of color in the nineteenth century could ill afford to relax and count their blessings. Those born free faced the possibility of enslavement and those freed during their lifetime struggled to escape the stigma of previous servitude. Even when all blacks in one society gained emancipation, the continuing existence of slavery elsewhere weighed on their existence. In addition, proponents of emancipation repeatedly had to choose between emphasizing women's rights or subordinating those claims in order to face the discriminations shared by black men and women alike.

The changing demography of free blacks in the nineteenth century does much to clarify the constraints on their lives (see table 4.1). The Haitian revolution, freeing a half-million slaves, raised the proportion of free people of color in the Caribbean from 25 to 45 percent of the total; for the Americas as a whole, it brought the proportion of free people of color from 41 to 49 percent. The freeing of seven hundred thousand slaves in the British West Indies in 1838 boosted the free population to over 55 percent of the total African-descended population of the Americas. The freeing of five million slaves in the United States in 1865 brought the free population to 85 percent of people of color in the Americas, yet over seven hundred thousand people were still enslaved in Brazil when emancipation took place there in 1888. By 1900, slavery had ended for the Americas but not for black people in general: as much as 20 percent of the sub-Saharan Africa population remained in slavery, and additional communities in the Old World diaspora included many still enslaved.

This section explores the experience and ambitions of free populations of color in three categories: their work and community, their political and sociocultural life, and their pursuit of education and elite cultural accomplishments. Within each of these categories, the choices differed over time. In the era of slavery, free people had greater autonomy than slaves in defining their cultural identity, selecting their language and religious practices. They could choose between emphasizing the local popular culture and aspiring to aspects of elite cultural activities. In politics, free people of color picked between advancing their own positions and carrying on a campaign for general emancipation. In postemancipation times, the resolution of one great problem revealed another challenge: the expanded racial discrimination of the postslavery age. Those just freed could ally with those already free to seek property, work, education, and citizenship rights. (For example, W. E. B. Du Bois, born free in Massachusetts, spent several years in the southern cities of Nashville and Atlanta.) Free people of color reaffirmed or adopted ethnic identities and—in the Americas—had to define their identity vis-à-vis other people of African ancestry as well as Amerindian, East Indian, and European populations. In Africa and the Old World diaspora, free people (including freed slaves) faced similar identity choices. Even after emancipation within a given society, there remained the uncompleted mission of ending slavery everywhere.

The labor of black people in the nineteenth century was principally agricultural, but they also worked as artisans, as domestic servants, and in transportation. Late in the century, they found employment as part of an expansion in industrial labor. The free communities of Africa consisted principally of peasants living in their ancestral homes. Their work was principally agricultural but also included such artisanal work as metal work, construction, textile manufacture, and transportation work. Elevated strata of merchants, landowners, religious specialists, and political elites existed as they had in earlier centuries, though in the nineteenth century a much larger portion of their wealth and power took the form of slave holdings. The expansion of slavery on the African continent in the eighteenth and nineteenth centuries and the numerous instances of manumission or escape resulted in a significant number of African free people being ex-slaves or slave descendants. These freed people of Africa formed the group most analogous to the free black people of the Americas and the Old World diaspora. In the nineteenth century, both categories of free Africans took advantage of the expanding opportunities to produce agricultural commodities for long-distance trade.

Latin America and the Caribbean had relatively large free populations of color as the nineteenth century began. Most had become independent peasants when they were able to purchase or otherwise occupy land. The ex-slaves of Haiti and Santo Domingo settled down primarily as peasants once they were free; those released earlier in Colombia, Mexico, and Brazil had already become peasants. As in Africa, employment choices in addition to agriculture included artisanal specializations in construction and metal work or employment in transportation. Women who were not farming worked primarily in domestic service or the clothing industry. Many of those freed in the nineteenth century had little choice but to become wage laborers or tenant farmers working closely with the plantation owners who had earlier ruled their lives. The balance among these three lifestyles varied from country to country, but the categories were consistent. In each territory, a few free people managed to become merchants or to gain formal education and become professionals in law, education, or government. In addition, people of color played a major role in military service, especially in the former Spanish territories. The free people of the United States took up occupations that echoed those elsewhere in the Americas. Prior to emancipation, free people in the American North and South worked primarily as artisans. After emancipation, the ex-slaves of the South sought to occupy or buy land, but most were forced to become tenant farmers. Here as elsewhere, upward mobility was possible in some cases through commerce, education, and military service.

One example of such enterprise took place in Barbados in the mid-nineteenth century. As sugar harvests declined and British sugar vessels visited the island less frequently, black mariners from the Barbados port of Speightstown built and sailed schooners that shuttled among the islands carrying foodstuffs and local manufactures. Coal-powered ships eventually displaced the schooners, but the Barbados mariners adapted by moving to other types of maritime work.

The shipping of the Indian Ocean, though greater in scale, included a similar mix of large and small vessels. The slave trade, as it expanded, relied heavily on slave seamen. Other maritime workers, often ex-slaves, were known as "lascars," and they worked in effect as indentured laborers aboard British ships. Africans constituted a minority among Indian and Arab crews.[28] As in the Atlantic, steam power gradually came to dominate Indian Ocean shipping, especially after the Suez Canal opened in 1869. This development brought new employment in establishing coal stations, refitting harbors, and in the engine rooms themselves—industrial work that relied on workers hoping to escape from slavery.

As emancipation came to each territory, one of the principal aims of freed persons was to own land. Planters, having lost all their slaves, sought other ways to attract or coerce cheap laborers as replacements. Their two principal programs were tenant farming and contract labor; both practices denied agricultural workers the opportunity to buy property. In Jamaica, for instance, court actions prevented ex-slaves from pooling their resources to buy land. As a result, many ex-slaves were faced with becoming tenants on land they had previously worked as slaves. Land tenancy for black people, therefore, began principally in the postemancipation era rather than before. In this manner, owners of large plantations sought to keep ex-slaves on the land.

Whenever and wherever the tenant-farming approach failed to garner enough workers, land owners recruited contract laborers. From 1840, such workers began arriving in the Americas from India, recruited especially for work in Trinidad and Guyana but also in other territories. (Walter Rodney provides a detailed description of the interactions, hostilities, and truces of the black and East Indian communities of Guyana in the late nineteenth century.)[29] Outside of the plantations, independent peasant communities of the Caribbean and South America produced cacao, coffee, and bananas for the market and food crops for their own consumption.

Some free blacks migrated, hoping for independence and a better life. The migrant community of Liberia, for example, came into being in 1820 when free and recently freed blacks from the United States began settling at points along the heavily forested West African coast. Their emigration was supported by the American Colonization Society, a complex mix of black and white abolitionists and white supporters of slavery. By 1843, over four thousand settlers had formed the nucleus of what grew into the Americo-Liberian population centered in the town of Monrovia. Liberia declared its independence as a republic in 1847.[30]

Beginning in 1835, another four thousand free blacks moved from Bahia to West African coastal towns between the Volta and Niger rivers, many of them expelled from Brazil after the 1835 Bahia rebellion. Over a longer period, at least another four thousand came from Britain, Canada, and the British West Indies to Sierra Leone. These New World blacks in Africa and the Africans who joined their coastal communities became major players in West African societies from the mid-nineteenth to the mid-twentieth centuries.

In the days before general emancipation, creole cultures developed more fully among free populations than among those in slavery. This led to the emergence of a range of national cultures among blacks of the Americas. The armed struggles of the Spanish-speaking countries such as Venezuela and Colombia surely developed the nationalism and the unity among blacks fighting to eliminate slavery. Yet a divergence and occasional conflict materialized between those seeking the self-sufficient lives of peasants and those participating in larger structures of the industrial and commercial economy. Blacks commonly took the liberal position in struggles with conservative parties during much of the nineteenth century, with varying success. In 1822, the black population of Cartagena supported Admiral José Padilla in a revolt against Simon Bolívar as he prepared to replace Colombia's liberal constitution with a centralized government, but they were defeated when the propertied families supported Bolívar. In Venezuela, the long Federal War brought victory to the liberals in 1863, with armies of black and mulatto peasants and ex-slaves defeating government forces. Brazil, more than any other state in the Americas, argues George Reid Andrews, defused racial tension in the years after independence.[31] The caste laws discriminating against free people of color were gone, and while discrimination remained, somehow social tensions diminished even as large numbers of white immigrants began to pour into the country.

Free people developed an expanding range of religious practices. Protestant Christianity dominated in the American North, where the African Methodist Episcopal Church was founded in Philadelphia in 1816 as the region's first independent black congregation. Free blacks of the American South increasingly formed Baptist congregations. Free populations in Catholic countries tended to stay close to that church. In these same lands, however, the practices of Santería and Candomblé, widely popular among slaves, also gained popularity among free people. In Jamaica, similarly, the magic cult of myalism grew among creole slaves and free people.[32] In Africa, however, some freed slaves left African religious traditions and adopted Christianity and Islam to help them get beyond slavery. Similarly, Islam in nineteenth-century Brazil served as a basis for protest against slavery. In the Old World diaspora, most people of African descent were members of the Islamic community, yet they were able to follow the cults of specific saints or participate in spirit-possession groups that affirmed their community identity.

The size and identity of black populations changed, sometimes surprisingly, over the nineteenth century. Large black and brown populations seemingly melted away in Mexico, Chile, and Argentina through a mixture of such factors as high death rates, migration, intermarriage, redefinition of identity, or failure to acknowledge the black populations that were still there. The same process took place in Ottoman lands of the Middle East. In contrast, black populations grew in Panama, the Dominican Republic, and Venezuela, as migrants arrived from Caribbean territories.

It was in the postemancipation era that the music and dance of merengue arose in Haiti and the Dominican Republic. This was music for the popular classes. The island's elite culture, which had thrived especially under the French in the eighteenth century, disappeared almost completely in the strife of revolution. Some formal and elite music and painting returned to Haiti after independence under the mulatto elite's patronage, but only the popular culture really thrived. Other musical developments among postemancipation populations included, in the United States, the continued polishing of spirituals, the development of the cakewalk dance, the uneasy overlap of white and black artistry in the minstrel shows of the late nineteenth century, and the musical practices that eventually became jazz and blues. In Trinidad, lively political and social commentary was put to music, and the genre of calypso emerged. In 1880s Cuba, Miguel Failde led in taming the rumba, creating the *danzón*, a form of music and dance that became popular among the middle classes. More generally, throughout Latin America, the slow and romantic bolero gained in popularity.

Political campaigns of the early nineteenth century kept free people of color in the Americas at a high level of activity. In the 1810s and 1820s, they pressed ahead on their campaign to eliminate caste laws in Latin America and were largely able to modify laws and constitutions to remove all formal restrictions on full citizenship for people of African descent. The next task was achieving a social equality that measured up to the letter of the law.

The evolution of the Dominican Republic was particularly unique and convoluted. The colony of Santo Domingo—the Spanish two-thirds of Hispaniola—was sparsely populated compared to French St. Domingue. Santo Domingo's population included a small white elite and a majority of highly mixed ancestry, many of them free. After admitting defeat in the wars of the Haitian revolution, Spain ceded its portion of the island to France in 1795. In 1801, Toussaint occupied the region to defend against the coming French invasion. Thus independent Haiti in 1804 included the whole island. In 1808, a counterrebellion gained control of the east, and the victors founded the first Dominican Republic. Spain regained the title to Santo Domingo in 1814 and then was expelled by the Dominicans in 1821. In 1822, Haitian President Jean Boyer occupied the east and again abolished slavery. In 1844, a Dominican uprising led by Pedro Santana created the second Dominican Republic. Conflicts with Haiti continued, but Spanish and U.S. intervention succeeded in guaranteeing the independence and leadership of the Dominican Republic's conservative party. The nineteenth-century history of the country is as unique as Haiti's. One curious result of this experience was that in the later nineteenth and especially the twentieth century

Dominicans tended to ignore or deny any African heritage, either biological or cultural, despite obvious evidence to the contrary.

In the United States, a series of conventions of free people of color set a broad political agenda for fighting slavery and struggling to gain access to education. Frederick Douglass and the medical doctor Martin Delany were prominent among the participating personalities. Their political campaigns included uneasy relationships with white philanthropists who intended to help the black cause—though not necessarily in the ways that black people had in mind.

As the American republics reached the postemancipation stage, several figures of African descent rose to high political office. In former Spanish territories, a number of black and mulatto leaders became president of their nations: Bernardino Rivadavia in Argentina (1825–1827), Vicente Guerrero in Mexico (1829–1831), Vicente Roca in Ecuador (1845–1849), Joaquín Crespo in Venezuela (1884–1886, 1892–1897), and Ulises Heureaux in the Dominican Republic (1882–1899). All the leaders of Haiti were black or mulatto, from Jean-Jacques Dessalines, who assumed power at independence, to Pierre Nord Alexis, elected in 1902. In the United States, Hiram Revels and Blanche K. Bruce were elected as U.S. senators from Mississippi in the 1870s, and twenty-two blacks were elected to the U.S. Congress. In all of these countries except Haiti, however, people of color virtually ceased to be elected to major public office after the end of the nineteenth century.

In Jamaica, a conflict in 1865 established postemancipation patterns that reverberated throughout the British Empire. After emancipation, white planters had used their influence in the colonial legislature to prevent blacks from buying land and thus escaping work on sugar plantations. They made it impossible, for instance, for groups of people to pool their earnings and buy land in common. Paul Bogle, a Baptist church leader, emerged on the island's eastern tip as the advocate of rural people demanding more voice in government. After two confrontations at the courthouse in Morant Bay, Governor Eyre sent in the troops. The subsequent ferocious repression resulted in the deaths of five hundred and the execution of Bogle and others. The British parliament responded to the excesses of Eyre and the legislature by removing the governor and imposing crown-colony government on Jamaica.[33] Crown-colony government was a double-edged sword. This reform reduced the power of the planter elite and therefore the abuse of ex-slaves, but at the same time it made it more difficult for black Jamaicans to seek elective office. The crown-colony model soon spread throughout Africa and the Caribbean, weakening local government and centralizing control of British colonies in London.

But it was not only the empires that made decisions and spread influences around the Atlantic and Indian Oceans. Free black people sailed among ports near and far and maintained overlapping networks. We know most about these networks from educated people, merchants and professionals, who wrote letters, newspaper articles, and books. For example, Nancy Prince left Salem, Massachusetts, and lived with her husband in St. Petersburg for nine years, where he became a member of the tsar's bodyguard. She later went to Jamaica as a teacher and missionary. Mary Seacoles, a Jamaican woman self-trained but highly effective in nursing, became famous on the battlefields of the Crimean War, where she tended wounded British soldiers. (Both women recorded their experiences in books.) But the largest numbers of these voyagers were wage workers, especially the ship crews and port longshore-men. Small vessels moved from island to island in the Caribbean and to the mainland—from Venezuela and Panama to New Orleans and Charleston. English-speaking communities linked the West Indies, West African ports, Britain, and the United States. One such community was the Fernandinos, who settled on Fernando Po from the Gold Coast and Sierra Leone when the British took the island in the 1820s, and who stayed even as the island became Spanish in the late nineteenth century. Portuguese speakers linked Brazil, Cape Verde, Guine-Bissau, the Bight of Benin, and Angola. For instance, a regular exchange of palm oil and Yoruba cloth for tobacco linked Lagos and Salvador up to the end of the nineteenth century.

Formal education and intellectual life for free people of color in the nineteenth century grew most rapidly in Britain, the British territories, the United States, and Liberia. Samuel Ajayi Crowther and Alexander Crummell were two leading Anglican churchmen whose lives spanned nearly the entire nineteenth century.[34] Crowther was born in Nigeria and Crummell in New York. Crowther was enslaved as a child but saved by the British navy. He was educated and became a teacher in Sierra Leone. Crummell was schooled in Massachusetts. Both studied and served in England, and both worked for many years in building the Anglican Church in West Africa. Crowther was ordained in England in 1845, set up mission stations in Nigeria, and served as bishop of the Niger from 1864 to 1890. Crummell moved from England to Liberia in 1853 and served for twenty years as missionary and teacher, after which he returned to the United States and settled in Washington. Among the luminaries with whom these men interacted were E. W. Blyden, Martin Delany, Frederick Douglass, James Africanus Horton, and George Washington Williams. In Latin America, in contrast, almost no blacks gained admission to institutions of higher education in the nineteenth century.

Trinidad is one exception. Its unusual combination of British rule and a mostly Catholic population created a situation in which Anglican, Catholic, and government schools became available. The parents of children of color became adept at playing one school off another to strengthen the curricula, and their children were able to advance intellectually along with the white children. Overall, the small educational institutions in Haiti, Trinidad, and the African coast—and the access of some black students to schools in New England and Europe—were essential in developing black scholarly traditions.

In the Old World during the early nineteenth century, a few key artistic leaders of African descent became widely recognized.[35] Aleksandr Pushkin, a descendant of Abraham Hannibal, achieved a reputation as Russia's greatest writer with his epic poem *Eugene Onegin* and many other works written in a short life that ended in 1837. Alexandre Dumas, whose grandmother was a Haitian slave and whose father achieved the rank of general under Napoleon, became France's most successful writer of romantic tales, including *The Three Musketeers* and *The Count of Monte Cristo*, both written in the 1840s. The Shakespearean actor Ira Aldridge was born in the United States and developed his career in Europe, performing before Pushkin and Dumas. Late in the nineteenth century, another wave of accomplished scholars and professionals reached the public eye. Among them were Joseph-Anténor Firmin, the Haitian lawyer who wrote a detailed criticism of scientific racism; Henry Sylvester Williams, the Trinidadian lawyer who convened the first Pan-African Conference; the Afro-British composer Samuel Coleridge-Taylor, best known for his 1898 composition "Hiawatha's Wedding Feast"; the Ohio-born poet Paul Lawrence Dunbar; and the American painter Henry Tanner, most famous for his 1893 work *The Banjo Lesson*, which showed a boy learning the instrument on the lap of an old man. Most energetic of all was W. E. B. Du Bois, whose long career of scholarship and activism began in 1895, when he received his Ph.D. in history from Harvard University, which published his dissertation, *The Suppression of the African Slave Trade to the United States of America, 1638–1870*.

Despite all the advances gained by free people in Africa and the diaspora during the nineteenth century, the growth in racialized power of a few great states tended to overshadow the free people and their accomplishments. In response, some sought to confront the forces of empire and simply lost out: Paul Bogle in Jamaica and the citizens of St.-Louis in Senegal who fought alongside al-hajj Umar against the French suffered this fate. Others attempted to join forces with the empire and mostly disappeared from view:

the activist E. W. Blyden, for example, switched late in life from supporting African nationhood to an alliance with British imperialism, but the shift in loyalty gained him little.

Empire Old and New

The term "empire" comes to the English language from the Latin *imperium*, itself a term drawn from the verb "to command." Empires are first of all structures of political domination in which a central state rules other regions. But because there are many forms for imperial domination, the term "empire" has rarely been defined carefully or its meaning debated. On the contrary, its scope has been extended metaphorically to other sorts of dominion or hegemony—economic, cultural, and intellectual. This section, which sets the struggle for emancipation in the context of global structures of dominance, focuses primarily on political empires but follows that discussion with an analysis of the role of empire in economic and intellectual affairs—especially in the interpretation of race—during the nineteenth century.

Africa in the nineteenth century experienced the rise and fall of several locally based empires and then the expansion of European-based ones. The Sokoto Caliphate, the largest African experiment to date in Islamic reform, created a great empire on the grasslands of the central savanna with a cavalry-based army. In another few years, the Zulu state expanded from a small chiefdom to a powerful kingdom with an army of tightly disciplined spearmen. In each case, the creation of the new state caused migrations and reverberations far from its frontiers. West of the Sokoto Caliphate, Fulbe activists created the state of Masina on the Niger River's inner delta; west of the Zulu kingdom, the Sotho leader Moshweshwe gathered refugees and firearms to create the Basuto state. (With the exception of the Sokoto, Masina, and Zulu states, all major African states of the nineteenth century relied principally on firearms in their warfare.) In Ethiopia, the Amharic kingdom expanded sharply in midcentury under the Negus Tewodros but was defeated by a British invasion. Under new leadership, the kingdom rebounded and conquered territory on all its boundaries under Negus Menelik II, even defeating an invading force from Italy in 1896. In Zanzibar, the Omani dynasty that gained power at the end of the eighteenth century expanded through commercial influence, dominating shipping along much of the East African coast and building diplomatic and market sway by sending expeditions for slaves and ivory deep into the African interior. The most successful of the Zanzibari adventurers was Tippu Tip, who made several voyages into the Congo's upper basin. There, in the 1870s, he set up a commercial regime that began to take on statelike attributes. Further south and earlier in the century, the Merina state of highland Madagascar had grown in strength and managed to conquer most of the island, building up large slave populations as it did.

Three powerful but short-lived states dominated the eastern and western ends of Africa's northern savanna in the last decades of the nineteenth century. Al-hajj Umar Tal of Senegal declared a jihad in 1858 and, with supporters from many parts of the western savanna, was able to establish a powerful state on the Niger's inner delta, destroying the Masina state as he did. Next came a decade-long confrontation with the French in the Senegal Valley. Following the death of Umar and the collapse of his regime, Samori Touré, whose impulses were more mercantile than religious, extended his control over much of the same area and fought the French effectively until the mid-1890s. In the Nile Valley, meanwhile, the British had taken control of Egypt in 1882 and sought to extend their control into the middle Nile region that Muhammad Ali had dominated during his long rule of Egypt (1805–1848). The result was a Muslim rising in which Muhammad ibn Abdallah, who was recognized as the Mahdi (a figure prophesized to guide the community), expelled the British and created a theocratic state dominating much of modern Sudan from 1881 to 1898. The British, determined to reconquer the area, built a railroad up the Nile to assure their supply routes and destroyed the Sudanese army in 1898 with early machine guns.

The endemic warfare accompanying the rise and fall of these states brought enslavement to a new height all across Africa's northern savanna in the last decades of the nineteenth century. At the extreme, male captives were slaughtered while the women and children were carried off. European empires, reacting to perceived threats from these growing states while desiring to extend their commercial domination of the African continent, turned in the 1880s to full-scale conquest and occupation, with the campaign against the slave trade and slavery as their principal justification. In Africa, the struggle for emancipation from slavery ended up with a new sort of bondage: imperial rule from afar.

Part of the fuel for the European invasions of Africa consisted of inflammatory reports coming back from missionary efforts. David Livingstone, the Scottish missionary, took three long voyages to Africa in the 1850s, 1860s, and 1870s. He traveled first to the upper Zambezi, then to the lower Zambezi, and then west from Zanzibar to the East African highlands and the upper Congo valley.[36] In each case, the areas of southern and eastern Africa that he visited were the sites of disastrous slavery expansion. Livingstone's accounts of his travels helped build a powerful audience among those in Britain seeking involvement in an international, humanitarian cause, and the antislavery campaign turned its attention toward Africa. The irony of Livingstone's campaign is that his intent was surely focused on combating slavery, but the end result was the conquest and belittlement of Africans. Similarly, the French White Fathers, Catholic missionaries who worked in Algeria and East Africa, sent home stories of the perils of slavery in Africa and the importance of imposing reforms on African societies. In addition to these missionaries, commercially oriented explorers such as Henry Morton Stanley and Savorgnan de Brazza helped draw European powers into Africa.

In one of the most curious turns of imperial adventure, King Leopold II of Belgium got interested in establishing an African empire. Seeking a way to gain large-scale imperial influence for his small, industrial country, Leopold linked up with Henry Morton Stanley, the journalist-adventurer who had already led an expedition from east to west across the African continent, and then began taking special interest in the Congo Valley. In a situation where British, French, German, and Portuguese interests competed for influence in Africa, Leopold played them against one another, gaining an extraordinarily free hand for himself. He organized the first International African Congress in Brussels, in 1882, and led in getting the European powers to agree to free trade and emancipation from slavery in Africa. A second congress, held in Berlin in 1885, extended this logic to establish an agreement on how the European occupation of African territories would be recognized. Within a year of the Berlin conference, Leopold had decreed that the whole of the Congo River basin was to be the Congo Free State under his personal rule. Germany moved even faster, claiming four regions in Africa (Togo, Cameroon, Namibia, and Tanganyika plus Rwanda and Burundi) and other regions in the Pacific as its colonies in 1885. Tippu Tip, the most powerful alternative to Leopold in the Congo, chose to avoid confrontation—in 1890, he left the upper Congo and journeyed with a portion of his entourage and his wealth in ivory to retirement in Zanzibar. Leopold's personal rule in the Congo led to brutal exploitation by his army and the companies to which he granted concessions. In 1908, he was forced to relinquish control of his colony to the Belgian parliament, and it became the Belgian Congo.[37]

European powers focused in the 1890s on wars of African conquest. In West Africa, the French pressed inland with their battles against Samori Touré and also conquered Dahomey from 1890 to 1892. In 1900, the French sent troops across the desert from Algeria, up the Congo River, and from West Africa to meet at Lake Chad and gain control of what is now Chad. English troops and diplomats went inland from the Indian Ocean to gain control of Kenya and Uganda. In West Africa, the British sent expeditions into southwestern Nigeria in 1893 and into northern Nigeria in 1898. In southern Africa, a private company, the British South Africa Company, led by the diamond magnate Cecil Rhodes, gained control of what is now Zimbabwe, Zambia, and Malawi. In the South African War from 1899 to 1902, Britain defeated Afrikaner forces in a successful but unpopular war. With the opening of the twentieth century, European powers turned to establishing firm administrative control over each newly conquered region of the continent. The French established federations of colonies—French West Africa and French Equatorial Africa—and the Portuguese expanded their control of Angola and Mozambique. In southern Africa, British efforts to pacify the defeated Afrikaners came mainly at the expense of the African majority of what became, in 1910, the Dominion of South Africa.

Empires expanded and shifted through the nineteenth century in the Old World diaspora, changing the conditions for emancipation. By 1815, Napoleon's quest for European empire had failed, leaving Britain and Russia as the greatest European powers. The Ottoman Empire still ruled much of the Mediterranean and Black Sea regions and the Arab lands north of Arabia. The Qajar Empire ruled Iran and the English East India Company ruled most of India on behalf of the British crown.

Muhammad Ali Pasha, the Albanian-born official who took over Egypt on behalf of the Ottoman Empire when Napoleon's armies withdrew in 1803 after five years of occupation, soon built up Egypt into a nearly independent state. Relying on European experts to build his military forces, in 1820 he launched a successful expedition up the Nile into Sudan, where he conquered the Funj Sultanate. Soon he was relying on slave soldiers from Sudan to prepare an expedition to invade Arabia. The Arabian expedition failed, but the expanded import of slaves to Egypt continued. At the same time, Egyptian production of cotton—with high quality, long-staple fibers—strengthened Egypt's economic position. When Muhammad Ali challenged his Ottoman overlords in 1835, however, the British allied with the Ottomans and defeated him.

Meanwhile France, seeking new imperial adventures after Napoleon's defeat, seized on a diplomatic scuffle to invade Algeria in 1830. It took at least thirty years before their conquest of Algeria was assured. By 1870, France had used diplomatic pressures rather than invasion to gain dominion over Tunisia.

Government in Latin American countries was primarily aimed at escaping imperial control: the wars of independence from Spain continued almost uninterrupted from 1810 to 1830, and resulted in independence for all but a few regions. The republics of mainland Latin America, however, then had to protect themselves against imperial adventures from the United States, Britain, and France. Mexico was especially vulnerable: it lost half its territory to the United States in the war of 1848–1850, and then suffered an occupation by French forces from 1864 to 1867. Britain did not seek to seize Latin American territory but gained great power through British dominance of trade and investment in the region.

Brazil, however, was unique, because it established its independence by proclaiming an empire. As the Portuguese monarchy returned from Brazil to Lisbon in the years following the Napoleonic wars, it was agreed to leave the heir to the throne, Dom Pedro, to retain control of Brazil. In 1822 and 1823, Dom Pedro gained support throughout Brazil and was proclaimed emperor. The Portuguese acceded to the change in 1825. In Bahia, where the dominant pro-Portuguese faction opposed independence, Antonio Pereira Rebouças, a talented young mulatto lawyer, organized patriotic conferences that set up an alternative provincial government, thereby providing essential support to Dom Pedro.[38] The imperial government of Brazil, allied rather consistently with conservative interests, avoided the civil wars of liberals and conservatives in other Latin American countries. The consensus achieved among the varying regional elites made it possible for Brazil to preserve large-scale slavery longer than any place else in the Americas.

The 1815 agreements of the Congress of Vienna ratified the British conquest of several French, Spanish, and Dutch territories in the Caribbean (and also in Africa and the Indian Ocean) but also forbade further seizures of islands by warring European powers. Consequently, each empire was left free to exploit its existing territories. The Cuban movement for independence, which brought the Ten Years' War of 1868–1878, nearly succeeded in expelling the Spanish but was crushed temporarily. When the Cubans rebelled again under leadership of poet and nationalist theorist José Martí, a parallel movement broke out in Puerto Rico. Then in 1898, the United States, not restricted by European agreements, entered the conflict and seized virtually all of Spain's empire. Thus, an American empire was added to the others in the Caribbean.

Beginning early in the nineteenth century, the United States sought to extend its economic influence widely in the Americas. The 1803 Louisiana Purchase initiated this expansion. From 1820 on, conflicts developed over whether the new territories would be slave or free states. Also in the 1820s, President James Monroe issued the "Monroe Doctrine," claiming that no great power other than the United States could intervene in the Americas. As the century went on, North American political figures became important in a range of Latin American adventures. The greatest of such was the Mexican-American war, in which the United States seized California and a huge area of the Rocky Mountains, annexing Texas as part of the package. Occasional involvement in the Caribbean opened possibilities for large-scale expansion of American influence at the end of the century.

The economic empires of the nineteenth century were not yet those of great corporations, which were to form in later years. Nor were the economic empires any longer simply those of nations, since the mercantilist policies of imperial monopoly ended in the wake of the Napoleonic wars. The empires were more properly those of industries—the linkages of raw materials, labor, production, and distribution for a related set of commodities: textiles, lumber, sugar, tobacco, wheat, or coffee. Thus the cotton-textile industry, which grew rapidly from the 1820s, relied especially on raw materials from the U.S. South and shipping services and manufacturing in Britain, the European continent, and New England. Sugar differed from cotton because it was processed mainly in the tropical territories where it was produced; coffee required relatively little processing once the beans were dried.[39]

In the case of these and other industries, slaves provided a substantial portion of the labor used throughout the nineteenth century. As of 1860, some twenty-five million persons lived in slavery in the Americas and in West and Central Africa, seven million of them in the Americas. Many of these individuals labored directly in the cotton, sugar, coffee, and tobacco industries or in the associated shipping and processing work. If one considers the number of wage workers (mostly in other parts of the world) involved in these same industries—even including the families of wage workers to make the comparison more consistent—it becomes clear that slave labor was still dominant in these industries in 1860. By 1900, the labor balance had changed dramatically, and slave workers had been mostly displaced by wage earners.

Another dimension of economic empire in the nineteenth century was the recruitment and voluntary migration of laborers into the Atlantic and African zones of the African diaspora. From the moment of the British emancipation of slaves in 1838, efforts began to hire contract laborers from India, China, and Africa for work in the Caribbean and, later, in Africa. The largest numbers of such recruits came from India, and they settled primarily in Trinidad, Guyana, Mauritius, Réunion, and South Africa. In Mauritius, the Indian immigrants became the majority of the population. Smaller numbers of Chinese workers came to the British West Indies, Cuba, and Indian Ocean colonies. (In fact, these were the tip of the iceberg of Indian and Chinese migration, as most migrants from both regions went to various parts of Southeast Asia.)

Beginning somewhat later, a larger number of migrants came from Europe to the Americas, some on their own and others responding to recruiters. These individuals settled down alongside or near black populations, and their arrival significantly changed the conditions of black life. In the United States, migrants came first from Ireland, Britain, and Germany, and then from Scandinavia and southern and eastern Europe. Spanish migrants came in large numbers to Cuba and Puerto Rico. For Brazil and Argentina, great numbers of Spanish and Italian migrants and smaller numbers of Germans and Portuguese settled down. Japanese migrants later came in significant numbers to Brazil and Peru; Greeks and Lebanese arrived as well. By 1920, thirty million migrants had come to the United States from Europe, seven million to South America, four million to the Caribbean, and nearly a million to Africa. Especially in Latin America, this immigration became known as "whitening."

Quite a different aspect of the global processes of the nineteenth century was the blossoming of intellectual empires. As the royal academies and salons of the eighteenth century gave way to secular universities in the nineteenth century, the production and publication of new scientific and humanistic knowledge grew rapidly. German, English, Scottish, and French universities asserted particular strength in developing what became a set of overlapping intellectual empires. The institutions of learning in Africa fell almost completely from view in this explosion of knowledge. The scientists and humanists of Latin America participated actively but as junior partners. Only in the United States were universities able to draw enough from European traditions to make North America a center of knowledge as well.

The creation of institutions of higher learning that focused on educating black people, especially in the United States but also in the Caribbean and in West Africa, would ultimately be of great importance. These included Fourah Bay College in Freetown (founded 1827), Liberia College in Monrovia (founded 1851), Ashmun College in Pennsylvania (founded 1854 and renamed Lincoln University in 1866), Wilberforce University in Ohio (founded 1856), and several institutions founded in the United States at the end of the Civil War in 1865, including Howard and Fisk.

These advances were significant, but substantial roadblocks still faced people of color in the professions and the sciences. Take, for example, the case of two young European naturalists, Alexander von Humboldt of Prussia and Aimé Bonpland of France. These two gained support from the Spanish crown and conducted five years of travels and researches throughout the Spanish territories of South and Central America between 1799 and 1804, concluding with a visit to the United States; they gathered information on geology, zoology, and physics. Humboldt, who became the more prominent of the two, collaborated with local scientists wherever he went and sought to acknowledge their contributions in his voluminous writings. But the structure of science and education at the time was such that Humboldt alone gained recognition for the discoveries he reported over the years to come.

Another major negative effect of the expanding European intellectual community on the lives of people of color came out of the effort to "make sense" of race. Eighteenth-century science had classified the species of plants and animals, verified the sense of grouping humans among the animals, and raised the question of racial differences among humans. Nineteenth-century science produced a distinct theory of evolution in Darwin's *Origin of the Species* (1859) and posed even more sharply the question of racial differences. In the public arena, the defenders of slavery and the propagandists for the superiority of European civilization were clear in asserting that the "Caucasian race," as they began to call it, was superior in intellect and culture to all other groups. Arthur de Gobineau, a French novelist, wrote one of the most influential such works, *On the Inequality of Human Races* (1853–1855), which described history in terms of comparative civilizations and argued that mixing races brought civilizational decline.

But the growing cadre of medical and biological scientists needed more objective criteria for their analysis. In the 1820s, Franz Gall of Switzerland proposed a science soon labeled "phrenology." He argued that the human skull's external shape, especially its irregularities or bumps, correlated with the character of individuals. Phrenological societies were founded, and traveling experts offered readings of individual characteristics. The practice became more a fad than a science and fell out of favor by the 1850s.

In the next development, groups of medical doctors formed anthropological societies at midcentury. They chose to measure the inside of skulls rather than the outside to identify and explain human differences. Paul Broca led in founding the Anthropological Society of Paris in 1859 and dominated it until his death in 1880. Working from a huge collection of skulls from around the world, his principal interest was on skull capacity and thus brain size, but he also measured ratios of skull width to length, the height of the forehead, and so forth. Broca, with his efforts at "craniology," claimed to show a clear hierarchy of races, especially with regard to brain size. In addition, he correlated brain size with social rank and criminal behavior within France. He argued that Negro brains, in addition to being relatively small, were of a dark color.

Meanwhile, in the mid-1880s a young Haitian diplomat, Joseph-Anténor Firmin, came to the Anthropological Society of Paris and asked to be admitted to the society's debates. Ultimately, Broca gave his assent. Within two years Firmin—who had a good education from the Lycée Pétion in Haiti and

a license to practice law but no medical training—had written a book reviewing and critiquing Broca's assertions on the hierarchy of race in physical
form.[40] Firmin's work used solid statistical arguments and went a long way
toward refuting Broca's claims. With time, the effort to distinguish human
races by brain size died out.

In Britain, meanwhile, the theory of natural selection in evolution led
John Galton to the idea of eugenics, which proposed that the most fit, most
intelligent individuals could be identified and they should be the ones most
encouraged to reproduce. Efforts to test and develop the ideas of eugenics were important to the creation of statistical techniques for correlation.
These same ideas also led to the beginning of intelligence testing, on the
assumption that "intelligence" was a discrete characteristic that could be
measured and inherited in a direct fashion.[41] The leading analysts of human
biology—the specialists in craniology and eugenics—each tended to argue
that races could be identified and ranked in a hierarchy. Yet in practice, their
descriptions of races and racial characteristics were always inconsistent
and changing, and they failed to establish any clear boundaries among racial
groupings.

At one level, the development of racism was a response to emancipation.
As blacks gained freedom from slavery, they appeared to some leading figures as a destabilizing element of society. Consciously or unconsciously,
it seemed that the confirmation of an ideology or science labeling them as
inferior would provide a basis for establishing new legislation to hold them
in place. This reasoning paralleled the response toward granting civil rights
to Jews. In the 1870s and 1880, a newly labeled and formal ideology of anti-
Semitism developed that claimed Jews were not so much a religious group
as a biologically separate racial group.[42] The elaboration of scientific racism and the development of new social restrictions on blacks and Jews—in
each case, after recent improvements in their legal status—reinforced one
another. Scientific and popular racism, while different from one other, fit
into a larger pattern.

Racial Restrictions

After the American Civil War ended in 1865, the civil rights of black people
were enforced and respected to a considerable degree for over a decade. Then
in 1877, Reconstruction was brought to a halt, and federal troops withdrew
from the South. This allowed the rise of postemancipation restrictions on
black citizens, which eventually evolved into segregation. In an early application of this idea, the state of Louisiana passed a law in 1890 decreeing that

railroad cars should henceforth have separate cars for black and white passengers. Homer Plessy was a Louisiana shoemaker who calculated his ancestry as seven-eighths white and one-eighth black. When he rode in a white car,
he was jailed. He sued to overrule his jailing in local and then state court and,
losing in each case, appealed to the U.S. Supreme Court. The court ruled,
in a nearly unanimous 1896 decision, that the Louisiana law did not violate
the Thirteenth Amendment to the Constitution (which abolished slavery),
nor did it violate the Fourteenth Amendment, which required equal protection under the law.[43] The court, in arguing that separate facilities based on
color could be equal under the law, opened the door to a fifteen-year period
in which southern states passed a large number of acts imposing racial segregation in transportation, education, employment, and residence.

This decision set the tone for most of the next century in the United
States, and it suggested the shape of things to come elsewhere in the African
diaspora. Blacks in the United States largely lost political representation in
the following decades. American control of Cuba and Puerto Rico expanded
American-style racial segregation to these territories. In the British Caribbean, crown-colony governments gave the British governors complete
power—as did their equivalents in Africa—with only a few appointed members of the legislative council to suggest alternate policies. The black populations could not even vote in municipal elections at the end of the nineteenth
century. In the French Caribbean, all inhabitants were formally citizens and
had formal rights to vote in elections for municipal offices. In practice, politics was reserved to whites and a small number of mulattoes. The Dominican
Republic, along with Haiti, was formally independent but was ruled, in practice, by a wealthy elite.

In Africa, the loss of political representation for blacks was perhaps more
severe—this was the era in which conquering Europeans set up residential
segregation in the small colonial cities along with different systems of law
("customary law") for Africans than for the Europeans who ruled them. In
Africa as elsewhere, black people were sometimes able to counter the new
restrictions. In 1894, three kings from what is today Botswana traveled to
London to petition Queen Victoria to retain direct crown government over
their territories rather than subject them to the local white-led government.
Their travels and speeches, translated for English audiences, gained them
support and approval for their request.[44]

The Spanish- and Portuguese-speaking countries from Mexico to Chile
did not experience the legalized racial segregation that came to the United
States and to Africa. However, black people of Latin America did undergo a
different negative social development: the "whitening" that came with large

FIGURE 2.2 [top] Ife royal couple. **FIGURE 2.3** [bottom] St. Maurice.

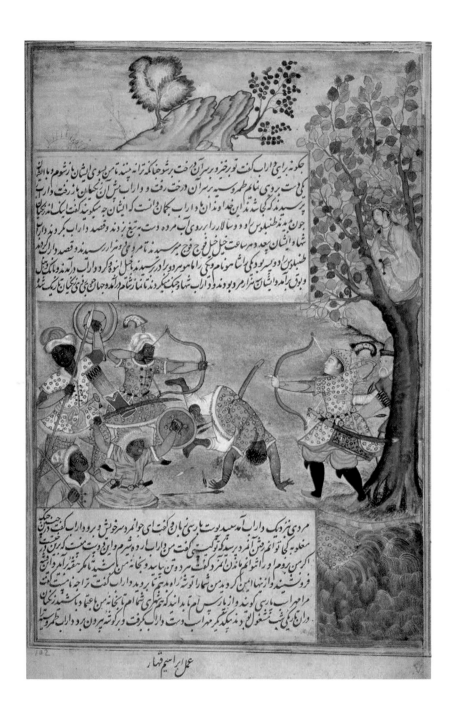

FIGURE 2.4 *Zanjis and Darab.*

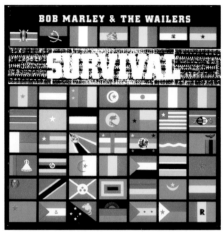

FIGURE 5.4 [left] *Charlemagne Péralte*, by Philomène Obin. FIGURE 6.2 [right] *Survival* album cover. FIGURE 6.1 [bottom] Urban Nigeria, by Jacob Lawrence.

FIGURE 6.4 [top] Master Mokhtar Gania. **FIGURE 7.1** [bottom] Oprah Winfrey with South African youth.

numbers of European immigrants. Millions of people from Spain, Portugal, and Italy, and smaller numbers from Germany, Greece, and Lebanon, settled in Latin America. Their numbers were largest in Brazil, Argentina, and Cuba but were also significant in Puerto Rico, Chile, Uruguay, Venezuela, Colombia, Peru, Mexico, and Central America. As a result, blacks became a smaller portion of the population, weakening their ability to compete for employment, education, and social services.

The struggle for emancipation throughout the African diaspora had made great advances. The victory of the emancipation campaign was perhaps exaggerated, as the continued existence of slavery in Africa was commonly hushed up. Colonial propaganda argued that African slavery was a gentle institution and, further, African society was so backward that normal standards of civilization did not apply. For Africa and the African diaspora as a whole, however, it was indeed true by the end of the nineteenth century that slavery was no longer the main problem. Instead, new sorts of discrimination against black people showed up at the end of the century: formal segregation, new institutions of colonial rule, and expanded immigration by whites that led to more difficult employment conditions and cultural recognition for blacks. As a result, in every part of the black world, it became clear that the social advance of black people required a stronger political position from which to advocate. The recognition of the nation as the appropriate unit for modern political existence made it clear that black people needed to insist on full recognition of their rights as citizens.

For the few nations led and principally populated by black people in 1900—Haiti, Liberia, and Ethiopia—the challenges of sustaining their recognition as nations remained formidable. They were small (except Ethiopia), weak, compromised, and often corrupt and oppressive. There is no need to paper over the abuses and inequalities within these regimes: Ethiopia, for instance, was only gradually transforming itself from monarchy to nation. But these nations struggled and survived under the most difficult conditions and did much to open the door to citizenship and nationhood for blacks everywhere. Their experience helps show the importance of long-term patterns and how the struggles of one generation are carried over into the next.

Suggested Readings

The rise of the Islamic theocracy based at Sokoto is described in concise but lively terms in Mervyn Hiskett, *The Sword of Truth: The Life and Times of the*

Shehu Usuman dan Fodio (New York: Oxford University Press, 1973). For a detailed and thoughtful study of the early days of the Sierra Leone colony, see Christopher Fyfe, *A History of Sierra Leone* (London: Oxford University Press, 1962).

Slavery and Antislavery

On the early stages of scientific racism, see William B. Cohen, *The French Encounter with Africans: White Response to Blacks, 1530–1880* (Bloomington: Indiana University Press, 2003); Philip D. Curtin, *The Image of Africa: British Ideas and Action, 1780–1850* (Madison: University of Wisconsin Press, 1964); Carl N. Degler, *Neither Black nor White: Slavery and Race Relations in Brazil and the United States* (Madison: University of Wisconsin Press, 1971). On a major slave revolt, see João José Reis, *Slave Rebellion in Brazil: The Muslim Uprising of 1835 in Bahia*, trans. Arthur Brakel (Baltimore, Md.: The Johns Hopkins University Press, 1993). On the early stages of abolition and emancipation in the Americas, see Robin Blackburn, *The Overthrow of Colonial Slavery, 1776–1848* (London: Verso, 1988). For the extraordinary and dismaying case of Sara Baartman, see Clifton Crais and Pamela Scully, *Sara Baartman and the Hottentot Venus: A Ghost Story and a Biography* (Princeton, N.J.: Princeton University Press, 2008).

Slavery's Expansion

For a survey of nineteenth-century expansion in slavery, see Patrick Manning, *Slavery and African Life: Occidental, Oriental, and African Slave Trades* (Cambridge: Cambridge University Press, 1990). For chapters on women in slavery in Africa, the Old World, and the Atlantic, see Gwyn Campbell, Suzanne Miers, and Joseph C. Miller, eds., *Women and Slavery*, 2 vols. (Athens: Ohio University Press, 2007). On West Africa, see Paul E. Lovejoy, *Slavery, Commerce and Production in the Sokoto Caliphate of West Africa* (Trenton, N.J.: Africa World Press, 2005); Sean Stilwell, *Paradoxes of Power: The Kano "Mamluks" and Male Royal Slavery in the Sokoto Caliphate, 1804–1903* (Portsmouth, N.H.: Heinemann, 2004); and Martin A. Klein, *Slavery and Colonial Rule in French West Africa* (Cambridge: Cambridge University Press, 1998). On Central Africa, see Robert W. Harms, *River of Wealth, River of Sorrow: The Central Zaire Basin in the Era of the Slave and Ivory Trade, 1500–1891* (New Haven, Conn.: Yale University Press, 1981). On Cuba, see Franklin W. Knight, *Slave Society in Cuba During the Nineteenth Century* (Madison: University of Wisconsin Press, 1970). On the continuity of slavery in North America and the Caribbean, see David Barry Gaspar and Darlene Clark Hine, *More Than Chattel: Black Women and Slavery in the Americas* (Bloomington: Indiana University Press, 1996); and Michael A. Gomez, *Exchanging Our Country Marks: The Transformation of African Identities in the Colonial and Antebellum South* (Chapel Hill: University of North Carolina Press, 1998). On the rise and fall of the East African slave trade, see Eve Troutt Powell, *A Different Shade of Colonialism: Egypt, Great Britain, and the Mastery of the Sudan* (Berkeley: University of California Press, 2003); William Gervase Clarence-Smith, ed., *The Economics of the Indian Ocean Slave Trade in the Nineteenth Century* (London: Frank Cass, 1989); Abdul Sheriff, *Slaves, Spices, and Ivory in Zanzibar: Integration of an East African Commercial Empire Into the World Economy, 1770–1873* (London: James Currey, 1987); Erik Gilbert, *Dhows and the Colonial Economy of Zanzibar* (Oxford: James Currey, 2004); Edward A. Alpers, *Ivory and Slaves: Changing Patterns of International Trade in East Central Africa to the Later Nineteenth Century* (Berkeley: University of California Press, 1975); and Leda Farrant, *Tippu Tip and the East African Slave Trade* (New York: St. Martin's Press, 1975).

The Pace of Slavery's Destruction

For an overview of British policy and practice in slave emancipation, see Seymour Drescher, *The Mighty Experiment: Free Labor Versus Slavery in British Emancipation* (Oxford: Oxford University Press, 2002). Stiv Jakobsson, *Am I Not a Man and a Brother? British Missions and the Abolition of the Slave Trade and Slavery in West Africa and the West Indies, 1786–1838* (Lund: Gleerup, 1972), provides details on the key actions and decisions in British emancipation. For an excellent history of Trinidad with a focus on issues of emancipation, see Bridget Brereton, *History of Modern Trinidad, 1783–1962* (Kingston: Heinemann, 1981). On the ambiguity of gradual emancipation in Peru, see Christine Hunefeldt, *Paying the Price of Freedom: Family and Labor Among Lima's Slaves, 1800–1854* (Berkeley: University of California Press, 1994); for Cuba, see Rebecca J. Scott, *Slave Emancipation in Cuba: The Transition to Free Labor, 1860–1899* (Princeton, N.J.: Princeton University Press, 1985). On emancipation in Latin America generally, see George Reid Andrews, *Afro-Latin America, 1800–2000* (Oxford: Oxford University Press, 2004). Perhaps the most effective of slave narratives because of its direct description of gender oppression and sexual exploitation is Harriet Jacobs, *Incidents in the Life of a Slave Girl*, ed. L. Maria Child (New York: Washington Square Press, 2003). For lives of major U.S. abolitionists see Jean M. Humez, *Harriet Tubman: The Life and the Life Stories* (Madison: University of Wisconsin Press, 2004); and

Margaret Washington, *Sojourner Truth's America* (Urbana: University of Illinois Press, 2009). On a key experiment in postemancipation reconstruction in the United States, see Willie Lee Rose, *Rehearsal for Reconstruction: The Port Royal Experiment* (Athens: University of Georgia Press, 1999). Robert Conrad, *The Destruction of Brazilian Slavery, 1850–1888* (Berkeley: University of California Press, 1972), traces emancipation in Brazil; John Hunwick and Eve Troutt Powell, eds., *The African Diaspora in the Mediterranean Lands of Islam* (Princeton, N.J.: Markus Wiener, 2002), documents the obstacles to emancipation in northern Africa. On the end of slavery in the Islamic world generally, see W. G. Clarence-Smith, *Islam and the Abolition of Slavery* (Oxford: Oxford University Press, 2006). See also Kristin Mann and Edna G. Bay, *Rethinking the African Diaspora: The Making of a Black Atlantic World in the Bight of Benin and Brazil* (London: Frank Cass, 2001).

Ambitions of Free Blacks

For insights into the general process of emancipation and postemancipation society, see Leo Spitzer, *Lives in Between: The Experience of Marginality in a Century of Emancipation* (New York: Hill and Wang, 1999); Jerome S. Handler, *The Unappropriated People: Freedmen in the Slave Society of Barbados* (Kingston: University of the West Indies Press, 2009); and Frederick Cooper et al., *Beyond Slavery: Explorations of Race, Labor, and Citizenship in Postemancipation Societies* (Chapel Hill: University of North Carolina Press, 2004). On the terrible demographic cost of creating the free community of Liberia, see Antonio McDaniel, *Swing Low, Sweet Chariot: The Mortality Cost of Colonizing Liberia in the Nineteenth Century* (Chicago: University of Chicago Press, 1995). See also Ibrahim Sundiata, *From Slaving to Neoslavery: The Bight of Biafra and Fernando Po in the Era of Abolition, 1827–1930* (Madison: University of Wisconsin Press, 1996); Donald R. Wright, *The World and a Very Small Place in Africa* (Armonk, N.Y.: M. E. Sharpe, 1997); Jan Vansina, *Art History in Africa: An Introduction to Method* (New York: Longman, 1984); and Tiyambe Zeleza, *A Modern Economic History of Africa* (Dakar: Codesria, 1993).

On the global connections of black political activists, see P. Olisanwuche Esedebe, *Pan-Africanism: The Idea and Movement, 1776–1991*, 2nd ed. (Washington, D.C.: Howard University Press, 1994); Imanuel Geiss, *The Pan-African Movement: A History of Pan-Africanism in America, Europe, and Africa* (New York: Africana Publishing, 1968); George Fredrickson, *Black Liberation: A Comparative History of Black Ideologies in the United States and South Africa* (New York: Oxford University Press, 1995); and Cedric J. Robinson, *Black Marxism: The Making of the Black Radical Tradition* (Chapel Hill: University of North Carolina Press, 2000). Among individuals who contributed significantly to pan-African thinking, see Martin R. Delany and Robert Campbell, *Search for a Place: Black Separatism and Africa* (Ann Arbor: University of Michigan Press, 1971); and biographical studies including Hollis R. Lynch, *Edward Wilmot Blyden: Pan-Negro Patriot, 1832–1912* (London: Oxford University Press, 1967); and John Hope Franklin, *George Washington Williams, a Biography* (Chicago: University of Chicago Press, 1985).

On the campaigns and trials of free blacks in the United States, see Nell Irvin Painter, *Sojourner Truth: A Life, a Symbol* (New York: W. W. Norton, 1996); Steven Hahn, *A Nation Under Our Feet: Black Political Struggles in the Rural South from Slavery to the Great Migration* (Cambridge, Mass.: Belknap Press, 2005); Jacqueline Jones, *Labor of Love, Labor of Sorrow: Black Women, Work, and the Family from Slavery to the Present* (New York: Knopf, 2009); Mary Niall Mitchell, *Raising Freedom's Child: Black Children and Visions of the Future After Slavery* (New York: New York University Press, 2008); Martha Hodes, *White Women, Black Men: Illicit Sex in the Nineteenth-century South* (New Haven, Conn.: Yale University Press, 1997); Frederick Douglass, *Narrative of the Life of Frederick Douglass, an American Slave*, ed. John W. Blassingame et al. (New Haven, Conn.: Yale University Press, 2001); Vincent Harding, *There Is a River: The Black Struggle for Freedom in America* (New York: Vintage Books, 1983); August Meier, *Negro Thought in America 1880–1915: Racial Ideologies in the Age of Booker T. Washington* (Ann Arbor: University of Michigan Press, 1988); Louis R. Harlan, *Booker T. Washington*, 2 vols. (New York: Oxford University Press, 1972–1983); Rackham Holt, *George Washington Carver, an American Biography*, rev. ed. (Garden City, N.Y.: Doubleday, 1963); and Sterling Stuckey, *Going Through the Storm: The Influence of African American Art in History* (New York: Oxford University Press, 1994).

On free people of color in Latin America and the Caribbean, see Andrews, *Afro-Latin America*; Chege J. Githiora, *Afro-Mexicans: Discourse of Race and Identity on the African Diaspora* (Trenton, N.J.: Africa World Press, 2008); Darien J. Davis, *Beyond Slavery: The Multilayered Legacy of Africans in Latin America and the Caribbean* (Lanham, Md.: Rowman and Littlefield, 2006); Franklin W. Knight, *The Caribbean: Genesis of a Fragmented Nationalism*, 2nd ed. (New York: Oxford University Press, 1990); Monica Schuler, *"Alas, Alas, Kongo": A Social History of Indentured African Immigration into Jamaica, 1841–1860* (Baltimore, Md.: The Johns Hopkins University Press, 1980); Ivar Oxaal, *Black Intellectuals and the Dilemmas of Race and Class in Trinidad* (Cambridge, Mass.: Schenkman Pub. Co., 1982); Rebecca J. Scott, *Slave Emancipation in Cuba: The Transition to Free Labor, 1860–1899* (Pittsburgh, Penn.: University of Pittsburgh Press, 2000); David Barry Gaspar and Darlene Clark Hine,

Beyond Bondage: Free Women of Color in the Americas (Urbana: University of Illinois Press, 2004); Kim D. Butler, *Freedoms Given, Freedoms Won: Afro-Brazilians in Postabolition São Paulo and Salvador* (New Brunswick, N.J.: Rutgers University Press, 1998); Robert Chaudenson, *Creolization of Language and Culture*, revised in collaboration with Salikoko S. Mufwene (London: Routledge, 2001); James Walvin, *Black Ivory: A History of British Slavery* (London: HarperCollins, 1992); and Norman E. Whitten Jr. and Arlene Torres, eds., *Blackness in Latin America and the Caribbean*, 2 vols. (Bloomington: Indiana University Press, 1998).

Empire Old and New

Aspects of empire in Africa and the African diaspora during the nineteenth century are explored in Joseph E. Inikori, *Africans and the Industrial Revolution in England: A Study in International Trade and Economic Development* (Cambridge: Cambridge University Press, 2002); C. A. Bayly, *The Birth of the Modern World, 1780–1914: Global Connections and Comparisons* (Oxford: Blackwell, 2004); Sugata Bose, *A Hundred Horizons: The Indian Ocean in the Age of Global Empire* (Cambridge, Mass.: Harvard University Press, 2006); Patrick Manning, *Francophone Sub-Saharan Africa, 1880–1995* (Cambridge: Cambridge University Press, 1998); Neil Parsons, *King Khama, Emperor Joe, and the Great White Queen: Victorian Britain Through African Eyes* (Chicago: University of Chicago Press, 1998); and Adam Hochschild, *King Leopold's Ghost: A Story of Greed, Terror, and Heroism in Colonial Africa* (Boston: Houghton Mifflin, 1998). For an important set of insights on the links of empire, nation, and race, see Eric Hobsbawm and Terence Ranger, eds., *The Invention of Tradition* (Cambridge: Cambridge University Press, 1993).

Racial Restrictions

A worldwide study of the expanding racial restrictions of the late nineteenth century has yet to be written. For comparisons in some regions of the African diaspora, see George M. Fredrickson, *White Supremacy: A Comparative Study in American and South African History* (New York: Oxford University Press, 1981); Joseph E. Harris, *Global Dimensions of the African Diaspora*, 2nd ed. (Washington, D.C.: Howard University Press, 1993); and Melville J. Herskovits, *The Myth of the Negro Past*, 2nd ed. (Boston: Beacon Press, 1990).

≡ 5 ≡

Citizenship, 1900–1960

I n July 1900, the first Pan-African Conference convened at Westminster Town Hall in London. The thirty-seven delegates, male and female, came from Africa, the Caribbean, Europe, and the United States under the leadership of Henry Sylvester Williams, a lawyer from Trinidad who resided in London. While the Congress was cautious in its declarations, the delegates nonetheless presented themselves as political leaders advocating for advanced rights and improved conditions for Africans and people of African descent on four continents. W. E. B. Du Bois gave a paper at the London conference, later published in his volume of essays, *Souls of Black Folk*,[1] in which he captured the heart and soul of the event:

> In the metropolis of the modern world, in this the closing year of the nineteenth century, there has been assembled a congress of men and women of African blood, to deliberate solemnly upon the present situation and outlook of the darker races of mankind. The problem of the twentieth century is the problem of the color-line, the question as to how far differences of race—which show themselves chiefly in the color of the skin and the texture of the hair—will hereafter be made the basis of denying to over half the world the right of sharing to their utmost ability the opportunities and privileges of modern civilization.

This small group of intellectuals and activists, convening at a time when the powers of empires and the organized white race were at their peak, nonetheless set an agenda for political and social activity during the century to come.

The sense of hope conveyed at the conference was shared by more than the black elite. The same year saw the composition of "Lift Every Voice" in the United States. For a local celebration of Abraham Lincoln's birthday, James Weldon Johnson, principal of a Jacksonville, Florida, school, wrote a poem. His brother J. Rosamond Johnson, the music teacher at the same school, provided the music, and the work was first performed on February 12, 1900.[2]

> Lift every voice and sing, till earth and Heaven ring,
> Ring with the harmonies of liberty;
> Let our rejoicing rise, high as the listening skies,
> Let it resound loud as the rolling sea.
> Sing a song full of the faith that the dark past has taught us,
> Sing a song full of the hope that the present has brought us;
> Facing the rising sun of our new day begun,
> Let us march on till victory is won.

The song spread quietly through black churches and assemblies in the American South and traveled north with the migrants. By the 1920s, it had become known as the "Negro National Anthem." Du Bois's pronouncement and the Johnsons' song articulated the hopes and acknowledged the fears of postemancipation generations of black people in the United States and beyond. The task these generations faced was navigating the rough seas of industry and empire—two forces that threatened to engulf their identities but that also held promise for great advancement and reward.

The hope of postemancipation generations continued to be conveyed in numerous ways beyond the Johnsons' lyrics. After the London conference, Du Bois traveled to France carrying 363 photographs of African Americans from Georgia, bound into three volumes, for display at the Paris Exposition of 1900 as part of the American Negro exhibit. The photos, which won a gold medal, conveyed urban and rural life, lives of comfort and of subsistence, and people of dark and of light color. It was accompanied by a sociological analysis of Georgia similar to the one Du Bois had just completed for black Philadelphia. The exhibit's emphasis, however, was on young, light-skinned, educated, middle-class blacks who reflected the achievements and hopes for progress of black Americans after the Civil War and emancipation (see figure 5.1). Three years later in West Africa, J. E. Casely Hayford, the Gold Coast lawyer and writer, published *Gold Coast Native Institutions*, a work

FIGURE 5.1 Citizens of Atlanta

At left is Mamie Westmoreland, a schoolteacher. At right is the "Summit Avenue Ensemble"—seated are Clarence Askew, Arthur Askew, and Walter Askew; standing are Norman Askew, Jake Sansome, and Robert Askew. These photographs, by Thomas E. Askew, are in the collection and exhibit by W. E. B. Du Bois, *Negro Life in Georgia, U.S.A.* (1900).

Source: Courtesy of the Daniel Murray Collection, Library of Congress, Washington, D.C.

of political analysis and advocacy. In it, he argued optimistically that the Fante polities of the Gold Coast and the larger Asante Empire of the interior were governed by constitutions comparable to Britain's and deserved to be granted self-government in the same way as the white dominions of Canada and Australia.[3]

Black visual artists at the beginning of the twentieth century also offered powerful statements that reaffirmed tradition while looking to the future. Artists of Liberia's Dan and Grebo ethnicities, in the aftermath of slave trade and imperial expansion, created masks conveying the earth's power. In 1907, sculptor Meta Warrick displayed in the Negro Building at the Jamestown Tercentennial Exposition fourteen dioramas with 130 plaster figures depicting the African-American experience, depicting scenes ranging from the arrival of twenty blacks in Virginia in 1617 to the home life of "the modern, successfully, educated, and progressive Negro." These works, while valued within the communities from which they came, were long ignored by outsiders or, as in the case of the Grebo sculptures, appropriated by other artists with little attribution.[4] Even so, they remain important for revealing the impulses of black people who expected to participate fully in a rapidly evolving world.

What stands out in the cultural creations of black people at the beginning of the twentieth century is the upbeat, confident, and even enthusiastic outlook they convey. Such positive expressions appeared especially in the Atlantic diaspora but also in the Old World diaspora and the African homeland. The nearly complete success of the movement for emancipation had created situations in which black people could hope—as they had not been able to hope for centuries—to build their lives without fear of enslavement.

The next step, it appeared, was to gain formal recognition of the citizenship of black people within the nations or colonies in which they lived. This chapter delves into the complex political, social, and cultural gains and the losses, triumphs, and compromises of the first half of the twentieth century as blacks everywhere strove to gain the rights of citizenship. As I will argue, this struggle for citizenship was not simply a campaign for rights to vote but a claim for freedom of expression and a call for the recognition of the value of black cultural achievements. In such a world of citizenship, one could express one's dreams and frustrations with security. The simultaneous campaigns for citizenship throughout the black world saw remarkable successes. They created robust national political movements, better understandings of what was shared throughout the African diaspora, and new appreciation within neighboring communities of black achievements.

Facing White Supremacy

The optimism of black communities would be difficult to sustain: achieving dreams of community advancement required running the gauntlet of white supremacy. This updated ideology differed from previous versions of racial and social discrimination because it was more systematic and more fully theorized. In earlier centuries, the oppression of black people and others worldwide relied on arbitrary and often brutal exercises of power, discriminating eclectically by religion, color, language, and ethnicity. But the white theorists of the late nineteenth century turned their inherited collection of discriminatory practices into a general social and biological theory with a hierarchy so explicit that it *required* discrimination rather than simply permitting it. What now arose was a coherent ideology, accepted by many though not all leaders who saw themselves as white and by many others in white communities and even communities of color.

This systematized ideology purported to explain both race and civilization. For race, it assumed the division of humanity into separate and distinct races with inherited biological characteristics. The attributes of individuals in each race were determined biologically at the racial level, and thus the races could be ranked in a hierarchy of efficiency and evolutionary development. For civilization, white supremacy posited the division of humanity into separate and distinct civilizations, each with common cultural characteristics that were passed on through learning and socialization. Each civilization had its strengths and weaknesses, but they too could be listed in a hierarchy. (Some peoples were thought to be so primitive that they possessed only race, since their culture had not yet evolved to the level of civilization.) The central logic of white supremacy was that the differences of individuals and societies *within* groups—racial or civilizational—were smaller than the differences *between* groups. Thus one could speak of the "typical Negro" or the "typical Caucasian" and expect each to be representative of their own group and sharply different from members of the other group. In addition, white-supremacist thinking, by accepting the logic of purity in race and in civilization, argued that any individuals or societies that could be pictured as "mixed" or "hybrid" were most likely to display the worst characteristics of each ancestry.

The authorities on which this set of beliefs rested included medical theorists of race such as Paul Broca, psychological theorists of eugenics such as John Galton, social theorists of race such as Wilhelm Marr (who classified Jews as a race rather than a religious group), legal-historical theorists of racial and civilizational hierarchy such as Arthur de Gobineau, orientalist theorists of civilization such as Sir Richard Burton, sociological theorists of social evolution such as Herbert Spencer, and leading practitioners of imperial expansion such as Cecil Rhodes.[5] While white supremacy did not become codified into a uniform set of rules, the ideas of these authorities combined to form a wider set of social movements sharing a sense of clear identity and triumphal advance for the white race. It took different forms in various parts of the world and interacted differently with previous conditions in each region, yet it was a worldwide phenomenon.

The obstacles imposed by white supremacy launched debates on the conditions of black people. In racial terms, was it the case that, regardless of their cultural upbringing, people of the black race were limited to inferior social and intellectual capacities? In civilizational terms, what disabilities did ex-slaves bring with them from their previous condition of bondage into the society of free people? Was it the case that slavery had created ingrained habits of laziness and servility? For black people slave and free, had African culture restricted them to primitive and inefficient skills and patterns of life? For those who rejected the ideology of white supremacy, other big questions arose. Did the very strength of the white-supremacist denial of black capacities suffice to overcome the efforts of blacks to gain full citizenship? Or, more insidiously and more practically, was it the case that new disabilities imposed on blacks in the very era of emancipation created new and more insurmountable limitations? From this point of view, racial segregation, limitations on education, restrictions against political participation, and a new specificity in the denigration of black culture presented new rather than old challenges.

White supremacy affected everyone. In Europe and North America, there were arguments about whether Irish, Italians, and Jews could be considered white. Amerindians in the Americas were put low on the hierarchy; mulattos and mestizos were highly suspect. The Arabs of North Africa and western Asia, along with the Muslims and Hindus of South Asia, were labeled as intermediate groups, and their civilizations were considered to have failed. The powerful ruling classes of great empires—in China, Japan, Iran, and the Ottoman state—were classified as inferior by this logic. White settlers in Australia, Africa, and the Americas came to expect better treatment than "nonwhites."

The peoples of the African homeland and diaspora were governed from the late nineteenth century to the 1960s by imperial and colonial autocracies and by racialized democracies. These governments, subscribing to white supremacy as an aspect of "Western" cultural and political hegemony, limited the access of black people to the enjoyment of citizenship for much of the twentieth century. In North America, centuries of racial hierarchy under European rule were now reinforced by formal, racial ideology. In the Caribbean, Spanish colonial rule was overthrown, but British, French, and Dutch domination continued, reaffirmed by American domination of Puerto Rico and sometimes Cuba, Haiti, and the Dominican Republic. Latin America's black communities, while not formally subjected to racial discrimination, found their interests subordinated to those of white immigrants and their political participation limited by property restrictions. In Africa, white supremacy struck with particular force as the continent was subjected to imperial rule from Europe. In the Old World diaspora, both the near diaspora at the edge of Africa and the Eurasian far diaspora, white supremacy had its effects as well.

Empires became the principal structures for the implementation of white supremacy, especially in Africa, but also in the Old World diaspora and the Caribbean. The African homeland faced the sharpest change in government and ideology. Emancipation had just begun in most parts of the continent. But the accompanying, sudden expansion of European colonization brought the shock of foreign rule and white-supremacist ideology. Africans had to learn to live under direct European colonial rule, a dominion aided in part by medical advances that protected colonial officials against malaria, Africa's greatest killer of newcomers.[6] These colonial powers became the monarchs of African lands, suppressing rebellions, collecting taxes, and leaning on their African subjects to adopt colonial ways. In general, Africans also had to show public obeisance to Europeans, bowing before them. Between 1890 and 1910, the per-capita taxes required of Africans rose by a factor of at least four. Villages that chose not to pay often found themselves facing a column of troops or police that burned their dwellings and then demanded the taxes plus reimbursement for what it cost to mount the disciplinary expedition. The troops and police were generally Africans under European leadership. African populations of tens of thousands of people in a newly defined British district or French *cercle* often found themselves living under the command of an inexperienced man in his twenties. Occasionally, the brasher of these young men imagined themselves as the repositories and guardians of all things Western. So it was with one district officer in Dahomey, who commanded pedestrians to walk abreast rather than single file on the newly repaired road from Abomey to Bohicon to slow the growth of weeds. For African subjects of these new empires, dealing with such powerful and often arbitrary figures required diplomacy and sometimes deviousness.

European empire also came to the near diaspora of Madagascar, Arabia, and North Africa, as France and Britain conquered territory after territory between 1830 and 1912.[7] These imperial governments gave little representation to any of their subjects, except that European settlers had formal political rights.[8] In North Africa, those of African ancestry were listed simply as Muslims. In independent Saudi Arabia, royal marriage practices brought some African women close to the seats of power and their sons, occasionally, to high rank, yet there was no formal recognition of African identity.

In the far diaspora of the Old World, from Europe to India, twentieth-century forms of government varied widely. The Ottoman, Russian, and Iranian empires controlled large areas, each including African-descended populations; after World War I, Turkey and the Soviet Union emerged as republics. Empire was the form in British India, in Indian Ocean islands, and later in Iraq and Palestine, as in French Syria and Lebanon. In none of these areas were black people able to gain significant political representation, nor were there aggressive campaigns to eliminate the remains of slavery. In the Old World diaspora, slave populations were slowly assimilated to free status under British and French colonial rule as well as in independent states. In Western Europe, blacks sometimes had the rights of citizens, but at other times they were considered as subjects of the empire rather than as citizens of the imperial homeland.

The Caribbean territories had two major forms of government. Haiti, the Dominican Republic, and (from 1902) Cuba were independent republics. Blacks had significant political representation in these countries, but elsewhere they had power only at the level of local government. The British, French, and Dutch colonial regimes continued to dominate the islands and the Guianas, and the communities of those territories had little opportunity for domestic political leadership. The United States began its Caribbean colonization through its conquest of Puerto Rico (1898), purchase of the American Virgin Islands from Denmark (1917), and periodic military occupation of independent states.

Latin America was remarkable in that it largely avoided the phenomenon of empire in the early twentieth century. It was governed principally by constitutional republics, though with episodes of military dictatorship. Black people, generally on the low end of the economic scale, were held there by limits on their wealth, not by formal prohibition of participation in politics or economy.

Large-scale migration by Europeans was another phenomenon of the imperial era. Some thirty million Europeans settled in North America between 1850 and 1920; about ten million more settled in South America, and another two million settled in northern and southern Africa (a significant portion of these migrants returned home). In South America, this phenomenon came to be known as "whitening," in that white workers got the best jobs and easier access to land. In the United States the same "whitening" phenomenon took place. Blacks and whites were often put in direct economic competition, with white immigrants taking jobs that would otherwise have gone to blacks and with blacks being brought in as strikebreakers against unionized white workers.

Racial segregation developed as a particular form of white supremacy, especially in the United States. Segregation came to be almost uniform in the American South: the removal of almost all blacks from the electoral rolls imposed a new sort of inequality on blacks. In the northern and western United States, it was not the rule but still a common practice. Black children went to public schools along with white children, but private schools, private clubs, churches, hotels, restaurants, and many other institutions outside the South implemented segregation in ways similar to those supported by law in the South. One of Woodrow Wilson's most dubious achievements after he became U.S. president in 1913 was to segregate federal government workplaces, rest rooms, and lunch rooms in Washington in order, as he put it, "to reduce friction." Segregation spread to other parts of the black world, especially Africa. In South Africa, where slavery had continued up to 1870 in the Boer republics, new residential restrictions, passports, and pass laws kept white and black populations separate except for the work of black domestics in white households and the shared work of blacks and whites on farms. In the cities of other parts of colonial Africa, whites established separate residential areas and created city centers principally to serve whites and the government. In the French colonies, these centers were known as *le plateau* in Dakar and Abidjan, and they were cleared of black inhabitants. In Dakar, this "cleansing" took place in part as a "necessary health measure" following an epidemic of plague. A parallel conflict took place with the "smallpox rebellion" of 1904 in Rio de Janeiro, when poor populations, largely people of color, objected to a government program of inoculation.

White supremacy advanced through military means as much as through ideology. The colonial wars of great powers—against the Amerindians of North and South America and the peoples of sub-Saharan Africa, North Africa, Southeast Asia, and the Pacific islands—were fought under this banner. By 1900, the ideology of white supremacy was in full swing and had brought many conquests. A few more occupations—for instance of Libya and Morocco—came after 1900. Then the great powers allowed imperial expansion to become imperial rivalry: they fought various small wars with each other, such as the Russo-Japanese war of 1905. Perhaps inevitably, the contending powers stumbled into a full-scale test of imperial might, and the war of 1914–1918 brought the Ottoman, Austro-Hungarian, Russian, and German empires to ruin. As a consequence, boundaries reshuffled, and Britain, the United States, and France emerged as the greatest powers.

The overall message was remarkably consistent: the dominant and overwhelmingly "white" interests treated people of African descent as biologically, socially, intellectually, and culturally inferior. People of color would do best to renounce their culture and trust white leaders to guide them, eventually, to positions of social responsibility. The ideology of white supremacy maintained its influence for no more than a century, but it had formidable and devastating consequences within that time.

Claims for Citizenship: Afro-Cuban Trailblazers

The breadth of black enthusiasm for constructing postemancipation societies collided with the multipronged ideology and practice of white supremacy. In this contest between the hopes of black communities and the plans of the hegemonic social order, black people guided their campaigns with a clearly defined goal: citizenship. Citizenship meant gaining full legal and political rights, opportunities for full and free expression, and recognition of black achievements by others within each nation.

What happened in Cuba from 1870 to 1950 reflected nearly the full range of social fates of black communities and the cultural responses to them. This section provides a preview, on a national scale, of the diaspora-wide struggle for citizenship during the twentieth century. The Afro-Cuban campaign for citizenship had an early start, reaching well back into the nineteenth century, and included rebellions, political alliances, campaigns to gain land, schooling, urban work, and cultural activities.

This will be a *dual narrative* of the Afro-Cuban experience. On one side, the narrative recounts social struggles in the late nineteenth and early twentieth centuries, including the campaigns of Afro-Cubans and their allies, and it will also include the actions of great powers and the larger currents of world affairs. On the other side, the narrative traces the ideas and expressions of Afro-Cubans as conveyed in their music, dance, visual, and literary creations. Overall, I argue that the Afro-Cuban case served as an avant-garde for black populations everywhere. Afro-Cubans were neither unique nor always first in their formulation of nationhood, citizenship, and modern culture, but overall they reveal a trendsetting case of black construction of postemancipation society.

It was wealthy planters who declared Cuban independence from Spain in 1868, but a cross-racial alliance developed, and people of color, slave and free, were among those who fought most relentlessly for independence. In ten years of war, Antonio Maceo rose through the ranks to become one of the most respected and uncompromising rebel generals. Yet Spain prevailed and regained full control of the island in 1878. To pacify blacks, the colonial regime adopted a measure for the gradual emancipation for the remaining slaves by 1886. Spanish reforms also opened the schools to people of color, and the resulting relatively high literacy of Afro-Cubans was reflected in the circulation of newspapers publicizing their legal and political claims. Sugar production expanded in the late nineteenth century, but now with U.S. investment in sugar mills and sale of cane lands to small sugar farmers known as *colonos*, most of them white, including immigrants. Chinese contract laborers had been brought in during the war, notably to work in cane fields. Other migrants arrived from Haiti and Jamaica to work in fields and mines. Cuban blacks, losing out in economic and legal contests to gain land in the sugar-rich center of the island, moved to the mountainous east.

Cuban nationalism survived its military defeat. A new prophet of independence, José Martí, arose to inspire the next campaign. Born in Cuba of Spanish parents, he was moved by the first war to call for "a nation for all and with all," sustaining the alliance of black and white from the first war. Martí wrote poetry, essays, and history on Cuban nationhood. His children's books were popular, portraying the place of Cuba in world history and civilization. Imprisoned whenever he came to Cuba, Martí spent the 1880s in New York as the consul for three South American nations. Martí prepared for rebellion especially in alliance with two heroic generals of the first war: Máximo Gómez, born in the Dominican Republic, and the Afro-Cuban Antonio Maceo. Yet Afro-Cubans pressed for reform as well as revolution: in Havana, Juan Gualberto Gómez led a campaign for urban rights. In response, in 1890, the Spanish conceded additional electoral rights to Afro-Cubans.

In the midst of this social tension, a musical fusion developed and gave form to the emerging national identity. The name given to this fusion was *son*: it began as the music of small rural bands but eventually became popular with urban audiences. Its antecedents were *rumba* from the slave and lower-class communities and *danzón* from white and middle-class communities. Drummers performed the *son* on sets of three barrel-shaped drums (known in Spanish as *tumbadora*, *conga*, and *quinto*, from biggest to smallest, and known in English simply as congas); smaller bongo drums and the marimbula (a bass version of the mbira) completed the ensembles.

Despite the popularity of Afro-Cuban music, there were pressures on black communities to abandon African traditions. White leaders and blacks aspiring for recognition by white society called for an end to the *cabildos de nación*, the African ethnic societies, and criticized Afro-Cuban religion as *brujería*, or witchcraft: they found these African traditions shameful. The African-descended population of Cuba at the end of the nineteenth century had declined to about 40 percent of the total from its earlier majority, but there were still fears that blacks would try to seize control of Cuba.

In February 1895, Martí and Gómez released the proclamation of independence drawn up by Martí: it restated the call for "a nation with all and for all" and explicitly urged black-white unity. Martí and Gómez landed in eastern Cuba, followed soon by Maceo and others. Soon rebel groups had formed all over the island. José Martí fell to Spanish bullets in June 1895, in the early days of the rebellion. In December 1896, as the combat had become more open, Antonio Maceo was killed when his group was discovered by a larger Spanish force. Gómez survived to lead the rebels, and by the spring of 1898, Spanish forces were on the defensive. Then in April 1898, the United

States intervened, turning the national Cuban conflict into a global contest between American and Spanish empires. The capture of Santiago de Cuba by an alliance of U.S. and Cuban forces brought the war to an end. Cubans were excluded from the peace negotiations in Paris, yet the United States would have to recognize the independence of Cuba.

The constitutional convention of 1901, held under U.S. military occupation, overrode U.S. recommendations and determined that Cuba would have universal manhood suffrage. That is, black men could vote regardless of their property, literacy, or previous status as slaves. This measure, which was never reversed, ensured that all political parties would seek the votes of Cubans of any color. The same constitution included the Platt Amendment, a measure enabling the United States to intervene in Cuba whenever it thought appropriate. In the initial occupation, lasting to 1902, American scientists consulting with the U.S. occupation forces declared Cuban blacks to be socially and intellectually inferior[Yet the continuing importance of veterans of the Cuban rebel movement—both black and white—was such that their alliance could not be denied even in this era of white supremacy.]

Parties formed: Moderate, Liberal, and Conservative. All sought black support, but none gave direct support to the needs of blacks. In response, a small group formed the Partido Independiente de Color in 1908. It received few votes in the presidential election but created a strong backlash. Martín Morúa Delgado, a Liberal Afro-Cuban member of the Cuban Congress, proposed a law making it illegal for a political party to be formed of people of any one race. The Morúa law was approved and the PIC outlawed. The law thus raised the question of whether it was possible, if blacks wished to be allied to whites, for them also to retain their own identity.

Shortly before the 1912 election, on the tenth anniversary of the Cuban republic, members of the PIC held an armed demonstration, parading in the eastern city of Santiago. Three weeks later, the Liberal president unleashed the army on the PIC and on many other blacks in the Santiago region, killing hundreds. Independent black action was discredited, and the number of black elected officials declined thereafter. But the Liberals were discredited too: the Conservatives castigated them for the murder of blacks, won the next election, and held power for years. Still, even in this era of racial polarization cross-racial groups nevertheless continued to function, as evidenced by the formation of the National Workers' Congress in 1914.[9]

All the while, the music continued, and with it the national passion of Cubans. As the *son* came to the city with migrants and musicians seeking work, a paired dance form developed out of the earlier line dances. Contests in Havana nightclubs developed the dance's most elaborate mode, while small parties in neighborhoods and villages sustained informal versions. At the same time, it became important to emphasize the African music's ancestry, and thus the term "Afro-Cuban" was coined, and it has remained as a descriptive term. By 1920, the *son* and Afro-Cuban music were known throughout the African diaspora.

Some of the instruments and the sounds were new, but some underlying patterns were old indeed. For the drums of the Niger-Congo tradition, the pattern was to sustain a repertoire with a wide range of percussion instruments, to modify the shape and sound of drums for performance of a new music and social function, and for the modified drums to be adopted everywhere the new music spread. The materials used for drums also changed—set screws ultimately supplanted nails and pegs to fix drumheads—yet the sound was essentially the same. Melodic instruments were added in larger numbers, but drums still provided the basic rhythm and served as solo instruments. This Cuban version of the Niger-Congo musical tradition adjusted easily to new technology and spread its influence widely in the twentieth century.

Education too remained a high priority in this country, which was already relatively well educated. Immediately after independence, Cubans of all descriptions poured into schools. By 1920, roughly 60 percent of Cubans were literate, nearly double the 1900 literacy rate, and the figures for blacks were quite close to those for whites. Blacks were a much smaller proportion of teachers than whites, but between 1900 and 1920, black teachers rose from 5 percent to 15 percent of the total.

The cultural flowering among Afro-Cubans was no simple response to political oppression. Neither was it a straightforward reaffirmation of ancient African values nor a leap into modernization. The many genres, audiences, and responses generated by this artistic outpouring, so riveting to the analyst, resist any clear categorization. Nevertheless, because of the heavily racialized interpretation of society in the twentieth century, the full range of cultural initiatives was somehow held together by the African ancestry of the artists, the subjects, and the audiences. Afro-Cubans, drawing on inherited techniques and genres, responded to the changes in their lives—especially emancipation, white supremacy, colonization, urbanization, nationalism, and industrial transformation—with expressions that affirmed their individual identity (in dress), the strength of their community (in communal music), the need for relaxation and entertainment after a day's work (in dance), and in many other feelings, conflicts, dreams, and frustrations.

Cuban politics slowly lapsed into dictatorship in the years from 1920 to 1950. Gerardo Machado came to power in 1925 as a Liberal, elected in place of an unpopular Conservative government. He began with a public performance of the *son* on his birthday and gained the initial support of the commoners. But by 1928 he was violating the constitution, pressing for a second term as president, and in 1933 he was overthrown by a popular uprising. After a brief interlude of popular reform that renounced the Platt Amendment, a U.S.-supported military coup brought Fulgencio Batista to power. Batista, who identified as white though he had Afro-Cuban ancestry, was able to retain power to 1958 and maintained popular support into the 1940s.

After 1929, the Great Depression caused incomes and public services to decline, and literacy rates began to fall, especially for blacks. In this era, and especially from 1937, the Cuban Communist Party rose in prominence through its support of trade unions and black-white unity in demands for employment rights and public services. A precarious balance of these forces continued through World War II and until the rise of the cold war. In 1947, Communist leaders were expelled from their positions in Cuban trade unions and in 1952, the Communist Party was banned. By 1950, Batista was relying on U.S. military support to retain power.

The emergence of the song "Guantanamera" provides an insight into the interplay of culture and citizenship in Cuba of the 1920s and 1930s. José (Joseito) Fernández, a young man of color from Havana, worked in the east in 1929 and composed a song based on an unsuccessful flirtation with a woman of Guantánamo. The chorus, "Guantanamera, guajira Guantanamera," includes a pun, in that the term *guajira* refers both to the peasant woman from Guantánamo and to the style of the song, a *guajira*. Back in Havana and still in his early twenties, Joseito gained a regular spot on radio programs, in which he used the song as a device for providing social, political, and cultural commentary. He adjusted the words of the song and the place and the woman to which it referred for the needs of each moment. The melody was not his own but had been known for decades, having emerged from the *son* tradition of the Cuban east. The song became important in the popular culture of Cuba in the 1930s, and it was to have an additional life several decades later.

During the social transformations of the 1920s and 1930s, the term *Afro-cubanismo* came to the forefront in cultural affairs. At the beginning of the 1920s, elite white and black cultural figures sought to deny and hide such aspects of black popular culture as *son*, *rumba*, and *Santería*: they favored an emphasis on Cuba's Spanish heritage. By the late 1930s, these same intellectuals had become fearful of the power of North American culture and the oppressiveness of the Cuban dictatorship, and they recognized the Afro-Cuban population and its cultural forms as the best defense of Cuban national culture. So they adopted the term *Afrocubanismo* to refer to the African heritage of the nation, though they still preferred to showcase music and dance that were far from the popular culture of black workers. At this same moment, a European and American craze for rumba brought additional prestige to an aspect of Cuban culture previously seen as "savage" by the elite.[10]

By the end of the 1940s, Afro-Cubans had done unusually well in advancing and sustaining their citizenship. Racial prejudice continued, unmistakably, but it was balanced by cross-racial alliances recognizing the place of Afro-Cubans in the nation and by the symbolic power of Afro-Cuban music's international prestige. The unusually high levels of Afro-Cuban literacy led to significant black employment in the public sector, which tended to offset the employment bias in the private sector. Yet economic inequality was unmistakable, and the era of depression and war weakened the economic and even educational position of Afro-Cubans. The Cuban nation as a whole found itself under the domination of foreign business and touristic interests and very close to an imperial power that was watchful and interventionist with regard to political trends in the country. Cuba had come far in the half-century since independence, and Afro-Cubans had benefited to a remarkable degree.

This review of Afro-Cuban campaigns for citizenship reveals some of the connections among class and racial groups, between politics and cultural production, and between local and global influences. The Afro-Cuban contributions became accepted as contributions to the Cuban national tradition, but with the disadvantage that sometimes the specifically black dimension of Cuban nationhood was forgotten. People in other regions of the African diaspora discovered similar stratagems for asserting their rights to full citizenship, perhaps in part through lessons learned from the Cuban experience and disseminated through the popularity of Cuban cultural production.

Rural and Urban Innovations, 1900–1920

The remainder of this chapter provides a dual narrative on a larger scale. Across the African diaspora, I trace the campaign for citizenship through major social processes and cultural commentaries of the black world. The social and cultural sides of the narrative correspond to the two main meanings of "citizenship" and to two main aspects of the strategy for gaining full citizenship. Citizenship, first, had the literal meaning of full political participation—the individual rights of black citizens in law and politics. By extension of that same meaning, citizenship granted to black people the recognition of their communities and community organizations. And especially for nations with dominantly black populations, citizenship meant not only individual rights but also the recognition of their right to nations—nations with the same status in international affairs as other nations, instead of being under the thumb of great powers.

Citizenship also had a figurative meaning, centered on the cultural recognition of one's peers—it meant freedom of expression, which, when exercised, brought esteem for the cultural accomplishments of blacks as individuals and in groups. Black people sought opportunities to express the loves, the joys, and the ambitions of full citizens rather than the laments of underlings. They hoped to receive the accolades of peers when they did well, to benefit from justice, to vote and to serve, to have recognition of their culture as valuable in itself and for its contribution to the larger society. Such a figurative citizenship in cultural affairs encouraged recognition of the political rights of literal citizenship. In this way, the early twentieth century brought interaction of the literal and figurative aspects of black campaigns for citizenship: cultural expression was not just a response to social life but was at times a way of creating the social conditions and roles of black people.

The details of black strategies for gaining full citizenship underwent wide and serious debate. The most famous example of such debate emerged, in the United States, out of the contrasting writings of Booker T. Washington (1901) and W. E. B. Du Bois (1903).[11] Washington, leader of the Tuskegee Institute in Alabama from its founding in 1888, favored practical training for blacks and an accommodationist approach in politics, in which black people would advance themselves by performing effectively within the boundaries set by whites. Du Bois, then teaching at Atlanta University, favored investment in the "talented tenth" of black youth and a more outspoken critique of racial discrimination to go with this focus on building a black elite. In every region, the advocates of confronting, accommodating, ignoring, and surmounting white supremacy found themselves in tension with one another, thus ensuring lively debate among black people at all levels regarding the best path to social progress. Leading figures who wrote and debated the strategy of black advance during the opening decades of the twentieth century included John Dube of South Africa, Blaise Diagne of Senegal, Kojo Tovalou-Houénou of Dahomey, Harry Thuku of Kenya, Manoel Querino of Brazil, and Jean Price-Mars of Haiti.

Gaining full citizenship required complicated strategies of race, class, and national identity. The task required cross-class alliances within black communities, cross-race alliances of blacks and neighboring communities, and ultimately diaspora-wide alliances of blacks. To tell the tale of the campaign for citizenship in the African diaspora, therefore, one must go beyond the lives of intellectual and political leaders: in practice, the most important advances for black people were those achieved in the lives of ordinary people. The interpretation here focuses especially on the anonymous members of black communities and those of other communities interested in social and cultural interchange with black people. Though unified in the desire for citizenship, black people had to campaign for it in a world divided by race and class. To tell the tale of the campaign, we need to keep track of class divisions, racial differences, and regional differences. Further, we need to keep an eye on the full extent of the African diaspora, to observe how a world of nations was crystallizing out of empires and understand the ways in which racial identity both hastened and slowed the formation of nations.

Blacks were distinguished by social class wherever they lived, even though they were linked to one another by racial category. (They were also separated by the regions and nations in which they lived.) Summarized simply, for postemancipation society these classes included rural communities (peasants, artisans, landless rural laborers, and a few large landowners), urban workers, the urban poor who struggle to achieve self-sufficiency, the business and professional leaders, and the political and social elite. The classes and class interests of black people, while different in each region because of the specifics of the economy, the historical experience, and the social organization, can be illustrated if not thoroughly analyzed by thinking in terms of class groups similar to those used to describe Afro-Cuban society in the previous section.

Racial categories relevant to the lives of people of African descent begin with the differences of black and brown within the community, the additional shadings of color among them, and the people of African ancestry who define themselves outside the black community. But other racial groups are important in the analysis. In Cuba, Afro-Cubans could only make progress toward citizenship in association with whites. Similarly, in other multiracial countries, blacks needed to reach accommodations with whites, Amerindians, Arabs, South Asians, and mestizos. (In Arab countries, despite all the intermarriage of blacks and Arabs, it is interesting that no separate "mixed" category has been defined—Arabic speakers are known as Arabs.) For countries that were majority black, their citizenship and nationhood were still in question until they gained recognition from nations dominated by other racial groups, especially whites.

In this narrative of a sixty-year campaign for citizenship, I alternate between social and cultural aspects of the story, a decade at a time. For the social side of the narrative, I explore the campaigns for literal citizenship in struggles over land, law, and elections as they interacted with the policies of imperial governments and the ideology of white supremacy. For the cultural side of the narrative, I emphasize expressive culture—especially music, but also dance, literature, visual art, film, and occasionally sports, plus religion and education. The narrative becomes tumultuous at times, shifting among rural and urban localities, national and diaspora-wide communities. But out of the tumult emerge the outlines of a remarkable era of transformation, in which black communities worked their way from the immediate consequences of emancipation to positions of citizenship and responsibility in national politics.

Society, 1900s

Black workers labored mightily in creating the twentieth-century world economy. Construction trades occupied many black workers—from earth moving by day laborers to carpentry and masonry by skilled artisans. The greatest construction project of all was the Panama Canal, on which thousands of Caribbean workers, especially from Jamaica and Barbados, worked for up to a decade. Many of them settled in Panama when the canal opened in 1913. The railroads of Africa were built in the early twentieth century, though they were meager and underfinanced reflections of those constructed earlier in Latin America, the Caribbean, and especially the United States. Railroads connected the lands to the oceans, and water transport linked the major ports. On all these lines of transportation, black workers were significant as wage employees, occasionally working their way up to key positions because of their skill. Maritime workers from the Caribbean took up jobs all around the Atlantic, building on their heritage in this line of work.

Most black people remained in the countryside, and most worked in agriculture. African peasant producers experienced considerable success in expanding cocoa and palm oil production in West Africa and coffee output in East and West Africa. Maize producers in southern Africa had initial success marketing their crops but were driven off their lands by white farmers in Rhodesia and South Africa. In Senegal, a steady expansion of peanut exports came about through the efforts of the Mouride Islamic order, which gained control of productive lands and put its believers to work on them. Slavery and forced labor persisted in Africa, though in 1905, the slave field workers in Banamba, in French West Africa, simply put down their tools and headed off in search of their homes.[12] Colonial governments throughout the African continent required farmers to grow cotton for sale, commonly at a loss. Most commercial cotton fiber came instead from the small farms and tenant plots of the U.S. South, produced now by free labor. In the Caribbean, sugar production expanded in the Dominican Republic and Cuba as it declined in other areas. Brazil's coffee industry was now challenged by that of Colombia and Guatemala. There were many ways to participate in building capitalism.

Industrial workers in the steel mills of Alabama, the gold mines of South Africa, the textile mills of Bahia, or the oil fields of Iraq labored according to an industrial discipline. Many more workers, male and female, earned piece-rates or hourly wages in the small firms servicing these great industries. Overall, three great classes of black workers arose in the twentieth century: a wage-earning proletariat, a self-employed peasantry, and a class of rural laborers and tenant farmers. In addition, the service workers and domestic servants of earlier times continued their work into the new century.

At the opposite end of the social order, imperial rulers organized the structure of politics and the economy. To begin with, empires provided control and discipline. Then they were to ensure production to cover the costs of administration and contribute to imperial advance. In colonial Africa, new systems of tax collection and administration were established by the regimes. African kings were now labeled chiefs, and as chiefs they were expected to serve as administrators for colonial governments more than as representatives of their constituents. Many people ended up paying double taxes, continuing old payments to their kings in addition to new payments to the colonial governments. Police systems set up throughout the continent also served as armies when it came time to put down rebellions; in fact, the roles of the police and army would remain confused in Africa for many decades.

In some cases, the imperial rulers acknowledged that colonial governments had gone too far. Stories began to leak out of the Congo Free State that agents of King Leopold's private government were using systematically murderous tactics to collect their quota of wild rubber. George Washington Williams, the African-American scholar and public figure, had traveled in Congo in 1890 and published a long, critical, open letter to Leopold but then died in 1891. In 1900, Edmund D. Morel, a British journalist who supported the British conquest of Nigeria, led in creating the Congo Reform Association to investigate and condemn the practices of the Congo Free State.[13] This movement's success led to the creation in 1908 of the Belgian Congo, with the Belgian government assuming control of the territory. Leopold lost his arbitrary power, but the Belgian colonial regime became heavily paternalistic, with church, state, and private companies all instructed to oversee the welfare of the inhabitants.

Migrants and stay-at-homes all had their social concerns, and the general search for the rights of citizens led black people to campaign for a range of specific reforms. Slavery must be the beginning of this discussion of social movements. Governments and anthropologists reported that African slavery was mild and provided many protections for those enslaved and argued that a hurried emancipation would be socially disruptive.[14] Since the widespread slavery of the African continent was largely forgotten outside the continent, those still in slavery had to rely on their own resources to gain freedom. In Sierra Leone, where Freetown had long been the center of liberated Africans, the government began emancipating the hinterland with a 1908 "free womb" decree, according to which the children of slave mothers would be free at age twenty-one.[15]

As the twentieth century opened, black people were virtually excluded from office throughout the diaspora; black electorates, where they existed, were small and commonly declining in size. With the exceptions of Haiti, Liberia, and Ethiopia, blacks rarely held executive positions in government; those who held high office were overwhelmingly appointed rather than elected. Representation to government relied primarily on pressure groups rather than parties. Petitions and demonstrations, rather than elections, constituted the principal activities in politics until after World War II, when the long processes of political mobilization began to bear fruit. One important pressure group was the National Association for the Advancement of Colored People (NAACP), founded in the United States in 1906 as an integrated organization. But it was telling for the times that the membership was overwhelmingly black and the leadership substantially white. An earlier organization, also relying heavily on the energies of lawyers, was the Aborigines' Rights Protection Society (ARPS), formed in the Gold Coast in 1897 to protest the proposed land law that treated all land as open to crown control. Auxiliary ARPS chapters developed in Nigeria and Sierra Leone starting in 1910. Yet another lawyer-based pressure group was the South African Native National Congress, formed in 1912 to oppose the Native Land Act, which removed most lands from access to African purchasers. Further, the Dahomean-born Kojo Tovalou-Houénou, who earned his law degree in France in 1912, became associated with the French human-rights organization *Ligue des Droits de l'Homme*.[16]

The problems facing black activists went beyond legal and economic limitations to include brutal intimidation, such as the practice of lynching in the United States. Vigilante mobs gathered to witness the execution, often by torture, of a person accused of a crime or offense. From 1880, the lynching of black men and women became a common practice in the American South, one that often followed accusations of rape or lustful behavior toward white women. The number of lynchings peaked in 1892. From 1900 to 1920, roughly sixty lynchings per year were recorded.

Overall, the social and cultural practices of black people in the early twentieth century coped in various ways with the dilemma of how to address the white-led hegemonic culture by confronting it, accommodating to it, ignoring it, or in some sense surmounting it. The ideology of white supremacy gave full credit to whites—what came to be known as Western Civilization—for creating the rapidly transforming world that was entering the twentieth century. In fact, construction of the modern world included a great deal more sharing and interaction than this interpretation allowed. More than that, the world of the twentieth century was evolving according to a global logic of its own rather than according to the plan of any select group, white or other. Black intellectuals addressed the distortions of white supremacist logic valiantly but without immediate success.

Culture, 1900s

For white supremacy to prevail, it was necessary to keep blacks—and other "nonwhite" communities—out of touch with one another. But the very spread of communication in this imperial era undercut the division on which white supremacy depended. White people who admired, shared, and appropriated the creations of blacks contributed, in their own way, to connecting black communities and challenging extreme forms of white supremacism. German culture historian Leo Frobenius and Belgian scholar Emile Torday reported in detail on the history and culture of the regions they visited in Nigeria and Congo. The sculptures purchased by European sailors along Africa's western coast appeared at the 1893 Chicago Exposition and began to enter museum collections in larger numbers and influence other artists. The brilliant young Spanish painter Pablo Picasso, for example, found what he was looking for in "conceptual art" in the sculptures of Dan and Grebo artists of Liberia (and other African artists) when he visited a Paris museum. The sculptures of Meta Warrick and the anonymous Liberians eventually circulated as widely as did the images of white superiority, and thus the condemnation of Africa and its cultural heritage, so widely accepted as the century opened, gradually weakened.

In the American South, for instance, music moved from rural to urban areas in a pattern similar to what occurred in Cuba. Blues music arose rather quietly in rural areas throughout the South, especially in the Delta area of the state of Mississippi, south of Memphis. The lyrics told individual tales of hard times, lost love, and bad luck. In this music, drums were of minor importance. The songs of hard times and heartbreak, often performed solo with guitar accompaniment, drew on the style of earlier work songs. W. C. Handy played an essential role in collecting, compiling, and composing blues music. Handy, born in northern Alabama in 1873, was a top student and a gifted musician who alternated between teaching and performing. From the 1890s, his tours in a minstrel band throughout the South (and in Cuba) acquainted him with a wide range of music and musicians. His famous compositions "Memphis Blues" (1912) and "St. Louis Blues" (1914) gave a name to the genre and showed that its popularity had spread to urban areas. Handy remained active as a composer and compiler of blues music until the 1940s.[17]

The works of black artists drew attention from white and black audiences, and some black artists produced increasingly with white audiences in mind. Ragtime music became a genre that fit this description: it was developed for black audiences in Missouri but rapidly became popular over a wide region and with white audiences. Ragtime music, played on solo piano or with a small band, developed before the turn of the century and reached the peak of its popularity among black and white audiences from 1900 to 1918, with later echoes and revivals in the 1930s, 1950s, and 1970s. The pianist Scott Joplin was the leading composer and performer of ragtime, most famously the "Maple Leaf Rag," which was distributed mainly through the sale of sheet music. Near the end of his life, he also recorded a number of piano rolls for player pianos. In addition, Joplin composed an opera, *Treemonisha*, telling the tale of an orphan girl found under a sacred tree who overcomes superstitious conjurers and provides education for her postemancipation community in the American South. The opera did not receive a full performance until the 1970s.

Jazz developed especially out of the New Orleans traditions of marching bands for funerals and small combos for night clubs. Here drums rejoined the black music of North America, thanks to the drum set or drum kit. Although the form of the drums owes much to European instruments, jazz drum sets were assembled in a group that facilitated multiple percussive sounds as part of a small band. The drum set thus fit the historic African tradition of a group of drums as musical foundation, and these instruments spread everywhere jazz went. Jelly Roll Morton became a key figure in popularizing jazz. Morton, who identified himself as a creole of color, had great initial success in introducing the jazz sound to cities from New York to Los Angeles starting in 1911.[18] Improvisation began to develop as the hallmark of jazz music. This urban music, upbeat in its musical form and lyrics, was played mainly to audiences of working-class blacks. By 1920, jazz music had spread to South

Africa and Europe, and it sustained local traditions in those regions as well as injecting innovations from the United States.

The broad appeal of ragtime and jazz represented early examples of "crossover." The actual term did not enter English usage until the 1950s in the United States, when it referred to black rock-and-roll musicians who gained a fan base among white audiences. But it is useful to apply the term more generally, since the concept has already been demonstrated in this narrative's description of the wide audiences reached by ragtime and jazz in the United States and the attraction of white art collectors and artists to African sculpture.[19]

With a timing little different from the previous cases, the music and dance of *merengue* blossomed in Haiti and the Dominican Republic in the early twentieth century. This rapidly paced music, with a simple beat that included regularly paced drum rolls, arose in the nineteenth century on both halves of the island, with each nation claiming to be the originator. This was music of the common people, more rural than urban. Military forces from the United States occupied both countries beginning in 1914. The presence of U.S. forces brought segregation to public facilities, but it also brought U.S. marines and Haitian and Dominican women together and introduced the island's music and dance forms to North Americans.

The spiritual side of African American rural life contributed as much to twentieth-century music as did the secular sounds of blues and jazz. The Negro spirituals of the nineteenth-century American South originated in the conditions of slavery. Sung a cappella by choral groups with male and female soloists, they drew especially on metaphors from the Old Testament to criticize slavery, express desires for liberation, and acknowledge the trials and tribulations of life. Drums were forbidden in most of the United States, but the spirituals remained percussive, through hand clapping, for instance. In postemancipation years, spirituals remained important in the church and social life of rural black populations. At the same time, they became attractive to more affluent communities. The Fisk Jubilee Singers at Fisk University in the post–Civil War era played a large role in formalizing spirituals for concert performance.[20]

Religious change continued in the Americas. Protestant churches were preponderant among blacks in the United States, though the denominations were numerous: Baptists, Methodists, AME and AME Zion churches, and many independent congregations. These bodies served as institutions of social welfare, and their ministers were members of a social elite. Catholic populations were largest in Baltimore and Louisiana, but they grew in other cities as blacks settled in areas where Catholicism was previously well established. Most blacks of Latin America and the Caribbean were Catholic, but a large minority shared or preferred the African-based religious practices of Candomblé, vodun, or Santería.

An unheralded but growing religious movement was that of Pentecostalism. This Christian movement, centering on possession by the Holy Spirit, originated in two stages. In Topeka, Kansas, in 1901, Rev. Charles Fox Parham of the largely white Holiness Movement observed the first instances of "speaking in tongues" (glossolalia) as confirmation of baptism in the Holy Spirit. He articulated the doctrine that speaking in tongues was the "Bible evidence" of that baptism. In 1905, the African-American preacher Rev. William J. Seymour learned of this tongues-attested baptism. As an invited preacher at a former AME church on Azusa Street in downtown Los Angeles, Seymour began the "Apostolic Faith Mission," which lasted for three years and helped thousands of participants receive the tongues baptism.[21] In this worship, clapping, shouting, and dancing facilitated the Holy Spirit's visitation. The worship of thousands of blacks and whites together under a black pastor added a social aspect to the religious experience. The basic concept of Pentecostalism, the visitation of individuals by the Holy Spirit within the practice of Christianity, was parallel to or perhaps inspired by Niger-Congo traditions of spirit possession.

Within a very few years, "Azusa pilgrims" had created congregations throughout the United States, especially the predominantly black Church of God in Christ and the predominantly white Assemblies of God. The Azusa pilgrims inspired other missions: a single American mission in South Africa led to the rise of the black Zion Christian Church and the white Apostolic Faith Mission. In Brazil, Swedish missionaries created the Brazilian Assemblies of God. With time, speaking in tongues and the direct experience of the Holy Spirit began to appear in other Protestant denominations and also among Catholics. Overall, this religious phenomenon of individual interaction with God seems to rely significantly on the spirit possession that historically had been well developed in Africa. One ironic consequence was that in Brazil, the Pentecostal movement long rejected any association with Afro-Brazilian religious practices.[22]

Black people in the early twentieth century found themselves caught between two conflicting views of the future. On the one hand was a vision of freedom, self-determination, and citizenship; on the other was a bleak picture of political and economic subordination and of social and cultural dependency ingrained after centuries of slavery, reaffirmed by racial categorization and fueled by imperial expansions and industrial work disciplines. Remarkably, communities all over the African diaspora in this difficult era found the resources and the will to respond creatively to these opposing expectations. In music, literature, and many other cultural arenas, black people created works that told the stories of their lives in striking, beautiful, and memorable terms. In so doing, these artists and performers spoke not only to their own communities but to black people more generally and beyond black communities to society as a whole. As a result, they deepened and transformed the cultural life of the twentieth century in general.

The cultural innovations came particularly from young working people both rural and urban. Some of their inventions, such as Afro-Cuban music, gained wide popularity after undergoing a transformation from local to cosmopolitan forms. The youth of these innovators, who were often in their early twenties, stands out in *son*, jazz, and dance. The middle classes too made their contributions to cultural change. It seems that educated black cultural figures did not replace or repress the culture of the untutored but rather studied, preserved, and built on it. W. C. Handy, for example, kept alive the work and spread the influence of unschooled blues musicians through his faithful transcriptions and his own compositions.

Society, 1910s

Land and land tenure remained central issues throughout the African diaspora, though the degree of black land ownership varied greatly from region to region. In the United States, blacks were rarely able to buy land except by migrating to areas outside the Old South. Elsewhere in the Americas, peasantries formed out of populations of free blacks, especially in Haiti, the Dominican Republic, Brazil, Venezuela, and Colombia. In the Old World diaspora regions of North Africa, Arabia, and the Persian Gulf, free blacks were able to gain modest land holdings. Sub-Saharan Africa was the great contrast, for there the great majority of the land was owned by local black populations.

Land remained a contentious issue. Governments subsidized land purchases by whites in the United States, Cuba, Brazil, North Africa, southern Africa, and East Africa. Governments also provided land grants or subsidized sales of land to corporations in the Belgian Congo, in French Equatorial Africa, in German Kamerun, in Cuba, and in other Caribbean territories. In African and Asian colonies, the colonial government claimed "unoccupied" land for its own disposal. In the United States, the Homestead Act provided an opportunity to gain title to unoccupied government land, and some blacks had been able to take advantage of this right. In Africa, land titles were held by oral contract, so governments could contest them. In the Americas, families of ex-slaves had often simply settled on land, working it for generations without formal title. In the Dominican Republic, this took the form of communal land holdings. In 1911, however, under the pressure of foreign sugar interests, the government abolished communal land holdings, and sugar companies were able to buy much of the formerly communal land. George Reid Andrews has labeled this set of processes as "enclosure," emphasizing that this was a general pattern, one echoing the earlier dispossession of peasant landholders in Europe.[23] The result was to force rural populations either to become agricultural laborers or move to the city.

The most extreme case of enclosure was in South Africa. There, following models from the United States and Algeria under French rule, the newly formed Union of South Africa adopted the Land Act of 1912, identifying "reserves" for the African ethnic groups and declaring that 90 percent of the land could only be owned by whites, while the remaining 10 percent of the land was to suffice for the 90 percent of the population labeled as nonwhite. The South African Native National Congress, led by black lawyers, formed in 1912 to contest this law.[24] They failed and soon also lost their rights to vote. But the organization persisted. Changing its name to the African National Congress in 1923, it remained in opposition for eighty years until it was elected to power in 1994.

Africans under European rule rapidly became discontented with the new regimes, especially as the colonial governments raised their demands for manpower and tax revenue. For the first two decades of the twentieth century, rebellions large and small broke out in every region of the continent. The 1915 rising led by John Chilembwe of Nyasaland is among the most famous, because Chilembwe was a Baptist minister who had studied in the United States. The 1905 rising of the Abe in the Ivory Coast shows how the French governor Angoulvant provoked a rebellion in order to force his superiors in Dakar to send in troops to burn numerous villages, collect indemnities, and "pacify" the colony.[25] Angoulvant's lesson, while rarely conveyed so forcefully, had become clear to colonized Africans by 1920: one needed to submit to the government and police.

Increasingly, therefore, enclosure pressed on young men and women to leave rural areas and seek work in the cities; once settled, they sent for their families to come as well. In the United States, black populations grew in the northern cities of Chicago, Detroit, and New York; in the southern cities of Atlanta and New Orleans; and in the border cities of St. Louis, Baltimore, and Washington. In mainland South America, black people moved similarly to the cities of Caracas, Medellín, São Paulo, Rio, Salvador, and Belo Horizonte; in the Caribbean, populations grew in Havana and San Juan. Migrants from Barbados, Jamaica, Trinidad, and the smaller islands sought employment on the Panama Canal, in the oil industry of Trinidad and Venezuela, in Cuban mines, on plantations of the Caribbean coast of Central America, and as seasonal agricultural workers in the United States. Caribbean maritime crews worked all over the Atlantic and set up port communities, especially in the United States, Britain, and France. Miners digging gold in Johannesburg and diamonds in Kimberley formed the core of growing urban populations. Blacks from the countryside of Morocco and Egypt joined the urban populations of Rabat and Cairo, and blacks in the Persian Gulf became workers in petroleum drilling and refining.

The overlapping institutions of army and police would be crucial to the lives of black people in the twentieth century. Normally, armies protect nations against foreign enemies and police forces keep domestic order within the community. Both provided prestige and social mobility to those who rose in their ranks. But often armies were used against domestic populations and police took to the streets to repress rather than protect. In Africa, most communities were disarmed and lived under the control of police forces and armies with African recruits and European officers. Conditions were similar in the Caribbean colonies. In the United States, there were few black police, as the urban race riots of 1917–1919 demonstrated. In Latin America, the numbers of black police were low compared to the size of black communities.

More than in the previous centuries, the twentieth century was dominated by military confrontation among great powers. The two global wars fought in the years 1914 to 1918 and 1939 to 1945 caused incredible destruction and loss of life. The presence of global and regional military action and posturing transformed the existence of black people wherever they lived. The homelands of black peoples were not the theater of major wars of the twentieth century, with some exceptions: Togo, Kamerun, Southwest Africa, and Tanganyika in World War I; Ethiopia with the Italian invasion of 1935 and North Africa in World War II. But wars shook up the established order, provided some opportunities for social mobility, and brought ideological change as well as opportunities for profit; mobilization and fighting were costly for those on the home front and for those in battle.

When war broke out in Europe in August 1914, it spread immediately to Africa. The German territories of Togo and Southwest Africa were immediately occupied by British and (for Togo) French forces. In Kamerun, the Germans held out for two years, and in Tanganyika the tireless and forceful General Von Lettow-Vorbeck resisted the British until after the armistice in Europe. Wartime meant forced labor for Africans, shortages of imported goods, and forced production of goods for the colonial government. The Senegalese Rifles, under French command, served on the front and as logistical troops in Europe. As the fighting wore on, Blaise Diagne, who had just won election to the Senegalese seat to the National Assembly, urged the recruitment of West African soldiers for the French army and convinced France to go along. Thousands were enlisted in 1918, most into the subject army of the Senegalese Rifles and some into the citizen army. Some of these advanced to citizenship and higher status.[26] Yet the same campaign of recruitment caused rebellions in several of France's West African colonies. As with the slave trade, in military recruitment doctors were used for triage rather than healing: they identified those fit for service and rejected the rest, offering them no further assistance. Recruits had no choice but to show up for induction. For Belgium during the Great War, the Congo was the only part of its territory not under German control.

When men in the British West Indies sought to volunteer for service in the war, their enlistment was opposed until the king and colonial secretary expressed an interest. A British West Indies Regiment was formed, separate from the regular army. No men of color were allowed to be officers, but A. A. Cipriani of Trinidad, of Corsican ancestry, became a captain in the regiment. These troops served mostly as labor battalions in Egypt. At the end of 1918, a portion of the group serving in Taranto, Italy, complained through their officers of discrimination and being assigned the work of laborers, not soldiers. The camp commander rejected the complaint and put the regiment under surveillance. On returning to Trinidad, these soldiers became a cohesive force for change, and Cipriani remained a reform leader for two decades.[27]

The United States entered World War I only in 1917 and then in the face of a strong antiwar movement. The United States also purchased the Virgin Islands from Denmark at the same time. Cuba, the Dominican Republic, Haiti, and Nicaragua, each under effective U.S. occupation, supported U.S. policy. Mexico produced petroleum of interest to both sides; the German Zimmerman Note to Mexico emphasized Mexican economic ties to Germany and slowed Mexico from following Allied policy. Other countries in the Americas declared neutrality until 1917 and then declared war, but they had little influence in the final peace conference.

After the war, the victorious powers seized the German colonies, dividing them among themselves while declaring the Germans to be brutal, ineffective rulers. Togo and Kamerun were divided among France and Britain, with France receiving the larger share; Southwest Africa was awarded to South Africa; and Tanganyika was divided among Britain and Belgium—the latter took over Rwanda and Burundi, two populous kingdoms bordering the African great lakes. Britain took from the Ottomans the lands that became Iraq and Palestine, leaving Syria and Lebanon to France. Later, the newly formed League of Nations ratified these appropriations, labeling them as Mandated Territories and requiring the colonial powers to send annual reports on their governance to the League.

The formal end to the war came with the Paris Peace Conference and the Treaty of Versailles (1919–1920). In addition to the great powers officially represented, many other delegations came to Paris to make their claims for recognition. Delegations from Egypt, Tunisia, India, and Vietnam came, along with a Pan-African delegation organized by W. E. B. Du Bois. These delegations, plus a 1921 delegation from the National Congress of British West Africa, were ignored by the great powers, but the colonial campaigns for nationhood and citizenship would not be dismissed so easily.[28]

Another central result of World War I was the Bolshevik Revolution in November 1917, which replaced the Russian Empire with the Soviet Union and put a communist party allied with workers and peasants into power. By 1921, socialist parties around the world had split, and communist parties formed in several countries of the African diaspora, challenging capitalism and racism: in Britain, France, the United States, Cuba, South Africa, Brazil, Iran, and India. Initially, the parties in Britain and France extended their influence to the empires of those countries; communist parties formed for other American countries in the 1930s.

The tensions of war and migration exacerbated the pattern of occasional antiblack riots in U.S. cities, leading to the huge 1917 riot of East St. Louis and then to as many as twenty riots in the United States during the summer of 1919. The largest uprisings of that year took place in Chicago; Washington, D.C.; Elaine, Arkansas; Charleston, South Carolina; Knoxville and Nashville, Tennessee; Longview, Texas; and Omaha, Nebraska. More than one hundred blacks were killed in these events; many more were left wounded and homeless. In Great Britain during the same summer, riots broke out in Liverpool, Cardiff, and London. Black communities, initially on the defensive, adopted a more militant stance in response to these attacks.[29]

Culture, 1910s

Dress is a basic element of culture—after all, one puts clothes on every day. At the same time, clothing and personal decoration communicate public comments and individual choices. They also play important roles for special occasions and celebrations. On the continent, African practices in dress had evolved over the previous three centuries through local fashion changes, textile imports, and borrowing from visitors. In the twentieth century, Africans faced direct pressure to adapt their dress to the standards of colonial masters as well as those of Christian and Muslim missionaries. Overall, however, the numerous, distinctive African styles clearly reveal a decision not to go over fully to the European style. The arrival of sewing machines throughout the black world at the end of the nineteenth century provided opportunities for innovation. In West Africa, for instance, a tradition developed that made fancy embroidery of men's shirts and women's gowns available to a wide constituency beyond the elite. The elaborate head wraps and gowns of women in Senegambia, the turbans in Muslim areas of the savanna, and even the simple dashikis worn by East African men affirmed an independence from European styles. With time, exchanges in dress styles between continent and diaspora became increasingly common.

Another central element in appearance and self-presentation is hair style. In Africa as in the Americas, continuities and changes in hair style for men and women provided a statement of social identity. Hairdressers and barbers served patrons in every black community. Madam C. J. Walker, catering to urban and upwardly mobile city people, became the first millionaire among African Americans through her development and marketing of hair-care products intended to grow and smooth the hair of black women. Born in rural Louisiana, she founded her hair-care business in St. Louis and in 1910 built the factory in Indianapolis that sustained her prosperity.

In some cases, one can trace the actual processes behind changing styles. Sally Price's research in the South American Dutch colony of Suriname reveals some dynamics of cultural innovation that probably have importance throughout the African diaspora. The men of rural Suriname wore capes made of large squares of embroidered fabric (see figure 5.2). Price collected and compared capes produced over the twentieth century and discovered a remarkable pattern in their evolution that she labeled "the centrality of margins." Seamstresses completing capes embroidered in an established pattern tended to add innovations at the edge, as they finished each piece. Over time, some of the embellishments not only survived but worked their way to the cape's center, only to be succeeded by new innovations beginning, as before, at the edge.[30] While the shape of the cape itself remained unchanged over the century, a succession of fashions in embroidered design appeared at the cape fringe and gradually moved to the center.

Visual art created in black communities appealed at times only to members of the community and at other times to broader audiences. Early in the twentieth century, black visual art consisted of folk art—recognized and collected for Africa but neglected everywhere else—and "academic" or professional art by those trained in painting and sculpture, especially in the United States. The work of academic artists in Latin America and the Carib-

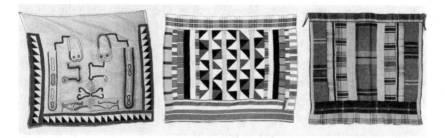

FIGURE 5.2 Saramaka Capes

Men's capes tailored by Saramaka women of Suriname, the first dated to 1900–1910, the second to 1920–1940, and the third to 1960s–1970s. Designs introduced at the margin of earlier capes work their way to the center of later capes, revealing the succession of styles.

Source: Photos courtesy of Richard Price and Sally Price. For more on
Saramaka textile arts, see Sally and Richard Price, *Maroon Arts:
Cultural Vitality in the African Diaspora* (Boston: Beacon Press, 1999).

bean included blacks as subjects, but blacks were not often the creators of such art. Recent scholarship has begun to assemble examples of turn-of-the-century visual arts from several traditions in the African diaspora—not only the work of African sculptors who inspired Picasso but also that of Cuban printmakers and installations such as bottle trees done in African-American rural communities. In Nigeria, a tradition of portraiture of elite figures in Yoruba cities originated early in the century.[31] Perhaps the best-known work of that time was that of academic artists in the United States. Meta Warrick Fuller was possibly the most prominent of these. As Meta Warrick, she had studied with the sculptor Rodin in France. In 1914, she created the *Awakening of Ethiopia*, a bronze sculpture of an erect young woman in pharaonic garb emerging from the wrappings of an Egyptian mummy. This work became an iconic statement of the unfolding renaissance in black creativity.

The progress of the twentieth century brought major changes in the language and literature of black people, especially in Africa but also elsewhere. The Indo-European languages of the Americas—English, Spanish, Portuguese, and French—came to be widely spoken in Africa as a result of Europe's conquest of the continent and thus expanded the dimensions of communication throughout the diaspora. Many African languages declined in influence under colonial rule, but some of them—Hausa, Swahili, Arabic, Yoruba, Lingala, and Wolof, for example—gained in influence and ultimately were reintroduced into the Americas. Hausa and Swahili, under imperial pressures, switched from the Arabic to the Roman alphabet. Yoruba, Zulu, and a few other languages developed significant bodies of text in the Roman alphabet under the sway of Christian missionaries. Amharic and Tigrinya of Ethiopia continued to be written in their own Semitic script; Somali, in the time of Muhammad Abdille's rebellion against the British from 1899 to 1920, was written in Arabic characters. The Afrikaans language developed more fully along with the political power of white Afrikaners; at the same time, over half the speakers of Afrikaans were people of color.

The twentieth century brought religious change to every area of the African diaspora but especially to Africa, where the rapid advance of Christianity and Islam changed the spiritual landscape. Christian missionaries from Catholic and especially Protestant orders flowed to Africa in the nineteenth century from Britain, France, the United States, and from such other countries as Germany, Sweden, Norway, Italy, Portugal, Canada, and more. They had the advantage of close cultural and perhaps political association with the colonial governments. The number of missionaries grew as colonial powers established their regimes more solidly. At the same time, black churches, especially in the United States, also supported missions in Africa.[32] While a wide range of issues in belief and ritual went through discussion during this expansion of Christianity, the question of polygyny came up particularly often. European and often African missionaries insisted on monogamy as a condition of membership in a Christian church. In the early days, converts were not uncommonly put in the position of breaking existing marriages in order to convert. On the other hand, some independent Christian churches allowed polygamy, and certain traditions of informal marriage or concubinage persisted alongside formal Christian marriage. Islamic missionary movements entered the twentieth century in association with the great states of the nineteenth century: those of Umar, Sokoto, Masina, the Mahdi, and even Samori. In the twentieth century, many more new believers were brought into the Islamic fold by religious orders and individual missionaries. Islam, spreading its word through the work of individual preachers and saints rather than with governmental support, gained as many adherents in Africa as Christianity.[33]

As with government, education changed sharply in Africa as the twentieth century opened. Schooling was mainly limited to the introductory level. In a few British territories, secondary schools and colleges allowed a small, overwhelmingly male number to receive education at levels that enabled them to become teachers, lawyers, clerics, and bureaucrats. Qur'anic schools in Islamic areas taught young children the verses of the holy book, basic literacy in Arabic, and calculation. Those who took their Arabic-language study to a higher level worked as interns with individual scholars, but no formal schools or universities existed for them to attend. For the great majority of African families, education still consisted of training from parents and instruction from elders at crucial turning points in life, such as the initiations that took place at adolescence.

In French territories, schooling was conducted in French only, primarily in state schools. A medical school for men in Dakar and a school for nurses were the main higher-level schools. The Belgian territories offered widespread primary education, mainly through mission schools, in four languages— Lingala, Kikongo, Swahili, and Tshiluba, plus Kirundi in Burundi and Kinyarwanda in Rwanda. There was some seminary education at advanced levels but no other secondary or university education. The British colonies offered strong government support for mission education, principally in local languages. Secondary schools, established rapidly in each colony, were conducted in English. Fourah Bay College in Sierra Leone and Fort Hare College in South Africa were the principal colleges in sub-Saharan Africa for most of the colonial era. In Portuguese colonies, Portuguese-language primary education in mission schools provided the only access to education; in Ethiopia, schools in Amharic continued for the elite. As Islam took hold in areas, Qur'anic schools spread quietly and usually without state involvement.

Throughout the diaspora, advanced training was available to small numbers of black men and women who were skilled, fortunate, or both. Medical and legal training were particular objectives of these students; it was possible to advance in the Protestant but not the Catholic clergy. In the United States, the Tuskegee Institute had gained great prominence as the center for Booker T. Washington's program of practical training. Howard University had become the most prestigious of the predominantly black schools; its first black president was appointed in 1926. Other leading schools, mainly founded at the end of the Civil War, were Hampton Institute, Fisk University, Lincoln University, and Wilberforce College. In addition to these private institutions, students of color could hope to gain access to public universities and colleges. Pedro Albizu Campos, for example, came from Puerto Rico to begin his collegiate studies at the University of Vermont. Students from Latin America, the Caribbean, and Africa generally had to go to Europe or the United States for college.[34]

Newspapers, even of small circulation, became very important to the development of black communities. The *Gleaner*, published in Kingston starting in 1804, began as the voice of Jamaica's planter class, but with the gradual rise of blacks to citizenship it ceded more and more space to their perspective. Black-owned newspapers were founded in Lagos, Cape Coast, Freetown, Havana, and Baltimore in the late nineteenth century, and in Chicago, São Paulo, New York, Los Angeles, and Paris in the early twentieth century. Writing also for literate black audiences were political activists such as W. E. B. Du Bois in the United States and J. E. Casely-Hayford, the Gold Coast lawyer and leader of the Aborigines' Rights Protection Society. Both published novels in 1911. Du Bois's *Quest of the Silver Fleece* portrays the choices between urban and rural existences, while Casely-Hayford's *Ethiopia Unbound* offers a vision of self-government on the Gold Coast. Yet another political figure, Solomon Plaatje of South Africa, was also at work on a novel, *Mhludi*, in 1911, but it was not completed until 1919 and was published only in 1930.

The limitations on university schooling for black people did not halt the development of scholarly analysis and intellectual debate. Samuel Johnson, of a well-established Oyo family, completed an extensive *History of the Yorubas* before his death in 1901; it was published in 1921. Solomon Plaatje published *Native Life in South Africa* in 1915 and a reader in SeTswana texts the next year. Washington and Du Bois carried out their famous debate on accommodation versus the "talented tenth" as strategies for black education. Du Bois later entered into debate with Marcus Garvey, emphasizing the dangers of militant nationalism. Garvey responded, echoing the earlier E. W. Blyden, that the "pure" Negro better represented the future than did mulattos.

A momentary high point in cross-racial discourse was the Universal Races Conference, convened at the University of London in 1911. It was organized by the German-born sociologist Felix Adler, founder of the Ethical Culture Society in New York. It gathered a remarkable array of intellectuals of various racial origins. Du Bois was a prominent participant; the meeting likely spurred his composition of his diaspora-wide overview, *The Negro*.[35] Dusé Mohamed Ali, a British-based intellectual of Egyptian birth and Sudanese ancestry, attended the conference, and soon thereafter started *The African Times and Orient Review*, a cosmopolitan monthly journal published between 1912 and 1918. The brutal national and imperial conflicts of world war, however, rendered such conferences impractical for many years.

So far, this account of twenty years of campaigning for citizenship identifies some impressive efforts at political advance and some equally impressive but more successful efforts at cultural innovation. Nevertheless, my narrative, while dividing the range of expressive culture by time period, social class, racial identity, and community, falls short of being orderly. The number of communities, artistic genres, and outlooks is too large to organize neatly. Dress is about individuals yet very much also about waves of fashion and how one wishes to be seen. Cuisine is about local communities, yet its elements come from everywhere. Music developed innovations in local communities, but sometimes the innovations gained devotees across great distances and cultural frontiers.

Nonetheless, I believe there is a coherence and a significance to the cultural production of the African diaspora in the twentieth century. To offer a musical metaphor, I argue that unifying this extraordinary variety of influences in cultural production is an underlying, polyrhythmic beat—a beat both literal and figurative. Shifting the metaphor, one can argue that the African Web—which linked the cultures and societies of Africa over the centuries—has extended to the diaspora, as ideas have been passed around systematically yet almost surreptitiously, invisibly. And while there have been leaders and stars in this social and cultural transformation, the essential impetus was the exchanges among ordinary people in each grouping.

Workers' Songs and High Culture, 1920–1940

The interwar years were a turning point for the ideology of white supremacy. Sophisticated calls for the rejection and replacement of African culture continued to echo throughout the black diaspora, and racial ideology became increasingly shrill among the expanding fascist and militarist parties—those in power in Italy, Germany, and Japan and those out of power elsewhere. At the same time, the sharp decline in European migration, the worldwide economic crisis, and the rise of an alternative vision in the Soviet Union and among its allied communist parties all tended to distract from race as the explanation of history. In this complex balance, the campaigns of black people for citizenship, including their growing linkage to one another, began to influence the overall pattern of social and cultural change.

Society, 1920s

The economic transformation of the twentieth century relied on new, expanded sources of energy: electrical and steam power, oil, and coal. The oilfields of Trinidad, Venezuela, Texas, and even the Persian Gulf depended substantially on black workers. So did the diamond and gold mines in South Africa and elsewhere in Africa, the tin mines in Nigeria, and the copper mines in Zambia and Congo. The deep gold mines of South Africa's Witwatersrand created an epidemic of tuberculosis among its workers and their families, as workers shifted daily between the heat of the mines and the unheated hostels in which they were housed. In Kilo and Moto, in the highlands of eastern Belgian Congo, as many as a hundred thousand recruits were put to work in placer gold mining under guard. The textile mills of Brazil, uneven in their success, also relied on black workers. Factory production developed in industry after industry. Caribbean migrant workers became seamen, port workers, construction workers, and agricultural laborers from Venezuela to North America and Europe. In the United States, black workers were important in the steel foundries of Birmingham and the textile mills of the Carolinas, in Chicago's steel and livestock industries and later in Detroit's automobile industry.

Drawing on this far-flung labor force was the most influential black social movement of the early twentieth century, the Universal Negro Improvement Association, led by Marcus Mosiah Garvey. Garvey was born in Jamaica and worked first as a printer. This artisanal background set much of his outlook, including his diaspora-wide perspective. He traveled throughout the Jamaican diaspora, visiting Central America, Britain, and the United States. While in Britain in 1913, Garvey worked as a printer on *The African Times and Orient Review* of Dusé Mohamed Ali, gaining an introduction to Islam from this mentor. He never met Booker T. Washington but was inspired by Washington's self-help vision. In 1916, Garvey settled in New York and there reorganized the UNIA and African Communities League that he had first created in Jamaica. The UNIA, with its statements of black assertiveness and destiny, suddenly gained immensely in membership in 1919 in response to the 1917 East St. Louis riots and subsequent attacks in Chicago and elsewhere.

The UNIA was aggressive in its reaction to these occurrences compared to the cautious response of the black elite characterized, for instance, by the NAACP. The UNIA began publishing *Negro World* in 1918 and sold copies openly and surreptitiously throughout the diaspora. Annual conventions and parades strengthened the organization and broadened its appeal. The UNIA sought not only to defend workers but to encourage entrepreneurs. The Black Star Line, incorporated in 1919, was intended to link the ports of the black world. At his height, Garvey declared himself provisional president of the Republic of Africa. But from 1922 he was on the defensive, especially because of an indictment for mail fraud spearheaded by J. Edgar Hoover of the U.S. Department of Justice. The charges claimed inaccuracies in solicitations of sales of Black Star Line stock. Internal dissension, the attacks of other black leaders, rejection by financiers, and government prosecution had their effect. Garvey served two years in prison and was released in 1927 to be deported to Jamaica. He later moved to England, where he died in 1940. Meanwhile, Garveyists in West Africa, South Africa, the Caribbean, Panama, and throughout the United States carried out local campaigns and often found themselves in trouble with officials. The echoes of the UNIA have yet to die down.[36]

While the UNIA focused on radical organization by race, communist and socialist parties focused on radical organization by class. Blaise Diagne, the first African elected to the French parliament (from Senegal in 1914) was affiliated with the French Socialist Party; the noted Trinidadian writer C. L. R. James was long a member of the Independent Labour Party of Britain; and Garan Kouyaté of Soudan (now Mali) organized transport workers on behalf of the French Communist Party. From the 1920s, black militants joined Communist Parties because of their anti-imperialist policies and their support for cross-racial unity—in Cuba, Sudan, South Africa, Venezuela, Brazil, the United States, and elsewhere. Many of these same militants, however, broke with communism when they felt that the party leadership had neglected the interests of blacks in particular or anti-imperialism in general.

Work in shipping and rail was especially susceptible to unionization. Labor organizations sprang up among African dockworkers in Marseille led by Garan Kouyaté of French Soudan, among railway workers in Sudan, among dockworkers in the Caribbean, and in the United States, with the Brotherhood of Sleeping Car Porters led by A. Philip Randolph. In South Africa in 1919, the immigrant worker Clements Kadalie helped found the Industrial and Commercial Workers Union (ICU), at first among Cape Town dock workers but then in other workplaces, as an industrial union that reached across specific trades. The ICU expanded dramatically to a claimed peak of two hundred thousand members, but Kadalie's arrest in 1928 and a split in the organization led to its rapid decline. Succeeding unions in South Africa were generally restricted to individual trades.[37] Kadalie lived out his life in South Africa as a supporter of the African National Congress. In Trinidad, the Trinidad Workingmen's Association formed in 1919 and successfully carried out strikes demanding wage increases for urban workers. The group also called for representation in the government for the general populace. In 1925, the first legislative elections in colonial Trinidad were held, with six elective seats for Trinidad and one for Tobago. The majority of legislators, however, were still appointed, and only 6 percent of the population was allowed to vote. A. A. Cipriani, president of the TWA, ran for the Port of Spain seat and held it for twenty years until his death in 1945.[38]

Remnants of an earlier system of labor survived, however, in Africa and parts of the Old World diaspora. In northern Nigeria, the former Sokoto Caliphate, elite men of the 1920s were still able to round up young women of their choice from non-Muslim villages to become concubines. Indeed, the documentation of concubinage in northern Nigeria of the 1920s is probably the most thorough available anywhere on that institution, though its practice doubtless survived in Arabia and parts of North Africa as well. And the government of Liberia was implicated in a scandal in the 1920s, when contract laborers recruited for work in the Spanish territory of Fernando Po were shown to have been enslaved.[39] This survival of slavery-like patterns, permitted by both imperial and independent governments, slowed the campaign for citizenship both locally and diaspora-wide.

Campaigns for political recognition went ahead regardless. In West Africa, African leaders of the four British colonies (Gambia, Sierra Leone, the Gold Coast, and Nigeria) lobbied for creating a united dominion on the model of those recently established in South Africa and Australia, but British officials rejected this proposal in 1921. In the French African territory of Dahomey, leaders of wealthy families sought French citizenship early in the century and by the 1920s began a series of newspaper campaigns to change government policy, partly by drawing attention to human-rights issues but especially by calling for more support of local business. When elections for three places on the Administrative Council were first held in 1925, Dahomean merchant Pierre Johnson won a seat. In the next election in 1928, Johnson and two colleagues swept the three seats.[40] Their election campaigns transfixed the colony, but still only a few hundred were able to vote. Over the next ten years, the government sought local allies against this nascent political party, put the owners of the main newspaper on trial, and eventually succeeded in derailing the movement.

Culture, 1920s

In the decades of the 1920s and 1930s—between the two great wars—new media entered popular culture. Radio, phonograph records, and motion pictures became widely available in the Americas and Europe, though less so in Africa and Asia. The black audience for these media was primarily urban working people. At one level, this period was one of separate national audiences. Nevertheless, transnational movements of black culture were also unmistakable.

The music recording industry expanded rapidly, and soon records were selling more than a million copies in the United States. In the 1920s, Bessie Smith became a recording sensation in blues music. While both jazz and blues traditions continued to evolve, the explicit emphasis on improvisation in jazz gave it a basis for evolving in multiple directions without losing its basic character. At the same time, jazz music crossed over to white musicians in the United States and in Europe and to black musicians in South Africa. Cuban musicians joined the U.S. music scene, especially in New York, so that son and jazz interacted from early on. In the early 1920s, a young New Orleans trumpeter with astonishing technical and musical skills, Louis Armstrong, gained a prominence that he would maintain for another half century. Amid these sounds, a heroic iconography of the black worker emerged in the 1920s, reflected notably in the murals and posters of Aaron Douglas. Newspapers such as the *Negro World* (New York), *O Clarim d'Alvorada* (São Paulo), and *Les Continents* (Paris) carried images of hulking, dark, young workers wielding their tools to produce goods and provide services—and also to defend themselves.

In contrast to these works aimed at an elite black audience and at whites ready to accept a black perspective, the remarkable dancer and singer Josephine Baker broke through to the widest levels of popularity in Europe. Baker began as a comedienne and dancer in her native Missouri, danced in New York, then arrived in Paris at age nineteen in 1925, where she immediately became a star in "La Revue Nègre" at the Théâtre des Champs Elysées, where, costumed in nothing but a feather skirt, she performed the "danse sauvage" with Joe Alex. She became most famous for "La Folie de jour" at the Folies-Bergère, where she was costumed simply in a skirt of fabric bananas (figure 5.3).[41] Her act drew on nudity and stereotypes of savages but also on visual gags and elegance, and she gained an immense following and unprecedented salary.

Marian Anderson, the operatic contralto from Philadelphia, was a performer of quite a different sort. After a childhood in church choirs, she worked with the Massachusetts-born black tenor Roland Hayes during her high-school years and adopted his practice of including spirituals in her classical recitals. Anderson then studied and toured in Europe in the 1920s and 1930s. She became most famous for singing German lieder and for her rendition of Schubert's "Ave Maria."

Movements to urban and industrial centers had just as great an effect on the expressive culture of South America. In Colombia and Peru, similar developments of music in black communities led to great popularity of new domestic forms, though not to much international impact. In Colombia, music known as *costeño*, referring to the Pacific coastal communities of black Colombians, developed through small bands that gained access to radio and recording beginning in the 1920s. Peter Wade has argued that the *costeños* were the Colombians who moved into Medellín and later Bogotá to work in the expanding industrial sector, and their music caught the essence of that urban lifestyle and so became relevant to succeeding urban settlers of other ethnicities.[42] Also in the 1920s, music known as *criollo* developed in Afro-Peruvian communities of the Peruvian lowlands and gained popularity in the cities. While the term *criollo* or "creole" has generally been controlled by white communities in Latin America, in this case *criollo* is clearly a reference to black people and to African cultural heritage.

The samba of Brazil and the beguine of Guadeloupe and Martinique reflect parallel developments of early twentieth-century urban musical tra-

FIGURE 5.3 Josephine Baker, c. 1926

Publicity photo based on Josephine Baker's performances at the Moulin Rouge, c. 1926.

Source: Roget-Viollet.

ditions that appeared principally in black communities. The beguine, played at a very rapid clip by groups of about ten players, relied heavily on wind and string instruments and laid the groundwork for the later *zouk*. In Brazil, the adoption of the samba beat was only part of a popular revival of Afro-Brazilian forms during the 1920s, which included a reorganization of Carnival to emphasize Afro-Brazilian music and dance. The tradition of "sambas," meaning parties and dances accompanied by drumming, had been long sustained in secular community life and also in the musical accompaniment to Candomblé ceremonies. Sambas now led to music and dance that became central to Brazil's national popular culture. The creation of major dance troupes with elaborate costumes to celebrate Carnaval in Brazil's twin cultural capitals of Salvador and Rio thus dates especially to the 1920s.

On both sides of the Atlantic, growing city populations created cosmopolitan centers where young people developed new forms of entertainment. Phyllis Martin has shown that migrants from the French Caribbean who settled in the 1920s and 1930s in Brazzaville, the capital of French Equatorial Africa, spread the sounds and instruments of Caribbean music.[43] Soon thereafter, musicians in Brazzaville—and in Leopoldville on the southern bank of the Congo River—began adopting Cuban rhythms and techniques and the Spanish language into their music. In addition, the presence of black Frenchmen from the Caribbean made it possible for young men from Brazzaville to join in football (soccer) games that were otherwise restricted to whites. From such bases as this, soccer spread to groups of boys throughout the continent.

In the Dominican Republic, the expanding barrios at the edge of town where poor people congregated gave rise in the 1930s to *bachata*, a form of sad music relying on guitars and maracas. Meanwhile, Rafael Trujillo, the long-term dictator of the Dominican Republic in the aftermath of the U.S. occupation, sought to strengthen his popular position by supporting a nationalized version of merengue, the more upbeat music and dance developed earlier. In addition, the slow, romantic *bolero* became popular among the middle classes of Santo Domingo, as it did in all other Spanish-speaking cities of the Americas.

For all these types of music, the availability of recordings on cylinders or disks was central to their dissemination. For eastern Africa, the early, rapid growth of British-dominated record industries in Egypt and in India helped expand musical culture. The most famous East African singer in the 1920s and 1930s was Siti Binti Saad of Zanzibar.[44] Born in about 1880 of parents with roots on the African mainland, she left her parents' village at about age thirty and moved to Zanzibar town, where she joined with a prominent violinist and learned to sing in the Arabic language and the Egyptian style known as *tarabu*. She sang as a soloist paired with a solo violin, backed with more strings and other voices. Her innovation was in singing *tarabu* songs in Swahili, though she continued to sing in Arabic and Hindi. Siti Binti Saad rapidly gained wide popularity, playing at clubs, ceremonial gatherings, and private parties, especially at evening festivities during Ramadan. Her style became famous throughout East Africa. In 1928, she traveled to Bombay to record songs in Swahili for the Gramophone label. Her success spread the prestige of the *tarabu* music and Swahili, and others imitated her style.

In the same region and time, another genre, a dance style known as *lelemama*, developed among women of Mombasa. In this genre, women created uniform costumes and gathered into rows, dancing sedately and singing songs that critiqued errant community members or the dancing abilities of other *lelemama* associations. One group, Kilingi, took its name from a noted warrior of Kamba ethnicity; another, Scotchi, wore costumes based on Scottish regimental garb. While freeborn women of important families contributed to the associations, the dancers were strictly slaves or ex-slaves. Even then, out of concern for modesty in this Muslim port town, the *lelemama* associations performed their dances privately. In addition to providing leisure-time activity and a venue for social critique, the *lelemama* associations served as mutual-support groups, and those elected to office within them gained prestige and influence. In the second generation of *lelemama*, from the 1930s, groups of women danced down public streets. Mombasa conservatives frowned on such displays, but some of the women's husbands cheered them on from the sidelines.[45]

Almost every region of the African diaspora saw musical innovations develop in conjunction with the social changes of the early twentieth century. In the mines of South Africa, where thousands of male workers lived in single-sex compounds, the men began performing in a cappella choruses and dance groups to the percussive beat created with the rubber boots they wore to work. This tradition spread north through the gold mines of southern Rhodesia to the copper mines of northern Rhodesia and the Katanga region of the Belgian Congo.

Somewhat akin to music and dance, film and sport provided venues in which black participants and black audiences were able to create occasional impacts. Oscar Micheaux, a pioneer film maker, shot and distributed numerous films to black audiences in the United States in the 1920s and 1930s. Paul Robeson, working in Britain, made several films emphasizing racial conciliation between whites and blacks and seeking to link diaspora blacks to Africa. One such film is his 1936 *Song of Freedom*. In sport, the heavyweight boxing champions Jack Johnson and Joe Louis became major symbols of black achievement, as did the runner Jesse Owens. More often in the early twentieth century, however, black athletes were segregated, as in the Negro baseball leagues of the United States. Along with the cross-racial practice of Brazilian *capoeira*. An important exception was cricket, where the West Indian teams developed great strength at the international level and individual West Indian players came to prominence in Britain.[46]

Meanwhile, a hymn appeared among Xhosa-speaking Christian communities of South Africa during the 1920s that gained popularity across the country. "Nkosi Sikelele Afrika," sung a cappella by a choir or community, called in eloquent tones for recognition of Africa as a nation and an end to suffering. Crowds singing this hymn shared in the powerful sense of destiny generated by its beautiful tones.[47]

Nkosi Sikelel'i Afrika	Lord God bless Africa
Maluphakanyisw'uphondo Iwayo	Let its fame be lifted up
Yizwa imithandazo yethu	Listen and hear our prayers
Nkosi sikelela	Oh Lord God bless
Thina lusapo Iwayo	We children of Africa
. . . .	. . . .
Morena bolota setjaba sa heso	God bless our nation
Ofedise dintwa le matshwenyeho	And stop all wars and suffering
O se bolote	And bless it
O se bolote morena	And bless it Lord, Oh God
Setjhaba sa heso	Bless our nation
Setjhaba sa Afrika	Our nation, Africa
Nkosi Sikelel'i Afrika	Lord God bless Africa
Maluphakanyisw'upondo Iwayo	Let its fame be lifted up
Yizwa imithandazo yethu	Listen and hear our prayers
Nkosi sikelela	Lord God bless us
Nkosi Sikelel'i Afrika	God bless Africa

The song and the manner of its performance indicates the growing assertion of nationhood and citizenship rights among black people along with the esthetic character of this claim on national destiny. Slightly different versions of the hymn developed, especially as it was translated into additional languages. The African National Congress, the South African political organization calling for citizenship rights for Africans, adopted "Nkosi Sikelel'i Afrika" as its hymn.

Remarkable achievements in black culture also emerged in New York City's Harlem during the 1920s. There, a literary elite, not wealthy but well educated and widely read, had a decade of resounding success: the Harlem Renaissance. The impetus for the Renaissance came from black people beginning to move in larger numbers to New York at the start of the twentieth century. They settled comfortably at the island of Manhattan's northern end. Then a series of key black figures came to Harlem. James Weldon Johnson left the U.S. diplomatic service and moved to New York in 1914. W. E. B. Du Bois moved from Atlanta to New York in 1910; Marcus Garvey arrived from Jamaica in 1916. After 1920, a flood of talented young writers arrived and benefited from each other's presence: Langston Hughes, Countee Cullen, Zora Neale Hurston, and Claude McKay were but a few.

Carter G. Woodson, in contrast, focused on building institutions for the study of black history. Woodson received a Ph.D. in history from Harvard University in 1912. While teaching high school in Baltimore, he led in forming the Association for the Study of Negro Life and History and the *Journal of Negro History* in 1916, and in 1926 he spearheaded the establishment of Negro History Week in February, the month of Frederick Douglass and Abraham Lincoln's birthdays.[48] Woodson also wrote widely and, along with Du Bois and William Leo Hansberry of Howard University, sought to link ancient Africa in general and Egypt in particular to the heritage of modern blacks.

By 1925, some of the literary and critical output of these writers came together in an anthology published in *Survey Graphic*, a magazine of progressive social reformers. Alain Locke, a professor of philosophy at Howard University, edited the collection, and it was republished immediately as a book, *The New Negro*. The volume's poems, fiction, and essays showed a concern for contemporary issues among urban blacks but also identified with African and Caribbean cultural heritage and the rural United States. Nathan Huggins, a major historian of the Harlem Renaissance, argued that this literary movement was an essential step in the development of black culture worldwide, though its activity was soon limited by the economic realities of the 1930s depression.[49] Ironically, however, over time it was Harlem that came to be celebrated rather than the black world's wider cultural connections.

[One recurring issue for black authors was whether to write in standard English or dialect.]Claude McKay occasionally attempted to capture the patois of his Jamaican homeland, and Zora Neale Hurston faced this issue in her analyses of Florida folk culture. In the 1930s, as a mix of black and white interviewers recorded recollections of aged former slaves for the Works Progress Administration, they adopted the convention of trying to reproduce the speech of the respondents. But no recognized written versions of Black English came out of these efforts. Even the Kreyol of Haiti, universal as a spoken tongue, became a written language only late in the twentieth century.

A parallel French-language network of creativity linked the Caribbean, France, and West and Central Africa. Jean Price-Mars, born and educated in Haiti, at a mature age wrote the anthropological *Ainsi Parla l'Oncle* (1928).

Other French-speaking intellectuals tended more toward literature and political essays. René Maran, born in Martinique, served in the French colonial administration of Chad. His novel *Batouala* (1921), a sharp critique of French colonialism and its effect on African life, won the prestigious Prix Goncourt. Thereafter, Maran joined with Kojo Tovalou-Houénou, a lawyer from a wealthy family in Dahomey, to publish a newspaper, *Les Continents*, where he became embroiled in a suit for defamation based on his reporting.

The always complex labels of identity for black people underwent periodic change during the twentieth century, as they had previously. As emancipation from slavery became more broadly assured and the focus of black activism turned more to gaining basic rights as citizens, new terms defining their identity gained popularity. In the United States, the word "colored" was replaced in most public discourse with "Negro" by 1915. The use of the latter was confirmed in Harlem with the rise of the "New Negro." A parallel and much broader transformation in identity was also taking place: in Jamaica in 1914, the Universal Negro Improvement Association came into being; during the 1920s, the term *nègre* was adopted in French-speaking areas of Africa, the Americas, and Europe; and also in the 1920s, the general term *negro* was revived in Brazil, where the terms *preto* and *pardo* had otherwise been used for black and brown.

On other levels, black people had to sort out their identities in the national, ethnic, imperial, and racial structures within which they lived and interacted. In the Caribbean and mainland Latin America, the larger number of racial and national communities complicated the notion of dualities. The Amerindian populations of mainland Latin America and the mestizo populations of the same areas left countries with more groups: white, African, Amerindian, and mestizo. In the Caribbean, while Amerindian populations were not numerous, other immigrant groups added white, East Indian, and Chinese settlers to Afro-Caribbean populations. In each case, one faced the question of whether to treat mixed populations (formed from black and white, black and Amerindian, and white and Amerindian individuals) as separate social groups or as a part of the black, white, or Amerindian population.

In South Africa, a parallel process of migration and mixing had left groups known as white, black, "colored," and Asian (each with identifiable subgroups, such as English and Afrikaners among the whites, Christian and Muslim among the colored, and various ethnic groups among the blacks). White academics there developed the notion of the "plural society" to use as an analytical term and exported it with some success to the Caribbean. This term, and the policies associated with it, tended to play the communities off one another and to sustain white leadership. It emphasized the boundaries between communities in contrast to the Latin American focus on *mestizaje*, or "mixing."

One vision of *mestizaje* was set forth memorably by José Vasconcelos, a former education minister in Mexico, in a 1925 essay entitled "The Cosmic Race." He urged the biological and cultural fusion of all races as a way to ensure social peace. This vision of an expected long-term consolidation of distinctive ancestries fit with the populist politics of the interwar years and with the studies undertaken by white scholars on black communities.

A somewhat different vision of mixing was that of *hispanidad*, which was articulated by the Puerto Rican scholar and activist Pedro Albizu Campos. Albizu Campos, the mulatto child of a black woman and white man who married after his birth, excelled in school and studied at Harvard but was then denied academic positions in the United States because of his color. He became active in the Puerto Rican nationalist movement and in the course of his theorizing developed the notion of *hispanidad* as a cultural umbrella for all who had been under Spanish tutelage, allowing a common identity of people of European, Amerindian, or African ancestry. Albizu Campos maintained his militant nationalism. He was jailed in 1936 and again in 1947 for his association with attempts to overthrow the U.S. government of Puerto Rico. (The term "Hispanic" became a U.S. census category years later and was used to denote all persons from a Spanish-language tradition.)

In the same era, African identities were modified, partly by colonizers, partly by pan-Africanism. The many divisions of ethnic and language groups within colonial territories provided multiple alternatives for identifying oneself. For example, a woman of the city of Dakar in French West Africa might have thought of herself as a Dakaroise, as of Wolof ethnicity, as Senegalese, as a subject of French West Africa, or as French—or, indeed as an African or a black woman. Each of these identities had its logic, but it was not obvious that one of them would be, dependably, her primary identity.

Society, 1930s

British and French empires reached the peak of their strength in the 1930s, especially in Africa but also in the Caribbean, Asia, and the Pacific. Systems of taxation, administration, and research were routinized, and an air of permanence settled over them. Was it possible that the people of the colonies would retain a permanent political connection to the nations that governed them? One reason for questioning the colonial regime's permanence was the jealousy arising in Germany and Japan that soon brought another war.

Another indication of impermanence appeared with the Great Depression of the 1930s. After the Wall Street financial panic, industrial production collapsed in the North Atlantic, followed by an even more serious collapse in the demand for agricultural products, causing prices and incomes for rural people to fall to a fraction of their earlier levels. Governments, lacking tax revenues, tried to raise taxes but ended up cutting services. African producers of cocoa, coffee, sisal, and peanuts tried to respond by expanding their volume of output, but only ended up with losses. One response to the crisis was a return to self-sufficiency: in depression and war years, when imported goods became impossible to get, people brought out the hand looms and increased the amount of their local textile production.

The economic crisis coincided with a virtual end to white migration. For Latin America, this meant that the demographic balance began to shift back toward black and brown people, and it reinforced a decline in the vision of "white republics." In the other areas of white immigration—the United States, the Caribbean, and parts of Africa, the vision of white destiny began similarly to give way to visions of racial accommodation.

Social conflict arose from economic dislocation. In the Dominican Republic, where the expanded sugar industry of the 1920s had brought many Haitians across the border dividing the island to become cane workers and to set up independent farms, President Rafael Trujillo determined that they were a threat to stability of his regime. In October 1937, his troops, aided by vigilantes, massacred at least fifteen thousand people of Haitian origin in the west of the Dominican Republic. This was an extreme example, but it fit into the increasingly merciless approach to conflict in that era.

The growth of industrial employment in the boom of the 1920s, followed by the massive layoffs of the 1930s, brought an expansion of labor organization within industrial workforces. Only gradually did black workers gain a substantial place in core heavy industries, such as steel and automobile production. Much more rapidly, however, black workers became important in transportation industries, light manufacturing, and mining. Uriah "Buzz" Butler spearheaded the organization of oilfield workers in Trinidad, an effort that peaked in a 1937 confrontation that paralleled a somewhat earlier strike of oil workers in nearby Venezuela. Railroad unions formed in French West Africa in the same era, and the Congress of Industrial Organizations in the United States gained influence in the automobile, electrical, and steel industries.

Of importance beyond their numbers in the labor struggles and social struggles of the 1930s were members of communist parties in every region of the African diaspora. Among the best documented groups was the Alabama

Communist Party. Other groups of black communists had significant success in building their movement in New York, Chicago, Cuba, South Africa, and Sudan. Communist parties formed in several countries of the Americas during the 1930s, including the Dominican Republic and Haiti. Garan Kouyaté of French Soudan organized actively among maritime workers in France; I. T. A. Wallace-Johnson organized workers in Sierra Leone. In practice, the activists of these communist parties worked most systematically in organizing workers and community members in their home areas, but they also sought to sustain the idea of cross-racial and transnational cooperation, and they did so especially by following leadership from the Soviet Union. For this reason, many black labor leaders and cultural leaders visited the Soviet Union during the 1930s, and some settled for long-term stays. George Padmore of Trinidad, who studied at Howard University in the United States, became an organizer and newspaper editor in Germany and then moved to Moscow, where he became an official of the Communist International.

The prelude to World War II came in Africa, when Italy invaded Ethiopia in 1935. Just at the end of the Spanish Civil War, Mussolini announced that Italy intended to gain control of Ethiopia, which it had failed to do in 1896. When his country came under attack, Emperor Haile Selassie fled, traveling to Geneva to address the League of Nations and call for support of Ethiopia's independence. The league declined to take any serious action and made its ineffectiveness clear. As Ethiopian troops fought for some months, black people throughout Africa and the diaspora took up a cry for defending Ethiopia against Italian conquest. While those campaigns had little effect on the Italian troops, they created organizations and networks that would be of great importance in coming years. Italy governed Ethiopia from 1936 to 1942, but once the general war broke out, British troops from British Somalia, Kenya, and Sudan rapidly displaced the Italians. After some years of military government, Ethiopia was returned to the monarchy of Haile Selassie.

Culture, 1930s

As memory has reordered the past, Harlem has come to be seen as the beginning and center of the black cultural Renaissance. While there is no doubt that the Harlem of the 1920s reflected a uniquely polished and advanced hub of cultural production, the perspective of the African diaspora puts it in a broader context. The elite artists of Harlem, rather than creating the Renaissance, drew on the outpouring of creativity that had been going on for decades in the countryside and cities across the continents. Harlem was a node in the expanded African Web. Even as Harlem declined as a center of black creativity in the 1930s, the overall creativity of the African diaspora continued unabated. Significant afterthoughts of the Harlem Renaissance appeared in the painting of William Johnson and especially in the work of Aaron Douglas. Douglas's angular works effectively conveyed a connection to African sculpture and also to the proletarian and Art Deco ethos emerging at the end of the 1920s and well into the 1930s.

An updated musical tradition appeared in the United States with the big bands and the swing tradition of the 1930s, especially under Count Basie and Duke Ellington. If the development of swing music is hard to pin down, the emergence of its accompanying dance, the Lindy Hop, seems clear. Key developments took place in the Savoy Ballroom in New York where, in the 1930s, the young Frankie Manning became the lead dancer and key choreographer. The showy and athletic movements of paired dancers drew in part on earlier cakewalk movements but went well beyond them. This dance craze, despite its popularity, did not yield the prestige of the preceding Harlem Renaissance in literature. It relied instead on ballrooms, big bands, and young people with leisure time and some spending money. It too crossed over to white audiences.

In the 1930s, a poetic movement known as *Négritude* arose, led by Léopold Sédar Senghor of Senegal and Aimé Césaire of Martinique. The two collaborated in producing a small periodical, *L'Etudiant noir*, in the late 1930s. Senghor's lyrical poetry celebrated the beauty of African bodies and cultural forms; Césaire's "Return to my Native Land" (1939) excoriated colonialism in Martinique. A wave of other African and Caribbean authors writing in French built on their achievements in the post–World War II years. Elsewhere during the interval between the two world wars, black writers composed poetry, history, and fiction in Portuguese (in Portuguese Africa and Brazil) and in Spanish (in the Caribbean and northern South America) at a more local level.

In a rare but powerful demonstration of public racial tolerance, the noted contralto Marian Anderson found herself at the center of a national celebration. In late 1938, officials at Howard University sought to rent Constitution Hall in Washington, D.C., owned by the Daughters of the American Revolution (DAR), for an Anderson concert. When the DAR refused to allow a black artist to perform, President Roosevelt's wife Eleanor publicly resigned from the DAR and, in the aftermath, an outdoor concert was arranged on Easter Sunday at the Lincoln Memorial. Attendance was officially estimated at seventy-five thousand, seating was not segregated, and the half-hour concert became a national and international sensation.

Paul Robeson, born in the same year as Marian Anderson in nearby Princeton, New Jersey, gained entrance by exam to Rutgers University, became an All-American football player, and then a lawyer, actor, and singer. He appeared in a 1924 silent film of Oscar Micheaux, *Body and Soul*, then starred in nine films during the 1930s, including *Showboat* (1936), in which he sang his famous rendition of "Ol' Man River" in his sonorous bass-baritone voice. Most of his films, however, were made in England (and included African scenes). As with other artists, Robeson found less racial discrimination in Europe than in the United States. In later years, he traveled extensively, performing vocal recitals of folk, national, and operatic music that carried a message of popular unity and racial interaction to people all over the world, though he came to be widely shunned in his home country because of his association with the Soviet Union.

To condemn the waning practice of lynching in the United States, the New York teacher and unionist Abel Meeropol wrote "Strange Fruit" in the late 1930s and set it to music. He presented the piece to Billie Holiday, the young but already famous vocalist. In 1939, she recorded it, over the objections of her company; it became a commercial success. With time, the song became her signature piece. Its success reflected not only her artistry but growing general support for civil rights. The mob violence of lynching was peculiar to the United States, but examples of racially motivated murders of blacks could be found in colonial Africa and in the rural and urban areas of Latin America.

Musical innovations appeared in churches as well as nightclubs. As spirituals became concert music, gospel music emerged to take their place in the black community. This religious music, which originated primarily in the 1920s, shifted its attention to the New Testament and the story of Jesus and focused more on cities than rural areas. The songs replaced the stories of enslavement and freedom with the experience of being close to God. Mahalia Jackson, who moved from New Orleans to Chicago as a teenager, rapidly became a leading voice in local churches. She began recording in 1937. Her lively and emotional style conveyed the sense of spiritual possession that grew within gospel music.

A related trend in literature and social analysis was the work of writers from outside black communities who drew heavily on black life and wrote for black as well as white audiences. The novelists included Carl Van Vechten in Harlem, Alejo Carpentier in Cuba, and Alan Paton in South Africa. Among social analysts, Melville Herskovits wrote on racism, African culture, and the diaspora; the Swedish economist Gunnar Myrdal surveyed black American society; Fernando Ortiz wrote on Afro-Cuban culture; and Gilberto Freyre wrote on Afro-Brazilian culture.

By 1930, Josephine Baker turned to singing and to film. She toured the United States in 1936 but encountered racial discrimination and negative reviews and so returned to France to complete a long career. While her early career and her fortune depended on her exotic, sexual, and comedic appeal, in later life she became prominent as a popular singer, a social reformer, and a heroine in the anti-Nazi French Resistance. Her career, while in many ways unique, anticipated the success of performers later in the century who would also draw huge audiences with lively, suggestive dance mixing sexuality and social commentary.

The main source of innovative artistic expression in the African diaspora, as before, was the black community—wage workers especially but also peasants and the urban and rural poor. Young enthusiasts from each community developed new forms, seizing on technological advances, and worked their way to stardom and into the artistic elite. Youthful artists who rose to prominence in this era included Louis Armstrong, Josephine Baker, Aimé Césaire, Billie Holiday, and Langston Hughes. Siti Binti Saad stood out for finding fame in her late thirties. The most skilled of the young artists drew large audiences and reached new communities. They went on to experiment with other possibilities, creating cosmopolitan and elite genres. In gathering large audiences through their work, these artists became linked to social movements. The wide interest in creative expression—whether in music, dance, literature, or even sport—made cross-class and cross-ethnic support for social movements possible. Controversies arose, however, when such artists appealed to broader audiences, modified their work, and appeared to leave behind their initial constituency. Louis Armstrong, for one, was subjected to such criticism. Those artists who managed to sustain their art and their audience continued to create and perform well into old age— particularly the musicians—and sometimes the old inspired the young to start the cycle again. "Father of the Blues" W. C. Handy, for instance, kept playing and writing well into later life.[50]

In accommodating hegemonic cultural pressures, artists of the African diaspora gained a lasting place in that culture as well as in the culture of black communities. For example, singer Billie Holiday and composer and band leader Duke Ellington were among the most celebrated American icons of the 1930s and 1940s.

Historical and sociological works by black authors appeared in larger numbers in the 1930s and 1940s. C. L. R. James of Trinidad published *Black*

Jacobins on the Haitian revolution in 1936, the same year that Du Bois's *Black Reconstruction* appeared. James's Trinidadian follower Eric Williams published *Capitalism and Slavery* in 1944. E. Franklin Frazier published studies of family, and St. Clair Drake published on urban and rural churches. Jomo Kenyatta of Kenya completed a thesis in anthropology at the London School of Economics under Bronislaw Malinowski and published a popular version of it as *Facing Mount Kenya*. Ralph Bunche, after a promising Harvard dissertation on the French administration of Togo and Dahomey, went into government service rather than academia and received a Nobel Peace Prize for his work on behalf of the fledgling United Nations in settling the 1948 war between Palestinians and Jews that resulted in the foundation of Israel. Black scholars did not, however, become prominent in the fields of anthropology or psychology, where the intellectual battles over the nature of race and racial hierarchy were fought. Franz Boas of Columbia University, who trained a generation of the leading anthropologists in the United States, argued consistently against the claims of scientific racism—speaking, for instance, at the 1911 Universal Conference. Of his students, Melville Herskovits specialized in the study of blacks in the diaspora and then in Africa. He became a close but combative associate of black American scholars.

The debate between Herskovits and E. Franklin Frazier in the early 1940s—on the contribution of African culture to Afro-American culture—marked an interesting cultural moment, in that it was the first debate of substance between a white academic and a black academic in which no race cards were played. Herskovits, the anthropologist with a geographically broad perspective who scrutinized race but not slavery, saw enough American similarities to the traditions of the Caribbean and Africa to conclude that the Afro-American tradition drew on Africa. Frazier, the sociologist who studied the United States only but analyzed both slavery and race, saw a complete explanation of Afro-American traditions in the experiences of slavery and emancipation. The debate has been revisited every generation since and remains of interest.

The years between the two world wars saw a veritable explosion of creative activity among black communities, and the resulting new forms gained a substantial following from those outside black communities. For black artists and intellectuals from the United States, the Caribbean, South America, and Africa, Europe was the place they could best hope to gain appreciative audiences. From the Caribbean came C. L. R. James, Aimé Césaire, and René Maran; from Africa came Kojo Tovalou-Houénou, Jomo Kenyatta, and Léopold Sédar Senghor. With the rise of Nazi Germany starting in 1933, however,

Europe became a place where the most vicious racist ideology was expressed and acted out.

The developments of the 1920s and 1930s tend to reaffirm the argument that cultural advances came before the social advances in the campaign for citizenship. Both in building the confidence of black communities and in softening the resistance to black rights in other communities, black achievements in both elite and popular cultural venues appear to have paved the way for social and political change. To pursue this possibility in detail, it is necessary to explore the audiences within black communities and beyond those communities.

Black Communities Break Through, 1940–1960

World War II brought the most casualties of any war in history. It was fought mostly outside the regions where the black population was numerous, but it depended heavily on imperial and racial struggles for domination. In this warfare among the great powers, the fate of black people was at stake, but blacks had little power in setting war aims or war strategies. Nevertheless, the outcome of the war dealt a near-fatal blow to notions of imperial and racial hierarchy. Thus the details of World War II are of importance to the story of the African diaspora.

Society, 1940s

The war in Europe broke out in several stages: the conquest of Ethiopia in 1935, the Nazi-Soviet Pact of 1939, the May–June 1940 German occupation of Western Europe, and the June 1941 German attack on the eastern front. The German takeover of Western Europe in May and June 1940 led to the capture of many black French troops. Vichy France, allied to Germany, maintained control over colonies in North Africa and West Africa, along with the French Caribbean and Asian colonies. General Charles De Gaulle declared the existence of the Free French resistance to the German conquest. Only in the interior colony of Chad did Félix Eboué, the one black governor of all of France's colonies, declare for the Free French and ally with the British. With support from the British in Nigeria, Colonel Jacques Philippe Leclerc, one of the few officers to declare for the Free French, landed in Cameroon and, with the support of African police, overturned the pro-Vichy government there. Eboué was then appointed governor general of French Equatorial Africa by De Gaulle. Leclerc led a small group of troops from Brazzaville to Chad, where he collected additional troops, mostly African. He attacked Italian bases in southern Libya in 1941, and at the beginning of 1943, he traversed the Sahara to attack the Italians in northern Libya and join with the British Field Marshal Montgomery as he moved from Egypt to Tunisia. Later, Leclerc led the armored division that liberated Paris in August 1944, though few African troops accompanied the final drive.

African territories were involved in the war from the time of May–June 1940. (Portugal remained neutral during the war, as did its African colonies.) In South Africa, the United Party government favored intervention on the side of the British, but many in the opposition National Party supported the Germans. South Africa did ultimately intervene as an allied power, and Prime Minister Jan Smuts emerged from the war as one of the architects of the United Nations. In the British territories in Africa, many men were recruited to provide support in India for the war against the Japanese. In Congo, the Belgian government set up substantial labor recruitment to collect agricultural and mineral products—including uranium—for the Allied effort.

In the Caribbean, the British territories gave active support to the war effort. The French territories, however, were ruled by pro-Vichy governors: they were able to do nothing to support the German war effort and were left alone. Most mainland Latin American countries declared war on Germany and Japan during 1942. They suffered economic isolation during the war but were not otherwise influenced greatly.

The United States entered the war in December 1941, following the Japanese attack on Pearl Harbor in Hawaii. Black soldiers were recruited to serve, though in segregated units. Blacks sent to New Guinea in an engineering troop were left in a malarial area, under the assumption that their race protected them from the disease; their white officers went to Australia for rest and recuperation. The U.S. government initially thought to pursue an anticolonial policy during the war. It considered supporting Lamine Guèye, the elected delegate of Senegal to the French National Assembly, as president of an independent Senegal if he would throw his support to the Allies. It also considered supporting the independence of the British and French territories in the Caribbean. As the war went on and as the British and French expressed their determination to hold on to these colonies, the Americans relented. Meanwhile, blacks in American and British military forces fought overwhelmingly in segregated units.

The end of World War II brought the defeat of powers that had explicitly avowed racial discrimination as war policies. More to the point, it revealed the horrors of the execution of millions of civilians during the war—Jews in the largest numbers, but also Romani (Gypsies) and suspected homosexuals and Communists. The postwar atmosphere was one in which popular movements rapidly arose to claim equality of political and economic rights and in which governments felt the need to offer concessions to these movements in the spirit of their war aims against racial discrimination.

Political activity accelerated after World War II, especially in areas under colonial rule, where there arose calls for workers' rights, civil rights, and national self-determination. These times saw the formation of political parties, broadening electoral enfranchisement, and multiple elections to varying offices. The 1945 Pan-African Conference in Manchester, England, included Africans, West Indians, and Americans. At it, Du Bois effectively passed the baton to the next generation, and Kwame Nkrumah of the Gold Coast took on the task of maintaining the Pan-African secretariat. In 1946, the postwar constitution of France integrated Guadeloupe, Martinique, Guiane, and Réunion into France as overseas departments with rights equal to the home departments. The other colonies were left separate and subordinate as a French Union. Aimé Césaire, mayor of Fort-de-France in Martinique, warned of the dangers of this halfway approach to ending the inequities of colonization. In his 1954 essay *Discourse on Colonialism*, Césaire condemned the bloody repression of the 1948 revolt in Madagascar and called on France to give the colonies full French status or complete independence. The alternative, he argued, was that the colonies would be taken over by the United States.

An alliance led by the United States, the Soviet Union, and Britain had brought World War II to a successful conclusion, with France and China as close allies. These powers created the United Nations in 1945 and began to set up a postwar world order based on an accommodation of communist and capitalist parties and regimes. But in 1947 and 1948, a sharp split occurred, especially over control of Germany, and the United States and the USSR then organized alliances to threaten each other with nuclear war for forty years. This era led to wars in Greece, Malaya, the Philippines, and Korea, but not at first in Africa or the Americas. Wherever communists were involved in nationalist movements—as in French West Africa, South Africa, Guyana, and Cuba, they came under careful scrutiny from the United States.

The years immediately after World War II brought a wave of union organization and strike activity throughout the diaspora. Strikes and boycotts in the Gold Coast during 1948 launched the movement for independence, and a year-long railroad strike in French West Africa beginning in 1947 brought the beginnings of racial equalization in salaries. Parallel labor confrontations took place in South African mines and in the automobile and steel industries in the United States. The rise of cold war confrontation in 1948, however, put limits on the demands of labor organizations.

In the same atmosphere arose demands for civil rights. In reaction, however, white supremacist groups were sometimes able to defeat the civil rights activists. In South Africa, community organizations led anti-pass activities, but the 1948 election of the Nationalist Party made *apartheid* the order of the day. Also in 1948, the United States announced the desegregation of its military forces. This provided one cause for the split in the Democratic Party in the 1948 election, in which southern Democrats formed the States' Rights Party (the "Dixiecrats"), with Senator J. Strom Thurmond of South Carolina as its candidate for president and with "Segregation Forever" as one of its slogans. (Many years later, it was revealed that Thurmond had a daughter through a liaison with a young black maid in his parents' household and had supported her from a distance.) Despite this resistance, the NAACP backed campaigns to desegregate various institutions in the North and West. A landmark case based on events in Topeka, Kansas, and argued by Thurgood Marshall reached the U.S. Supreme Court in 1954. In *Brown v. Board of Education*, the court ruled to overthrow the previous "separate but equal" logic and affirmed that segregation in public schools was unconstitutional. Yet the decision was to be implemented, the court ruled, "with all deliberate speed," so that it had little effect over the next decade.

The end of World War II brought rapid independence for several countries of South and Southeast Asia. Indonesia, India, Egypt, and Yugoslavia combined to convene a 1955 conference of nonaligned nations in Bandung, Indonesia. No countries from the Americas were represented, but four North African countries attended, as did Kwame Nkrumah of the Gold Coast, though it was not yet independent. An effort to create a third way and a Third World was under way.

Culture, 1940s

If the elite accomplishments of the 1920s and 1930s left a deep mark in the collective memory, the artistic innovations within black working communities of the 1940s and 1950s had a powerful effect on social organization. The twentieth century's middle two decades, the 1940s and 1950s, were a time of growing connections among regions. An outstanding example of connections across the diaspora is the research and performance in dance by Katherine Dunham and her troupe. Dunham, from Chicago, studied anthropology and dance in the 1930s, beginning her Caribbean travels with a grant from the University of Chicago. Her studies depended especially on Haiti, but also on Cuba, Jamaica, Brazil, and Trinidad. Her dance troupe, drawing heavily on African-inspired dance of the Caribbean and South America, gained fame in the 1940s, with Broadway and film performances. In 1945, she opened a dance school in New York, emphasizing her distinctive method of study; in 1947, she took her troupe to Mexico and then to Europe, where she performed for nearly fifteen years.

The music of Trinidad spread in a different fashion. Trinidadian-based calypso had become a major form of Caribbean music: in contests among musical groups, singers improvised lyrics with humorous social and political commentary. Drums had been banned periodically in Trinidad, but in the 1930s and 1940s musicians in Port of Spain began experimenting with sounds made by striking raised areas of biscuit pans and other metallic containers and assembled a range of Afro-Caribbean elements into a lively cultural complex. An early steel pan known as "pingpong" had four distinct tones. These early pans were played as drums; later on they were slung from the performer's neck. By 1944, Lord Kitchener, the most prominent of the calypso singers, was praising the steel pans, suggesting that they be sent to combat Hitler. In 1946, the developer of a fifteen-tone pan played renditions of Schubert's "Ave Maria," setting a tradition that would be extended to competitions that had bands of as many as one hundred members. Playing the classical pieces helped establish the new instrument's sound quality and prestige as well as develop the discipline and musicianship of performers. After hours, the players from the "Behind the Bridge" section of Port of Spain used smaller ensembles to play livelier music for parties. From Trinidad, the steel pans gained favorable attention in Britain and spread all over the Caribbean, gradually working their way into many musical genres.

In the late 1940s, the young American trumpeter Dizzy Gillespie—an early participant in the bebop movement within jazz—became a leading devotee of Cuban music, exemplifying the overlap of American jazz and Afro-Cuban music that reflected musical change throughout the diaspora. Cuban drums became popular all along the western coast of Africa; musicians in Congo and Angola commonly sang in Spanish during the 1940s and 1950s. The High Life cabaret music that developed in the Gold Coast during the 1940s, led by the big band of E. T. Mensah and the Tempos, drew at once on orchestration from the New World, village songs, and a cheerful sense of national identity. Mensah's regular tours in Nigeria laid the groundwork for a musical scene that exploded in the 1960s.

Back in the Caribbean, Afro-Cuban big bands grew in popularity, and new forms of dance developed along with the music's recognition. Mambo was the name under which the dance of *son* spread to other countries, the *cha-cha-chá* (later known in English as cha-cha) spread in the 1940s and 1950s as a simplified dance form, and salsa became the Puerto Rican form of *son*, with little change in the beat but a distinctive orchestration. The style of these forms changed somewhat over time: salsa and mambo came to be danced at a rapid tempo and rumba at a slower one.

After World War II, the newly formed United Nations Educational, Social, and Cultural Organization (UNESCO) organized an exhibit of contemporary painting in Mexico City and included a set of Haitian paintings in tempera. Those works gained wide acclaim and the name Hector Hippolyte, the exhibit's outstanding painter, became well known in art circles. During the war, Hippolyte, a self-trained artist, had come to the studio set up in Port-au-Prince by DeWitt Peters, a conscientious objector from the United States who arranged to do alternative service by teaching art in Haiti. Peters provided the studio and materials; Hippolyte and other artists created painting and sculpture with themes taken from Haitian daily life and the spiritual worlds of vodun and Christianity. The paintings were at once representational, abstract, and caricatures and featured imaginative use of color and space and little reliance on perspective. The Anglican cathedral of Port-au-Prince engaged the painters to create murals for its walls. Critics welcomed the artistic skill and the social values of the artists but consistently interpreted the work as "primitivist." The critics gave credit to the artists for their recuperation of African traditions but little recognition for expressing modern ideas. While many artists addressed the spiritual, the political was not absent, as revealed in the well-known painting of Philomène Obin celebrating the Haitian nationalist figure Charlemagne Péralte (see figure 5.4). In any case, the popularity of Haitian painting and sculpture at home and abroad gave rise to an extraordinary outpouring of creative work, ranging in quality from the mundane to masterpieces.

The literary output of black authors expanded with each decade. For instance, the Nigerian author Amos Tutuola published, in 1946, *The Palm Wine Drinkard*, a long Yoruba fairy tale, written in an English heavily influenced by Yoruba syntax, that has charmed readers ever since. But perhaps the most outstanding writer of the 1940s was Richard Wright, whose *Native Son* (1940) and autobiographical *Black Boy* (1945) gained wide acclaim. Wright was born in Mississippi and moved as a youth, like many from his homeland, to Chicago. There he became active in the political and cultural activities of the Communist Party during the Depression years. *Native Son* told the disastrous story of a young black man who became involved in the racial and sexual politics of radicalism: it became a national bestseller. Wright left the Communist Party in 1944, labeling it "the god that failed." He settled in France after World War II and became a French citizen in 1947.

FIGURE 5.4 *Charlemagne Péralte*, by Philomène Obin

Painted in 1970 by Philomène Obin. The painting refers to the leader of the Cacos rebels, killed and crucified on his front door by U.S. Marines in 1926. Péralte's mother is pictured next to him.

Source: Courtesy of Flagg Tanning Corp., Milwaukee, Wis.

Society, 1950s

Decolonization began immediately after World War II, with the Japanese-occupied Philippines and Indonesia gaining independence in 1946 and 1947 and with British India becoming the two independent countries of India and Pakistan in 1947. But for African or Caribbean colonies to become independent was quite a different matter: the colonial officials of the day asked whether blacks were "ready for self-government."

The Republic of Sudan gained independence at the start of 1956 and thus initiated sub-Saharan African decolonization. Yet Sudanese independence has gained little attention in accounts of the African diaspora, perhaps because it has been considered as an exception rather than the norm. Realistically, however, and despite all of the country's crises, Sudan must be seen as having an importance in the history of Africa and the Old World diaspora for the twentieth century that equals its importance since the days of Nubian kingdoms and Nilotic migrants.[51] Sudan lies astride the boundary of sub-Saharan Africa and the near diaspora of the Old World. Sudan's colonial era began with the British conquest of 1898, after which it was known as the Anglo-Egyptian Condominium of Sudan, under the fiction that Britain and Egypt shared in ruling the colony. In the north, the Arabic language and the Islamic religion predominated across a large ethnically and economically varied region. The three provinces of the south, with about one-quarter of the colony's population, were kept isolated from the north by the British government and maintained as a preserve for Christian missionaries. In the north, a lively set of social movements arose representing religious groups, trade unions, a Western-educated elite, and professional soldiers. Only in 1947 did the British allow the first elections, and only in 1948 was the south opened to political participation. Religious and secular parties formed by 1950, each calling for independence, including the possibility of union with Egypt. Independence came in 1956 to a government of the National Unionist Party led by Isma'il al-Azhari, a coalition of Arab secular and religious interests. By June 1956, a coalition of the Umma and the People's Democratic Party forced al-Azhari's resignation, but this government remained ineffective in the face of growing radical and trade-union movements. Then in 1958, Prime Minister 'Abdallah Khalil turned to the military for support, and General Ibrahim 'Abbud took power until he was overthrown in the general strike of 1964. Overall, though the country was rich in natural and especially human resources, the colonial and postcolonial experience of Sudan became emblematic of the many unresolved issues of the African diaspora: religion, national identity, political community, social class, and social policy.

In the Gold Coast, Kwame Nkrumah, the American-educated Pan-Africanist leader, made an eloquent claim for self government with the phrase, "Seek ye first the political kingdom, and all else shall be added unto you." (This revision of the Christian gospel was all the stronger given that Nkrumah undertook early training for the priesthood.) George Padmore, Nkrumah's political counselor and the Trinidadian activist who had earlier campaigned among blacks for the Communist International, put forth the choice to African leaders with the title of his 1956 book: *Pan-Africanism or Communism?* Under Nkrumah's leadership, the Gold Coast gained independence in 1957 as Ghana. Within three years, dozens of new nations were gaining formal recognition. For Africa, one might argue that Africans were simply regaining what they had lost less than a century before. The difference, however, was that the independent nations of Africa and the Caribbean and the black elected officials in the United States and other multiracial nations had a fuller legitimacy than ever before in the recognition of their office by powers large and small.

Struggles for autonomy and independence turned violent, however, when the rulers refused to grant concessions. In Kenya, the Kenya Land and Freedom Army began to form among Kikuyu men seeking to end British occupation of their lands. The British declared a state of emergency in 1952 against this movement, which came to be known as Mau Mau. The years of fighting were overshadowed by the internment of thousands of Kenyans. The uprising was stifled by the end of the 1950s. Other wars for national liberation broke out in this era. Of them, the Algerian uprising in 1954 launched the guerilla struggle that finally won independence in 1962. In South Africa, the African National Congress split. The departing faction took the name of the Pan Africanist Congress and rejected alliances with whites, announcing its preparation for military action. The Cuban Revolution, victorious in 1959, was not led primarily by blacks, yet the call for greater national independence resonated with black Cubans, who had much to gain from major change.

By the mid-twentieth century, Africa and the African diaspora had developed a remarkable set of political theorists and practitioners who played a crucial role in the great political realignment to come. These men drew on the full experience of black social struggle and its cultural expression to articulate the main directions of the black political fight in the 1940s and 1950s. Many could be listed but four individuals in particular give a sense of how the long push for citizenship gained some signal victories: Nelson Mandela of South Africa, Rev. Martin Luther King Jr. of the United States, Frantz Fanon of Martinique, and Kwame Nkrumah of Ghana. Mandela was the most gifted of them as a practical political leader, relying on sheer staying power to lead in redefining the South African nation. In a 1953 speech to an African National Congress group entitled "No Easy Walk to Freedom," Mandela laid out the analysis and strategy he was to pursue for the next fifty years. King, the most effective visionary and moralist, conveyed a memorable image of a society beyond racial and economic prejudice. Fanon, with the sharpest analytical mind, analyzed the contradictions of colonial society and skillfully predicted those of postcolonial society. Nkrumah opened the pathway to achieving national independence through politics rather than war and formulated arguments for African unity to counter the neocolonial interference of great powers and global corporations.

In 1954 and 1955, two campaigns organized by black women made powerful claims for equal rights. In Montgomery, Alabama, the arrest of Rosa Parks for refusing to give up her seat prompted a year-long black boycott of the city's segregated buses. Rev. Martin Luther King Jr. emerged as the inspiring spokesperson of this desegregation movement, and the daily organization of the bus boycott by women from clubs, churches, and labor unions kept it going until they achieved complete victory. In Johannesburg, women led a 1955 bus boycott to protest sharp fare increases and then organized a 1957 national march on the capital of Pretoria to protest a law forcing black women to carry identity passes. The South African women lost that battle but made their political point. With these social movements of the 1950s, it became clear that racial discrimination had been discredited though not eliminated from the world.

The United States too had few black elected officials in the years before 1960. Most prominent among them was Adam Clayton Powell Jr. of the Abyssinian Baptist Church, elected to New York's city council in 1941 and the U.S. Congress in 1944. To indicate his interest in the politics of decolonization, he attended the Bandung Conference of nonaligned nations in 1955. So did the writer Richard Wright.

Culture, 1950s

In the late 1940s, young musicians in the American South combined elements of jazz and gospel to form vocal music backed by piano or guitar and a small band that came to be called "rhythm and blues." Fats Domino of New Orleans had early and durable success in this genre, which became popular with young blacks and then young whites. Alan Freed, a Cleveland radio broadcaster who became popular by playing this music, applied the term "rock and roll" to it. Freed organized the first rock-and-roll concert—the "Moondog Coronation Ball"—and scheduled it for March 21, 1952. As many as thirty thousand young people arrived—half white and half black and far in excess of the space available—and a riot occurred when police decided to end the event. Freed went on to great fame, and the black rhythm and blues dubbed rock and roll came to be performed by black or white artists for black, white, and (increasingly) mixed audiences. This music saw the burgeoning of cultural "crossover." Among the early rock-and-roll successes were Little Richard, Chuck Berry, Bo Diddley, and Ray Charles. Elvis Presley, a white Southerner knowledgeable in black music, emerged as the most successful of all.

In visual arts, African-American painters such as Jacob Lawrence, Lois Mailou Jones, and John Biggers, whose work began under the influence of the Harlem Renaissance, showed increasing interest over time in African and

Caribbean themes and subjects. New painting traditions emerged in other regions also. In Barbados, black students working with established white painters began to paint and exhibit. An influx of expatriate artists enriched the island scene, and by the 1950s an Afro-Barbadian school of painting had been established.[52] In Africa, sculptors expanded the volume and updated the styles of their carvings, producing initially for their home market and, increasingly, for export (see figure 5.5).

FIGURE 5.5 Arowogun of Osi with Carvings

This sculptor of the town of Osi, shown near the end of his life in c. 1990, gained a wide reputation throughout western Nigeria. Others in his workshop produced religious sculpture, including a well-known set of bas-reliefs portraying the stations of the cross.

Source: Courtesy of Daniel Biebuyck, ed., *Tradition and Creativity in Tribal Art* (Berkeley: University of California Press, 1969).

In the last days of the Belgian Congo, guitarist and vocalist Franco formed OK Jazz in 1956 and launched his more than two decades of dominance of the "African rumba." He based his style on Cuban *son* but put great emphasis on melodious electric-guitar solos and lyrics sung in Lingala. His sound transformed popular music throughout sub-Saharan Africa.

Katherine Dunham's tours had done much to build an international audience for the dance of black communities. The influence of such dances, with their lively, elegant, sensual movements, went far beyond the communities that created them. These movements became central to competitive ballroom dancing as it became codified in the British-based "International Style" of the 1950s, which has since remained dominant. Of the International Standard ballroom dances, the waltz, quickstep, and Viennese waltz came from Europe; the foxtrot came from the United States (a later form of the cakewalk); and the tango came from Argentina (where it developed among poor and especially black communities). Of International Latin American dances, the rumba and cha-cha were born of Cuban models, jive came from American swing, samba from Brazil's black communities, and paso doble from Spanish roots. The original forms provided the essential foundation for the newer dances. Few black people danced in the competitions, in which British and Norwegian dancers often dominated, yet the African diaspora origin of the dances was remembered.

Religious change and in some cases conflict continued throughout the African diaspora. The religious map of Africa had largely settled down by 1960 (see map 5.1). Sub-Saharan lands that became overwhelmingly Islamic are (by their present names) Mauritania, Senegal, Mali, Niger, Chad, Guinea, and Somalia. The mainly Catholic territories are Angola, Congo-Kinshasa, Rwanda, Burundi, Congo-Brazzaville, Gabon, and Madagascar. The mainly Protestant territories are Zimbabwe, Zambia, Kenya, Ghana, and Liberia.

Religious diversity characterized the other half of African nations. By 1960, the territories that had at least two major religious dominations included Guiné-Bissau, Sierra Leone, Liberia, the Ivory Coast, Burkina Faso, Togo, Benin, Nigeria, Cameroon, the Central African Republic, Sudan, Ethiopia, Uganda, Tanzania, Mozambique, and South Africa. The ancestral African religious traditions remained strong in several areas of the continent—especially along the West African coast—and they reinvented themselves to remain relevant to contemporary concerns, as James Fernandes showed for the religion of Bwiti in Gabon. Thus the emerging nations of Africa, more than those of any other region, faced the task of working out domestic religious toleration. It would not be easy.

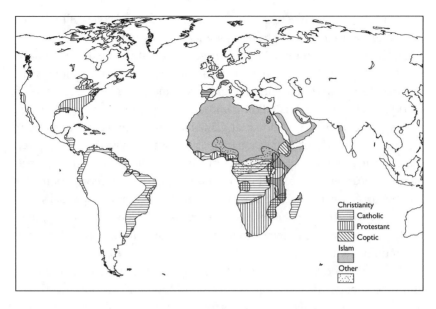

MAP 5.1 Religion in Africa and the Diaspora, 1960

In the Americas, significant changes in religious affiliation continued to take place. Islam grew in North America and the Caribbean, while previously Catholic Latin America experienced conversion to Protestant and Evangelical churches plus a modest growth in Islam. The African diaspora in Europe, mainly Christian in early times, became increasingly Islamic, and the remainder of the Old World diaspora continued to be overwhelmingly Muslim.

The outburst of twentieth-century creativity and renewal drew on underlying patterns of African culture—in simplest terms, on drums, dancers, and griots—and drew even more on the previous three centuries of struggle with slavery and its consequences. The success of black popular culture is in part a consequence of deprivation. African societies, at home and abroad, lost their elites in the era of slavery. At the dawn of the twentieth century, little black elite culture existed in the countries of the diaspora. On the continent, African monarchies had been weakened, and those that survived had been turned into exploitive, alienating powers by their association with enslavement. So the great artists in black communities, with no kings or courts to call on them to celebrate the monarchy, played instead to the communities in which they lived. The direct, earthy, ribald, critical, and profound culture of the common people received the creative attention of the best black artists. Their names are mostly lost to us, but the forms and styles of their creations survive to this day in the many works they engendered.

For black communities, the various genres of cultural expression have included statements to sustain the community in slavery, under colonialism, in rural life, and in the transition to urban and industrial life; statements of broad identity that marshaled the community to common action; and statements of the human condition that gained appeal beyond black communities. For individuals, black cultural expression has given voice to the desires and dilemmas in their search for security, love, and acknowledgment; it has elevated the experience of ordinary people to a high level of recognition. The creative artists, in taking advantage of new technology and new social situations, expressed old messages in new, intriguing fashions. In so doing, they spoke to the need for citizenship in figurative and literal terms, for black communities and for others as well.

The two previously predominant dualities—white and black, dominant and subordinate—denoted a prime aspect of life in Africa and the African diaspora. But the disadvantage of this formulation was its failure to account for the importance of relations among different black communities or the relations between black communities and other communities, be they Asian, Amerindian, or European in ancestry. In particular, this formulation does not encompass the degree to which white and black communities have been neighbors in parallel rather than in hierarchical relationships. Over time, this dimension of the lives of black people has become somewhat more prominent.

Massive social and political changes in the lives of black people began to mount up at the end of the 1950s: political independence in Africa and the Caribbean, legal victories in the United States and Latin America, and accelerated advance in education and health conditions throughout the black world. There were many casualties, many defeats, and a continuing stream of racial discrimination at every level. Yet by the end of the 1950s, a crucial turn had been made. The ideology of white supremacy had lost its credibility and its primacy, though the reality of its dictates might last for a long time. Pan-African visions of a united Africa or a united black world were not to succeed, but the growing ties of recognition among blacks worldwide were a far cry from the rejections of blackness of the early twentieth century.

The renewed popularity of the song "Guantanamera" provides an example of the linkage of literal and figurative citizenship. In 1958, in the last days of Batista's unpopular Cuban regime, the composer Julián Orbón put the opening words of José Martí's poem "Versos Sencillos" to the well-known melody. The lyrics, emphasizing simple values of honesty and love of the countryside, brought the song another round of popularity. When it came to New York in the wake of the Cuban revolution of 1959, the American folk singer Pete Seeger arranged a recording in Spanish and English, and in this form the song enjoyed worldwide success as a musical symbol of a sort of global citizenship.

City and Nation

The city and the nation are social realities of our time, but they are also concepts that we use to organize history. The nation began to emerge, in the late eighteenth century, as the leading form of government and social organization. Haiti and Liberia stand out as early black nations; the United States and Brazil stand out as early, multicultural nations with large black populations. Nationhood came gradually to all black people. National identity brought rights to vote, to hold office, and independence for a growing number of black territories held under colonial rule. For such countries as Egypt, Arabia, and Morocco, with significant but minority black populations, nationhood came late and the recognition of black identity came even later.

In the same era, cities grew from ports and administrative nodes to metropolitan centers. Suburbs developed alongside the cities, and many lives involved mobility among rural, urban, and surburban settings. Thus the African diaspora began to grow more connected, linking people from city to countryside as well as from continent to continent. Opportunities seemed greater in cities, so people moved there, but found urban life demanding.

Urbanization took hold not all at once, but over the course of a century. Black urbanites of the nineteenth century helped to establish the forms of New World city life in the industrial age, and we preserve a record of that influence especially in the music they created. By 1960, black people had become primarily urban in North America, South America, and Europe. Similarly, blacks in old and new cities of twentieth-century Africa set social patterns there. In parallel but less well documented ways, blacks contributed to urban life in the North African cities of Rabat, Algiers, and Alexandria, as well as in Istanbul and Jidda.

Twentieth-century cities came to require literacy of their inhabitants for survival, but they did not necessarily reward them for reading. Education and literacy became desirable not only for the leaders of society but for all who attempted to live at levels beyond the very basic. For black communities everywhere, education was recognized as a key to social mobility. Yet formal education of children meant that families and communities had to give up some of the role in their socialization that they had previously enjoyed. It also meant losing the labor of children who were in school instead of working. It is important to distinguish between cases where the community controlled childhood education and cases where families had to submit to a dominant outside influence to get formal education for their children. State schools, for example, were surely beyond the control of most families, and while religious schools might respond to the desires of parents, they might also be under the control of foreign missionaries. The growing number of families able to get education for their children also had to campaign for more resources for their schools, for stronger curricula, and for their children's advancement.

In the late 1950s, a Brazilian reporter, following a lead from associates in São Paulo, located Carolina Maria de Jesus, a black single mother of three children living in the city's *favela*, or slum. This poverty-stricken woman had a diary that chronicled life in the rapidly growing *favelas* of Brazil's largest city. After interviews and negotiations, she agreed to have her diary published. When it appeared in 1960 as *Quarto de Despejo*, her chronicle of life in the city from 1955 through 1959 gained wide attention and sympathy.[53] The hope was that expanding poverty could somehow be limited and that the example captured in Carolina Maria's words would inspire migrants to the city to seek and achieve a better life, or that the unhappy lives of migrants to the city could be replaced by reliance on such skills as Carolina Maria's way with words to elevate the poor to a decent existence.

> The children eat a lot of bread. They like soft bread, but when they don't have it, they eat hard bread.
>
> Hard is the bread that we eat. Hard is the bed on which we sleep. Hard is the life of the *favelado*.
>
> Oh, São Paulo! A queen that vainly shows her skyscrapers that are her crown of gold. All dressed up in velvet and silk but with cheap stockings underneath—the *favela*.
>
> The money didn't stretch far enough to buy meat, so I cooked macaroni with a carrot. I didn't have any grease, it was horrible. Vera was the only one who complained, yet asked for more.
>
> "Mama, sell me to Dona Julita, because she has delicious food."[54]

Twenty years later, after the death of Carolina Maria, the same reporter sought out her children to review the later stages of her life. Her subsequent books did not sell as well, and it was concluded that, in Brazil and the world of the 1970s and 1980s, urban poverty was no longer seen as an exception and perhaps no longer even seen as a soluble problem.

Like many others, Carolina Maria had her citizenship. She could listen to the radio, read and write, sell the paper she gathered in the street, and vote in years when elections were held (though a 1964 military coup halted serious elections for twenty years). The problem still to be resolved for Carolina Maria, her children, and countless other black people was the ongoing struggle for equality.

The rapid and worldwide economic growth that began after World War II continued up to 1960 and then came to an end. The sudden economic stagnation clashed sharply with the high hopes arising in black communities with the social victories of the 1950s and 1960s. The next step on the black agenda, once citizenship had been gained, would apparently be a campaign for wider social equality. This would be a tall order. The very cities that housed a growing proportion of black people offered opportunity, but they also brought frightening new problems. In the time to come, black people would gain prominence as athletes, performers, and political leaders—arguably, they would be symbols of their age. Yet equally important as a symbol of the age to come was Carolina Maria, the talented and insightful single mother struggling to make ends meet.

Suggested Readings

W. E. B. Du Bois's famous statement on "the problem of the twentieth century" and many of his other writings are contained in Eric J. Sundquist's *The Oxford W. E. B. Du Bois Reader* (New York: Oxford University Press, 1996). James Weldon Johnson, who wrote the lyrics for "Lift Every Voice," later wrote *The Autobiography of an Ex-colored Man* (Boston: Sherman, French & Co., 1912).

Facing White Supremacy

Shawn Michelle Smith, in *Photography on the Color Line: W. E. B. Du Bois, Race, and Visual Culture* (Durham, N.C.: Duke University Press, 2004), provides numerous images and a multilayered analysis of the outlook of Du Bois and others in the U.S. black elite. For a contemporary review of black cultural achievement in the early twentieth century, including a focus on Meta Warrick Fuller, see Benjamin Griffith Brawley, *The Negro in Literature and Art in the United States*, 3rd ed. (New York: Duffield, 1929). On the formation and rise of the NAACP, see Charles Flint Kellogg, *NAACP: A History of the National Association for the Advancement of Colored People* (Baltimore, Md.: The Johns Hopkins University Press, 1967). J. E. Casely Hayford's argument for extending self-government in British West Africa is presented in his *Gold Coast Native Institutions: With Thoughts Upon a Healthy Imperial Policy for the Gold Coast and Ashanti* (London: Sweet and Maxwell, 1903). Leo Frobenius published the catalog of his studies in West and Central Africa in German, and it was translated immediately into English. See Leo Frobenius, *The Voice of Africa; Being an Account of the German Inner African Exploration Expedition in the Years 1910–1912* (New York: B. Blom, 1968). For the effects of colonial rule in Africa, for instance in French territories, see Patrick Manning, *Francophone Sub-Saharan Africa, 1880–1995*, 2nd ed. (Cambridge: Cambridge University Press, 1998). The early twentieth-century expansion of U.S. imperial influence to the Caribbean and its later backlash are traced in Walter LaFeber, *Inevitable Revolutions: The United States in Central America* (New York: Norton, 1983). On the gentler but unmistakable influence of white-supremacist thinking in Latin America, see George Reid Andrews, *Afro-Latin America, 1800–2000* (New York: Oxford University Press, 2005). For a comparison of white supremacy in the United States and South Africa, see George M. Fredrickson, *White Supremacy: A Comparative Study in American and South African History* (New York: Oxford University Press, 1981).

Claims for Citizenship: Afro-Cuban Trailblazers

The excellent literature on the history of Afro-Cuban communities and their place in Cuban national history is deserving of wider attention and comparison. See Rebecca J. Scott, *Degrees of Freedom: Louisiana and Cuba After Slavery* (Cambridge, Mass.: Belknap Press of Harvard University Press, 2005); Robin Moore, *Nationalizing Blackness: Afrocubanismo and Artistic Revolution in Havana, 1920–1940* (Pittsburgh, Penn.: University of Pittsburgh Press, 1997); Alejandro de la Fuente, *A Nation for All: Race, Inequality, and Politics in Twentieth-century Cuba* (Chapel Hill: University of North Carolina Press, 2001); Aline Helg, *Our Rightful Share: The Afro-Cuban Struggle for Equality, 1886–1912* (Chapel Hill: University of North Carolina Press, 1995); Ada Ferrer, *Insurgent Cuba: Race, Nation, and Revolution, 1868–1898* (Chapel Hill: University of North Carolina Press, 1998); Jana K. Lipman, *Guantánamo: A Working-Class History Between Empire and Revolution* (Berkeley: University of California Press, 2009); Stephan Palmié, *Wizards and Scientists: Explorations in Afro-Cuban Modernity* (Durham, N.C.: Duke University Press, 2002); and Louis A. Pérez Jr., *Cuba Under the Platt Amendment, 1902–1934* (Pittsburgh, Penn.: University of Pittsburgh Press, 1986).

Rural and Urban Innovations, 1900–1920

On strategies for the pursuit of citizenship, see Booker T. Washington, *Up from Slavery, an Autobiography* (Garden City, N.Y.: Doubleday, 1963); August Meier, *Negro Thought in America, 1880–1915: Racial Ideologies in the Age of Booker T. Washington* (Ann Arbor: University of Michigan Press, 1988); and John W. Cell, *The Highest Stage of White Supremacy: The Origins of Segregation in South Africa and the American South* (Cambridge: Cambridge University Press, 1982). On the documentation of African culture by Leo Frobenius, see Eike Haverland, ed., *Leo Frobenius on African History, Art, and Culture* (Princeton, N.J.: Markus Wiener Publishers, 2007). For general overviews of black visual art and music in the early twentieth century, see Richard J. Powell, *Black Art: A Cultural History* (London: Thames and Hudson, 2002); John Storm Roberts, *Black Music of Two Worlds: African, Caribbean, Latin, and African-American Traditions*, 2nd ed. (New York: Schirmer, 1998); and J. H. Kwabena Nketia, *The Music of Africa* (London: Gollancz, 1975). A remarkable study of multilingual communities in colonial Gold Coast and independent Ghana is M. E. Kropp Dakubu's *Korle Meets the Sea: A Sociolinguistic History of Accra* (New York: Oxford University Press, 1997). Johannes Fabian, in *Language and Colonial Power: The Appropriation of Swahili in the Former Belgian Congo* (Cambridge: Cambridge University Press, 1986), shows how colonial powers and local communities negotiate to create a common language. In material culture, see Erik Gilbert's *Dhows and the Colonial Economy of Zanzibar* (Oxford: James Currey, 2004); in music, see Peter Manuel's *Caribbean Currents: Caribbean Music from Rumba to Reggae* (Philadelphia: Temple University Press, 1995); and in literature, see W. E. B. Du Bois's *The Quest of the Silver Fleece* (New York: Harlem Moon, 2004). For a long-term social history of France's West African army, see Myron J. Echenberg, *Colonial Conscripts: The Tirailleurs Sénégalais in French West Africa, 1857–1960* (Portsmouth, N.H.: Heinemann, 1991). On civil-rights struggles in South Africa, see Shula Marks, *The Ambiguities of Dependence in South Africa: Class, Nationalism, and the State in Twentieth-century Natal* (Baltimore, Md.: The Johns Hopkins University Press, 1986). On the survival of slavery in twentieth-century Africa, see Suzanne Miers and Richard Roberts, eds., *The End of Slavery in Africa* (Madison: University of Wisconsin Press, 1988).

Workers' Songs and High Culture, 1920–1940

The extraordinary cultural output of the 1920s and 1930s is chronicled in a number of excellent studies. On the Martinican writer René Maran, see Femi Ojo-Ade's *René Maran, the Black Frenchman: A Bio-critical Study* (Washington, D.C.: Three Continents Press, 1984). Other studies of writers in the

French language include Lilyan Kesteloot's *Black Writers in French: A Literary History of Negritude* (Washington, D.C.: Howard University Press, 1991) and Robert Cornevin's *Littératures d'Afrique Noire de Langue française* (Paris: Presses Universitaires de France, 1976). On the Harlem Renaissance, see Nathan Huggins's *Harlem Renaissance* (New York: Oxford University Press, 1973) and Arnold Rampersad's *The Life of Langston Hughes*, 2 vols., 2nd ed. (New York: Oxford University Press, 2002). On U.S. artists prominent in the 1930s, see Jacob Lawrence, *The Toussaint L'Ouverture Series: A Visual Narration of the Liberation of Haiti in 1804 Under the Leadership of General Toussaint L'Ouverture*, ed. James M. Buell (New York: Religious Communities for the Arts, 1982); Bennetta Jules-Rosette, *Josephine Baker in Art and Life: The Icon and the Image* (Urbana: University of Illinois Press, 2007); Henry Louis Gates Jr. and Karen C. C. Dalton, eds., *Josephine Baker and* La Revue Nègre: *Paul Colin's Lithographs of* Le Tumulte Noir *in Paris, 1927* (New York: Abrams, 1997); Marian Anderson, *My Lord, What a Morning: An Autobiography* (Urbana: University of Illinois Press, 2002); David Margolick, *Strange Fruit: Billie Holiday, Café Society, and an Early Cry for Civil Rights* (Philadelphia: Running Press, 2000); Michelle Scott, *Blues Empress in Black Chattanooga: Bessie Smith and the Emerging Urban South* (Urbana: University of Illinois Press, 2008); Gena Caponi-Tabery, *Jump for Joy: Jazz, Basketball, and Black Culture in 1930s* (Amherst, Mass.: University of Massachusetts Press, 2008); Joel Dinerstein, *Swinging the Machine: Modernity, Technology, and African American Culture Between the World Wars* (Amherst: University of Massachusetts Press, 2003); and Sterling Stuckey, *Going Through the Storm: The Influence of African-American Art in History* (New York: Oxford University Press, 1994).

On the struggles within independent Liberia, see Ibrahim Sundiata, *Brothers and Strangers: Black Zion, Black Slavery, 1914–1940* (Durham, N.C.: Duke University Press, 2003). On the national movement in colonial Dahomey from the 1920s to 1940s, see Patrick Manning, *Slavery, Colonialism, and Economic Growth in Dahomey, 1640–1960* (Cambridge: Cambridge University Press, 1982).

The labor and political struggles of Trinidad set the tone for the British West Indies: see Bridget Brereton's *A History of Modern Trinidad, 1783–1962* (Kingston: Heinemann, 1981). For parallel movements in other regions, see Marison de la Cadena, *Indigenous Mestizos: The Politics of Race and Culture in Cuzco, Peru, 1919–1991* (Durham, N.C.: Duke University Press, 2000); Philippe DeWitte, *Les Mouvements nègres en France, 1919–1939* (Paris: Harmattan, 1985); W. E. B. Du Bois, *An ABC of Color* (New York: International Publishers, 1969); and Joe W. Trotter, *African Americans in the Industrial Age: A Documentary History* (Boston: Northeastern University Press, 1996).

Pan-African movements rose from abstract principles to political campaigns. See J. Ayodele Langley, *Pan-Africanism and Nationalism in West Africa, 1900–1945: A Study in Ideology and Social Classes* (Oxford: Clarendon, 1973); and Edmund David Cronon, *Black Moses: The Story of Marcus Garvey and the Universal Negro Improvement Association* (Madison: University of Wisconsin Press, 1955). On the rise of the Rastafarian movement in Jamaica, see Leonard E. Barrett, *The Rastafarians: Sounds of Cultural Dissonance*, rev. ed. (Boston: Beacon Press, 1988).

Du Bois wrote a global study early in the twentieth century in *The Negro* (1915); he returned after World War II to write *The World and Africa* (New York: International Publishers, 1946). Also on radical and Pan-African analyses of the 1920s and 1930s, see Winston James, *Holding Aloft the Banner of Ethiopia: Caribbean Radicalism in Early Twentieth-century America* (London: Verso, 1998); W. E. B. Du Bois, *Black Reconstruction* (Millwood, N.Y.: Kraus-Thompson, 1976); Cedric Robinson, *Black Marxism: The Making of a Black Radical Tradition* (Chapel Hill: University of North Carolina Press, 2000); Maghan Keita, *Race and the Writing of History: Riddling the Sphinx* (New York: Oxford University Press, 2000); and C. L. R. James, *The Black Jacobins: Toussaint L'Ouverture and the San Domingo Revolution* (London: Penguin, 2001).

Black Communities Break Through, 1940–1960

On Africa in World War II, see David Killingray and Richard Rathbone, eds., *Africa and the Second World War* (Basingstoke: Macmillan, 1986); and for the life of the black governor who helped turn the tide for the Free French, see Brian Weinstein, *Eboué* (New York: Oxford University Press, 1972). On the 1945 Manchester Pan-African conference and its aftermath, see Ras Makonnen, *Pan-Africanism from Within* (New York: Oxford University Press, 1973). For an eyewitness report on the 1955 Bandung Conference, see Richard Wright, *The Color Curtain: A Report on the Bandung Conference* (Jackson: University Press of Mississippi, 1995). On the politics and independence of Sudan, see Tim Niblock, *Class and Power in Sudan: The Dynamics of Sudanese Politics, 1989–1985* (Albany: State University of New York Press, 1987); and Heather J. Sharkey, *Living with Colonialism: Nationalism and Culture in the Anglo-Egyptian Sudan* (Berkeley: University of California Press, 2003). On the independence movement of Ghana, see J. Godson Amamoo, *The New Ghana: The Birth of a Nation* (London: Pan Books, 1958); and Immanuel Wallerstein, *The Road to Independence: Ghana and the Ivory Coast* (The Hague: Mouton, 1964). For an early and unsuccessful war for national liberation, see Joseph Kariuki's *Mau Mau Detainee: The Account by a Kenya African of*

His Experiences in Detention Camps, 1953–1960 (London: Oxford University Press, 1963). For the beginnings of postcolonial politics, see Ronald W. Walters, *Pan Africanism in the African Diaspora: An Analysis of Modern Afrocentric Political Movements* (Detroit, Mich.: Wayne State University Press, 1993).

On postwar pan-Africanism, see George Padmore, *Pan-Africanism or Communism* (Garden City, N.Y.: Doubleday, 1971); Colin Legum, *Pan-Africanism, a Short Political Guide* (Westport, Conn.: Greenwood Press, 1976); Nelson Mandela, *No Easy Walk to Freedom: Articles, Speeches, and Trial Addresses of Nelson Mandela* (London: Heinemann, 1965); and the American Society of African Culture, *Pan-Africanism Reconsidered* (Berkeley: University of California Press, 1962).

For the contending views of black consciousness, see C. L. R. James, *Beyond a Boundary* (New York: Pantheon, 1983); Aimé Cesaire, *Discourse on Colonialism* (New York: Monthly Review Press, 2000); Frantz Fanon, *Toward the African Revolution: Political Essays*, trans. Haakon Chevalier (New York: Grove Press, 1988); Frantz Fanon, *Wretched of the Earth*, trans. Richard Philcox (New York: Grove Press, 2004); Tommy L. Lott, *The Invention of Race: Black Culture and the Politics of Representation* (Malden, Mass: Blackwell, 1999); George Fredrickson, *Black Liberation: A Comparative History of Black Ideologies in the United States and South Africa* (New York: Oxford University Press, 1995); and Irene Gendzier, *Frantz Fanon: A Critical Study* (New York: Pantheon, 1973). On Martin Luther King Jr., see the first volume of the three-volume biography of Taylor Branch: *Parting the Waters: America in the King Years, 1954–1963* (New York: Simon and Schuster, 1989).

City and Nation

Bill Freund, *The African City* (New York: Cambridge University Press, 2007), conveys at once the uniqueness of African cities and the general problems of twentieth-century urbanization; see also John Iliffe, *The African Poor: A History* (Cambridge: Cambridge University Press, 1987). For the remarkable voice of a mother in the Brazilian slums, see Carolina Maria de Jesus, *Child of the Dark: The Diary of Carolina Maria de Jesus*, trans. David St. Clair (New York: Mentor, 1962); and Robert M. Levine and José Carlos Sebe Bom Meihy, *The Life and Death of Carolina Maria de Jesus* (Albuquerque: University of New Mexico Press, 1995).

⟹ 6 ⟸

Equality, 1960–2000

istant relatives became reacquainted in 1966 at Dakar, the lively capital city of Senegal and major port on the western tip of the African continent. With over forty African and Caribbean countries suddenly independent and self-governing, the idea of a global celebration of African culture proved irresistible. Here, near the geographical center of the black world, such a celebration unfolded in June 1966: the Black and African Festival of Arts and Culture (FESTAC). Among those in attendance were Katherine Dunham and Langston Hughes of the United States, Aimé Césaire of Martinique, Wole Soyinka of Nigeria, Cheikh Anta Diop of Senegal, and many other writers, visual artists, musicians, and filmmakers.

Alioune Diop led in organizing this postcolonial celebration and reunion. Diop, the Senegalese writer who since 1946 had sustained the Society of African Culture and its publication, *Présence africaine*, had dreamed of such a gathering for years. He had previously convened conferences of African artists and writers (in 1956 in Paris and 1959 in Rome) that served as a sort of rehearsal for the much larger FESTAC. The Dakar meeting drew cultural figures from every medium. It was conducted primarily in French and English but touched also on the traditions dominated by Portuguese, Spanish, Arabic, and many other African languages. Meetings and performances took place all over the city, and a craft village was even constructed at Soumbédioune on a bluff overlooking the fish market.

Among the most popular performances were those by the Ballets africains de Guinée. This dance troupe, founded in the 1950s by Keita Fodéba, featured elaborately staged versions of the acrobatic folk dances of his homeland.

Music included the sounds of the *kora* (a harp), the *balafon* (a xylophone), and drums—especially *djembes*, kettle-shaped instruments with laced drumheads that could be played while held between the legs. When Guinée became independent in 1958 (the sole territory among France's colonies to challenge Charles de Gaulle and claim its freedom), the accomplishment represented a powerful statement of African nationalism. President Ahmed Sékou Touré supported Fodéba and the Ballets africains, arranging international tours in Africa, Europe, and America. The ballet troupe was enthusiastically received and spread the prestige of African dance and music, and the djembe drum became widely appreciated for its sound and its association with African nationhood.

FESTAC celebrated black cultural achievement, but it also provided an opportunity for critical commentary. It was there that Nigerian writer Wole Soyinka expressed his disdain for the notion of "Négritude" championed by the poet Léopold Senghor, then serving as president of Senegal. Soyinka argued that a tiger did not need to proclaim its "tigritude." Another outspoken attendee was Martinican writer Aimé Césaire, who founded the poetry of Négritude with Senghor and now was also an elected official, serving as mayor of Fort-de-France. Césaire presented a production of his 1963 play, *The Tragedy of King Christophe*, set in revolutionary Haiti but commenting fiercely on dictatorship in the postcolonial twentieth century—most obviously with regard to François Duvalier in Haiti but also in reference to the regimes emerging in African countries.[1]

The conference reinforced Dakar's position as a pan-African cultural center. One of its brightest stars was Cheikh Anta Diop, the Senegalese historian and archaeologist. Diop directed his radiocarbon-dating laboratory in Dakar, where he was in the midst of a remarkable wave of publication on ancient Egypt and Nubia, the African continent's cultural history, and the desire to form an African federation. Mercer Cook, an African-American literary scholar then serving as special envoy to Senegal, later translated some of Diop's work into English. Diop's vision of the unity and connection in Africa's past, especially the heritage of the Nile Valley and Egypt, resonated with many African-American readers. Meanwhile, the University of Dakar, created in 1959 as an expansion of the previous medical school, became Cheikh Anta Diop University in 1987.

High Tide in Politics and Culture: The 1960s

The decade of the 1960s marked a time when black people consolidated extraordinary gains in citizenship and nationhood. In that same decade, innovations in popular culture brought new unity to blacks and linked them to allies and admirers among whites and other groups. Connections and reconnections across the African diaspora formed with greater ease. In contrast to the previous half century, political change caught up so that it took place together with cultural advance, rather than with culture in the lead.

In this era of triumphant nationhood, stories are usually told country by country, so that civil rights campaigns in the United States are recounted separately from antiapartheid activism in South Africa and from the politics of Africans and West Indians in France. Similarly, Congolese *soukous*, Brazilian bossa nova, and Algerian *rai* are treated as discrete musical genres. But in this chapter (as earlier in this book) the stories are told in narratives linking all the regions of the African continent and African diaspora. Thus the national stories, some familiar and some new to readers, may appear different when they are shown in parallel and in interaction with each other. While it is not possible to identify or present all the connections among aspects of African diaspora life in the late twentieth century, this concluding review of events since 1960 should make it clear that broad patterns and global interactions remain as significant today as they were in earlier centuries.

The narrative in this chapter includes a greater emphasis on politics than the previous chapter, because from the 1960s, blacks progressively regained the influence in government that had all but disappeared at the end of the nineteenth century. Yet the achievements, however satisfying, came at the cost of many losses and disasters. The political disasters of civil war, massacres, and apartheid were paralleled by the cultural setbacks of continuing educational inequality and new forms of racial discrimination.

FESTAC provided one of the many moments of cultural and political triumph in the African diaspora in the 1960s. The remainder of this chapter traces other high points of the late twentieth century. It shows how, out of these achievements, people throughout the diaspora began to envision full-scale social equality for themselves and pursued the reality behind that vision. But not all was triumph: the chapter also recounts the continuing resistance to citizenship and equal rights for blacks, plus natural and human disasters. By the 1970s, the frustrations brought by the resurgence of old obstacles to black equality had generated the growth of radical responses in black politics and culture. Overall, the experience of the 1970s and 1980s brought mixed results for black communities, with economic hard times and political dictatorship offsetting new achievements in popular culture and higher education. In the 1990s, the achievement of majority rule in South Africa and the elimination of apartheid brought a wave of expanded connections across the diaspora. These connections are explored here in terms of democracy, modernity, diaspora, and equality. But the goal of equality proved elusive on several levels. Divisions grew within black communities, economic globalization left the African diaspora behind, and the HIV/AIDS crisis struck black people disproportionately. Yet the basic strategy of blacks in this era remained in place. It was to gain equal rights in citizenship and to use citizenship as a platform for claiming the full social equality of blacks—in economy, education, political status, and cultural recognition. This program gained ever wider understanding and approval, though implementing it was uneven at best.

Milestones of Black Achievement

The long twentieth-century campaign for civil rights and national recognition was bearing fruit. In 1960 alone, sixteen African countries gained independence. By the end of 1964, thirty African countries, five Caribbean countries, and eight countries of the Old World near diaspora had seats in the United Nations—as did the apartheid regime in South Africa. (By 1983, the total rose to forty-two sub-Saharan African countries, fourteen Caribbean countries, and ten Old World diaspora countries.)[2] The international recognition of black-led political units closely paralleled the domestic advances in civil rights and voting rights in Africa, the Caribbean, and the United States. Voting rights had been suddenly granted to millions of Africans during the 1950s, self-government advanced in Caribbean territories, and civil rights campaigns in the United States culminated in the 1963 March on Washington (where Martin Luther King Jr. gave his memorable "I Have a Dream" speech) and in the passage of the 1964 Civil Rights Act.

The years 1960 to 1968 witnessed the continuation of a sort of honeymoon in international black politics that began with the independence of Sudan in 1956 and Ghana in 1957. Even difficult struggles such as the long crisis in Congo could be interpreted as an advance over the previous absence of black participants from the political stage. Fifteen French African colonies gained independence in 1960, and the Ivory Coast and Senegal, representing the two main political factions, vied for leadership among them. Nigeria gained independence after Ghana. Sierra Leone and Gambia soon followed, then Uganda, Tanzania, and Kenya. (In 1964, the people of the two islands of Zanzibar overthrew the ruling elite, known as Arabs, and joined with Tanganyika to form Tanzania.) An optimistic vision of African socialism, harking back to an imagined earlier time of communal society, was espoused by leaders in Senegal, Guinea, Mali, Ghana, and Tanzania.[3]

The wave of independence brought a great advance in black international politics, though there remained a tinge of paternalism in the phrase "new nations." The principal complication, however, was that international politics were balanced and intertwined with domestic politics: ethnic politics in Africa and the politics of color in the diaspora of Old and New Worlds. (In fact, the politics of color also played a role in such African nations as South Africa and Kenya, and ethnic politics played a role in such American nations as Trinidad and Guyana.)

Meanwhile, the British West Indian territories came to independence, though with contentious changes. The challenges to crown-colony government had led in 1958 to a West Indies Federation, including ten British West Indian territories, scheduled for independence in 1962. In 1961, Jamaica voted to leave the federation on the grounds that it would fare better economically on its own, and when Trinidad and Tobago followed suit in 1962, the federation collapsed.[4]

The political successes and struggles in Africa and the Caribbean encouraged blacks in the United States in their campaign for full political rights. Along the way, a civil rights hymn, "We Shall Overcome," provided strength for those who faced beatings and jail because of their participation in demonstrations for voting rights and desegregation. The song, which has its roots in spirituals, was given new lyrics by members of the Food and Tobacco Workers Union in a 1945 strike in Charleston, South Carolina. The Highlander Folk School in Monteagle, Tennessee, provided support for the strikers, learned the song, revised it further with the assistance of folk singer Pete Seeger, and began teaching it as "We Shall Overcome" from about 1950.

> We shall overcome
> We shall overcome
> We shall overcome some day
> Oh, deep in my heart
> I do believe
> We shall overcome some day

In 1953, the Highlander School shifted its emphasis from labor organizing to the desegregation of schools and community facilities. (Rosa Parks attended the 1955 desegregation workshop.) When participants in a 1959 workshop were raided by police, they sang "We Shall Overcome." The song had found its mission and spread rapidly through the civil rights movement from 1960: it became an anthem adopted in other countries with parallel social movements.[5]

The atmosphere of the 1960s, with its persistent challenges to racial discrimination combined with the cosmopolitan connections resulting from national independence, produced confident new creations in film, music, dress, language, and literature. The emphasis in cultural creation now turned less to European models and more to African roots in search of visions of the past and models for the future. These cultural changes took place under conditions of dramatic economic transformation—globalization—and of continuing urbanization, especially for Africa. In the 1960s and 1970s, black musicians in varying parts of the world expanded their audiences: Harry Belafonte in the United States, Mighty Sparrow in Trinidad, Franco and Rochereau in Central Africa, King Sunny Ade in Nigeria, Milton Nascimento in Brazil—each with their stylistic innovations and all appealing to urban working people. Out of the U.S. urban scene came new musical forms. Saxophonist John Coltrane went beyond brilliant performance to develop a new, influential approach to jazz composition and performance that was spiritual, avant-garde, and cerebral. Most commercially successful was the Motown sound that originated in Detroit, where blacks made up a major proportion of the automobile work force. Berry Gordy, who was born in Detroit and worked for a time on an auto assembly line, became a songwriter and then a music producer. From 1959, he handled groups such as the Supremes and the Jackson Five and solo acts such as Marvin Gaye. Motown reigned supreme in North American popular music for almost twenty years.

In this era even more than in previous times, leading black athletes became public symbols important to the self-confidence of their communities. Perhaps the most prominent athlete of the 1960s was Pelé (Edson Arantes do Nascimento), the dazzling Brazilian forward who scored over a thousand goals in the era of Brazil's domination of the world's most popular sport, soccer football. Nearly equally renowned was the American boxer Cassius Clay, who became heavyweight champion in 1964 and then revealed himself as a member of the Nation of Islam, taking the name Muhammad Ali. When Ali refused to accept induction into the U.S. Army in 1967, at the height of the Vietnam War, he was stripped of his title and boxing license. In the 1970s, he won a reversal through the courts, regained his title, and eventually retired to become an elder statesman in sport. In addition to these black athletes from big countries, the recognition of national independence for African and Caribbean countries enabled them to participate in the Olympics and in global competitions in major sports. The West Indies had already gained prominence in cricket. Cuba had championship middleweight and lightweight boxers. The spreading independence also brought Caribbean sprinters and East African distance runners to prominence. Kipchoge Keino set the pattern for East African runners. This mailman, who trained himself working at high altitudes, won the attention of crowds as he raised the flaps on his cap at the beginning of his final kick. He won the 1,500meter run at the 1968 Olympics and returned in 1972 to win the 3,000meter steeplechase.

The Meaning of Equality

The contradictions of success and recurring limits in the campaign for citizenship brought the formulation of a new and more ambitious objective: black communities began calling for social equality. The need for this new social strategy was demonstrated by the continuing discrimination against black people even as they produced impressive achievements in politics and cultural output. The continuing resistance by the defenders of white supremacy slowed but did not halt the claims for citizenship. If citizens' rights gained widespread approval in formal terms, the practical implementation of those ideals left much to be desired. The education of black people at elementary and higher levels trailed dramatically behind that of the most privileged communities, especially in Africa. Health conditions for black people were greatly inferior to the average for the Atlantic world as a whole. Most especially, economic inequality, which placed black people at the low end of global economic welfare in sub-Saharan Africa and at the low end of national economic welfare in the diasporas of the Atlantic and the Old World, remained an intractable problem. Even the struggle to achieve cultural recognition, overcoming stereotyping and disdain from hegemonic cultural influences, was no easy task.

But what was the meaning of "social equality"? It called for far more than the earlier black claims for voting rights and rights to form nations, but it was not necessarily a claim for blacks to become the same as all other groups. The elements of social equality were the elimination of hierarchy and discrimination in education, health, employment, property rights, family conditions, and in the acceptance of the validity of their cultural production. More crudely and basically, "equality" meant a situation where black people were no longer placed at the bottom of every social category. A new campaign of diaspora-wide social activism sprung up to pursue this goal.

Equality was a most attractive goal, but it proved to be difficult to achieve, partly because it was difficult to measure. Was there a way for black communities to gain social equality and yet retain their distinctive cultural traditions? Would equality of belief mean that all had to share the same basic beliefs, or would it mean tolerance and equal status for differing and even contradictory beliefs? With reference to existing social hierarchies, would equality mean that blacks would be assimilated into the standards set by other racial, ethnic, or national groups? In searching for measures of equality, the pronouncements of key leaders became important. Nelson Mandela's 1953 speech "No Easy Walk to Freedom" became a widely cited statement of hoped-for equality, as did the 1963 "I Have a Dream" speech by Rev. Martin Luther King Jr. As a more militant statement of the need to seize equality, the psychological and political writings of Frantz Fanon also gained wide readership.[6]

In the United States, a turning point in popular understanding arose in 1967 with the publication of *Roots*, a semiautobiographical family history by Alex Haley, which was immediately made into the first television miniseries. This tale, presenting a story of black Americans as an immigrant narrative parallel in many ways to the stories of white immigrants, gained wide popularity in this nation of immigrants. In the same year, the brief but prominent campaign for president by Congresswoman Shirley Chisholm of New York again made the point for full citizenship of African Americans.

Much of the campaign for equality involved identifying and stigmatizing discriminatory behavior. The term "racism," coined in the 1930s in response to the rising persecution of Jews in Europe, became widely used in English and other languages to refer to antiblack discrimination as well. The rhetoric of opposition to racism gave an opportunity to people of all racial groups to join the campaign against discrimination and to express support for the ideals of racial equality. Indeed, the very success of the campaign for identifying and challenging antiblack racism fed the expansion of parallel movements for social equality in many areas of society. For example, a new wave of activism for women's rights emerged in the 1960s and grew in force in the 1970s, most obviously in the United States and the countries of Western Europe, but in practice in many more parts of the world.

Some of the steps toward achieving equality had to take place within the minds of black people. Among the attributes of full social equality was the ability to establish one's own identity, both as individuals and in groups. This need helps explain why so many individual and group identities shifted in black communities. National identities were created with the independence of African and Caribbean states—for example, people gave up their Portuguese identity to become Cape Verdean, and the new nations of Ghana and Mali took the names of ancient kingdoms.[7] In the late 1960s, people of African descent in the United States rather suddenly changed their racial identity from "Negro" to "black." Malcolm X's critique of the term "Negro" may have had something to do with this shift, and the growth in black pride and such phrases as "black is beautiful" facilitated the switch. (At the time, French speakers had already adopted the term *noir* [black] rather than *nègre*.) In South Africa, the government identification of Bantu-speaking Africans as "the Bantu" led to a firm rejection of this label, and the subsequent adoption of "black" identity underscored the strength of the Black Consciousness movement in the 1970s. Many individuals took new names to confirm their control of their identity: the case of Malcolm X is paralleled by that of Kwame Toure (formerly Stokely Carmichael) and those of many thousands more. Styles of dress and hair care changed in a parallel response.

Advances in Health and Education

Medical services expanded in cities and rural areas, and the health conditions of people in Africa and the diaspora improved dramatically after 1960. The per capita expenses on health were low when compared to the rest of the world, but the rise in black self-government meant that medical expenditures rose at a rapid rate. For typical sub-Saharan African countries, the life expectancy at birth rose from thirty-five years in the 1950s to fifty years in 1990. In an important campaign relying on widespread international cooperation, smallpox was eliminated throughout the world, with particular benefits for Africa. African infant mortality rates, while always higher than those for any other continent, fell from over 150 per thousand to under fifty per thousand in the same time period. For Latin American and Caribbean countries, life expectancy typically rose from fifty-five years in the 1950s to near seventy years in 1990, and infant mortality rates declined from fifty per thousand to ten per thousand. These improving health conditions reflect medical advances such as the availability of antibiotics, but they also demonstrate the greater ability of local communities to demand health-care facilities from their governments and to improve public-health conditions regardless of government activity. Still, there were new health problems as well. One scandal emerged from the effort of Nestlé and other canned milk producers to sell their product to nursing mothers in African cities as a substitute for breast milk. When the mothers diluted the canned milk with unsterilized water, their children came down with infections. For a time in the 1960s, mortality rates for infants in Nigerian cities were higher than for rural breast-fed infants. In response to an international outcry, Nestlé became an advocate of breast feeding and found other ways to market its products.

From independence in 1960, elementary schools went up all over Africa. Elementary schooling had expanded in the 1950s, but independence changed the priority given to education. State schools especially grew in number, and in some cases they took over mission schools. Teachers included some from overseas such as missionaries or Peace Corps volunteers, but most were from the home country. By 2000, roughly half of adult Africans were literate, though usually this meant literacy in a second language rather than their first language.

Especially in Africa, the expansion of education brought up difficult questions on the place of local languages in literacy and education. By and large, the postindependence governments stuck with decisions made by colonial regimes. Efforts in former French colonies to develop literary and instructional languages other than French met with little success, as French had occupied that space too fully in the colonial era. As a result, major languages such as Mandinka, More, and Wolof are hardly written at all. In East Africa, Swahili gained confirmation as an official language and a language of instruction, and it sustained itself alongside English. Lingua francas developed widely for speech and song—Lingala in Congo, Sango in Central Africa, Hausa in West Africa, Xhosa in southern Africa—but without becoming languages of instruction. Television and radio, however, allowed for widespread diffusion of vernacular languages. Arabic gained increasing recognition as a language of instruction and public discourse, along with the continuing spread of Islam. Aid campaigns, especially from Libya and Saudi Arabia, helped build mosques and schools throughout Africa, and students were encouraged to attend Arabic-language universities in North Africa and the Middle East.

In the near diaspora of the Old World, since Arabic was the native language of the black and brown people of North Africa and the Arabian peninsula, the expansion of secular schools and the additional support for religious schools meant that literacy rose there as well. The French language continued to be important in the former French colonies of Morocco, Tunisia, Algeria, and Madagascar, especially in elite schools.

Latin American and Caribbean elementary schools expanded and literacy rates improved in the late twentieth century, whether in countries with elected, colonial, or dictatorial regimes. Where creole languages existed, education was in the standard language: English in the English Caribbean, French in Haiti and the French Caribbean, Dutch in the Dutch territories. Spanish remained the language of elementary instruction in Puerto Rico under U.S. rule.

The arguments for expanded education were made more in terms of class than race or ethnicity. Thus when the Brazilian educator Paolo Freire published *Pedagogy of the Oppressed* in 1970 (in Spanish, as he was then in exile during the Brazilian dictatorship), he fueled a social and intellectual movement spreading from Latin America to much of the world.[8] This educational movement, in largely Catholic Latin America, drew on liberation theology, a philosophy developing at the time under the leadership of Gustavo Gutiér-rez, a Peruvian priest. Liberation theology in turn based its arguments in part on the critique of poverty that came from the Catholic Church's Vatican II Council (1962–1965). Cuba's revolutionary regime carried out major literacy campaigns in the 1960s, and literacy there reached uncommonly high levels. In the United States, the 1960s began the era of school desegregation and greater black school attendance. As reported in official statistics, the propor-tion of black children ages five to six enrolled in school rose from 69 percent in 1954 to 96 percent in 2002.

College and university education for black people expanded as never before. The new students took up the slim but potent intellectual tradi-tion that had been maintained in a few institutions in previous times. In the United States, the Negro colleges, many of them founded in the aftermath of the Civil War, had provided a nearly unique opportunity for higher education for people of African descent. They now became known as Historically Black Colleges and Universities: Howard, Hampton, and Tuskegee became espe-cially prominent among them. Universities elsewhere in the black world had provided educational opportunity for a few black scholars: Fourah Bay Col-lege in Sierra Leone, Fort Hare College in South Africa, and the medical col-lege at Dakar, along with the private instruction of students in regions near Timbuktu, where the Madrasa Sankoré had earlier thrived. African students had also traveled to study at universities in Britain, France, Portugal, and in Cairo, at the religious al-Azhar University and the state-supported Cairo University.

The 1960s brought the first admission of large numbers of blacks to col-lege and university education in the United States, Africa, the Caribbean and, to a lesser degree, in Latin America. In this same period, college and university curricula began to recognize and expand the study of the lives and conditions of black people. Area studies and ethnic studies emerged as schol-arly fields. African studies began in the 1950s in the United States, Europe, and Africa and expanded in several disciplines and in their interdisciplinary combination.[9] Latin American studies had begun earlier. After some delay, scholarship in Latin American studies came to give substantial attention to Afro-Latin Americans. Black studies rose in the 1960s, especially in the United States, as a concomitant to the political mobilization of black com-munities.[10] Black studies led in the establishment of a wider movement of ethnic studies, which had influence in the Caribbean and Europe but did not gain the systematic recognition accorded to area studies. Overall, African studies and black studies eventually achieved rough parity with studies of other areas, but black scholars were long neglected in this change. In addition, a substantial expansion in the study of slavery in the United States and elsewhere in the Americas, and related studies on the Atlantic slave trade, emerged in this period. African universities were founded but rarely had the strength to support departments that could compete on a worldwide basis. On the other hand, black scholars in the United States, Britain, and some other countries reached positions of importance, and a few historically black colleges and universities, notably Howard University, gained a place at the table of top U.S. research institutions.

Crises and Reverses

The great waves of social accomplishment coursing across the African diaspora did encounter obstacles. The mountains of previous prejudice and hierarchy stood firmly, sometimes barely eroding as the waves of change crashed against them. The tide of black activism, even at its peak, encountered disappointments and disasters, in part because the advances brought black people into exposed positions on political and cultural stages, where they became vulnerable to divisions among themselves and to counterattacks from outside their community.[11]

Within sub-Saharan Africa, the great political conflict of the early 1960s came in the Congo, which moved hurriedly to independence as the Belgian colonial regime suddenly realized it could no longer deny even local elections to the colony's population. The sudden national elections created a parliament with three groups: an ethnically based party centered around the capital Leopoldville (Kinshasa), a regionally based party led by elite families in the copper-rich southeast, and a loose coalition called the Mouvement National Congolais. The latter had support in several regions and was led by Patrice Lumumba, who had participated in international pan-African meetings. Lumumba became prime minister, but his independence-day condemnation of Belgian colonialism put him in confrontation with the former rulers. The Congolese army soon mutinied against its Belgian officers. Then one opposition party leader challenged Lumumba's leadership and another announced the secession of Katanga province, in association with the copper mining firms. Lumumba sustained his position in the summer of 1960, appealing to the United Nations and the United States to support the integrity of the new nation and UN member state. When no help was forthcoming, he turned to the Soviet Union for aid. This request was sufficient to galvanize his opponents. Joseph Desiré Mobutu, the reporter who became Lumumba's defense minister, seized power and turned Lumumba over to his enemies in Katanga, who executed him in January 1961. Both Belgian officials and the U.S. Central Intelligence Agency were implicated in these events. From there, Congo underwent four years of civil war, armed UN intervention, and the seizure of large portions of the country by mercenary-led armies. In the end, it was Mobutu who seized power again in 1965. By 1967, he was even able to host a continent-wide political meeting in his capital.

In the Caribbean, the unfolding Cuban Revolution echoed the principal events taking place elsewhere during the early 1960s. The conflict of Cuban nationalism and U.S. hegemony soon became a cold war conflict pitting strategies of isolation and containment against revolutionary nationalism. The initial conflict was national, as Cuba moved to take over the holdings of U.S.-based sugar companies. The next conflict was social. At this time, wealthy and professional Cubans found their options limited and many began to leave, going especially to the United States. Eventually, the racial dimension of the revolution emerged, as most people of African descent remained in Cuba and their proportion of the population grew. The U.S.-backed invasion that failed at the Bay of Pigs in 1961 further galvanized Cuban nationalism. Then the Soviet Union's attempt to place missiles on Cuban soil brought the brief but terrifying threat of nuclear war in 1962. In 1965 and 1966, Che Guevara traveled to the highlands of eastern Congo-Kinshasa in an unsuccessful attempt to build a rebellion against Mobutu.

The rejection of legal initiatives to gain citizenship rights led to the development of more radical approaches. In South Africa, the 1960 Sharpeville Massacre—in which over sixty unarmed demonstrators were killed by police bullets—confirmed that in that nation armed struggle and confrontation rather than legal political agitation was to determine the path of racial politics. In 1964, the government of South Africa put leaders of the African National Congress, arrested the previous year at Rivonia, on trial for treason. The ANC, denied any outlet for legal political participation, had turned to gathering international support for military action against the apartheid state, and its leaders were in hiding at Rivonia. Of the fourteen men charged (four of them white), eight were convicted and served long terms.[12] Nelson Mandela remained in prison until 1990.

A similar disappointment arose in Mississippi, where a voting-rights campaign developed the Mississippi Freedom Democratic Party. The MFDP overcame intimidation to register many black voters and present a slate of delegates at the 1964 Democratic National Convention. These delegates claimed that they rather than the regular Democrats of Mississippi represented the principles of the party. When the convention rejected their petition, the door opened to more militant approaches. One of those responses arose in northern U.S. cities with the growth of the Nation of Islam, which had come into existence thirty years earlier as an independent Islamic community of blacks highly critical of "white devils." The group's slow growth was accelerated by greater black assertiveness and through the energetic preaching of Malcolm X, who converted to Islam while in prison and adopted the last name of X to emphasize how his original name had been taken from his ancestors in times of slavery. At the height of his influence in the Nation of Islam, Malcolm X broke from the organization, took the hajj, became an orthodox Muslim, and adopted a pan-African rather than black nationalist posture. He was assassinated in his New York mosque in 1965. Another militant response was that of the Black Panther Party, beginning in California in 1968. Armed with rifles and the writings of Frantz Fanon, the Panthers demonstrated their right to bear arms in a meeting of the California state legislature. Thereafter until the mid-1970s, this militant group carried on a program of community organization and opposition to police forces in a movement spurred on by, among other things, the actions and philosophies of the Red Guard in China's Cultural Revolution. Many Black Panthers died from police bullets, and the principal leaders were tried and convicted on charges related to these events.

Two great crises struck West Africa in 1967, one environmental and one political. The rains failed for several years in a row in the grasslands of the savanna and Sahel from Senegal to Chad; both farmers and pastoralists had to struggle through a devastating famine. The drought was associated with El Niño events of the Pacific, but its effects were made more serious by the results of colonial policies that had overextended farmlands and discouraged people from migrating when the drought hit. In Nigeria, meanwhile, a civil war broke out that was to bring about as many as three million deaths through warfare, famine, and disease. Following a political stalemate dividing the north and south of the country and a military seizure of power, the killings of minority Igbo residents in northern cities led to the declaration of secession by the dominantly Igbo southeastern region, which took the name Biafra. Mobile war in the early stages gave way to a war of attrition. International aid arrived far too late to prevent the famine, and Biafra formally surrendered in 1970.

Less immediately disastrous but still disappointing were the developments in urban life. Early black urbanites at the opening of the twentieth century had set the tone for social life in many twentieth-century cities. (Later black arrivals from the countryside found cities both the source of hope for advance but also prisons with multiple levels of hierarchy.) Latin American cities grew at rapid rates in this era, and those with large black populations included the major Brazilian cities, especially São Paulo and

Rio, Caracas in Venezuela, and Bogotá and Cartagena in Colombia. The cities of the Caribbean grew at rates similar to those in mainland Latin America. Havana had long been a major metropolis, but it was now joined by several others: Santo Domingo, Port-au-Prince, Kingston, San Juan, and Nassau. Each of the larger Caribbean islands came to have at least two major cities (and on the two-country island of Hispaniola, Santo Domingo and Santiago in the Dominican Republic and Port-au-Prince and Cap Haitien in Haiti). By 2000, the Caribbean had become well over 50 percent urban. But millions of additional Caribbean migrants had gone to cities outside the region. New York became the largest or second-largest city for Puerto Ricans, Dominicans, Jamaicans, and Barbadians; Caracas was the second city for Trinidadians; Paris was the second city for Martinicans. As islanders moved to Caribbean cities, tourists from North America and Europe crowded into new beach resorts, which grew as the prerevolutionary resorts in Havana declined.

African cities were built in a hurry and on the cheap, so they lacked elegant boulevards and efficient transit systems. Leopoldville, the capital of Congo, had grown in population from fifty thousand in 1945 to four hundred thousand at independence in 1960; by 1980, with its name officially changed to Kinshasa, the city had a population of 2.5 million. Nairobi became the East African metropolis. Lagos, as it expanded to the west and north of the island on which it began, became famous for its traffic jams. Nonetheless, each African city developed its own character and, for some of them, a clear charm (see figure 6.1). Abidjan, built on islands and peninsulas around the Ebrié lagoon, made it easy to see one quarter from another. And in Yaoundé, the Cameroonian capital built among hills, the distinctive architecture of government and commercial buildings provided impressive vistas. In Yaoundé as elsewhere in Africa, home construction was carried out in bits and pieces, with persistence paying off. A family had first to get access to land and then obtain cement blocks to begin building. Construction might take years, as families gathered money to pay wages, materials, and fees.

Many people who came to urban areas were not able to settle as homeowners or renters; rather, they lived as squatters in makeshift quarters that gradually blended into the structure of growing cities. These areas became known as *bidonvilles* in French (after the *bidons* or oil drums used in constructing housing), "shantytowns" in English, *barrios* or *barrios chabolas* in Spanish, and *favelas* in Portuguese, as well as by many similar terms in the African languages. In South Africa, where the government maintained more control of settlement than in most places, "townships" were created in the mid-twentieth century for black and colored populations, including

FIGURE 6.1 Urban Nigeria, by Jacob Lawrence

Jacob Lawrence, who came to prominence in the United States in the 1930s, visited and painted in Nigeria in the 1960s. This image in tempera, gouache, and graphite, *Street to Mbari*, is a 1964 street scene in Lagos.

Source: Courtesy of the National Gallery of Art, Washington, D.C.

District 6 outside Cape Town and Soweto (for "southwest township") outside Johannesburg. Somehow the inhabitants of these shantytowns gained access to electric power, water, schooling for their children, and a system of urban transportation. The largest and most rapidly growing of all these shantytowns were the *favelas* of São Paulo and Rio de Janeiro, but those of Kinshasa, Lagos, Caracas, Abidjan, and Nairobi—as well as Rabat, Cairo, and Jidda—were not far behind. The "ghettoes" of cities in the United States were different from black neighborhoods elsewhere in African-diaspora cities, in that black and especially poor populations gravitated toward the center rather than the edges. Bank policies, supported by the U.S. government, provided home loans to enable white families to purchase suburban homes but denied credit to black families.

In Europe, black populations in cities grew from the small enclaves that had long existed into major communities. The rapidly increasing postwar populations of the Caribbean spurred the expanding migration of students, workers, and job seekers to London, Paris, Liverpool, and Marseille. Similar flows from Africa grew, especially after 1960. One result was that Notting Hill becoming the principal black section of London, a place where an annual August celebration of Carnival became a major social event. Similarly, Brazilian settlers in Paris, white and black, organized celebrations of Carnival in the Brazilian style in the 1970s. There as elsewhere in Europe, the settlement of large black populations brought a period of fierce racial discrimination by conservative nationalistic groups and by white workers who feared displacement. For example, when the Dutch colony of Suriname gained its independence in 1975, the people there were given a choice between Dutch and Surinamese citizenship. While most stayed in Suriname, many thousands settled in the Netherlands, especially Amsterdam. Only later did cordial relations among communities emerge.

The Sixties

The era of the 1960s brought great promise for black people, although it did not carry them into the Promised Land. The long campaign for citizenship brought results in the recognition of national independence for some fifty nations in which black people were numerous, and it brought formal recognition of civil rights in several major countries with multiracial populations. Blacks gained positions of political leadership, black innovations in popular culture gained wide audiences, and black communities carried on aggressive campaigns against racial discrimination.

In regions of the world beyond the African diaspora, the era of the 1960s brought somewhat different perspectives. It was an era of massive revolutionary upheaval in the Cultural Revolution of China, paralleled by the contemporaneous Revolutionary Offensive in Cuba. For the dominantly white areas of Europe and North America, the decade of the 1960s is often recounted as a time of student upheaval, popular cultural innovation, and the formation of a radical New Left. This was the era of the war in Vietnam, in which U.S. troops, along with Western allies, fought against the communist-led forces of Vietnam, which had Chinese and Soviet support—a struggle both about nationalism and the cold war. It was also a moment of reform movements within socialist states, especially in Czechoslovakia.

In practice, the varying experiences of the sixties overlapped each other. As experienced by black people, the sixties unfolded in response to events both outside and inside their community. The effects of China's Cultural Revolution, the influence of expanded college education, and the rise of a global youth culture became important in Africa and the diaspora. At the

same time, the experience of blacks in the sixties came out of the long struggles of their own communities for citizenship and equality. The sixties of
black people included Fanon as well as Marx, black as well as white college
students, anticolonial warfare in Angola and Mozambique as well as Vietnam,
antiracism in Johannesburg as well as Birmingham, and the new demands of
black as well as white women. In the increasingly class-conscious era of the
1960s, blacks tended to see themselves and were seen by others as workers
and perhaps also as rural people.

The 1960s brought an era of unprecedented steps toward the goal of racial
equality: the near elimination of colonial rule, the discrediting of racial discrimination, and the return of black people to positions of political responsibility in both the New World and the Old World. Confident works of popular
culture buoyed the energies of black people and brought admiration from
their neighbors. The movements for decolonization and civil rights reshaped
the world and proposed an expanded vision of social equality. These social
changes reverberated around the planet, constituting a central aspect of
"the sixties" and a fundamental change in the political and social balance of
the world.

New Inequalities, 1970–1988

The social changes favoring blacks as individuals and in groups could not
continue without interruption, though achievements of blacks as individuals and in groups continued. Yet so also did explicit examples of racial discrimination and the subtle limits on black people that came to be known as
"institutional racism." To a certain degree, these two trends were more of
the same struggle that had gone on for generations. Yet there were also new
forms of social advance for blacks and new obstacles to black equality. On
the positive side, the notion of social equality for people of African descent
gained steadily wider acceptance as it moved forward in the company of
campaigns against discrimination by gender or religion and with newer
campaigns against discrimination by age and by disability. On the negative
side, economic stagnation, ecological crisis, charges of reverse discrimination, discrimination in international law, and growing divisions within black
communities each required new tactics to combat them. The new decade
brought spectacular advances for new elites, especially in entertainment
and sports, and for some in politics. But in the 1970s, it became clear that
there would remain many hindrances to black equality and that several new
sorts of inequality were emerging. With political responsibility came greed

and corruption. Former colonial powers could now choose to neglect the nations for which they had earlier held responsibility. Conditions of education and health improved markedly but brought limited economic rewards.

Global Stagnation and Restructuring

In every corner of the world, the long postwar economic boom gave out at the end of the 1960s. Unemployment rates rose, agricultural prices fell, and for a time both workers' incomes and corporate profits declined. Encouraged by low interest rates and slowing economic growth, African and Latin American countries borrowed heavily from groups of banks organized by the World Bank at the end of the 1960s. Then an economic crisis in 1973 and 1974 put many countries in dire straits. The trigger was the October 1973 war in which Egypt and Syria attacked Israel in attempt to reverse their defeat in 1967. When the United States and the Netherlands gave strong support to Israel and repelled the attacks, the OPEC cartel (with Arab voices dominant but not exclusive) doubled the price of crude oil and then doubled it again. In addition, Arab countries halted oil shipments to the United States and some European countries. The war was brought to an end, but prices of petroleum products and many other manufactures rose rapidly. Currency markets were thrown out of joint, gold prices skyrocketed, and—most important for debtor nations—interest rates rose suddenly to nearly 20 percent per year. The interest burden on loans was now so high that many countries were threatened with default. The International Monetary Fund took hold of the situation and made debt repayment—including the new, higher interest rates—its top priority. It developed the notion of "structural adjustment policies," requiring debtor nations to cut back on public services.[13] The result was sharp reductions in spending on schools, health, infrastructure, and government service generally. The structural adjustment programs continued for about thirty years.

Empires were disappearing in the aftermath of World War II, yet the hegemonic power that had sustained empires rapidly took new forms. The global socioeconomic system thus came to operate at a new and more complex scale. Most unmistakably, giant corporations stretched their influence far beyond their home country. Leaders included the Dutch-British petroleum firm Shell Oil, the U.S. automobile firm General Motors, the Swiss food distribution firm Nestlé, the Japanese shipping firm Mitsubishi, and the German chemical firm Bayer. In addition, semigovernmental organizations of worldwide scope took form and expanded rapidly. The United Nations, created in 1945 to replace the defunct League of Nations, is the most obvious example. Organizations that developed under the UN umbrella included the World Health Organization and UNESCO, the educational and cultural organization that became so important in helping small and poor nations contribute to global cultural discourse. The World Bank and the International Monetary Fund, founded in 1945 and based in Washington, D.C., served as a consortium of the wealthy nations and big banks focused on stabilizing the world economy.

For blacks, who had just regained entry to formal politics, it immediately became necessary to launch superpolitical activity at the global level. Of course, black activists had devoted themselves to creating international organizations for many decades. The Universal Negro Improvement Association had a broad and impressive influence in the 1920s. The periodic Pan-African Congresses, beginning in 1900, were highly influential in creating political goals. When the Organization of African Unity formed in 1963, the scope of pan-Africanism narrowed for a time from the whole African diaspora to the home continent alone. On the economic front, OPEC has come to include significant representation of black populations: Venezuela was one of the five founding nations in 1960, and Nigeria joined later, along with two other African countries, Algeria and Libya. Other countries important in oil production with large black populations include Angola, Gabon, Trinidad and Tobago, and the United States.

Kwame Nkrumah envisioned the creation of a United States of Africa through federation of newly independent African nations. The idea gained a few steps but no more. Ghana and Guinea declared themselves to be united in 1958, and Mali joined the union in 1960. But Felix Houphouet-Boigny, the principal leader of Ivory Coast since 1946, had become closely tied to France and joined the pro-American President Tubman of Liberia to form the Monrovia Group of African states. This group favored a "moderate" policy in opposition to the smaller Casablanca Group of states that included Nkrumah and his pan-Africanist allies. Soon after, a truce was arranged and the two groups met in Addis Ababa, Ethiopia, in 1963, to form the Organization of African Unity, which included all independent African states.[14] Excluded from the OAU were the white-ruled territories, mostly in southern Africa.

Quite a different organization relevant to the lives of black people is the Organization of the Islamic Conference, formed in 1969 to hold annual conferences to discuss concerns common to nations with large Islamic populations.[15] Thirteen African countries became charter members, and ten more joined in the 1970s. Since then five more African countries and two Caribbean countries (Guyana and Suriname) have joined. The nations with the largest Muslim populations of African descent that have chosen not to affiliate with the OIC are (in rough order of the size of their Muslim population) Ethiopia, the United States, Congo-Kinshasa, Eritrea, Tanzania, Kenya, and Malawi. Another set of international meetings, organized beginning in 1986, is that of the Francophone countries, that is, the countries where French is spoken as a significant language. Following years of annual meetings of Francophone African states with the French president, Léopold Senghor of Senegal and Habib Bourguiba of Tunisia led the way in organizing a more formal organization to sustain the use of the French language—partly to offset the expanded use of English. The organization became permanent, with biennial conferences, and includes a system of cooperation among French-language universities.

Great powers, though relinquishing political control of colonies, sought to maintain global military power. Thus the United Kingdom, in giving up its colonies, sought initially to retain a set of island military bases from Africa to Australia. The United States, the dominant partner in the cold war alliance, encouraged this continued British presence. The British gradually narrowed their plan down to the Chagos Islands, two thousand kilometers northeast of Mauritius but part of that colony. As Mauritius became independent, its government agreed to cede the islands to Britain, creating what became known as the British Indian Ocean Territory. More quietly, the Maurician authorities allowed the British to remove the Chagos Islands population (known as Zilois) from their homes and deposit them as refugees in Mauritius—though this later caused a political scandal. Then in treaties of 1966, 1972, and 1976, the British leased one of the Chagos islands, Diego Garcia, to the U.S. military. Diego Garcia later become central to U.S. military activities in Afghanistan, Iran, Iraq, and elsewhere in the Indian Ocean region.

Black Power and Revolutionary Nationalism

The years 1968 through 1980 were dominated by militant black politics and by wars of national liberation that had varying degrees of success. The phrase "Black Power," enunciated by Trinidadian-born activist Stokely Carmichael in 1966 in the United States, resonated for at least two decades.[16] Militant black nationalism reaffirmed the waves of revolution coursing through the Third World, as it was then known, with Ernesto "Che" Guevara, the Argentine-born activist of the Cuban revolution, as one of its heroes and symbols. Revolutionary nationalism had some successes in the African diaspora, but it ran rapidly into its limits. The main limiting factors were the growing power of dictatorships among black people and new pressures from without, especially the ideology and practice of neoliberalism.

Black-power movements ranged in tactics from mass demonstrations to armed struggle. In the Portuguese African territories, rebellions gathered force, but the Portuguese were unyielding, drawing on NATO support to carry on the conflicts. They also succeeded in assassinating opposition leaders Eduardo Mondlane of Mozambique in 1969 and Amilcar Cabral of Guiné and Cape Verde in 1973. Ultimately, however, the rebel soldiers convinced the Portuguese army of the justice of their cause. In a 1974 revolution, the military overthrew Portugal's government and moved rapidly to grant independence to the African colonies. Conflict died down for a time in Mozambique, but in Angola, South Africa and the United States supported the National Union for the Total Independence of Angola (UNITA) forces opposing the Popular Movement for the Liberation of Angola (MPLA) government, and the fighting there continued for more than twenty more years.

Among Catholic theologians working with poor and dispossessed communities, the notion of liberation theology began to emerge. Dominican father Gustavo Gutiérrez of Peru gave the concept a formal voice in a 1971 book.[17] While the theology was principally religious, its precepts led its practitioners into conflict with political authorities and later encouraged some to run for and win public office. In sharp contrast to Latin America, liberation theology did not gain many adherents in Africa. Perhaps some of this can be attributed to the fact that into the 1970s, the top positions in the Catholic hierarchy of Africa were held by European rather than African priests. A secular ideology that maintained many parallels to liberation theology emerged in South Africa in the Black Consciousness movement. Steve Biko was its principal spokesperson. Biko became a leader of the South African Student Organization in 1969 and then went on to participate in claiming civil rights on many fronts through a coalition of many groups, one independent of the ANC and its campaign of armed struggle. One event prompted by this organization was the 1976 Soweto uprising of young people. Schoolchildren were protesting the imposition of the Afrikaans language in their classrooms. The police shooting of eleven-year-old Hector Petersen brought several days of violent protest and worldwide attention. Biko, banned for much of this time and detained repeatedly, was arrested again in 1977 and died from a beating in prison shortly thereafter.

Other governments moved to the left, adopting socialist or communist affiliations. In Jamaica, the People's National Party government of Michael Manley began nationalizing major economic resources such as aluminum mines and opening closer ties with Cuba. Manley encountered strong opposition from the United States and from domestic business interests, who united behind the Jamaican Labor Party of Edward Seaga. In a key moment of this long contest, musician Bob Marley called Manley and Seaga to the platform during a 1978 concert and lectured them on the need for a more civil style of politics. African governments moving to the left included the "Afro-Marxist" regimes of Benin, Congo, and Ethiopia. In each case, military governments formed themselves into political parties that adopted socialist polities and allied with the Soviet Union in international politics. To these Afro-Marxist regimes were added those of the former Portuguese territories, which gained independence when their long wars for national liberation ended with the 1975 revolution in Portugal.

The overlap of national liberation struggles and cold war confrontations took on a decidedly African-diaspora cast as Cuba and the United States became central participants. When the Angolan independence of 1975 placed the Marxist MPLA in power, South African troops invaded Angola from Namibia and pressed very close to the capital of Luanda. Cuban troops were instrumental in holding off the invaders, and the South Africans pulled out in 1976. The Cuban troops included many blacks whose ancestors arguably came from Angola four generations earlier in the late stages of the slave trade. In the wake of this assault, a second proindependence party, UNITA, led by Jonas Savimbi and popular among the Ovimbundu of southern and central Angola, gained continuing support from South Africa and the United States and continued the fight. Cuban involvement in African politics continued as they backed the Marxist Ethiopian regime, helping it to turn back a 1978 invasion from Somalia. Additional Cuban troops went to Mozambique, Guinea, and Guiné-Bissau.

Uprising: From Reggae to Rap

The most distinctive cultural trend to come out of Caribbean cities in the late twentieth century was reggae music and Rastafarian culture from Jamaica. The Rastafarian movement began in the 1930s as groups in the cities and countryside took up the worship of Ras Tafari of Ethiopia as the living God. Ras Tafari, the regent of Ethiopia, became king in 1930 under the throne name of Haile Selassie and was worshipped from afar. The Rastafarians drew on a mixture of Jamaican maroon tradition, East African ritual, and Old Testament theology: life in Jamaica was that of the slaves in Babylon, a hell on earth. Equally important, this outlook gained reinforcement from the frustration of Caribbean migrants whose ambitions met racial discrimination in Central American and North American lands. This messianic religion and its migratory connections interacted with a developing youth culture of Kingston and with local bands creating music based in part on imports from the

United States. The Wailers—Bunny Wailer, Bob Marley, and Peter Tosh—were one such group. They formed in 1963, and by 1964 they had a local hit in "Simmer Down." For the duration of the 1960s, they struggled in a lively Jamaican music scene. They were drawn steadily to the Rastafarian religion and wrote songs that would later gain wide attention and. In 1973, the Wailers released their first two record albums, recorded in England. Marley became the lead singer, and they developed a sound that resonated with the black revolutionary, countercultural consciousness of the day and attracted wide attention to Rastafarian practices. The first album, *Catch a Fire*, spread the reputation of reggae far and wide; the second, *Burnin'*, included "Get Up, Stand Up," a clarion call for the dispossessed to "stand up for your rights." By 1974, the Wailers had broken up, but the music continued. This was one of the cases where black cultural traditions, in nurturing ties among various regions of the diaspora, created a powerful and original cultural form and social movement.

For over a decade, the reggae sound—relying on a distinctive slow beat led by electric guitars, backed by drums, and characterized by lyrics expressing hope and determination for people of modest means—linked the regional and social elements of the African diaspora and provided inspiration and comfort to people beyond the diaspora, notably whites. It also resonated with the widespread celebration of marijuana in the youth culture of the time.[18] It was a remarkable case of Jamaican national music that became world music (see figure 6.2). Local bands developed versions of reggae in Brazil, West Africa, southern Africa, Europe, North America, and throughout the Caribbean. Reggae, as the music of love and rebellion, affirmed black identity, black nationalism, and the critique of capitalism. It filled stadiums in Zimbabwe and Rome.[19] The music continued even as the artists met their end: Bob Marley died of cancer in 1981; Peter Tosh, who split from Marley in the 1970s, was killed by Kingston robbers in 1987.

One way that reggae spread was by linking to earlier musical trends. So it was with *sega*, a musical genre of Mauritius with origins in the nineteenth century that combined Mozambican and Malagasy traditions in music and dance. Long despised for its link to slavery, *sega* was "rediscovered" by Jacques Cantin, a creole intellectual, and made popular by performer "Ti-Frère" Alphone Ravaton. The music became prevalent in a time of community reaffirmation by African-descended creoles, largely Catholic, who were a minority in contrast to the Muslim and Hindu Indian-descended majority. A new rhythm, closer to that of reggae, gained the label of *seggae* and became a popular aspect of an expanding Maurician tourism industry.

The innovations in films produced by black-led companies in the late twentieth century were impressive, but for lack of funding they relied less

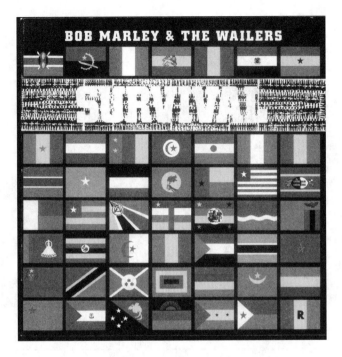

FIGURE 6.2 *Survival* album cover

Survival, record album by Bob Marley and the Wailers, 1979. The album includes a portion of the 1789 image of the "Brookes" slave ship and the flags of forty-nine African nations. Note that the flags of Caribbean nations are not included.

Source: Courtesy of Island Records.

on advanced technology than did music producers. The leading black film-makers became highly skilled with low-budget films. Ousmane Sembène of Senegal was the pioneer. This novelist-turned-filmmaker produced nine films beginning in 1966; much of the dialogue is in Wolof rather than French. A network of support developed with the emergence of FESPACO, a biennial film festival in Ouagadougou, beginning in 1969, and led ultimately to awards for African filmmakers at the Cannes Festival.

Governments also manipulated identities. In the 1970s, as Joseph Désiré Mobutu changed the name of Congo to Zaire, he started an authenticity campaign that required every Zairian to adopt an "authentic" name, changing his own to Mobutu Sese Seko. The singer Rochereau, for instance, changed his name to Tabu Ley. More commonly, the name changes on both sides of the Atlantic were individual and voluntary. The implicit point was the ability of each generation in this era of self-determination to define its own

FIGURE 6.3 *Untitled*, by Seydou Keita

Untitled photo, c. 1960, by Seydou Keita, Bamako, Mali. Seydou took photos from 1959 to 1971, then halted under government order. In the 1990s, after a return to democratic government, his photos became attractive to international art collectors.

Source: Courtesy of Jean Pigozzi.

identity, and indeed for each individual to do the same. Carrying this wave of self-definition into the visual realm, the Malian photographer Seydou Keita created elegant portraits of clients that highlighted their individuality (see figure 6.3).

Another form of manipulated identity, supported by the corporate sector but widely adopted in mass popular culture, was beauty contests or "pageants." The place of black women in these contests provides a sort of index of changing cultural standards. The Miss World beauty pageant began in the United Kingdom in 1951, and the Miss Universe pageant began in the United States in 1952. The first black Miss World, from Grenada, won the crown in 1970. South Africa had sent two contestants in that year: a white "Miss South Africa" placed fifth; a black "Miss Africa South" placed second. In the Miss Universe pageant, the first black winner was from Trinidad and Tobago, in 1977. The Miss America campaign had begun in the 1920s, and the first black winner was in 1984.[20] The pattern of gradual inclusion of black women among beauty-contest winners is clear, but the meaning of the pattern is open to discussion. Did worldwide standards of beauty adjust so as to include standards of Africa and the African diaspora? Or did blacks find ways to adjust their culture to fit standards of beauty defined by the elites of the United States and United Kingdom?

In a segment of society apparently far from beauty pageants, a different sort of musical rebellion emerged out of depressed black neighborhoods in cities of the northeastern United States, beginning at the end of the 1970s. "Rap," involving rapid-fire verbal dexterity and complex lyrics spoken over a percussive beat, emphasized the anger of the young male artists at the social inequalities surrounding them. Though evidently original in its form, rap also drew on Niger-Congo traditions, as speaking through music is widely known and practiced on continent and diaspora.[21] Rap spread across many lines and became better known as "hip-hop," to account for the entire cultural complex of dress, music, and style of social interaction. It became a moneymaker in a way that reggae never was, with individual musicians and the recording companies gaining great wealth. Hip-hop remained a form of protest against social inequities, but it never became a social movement.

In more affluent segments of black and mixed communities, technology changes began to have sharp effects. Michael Jackson, drawing on the Motown tradition, took the lead in fusing music, dance, and video. His *Thriller* album of 1984 was not only the highest-selling album up to that time, but the elaborate videos released with it set a new standard. The references to earlier works were no longer limited to musical quotes but included film clips as well. Dance now was performed at such a high technical level that it was more for watching than for participating. Jackson had taken advantage of the possibilities brought by the emergence of MTV, which first appeared on television screens in 1981.

Dictatorship and Neoliberalism

The 1980s were a time of contradictory social change for the African diaspora. The military struggles of the national liberation wars either were successful or died down. In their place arose popular mass movements in some places, dictatorships in other places, and governments dominated by neoliberal ideology, especially in the United States and Britain, with close alliances to major business interests.[22] In 1980, Zimbabwe finally gained its independence, as a combination of guerilla war and multiparty negotiations ended the white minority regime and created a parliamentary government with Robert Mugabe as president. Bob Marley and the Wailers sang at the independence day celebrations, and the *Survival* album, featuring Zimbabwe and covered with images of African flags sold in great quantities. In 1983, the young military officer Thomas Sankara came to power in Upper Volta and led a movement for national renewal that created great enthusiasm at home and abroad for his self-help schemes. The country was renamed Burkina Faso, drawing terms from the two major languages of the country to mean "land of the incorruptible." Both the governments of Zimbabwe and Burkina Faso, however, lapsed into dictatorship with time, in a pattern that proved remarkably general.

For the first half of the twentieth century, black people lived under authoritarian and colonial governments and had virtually no representation; this pattern could not change overnight. In the 1960s, the newly independent nations of Africa and the Caribbean mostly began with parliamentary governments modeled after those of Europe. But the need for national unity, the fear of subversion, and the prestige of the Soviet model prompted the rise of many one-party governments. Then when the parliamentary governments failed in one way or another, military coups brought dictators to power. In the diaspora, monarchies held power in Arabia and Morocco, dictators held power in Haiti and the Dominican Republic, and the military seized power in Brazil and Libya.

More dictatorships emerged in sub-Saharan Africa in the 1970s. Most were military in origin, but in some cases one-party states held on. The military regime of Idi Amin in Uganda came to power in 1972, moved rapidly to expel all Ugandans of Indian ancestry, and later was brought down by an invasion from Tanzania. Military regimes held power in much of Latin America during the 1970s, and authoritarian governments held on in North Africa and Madagascar. Opposition to dictatorship arose both through popular mass movements and through new military coups. In the 1980s, the military fell from power in most of South America. Military and other authoritarian governments faced challenges from an aroused populace in a number of Caribbean and sub-Saharan African countries. In two of Africa's most difficult experiences, the 1975 independence of revolutionary nationalist regimes in Angola and Mozambique led rapidly to civil war. Domestic opposition and especially foreign intervention led to another two decades of war in both countries. In Mozambique, the shadowy Renamo movement built its strength by seizing children and training them as soldiers. Similar instances of impressing child soldiers arose elsewhere on the continent. Overall, the national liberation movements of the 1970s had partial success in overthrowing colonial regimes but had less success in establishing or maintaining governments with broad popular support.

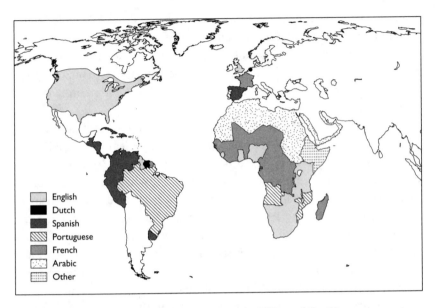

MAP 6.1 Language of Government in Africa and the Diaspora

The rise to power of neoconservative political movements in the great powers, especially during the 1980s, provided additional challenges for black political movements in general and for revolutionary nationalists in particular. Government shifts in two major countries, the United States and Britain, sent conservative ripples across the global pond. Margaret Thatcher's selection as prime minister of the United Kingdom by her victorious Conservative Party (1979–1990) and Ronald Reagan's election as president of the United States (1981–1989) brought governmental restrictions of social policy, expanded military programs, greater emphasis on the private sector, and a shift in class orientation toward an emphasis on wealthy, corporate, and privately employed constituents. The results shifted the domestic and international policies of both countries in education, employment, and in foreign affairs. Both regimes provided reassurance to the minority regime in South Africa, and the United States invaded Grenada in 1983.

In Grenada, a popular group, the New Jewel Movement, seized power in 1979 under Maurice Bishop, a young lawyer. But by 1983, dissension between its leaders ended in Bishop's killing by his close colleague, Bernard Coard. In the aftermath, U.S. forces invaded and oversaw the creation of a new government.

In South Africa, the United Democratic Front formed in 1983 as a coalition of several antiapartheid organizations, including in effect the banned African National Congress. Students and young people of Soweto rebelled again in 1985. This time the actions the angry crowds took included tying automobile tires ("necklaces") around accused government spies and then burning them to death. Meanwhile, assassinations by the secret police continued. At the same time, the antiapartheid movement gained new supporters, and calls for a "new nation" and "new culture" arose from protestors of all ethnicities.

In this atmosphere of renewed popular mobilization, Reverend Jesse Jackson launched a presidential campaign in the United States in 1984. Calling his movement a "Rainbow Coalition," he sought to ally people of all ethnicities in a drive to give priority to advances in health and education. His campaign included an international dimension, and while Jackson did not come near to gaining the Democratic Party nomination, his efforts gave attention to the foreign-policy concerns of black Americans, notably their critique of South Africa's apartheid regime. Yet Ronald Reagan, the winner of the 1984 election, supported a policy of "constructive engagement" in southern Africa, effectively supporting South Africa's Nationalist Party government.

TransAfrica, a black political lobby founded in the United States in 1977 and long led by Randall Robinson, developed with particular attention to representing the opinions of black Americans in international issues. Its first major campaign took place in the 1980s, against the selling of South African Krugerrands (gold coins sold by the apartheid government). The success of this drive led to similarly effective efforts to get U.S. companies and universities to divest their security holdings of companies doing business in South Africa. In later years, TransAfrica gave attention to events in Haiti, Sierra Leone, Venezuela, and elsewhere.

By the late 1980s, as the United Democratic Front formed to unite people of all ethnic groups in public opposition to apartheid, the term "black" had been adopted on an even broader level and came to include those otherwise known as African, Colored, and Asian. War continued in Angola throughout the 1980s, reaching a peak at the 1987–1988 battle of Cuito Cuanavale, where Cuban troops halted a South African drive toward Luanda. In the aftermath, South Africa withdrew its troops, entered multiparty discussions, and gradually agreed to give up control over Namibia, which gained independence in 1990. As part of the arrangement, Cuban troops withdrew from Angola. Even so, the war there continued but at a lower intensity.

Literate Culture

By the 1980s, the results of the previous thirty years of expanded education in black communities became apparent. That is, in the 1960s blacks returned to the political stage, and by the 1980s they had gained more space on intellectual and cultural stages. The expansion of both secondary- and university-level education prepared many thousands of black people for entry to the higher levels of society. For secondary schools, the patterns of increased investment in education paralleled those for elementary schools. In the Africa of 1960, only a limited number of secondary schools existed in each country, and most were boarding schools. By 2000, such schools were much more widespread, and in urban areas they did not need to be boarding schools. In the United States, the issue was not the number of schools but the attendance rates and degree of segregation. In city after city, courts ordered schools to be integrated by busing students from segregated neighborhoods. Some integration schemes proceeded smoothly; others, like that of Boston, brought a decade of contention and the flight of white families to the suburbs. Overall statistics, however, showed that, of blacks over age twenty-five, 15 percent were high-school graduates in 1954 and 79 percent in 2002.

University-level education underwent great changes everywhere in the black world. Africa in 1960 had only three universities outside of South Africa and Egypt. By 2000, all but the tiniest countries had a series of universities, some of them fully equipped, as with the University of Ghana and Cheikh Anta Diop University of Dakar. At the other extreme were small religious schools that claimed university status primarily on hope. Most Caribbean universities came into being in this period, though the University of Havana dates from the eighteenth century. Latin American countries began expanding university systems earlier in the century and continued to open new universities after 1960. Brazil, for instance, created federal universities in nearly all of its states, in addition to state and religious institutions. In the United States, too, the number of universities expanded, though from a comparatively strong base. The proportion of U.S. blacks over age twenty-five with a college degree grew from 2 percent in 1954 to 17 percent in 2002.

In the years from 1980 forward, black writers from many parts of the world were at once critically acclaimed and commercially successful. A harbinger of things to come was Chinua Achebe's *Things Fall Apart*, a novel published in 1958 when the author was twenty-eight, which tells of a father's tragedy and his son's adoption of another path in the era of colonization. It is perhaps the most widely read African novel. Fellow Nigerian Wole Soyinka, a playwright and essayist, was awarded a Nobel Prize in 1986. The Kenyan author Ngugi Wa Thiong'o became a successful writer of novels in English and then stopped producing in that language to help build a Gikuyu-language literature. The Senegalese poet Léopold Sédar Senghor and the Angolan poet

Agostinho Neto each became president of their countries. From the Caribbean, poet Derek Walcott won a Nobel Prize in 1992, and Nancy Morejón of Cuba is also read widely. In the written works of these authors, the medium was little changed but the expression within the medium developed considerably. From the United States, Alice Walker wrote of the American South in *The Color Purple*, and Toni Morrison, after a series of deep yet successful novels, won a Nobel Prize in 1993. Thereafter, the stream of major literary awards to black authors returned to a trickle, but the level of literary output continued to grow. These authors wrote primarily in English, French, and Portuguese; the development of literary culture in creole languages and in non–Indo-European languages was slower and more uneven, but it remains a real possibility for the future.

Black intellectuals in the humanities and social sciences also came to greater prominence during the 1980s. Among the most prominent black scholars have been historian John Hope Franklin, philosophers Paulin Hountondji and Valentin Mudimbe, economist W. Arthur Lewis, political scientist Ali Mazrui, and literary scholar Henry Louis Gates. Two Jamaican-born sociologists gained great prominence: Stuart Hall in the United Kingdom and Orlando Patterson in the United States. More slowly, blacks gained recognition in engineering, mathematics, and computer science, and in the physical and biological sciences.

Democratization and Globalization, 1989–2000

The worldwide patterns of the 1990s moved in two directions—toward greater political social democracy and toward corporate globalization. Sometimes these two patterns reinforced each other; at other times, they conflicted rather directly. This section, in portraying the African diaspora during the final decade of the twentieth century, addresses both the long-term developments in the lives of black people and the short-term developments of the recent past. Both long-term and short-term issues are presented under the four headings of democracy, modernity, equality, and diaspora.

Democracy

The headlines of the year 1989 gave particular attention to the great prodemocracy demonstrations at Tiananmen in Beijing from April to June, to the opening of the Berlin Wall in November, and to the fall of communist regimes in Poland, Czechoslovakia, Hungary, the German Democratic Republic, and Romania. Earlier in 1989, there had been agreements and the end to military occupation in Afghanistan, Cambodia, and Namibia. In all these cases, demands for democracy arose among urban workers, rural people, and especially professionals, calling for an end to arbitrary restrictions by government, greater economic openness, and greater popular participation in governance.

The ideas of democracy and citizenship are closely related. In the lands of the African diaspora, participation in this sudden wave of democratization movements linked automatically to the long campaign to citizenship. For black people, therefore, campaigns for democracy launched in 1989 were not new campaigns but rather new phases of political programs that had gone on for generations. Democratization movements were understood with equal clarity as restatements of protest against the dictatorial governments that arose in Africa after the end of colonial rule. Activists in Africa and the Americas readily took up the term "civil society" to refer to the many layers of the general population that found themselves in opposition to "the power," referring to the state, the military, the police, and social organizations that were under government control.

In West and Central Africa, the most outstanding democratization movement was the series of "national conferences" that began in Benin. There the Marxist-oriented military government faced a long series of work stoppages by unpaid public employees, leading to a threatened national strike in December 1989. Newspapers, long forbidden or otherwise discouraged, now flooded the streets and offered news and critical commentary on every subject. The government backed down from confronting its workers and agreed to convene a national conference that would include "all the active forces of the nation." In a remarkable nine-day meeting in February 1990, representatives from throughout the country appointed a prime minister and selected members of a high commission to prepare a new constitution. In the most crucial moment of the process, President Mathieu Kérékou addressed the conference and effectively ceded power to its leadership. In the language of the time, it was a struggle between "civil society" and "the power." Videotapes from the Benin events circulated all over French-speaking Africa, and within two years nine other African nations had national conferences. Catholic bishops—now of African birth—were selected to preside over most of these conferences. In another nine countries, the popular demands for similar national conferences were deflected only by the adoption of other reforms or, as in Cameroon and Ivory Coast, by a police-backed government clampdown.[23]

Southern Africa experienced its own unique democratization. Namibia held elections under UN auspices in late 1989, and in 1990 became independent with a government headed by Sam Nujoma, the longtime leader of the main liberation party, SWAPO. And on February 11, 1990, Nelson Mandela strode out of Pollsmoor Prison in South Africa, released by President F. W. De Klerk after twenty-six years of imprisonment. Mandela, then seventy-one, demonstrated remarkable energy and political skill. He first met with crowds throughout South Africa. Then for several weeks he traveled throughout Africa, offering thanks to supporters of the antiapartheid movement. Thereafter, he traveled to Europe and to the Americas, meeting large crowds and government officials at each stage. In South Africa, it took four years of complex negotiations, mutual recriminations, and continuing violence, but in 1994, Nelson Mandela assumed office as president as a result of the first national election in which all adults were eligible to vote. "Nkosi sikelel'i Afrika" became the national anthem of South Africa, and a new flag recognized the many constituencies of what was called by many South Africans their "new nation."

Why did change come to the South African bastion of white supremacy? A long list of factors combined: the international solidarity of black people in opposing the regime, the growing isolation of white supporters of the regime, the expanding black-white alliances inside and outside South Africa, the effectiveness of the long-term alliance of the African National Congress and the South African Communist Party, and the remarkable force and diplomatic skill of Nelson Mandela. Of all these factors, black solidarity mattered most in the long term and Mandela's skills were crucial in the short term.

The democratic changes of the Americas in this era were less spectacular but no less significant. Haiti was no longer the sole nation with a significant number of elected black officials. Military regimes had formally relinquished power in Brazil and Argentina, and presidential elections at the end of the 1980s confirmed that civilian government was back to stay. In Brazil, by the end of the 1990s, President Fernando Henrique Cardoso publicly denounced racism and supported the creation of affirmative-action programs in university education and employment. In a parallel change, a new constitution of Colombia (ratified in 1991) officially recognized African ancestry, thereby changing school curriculums to include study of African heritage and giving Afro-Colombians the right to claim land. This change substantially advanced the social status of Afro-Colombians but required careful readjustment in relations among blacks, whites, mestizos, and Indians. In the United States, the number of elected blacks grew substantially: in 1990, twenty-four black representatives were elected to the U.S. Congress from all regions of the country. (In 1955, Adam Clayton Powell and Charles Diggs had been the only two black members of Congress.)

But also in late 1990, the wave of democratization campaigns met the jolt of a new sort of threat. In August, Iraqi troops suddenly occupied the neighboring state of Kuwait. Iraqi President Saddam Hussein announced the latter country's annexation and sought to exploit its petroleum reserves. A massive confrontation of Iraq with the United States and its allies dominated world affairs for much of the next year and would recur in later years. Surprisingly, however, the U.S. preoccupation with the military and diplomatic buildup for the Iraq campaign provided the opening for a sudden change in the politics of Haiti. In the aftermath of dictator Jean-Claude Duvalier's fleeing the country in 1986 in the face of popular pressure, national elections had finally been arranged. Marc Bazin, a World Bank economist who had U.S. support, was expected to win, until Jean-Bertrand Aristide declared himself a candidate in November 1990. Aristide was a former Catholic priest of the Salesian order. The group that backed him, *Lavalas* (Avalanche), was a popular movement that backed his liberation-theology approach and criticized the various elite and military factions contending for power. Aristide won the December election overwhelmingly and assumed office. In June 1991, however, his government was overthrown by a military coup with the assent if not the encouragement of U.S. officials.[24]

These and other events showed that democratization movements in the African diaspora were more than faint reflections of the collapse of the Berlin Wall. They were lively chapters in the long history of black campaigns for citizenship and, as the cases of Benin, South Africa, and Haiti show, each involved strikingly original approaches to the worldwide call for democratization. At the same time, politics had not become a simple matter of steady progress, especially as is shown by the beginning of a new set of disastrous conflicts in West Africa. A new outbreak of violence began in 1989, as Charles Taylor led a small army into Liberia from Ivory Coast. This invasion provoked an uprising that overthrew the military ruler, Samuel Doe. Doe's torture and execution were recorded on videotape and broadcast widely in Africa. New parties entered the fray, funding their arms purchases through the sale of diamonds, and civil war continued until it was finally halted by a West African peacekeeping force led by Nigeria. In the wake of this conflict, similar civil wars emerged in neighboring Sierra Leone in 1991 and in Guiné-Bissau thereafter.

Modernity

The long debate about modernity—its origins and influence in the world—gained a new label in the 1990s: "globalization." The vision of globalization, centering on planetary interactions in economics, culture, and politics, was often expressed as the sudden opening of new global interconnections in the aftermath of the cold war. With further reflection, however, analysts came to see that this was only the latest expression of a familiar story of large-scale social changes that have taken place every century or so. That is, "globalization" was really another term for "modernity," and the new debates about globalization were little different from the older debates about the dramatic changes separating modern life from previous times. In those debates, one of the most important distinctions among interpretations is between those that allow for the inclusion of Africans in the story of modernity and those that exclude black people from a modernity that is seen as the property of narrow groups defined variously as "civilized" peoples, the white race, or highly educated elites.[25]

The experience of the African diaspora teaches one to seek out a vision of modernity based on interaction, not purity. Instead of inventiveness resulting from isolating the Best of the West, where they can create in splendid isolation, it has come from exchange of ideas and experience. True, there is commonly a struggle over who gets control of the benefits of innovations, and sometimes that control is tightly guarded by a small group.

The economic story of modernity centers on expanded productivity and the accumulation of great amounts of wealth that can be invested in further productivity. In an era of rapidly flowing international investment, decisions were made to invest elsewhere than in Africa, to invest minimally in Latin America and the near diaspora of the Old World, and to invest minimally in urban areas with large black populations. In an era when social discrimination against black people was being challenged at national levels, the continuing economic discrimination at the international level was striking.

Regardless of whether corporate investment was available, black populations around the world continued their movement into cities (see map 6.2). São Paulo, Rio de Janeiro, and Cairo were among the biggest cities of the world, with populations of some twenty million each. Six cities of sub-Saharan Africa had populations of over five million by 2000, and many more had populations of over a million. In terms of total black population, the major U.S. cities in 2000 were New York, Chicago, Detroit, Philadelphia, Los Angeles, and Houston. In terms of the proportion of blacks in urban populations, the major cities were Atlanta, Washington, D.C., Birmingham, New Orleans, and Baltimore. The contrast between U.S. and Canadian cities was remarkable: the

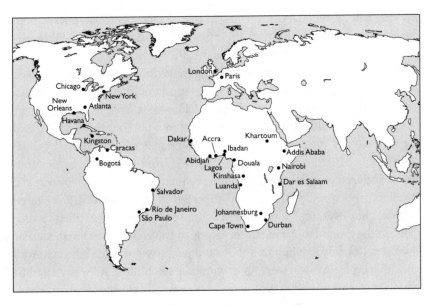

MAP 6.2 Major Cities of the Black World, 2000

two countries shared the same economic system, and numerous Caribbean immigrants settled in Montreal and Toronto, but the centers of Canadian cities remained vibrant and cosmopolitan rather than becoming ghettos.

Modernity has brought the successful handling of social and ecological crises, but it has also brought disasters. The disasters of Central Africa in the mid-1990s—which are known as "genocide" but can perhaps be best understood as "fratricide"—are failures of the modern world rather than remnants of premodern times. The Hutu and Tutsi populations of Rwanda and Burundi were "ethnic" groups in only the most restricted sense—they shared the same language, religion, and culture and differed mainly in statements about their ancestry and labels on their identity cards. On the other hand, a quiet social dislocation had been taking place since the mid-1980s, as HIV/AIDS infection spread widely throughout Rwanda, Burundi, and all of highland East Africa.

Political disaster struck in 1993 and 1994. In both countries, paramilitary Hutu militias preaching extermination of Tutsi oppressors gained the freedom to do their worst. In Burundi, a 1993 coup by the Tutsi-led military seized and executed President Melchior Ndadaye. Hutu militias then massacred groups of Tutsis and fled the country before the Tutsi military clamped down. Efforts by leaders of both countries to mediate their situations brought them to Tanzania for meetings with President Julius Nyerere and United Nations officials. Then, on April 6, 1994, as the presidents of

Rwanda and Burundi were returning from one such meeting, a missile fired by unknown assailants brought their plane down as it approached the airport in Kigali, Rwanda, killing all on board.

With that incident, the massacres began. Within a day, the Hutu-based Rwandan military had killed most top government officials. Hutu militias, urged on by their partisan radio station, Radio Mille Collines, executed virtually all Tutsis in Kigali and then fanned out into the countryside to expand their mission. At the same moment, the Rwandan Patriotic Front, a Uganda-based force of Tutsis who had been expelled from Rwanda in earlier conflicts, declared war and rapidly occupied much of the country. French and Belgian forces quickly removed most foreigners from Rwanda. The United Nations, however, took a noninterventionist approach, overruling its officials on the ground in Rwanda, since none of the great powers wished to be involved. Roughly five hundred thousand people were killed between April and July; typically, men were shot; women and children were executed by hand. Rape, as is typical in such massacres, was at an elevated level. It is hard to explain how a society of neighbors, whatever the balance of intermarriage and enmity, can so suddenly turn to systematic murder.

In July, the United Nations reversed its policy and sent troops into Rwanda. By this time, the RPF controlled the majority of the country, and fearful Hutu populations began fleeing to the west, crossing the border into neighboring Zaire. The UN troops halted the massacres and the forward movement of RPF forces, which fit France's political agenda in particular. The RPF established itself as Rwanda's government, and the situation there quieted, albeit under a well-armed regime and with the problem of sorting out the genocide's repercussions.[26]

Social disasters in another part of Africa brought a response that demonstrates the creativity of modernity. In South Africa, once the elections of 1994 brought a coalition of black and white to govern, a Truth and Reconciliation Commission was appointed as a source of social healing. In an effort to heal national wounds and enmities, the ANC government adopted and expanded a model developed in Latin American countries such as Argentina, Uruguay, and Chile to acknowledge and repudiate the abuses that had occurred under their dictatorships.[27] The TRC held public hearings that allowed people on each side to express their anger or grief and in some cases to beg forgiveness, and a huge amount of documentation was made public. During these hearings, the necklace killings, assassinations by police, and other painful events were reviewed in public, televised testimony. Many of the problems caused by generations of discrimination and violence remain unsolved, but the TRC arguably succeeded in creating a new and much broader national identity for South Africa by initiating this common forum for expression. While the TRC still has its critics, it was an effort at social reconciliation on an unprecedented scale.

Addressing issues of reconciliation and equality at a still larger scale, activists across the African diaspora have raised the call for *reparations* to black people in compensation for the losses suffered through enslavement and racial discrimination. This call, raised most explicitly by Frantz Fanon in 1961, has led to complex discussions since.[28] Reparations have been collected by victorious powers from defeated enemies, but in a new development, the governments of West Germany and East Germany paid reparations to the state of Israel as a response to the execution of Jews in World War II. While virtually all of those enslaved have now passed on—as have the oppressors of the enslaved—and while the effects of racial discrimination were surely greater in the past than in the present, it is undeniable that the effects of slavery and racial discrimination remain with us today and that they reproduce inequalities in today's societies. One question raised by the call for reparations is whether there is some way to respond to these inequities of the past in the name of our common humanity.

Equality

At the beginning of the new millennium, the organized campaign of black people for social equality had gone on for over a generation. What results were gained in that time? What views emerged in black communities about the value and effectiveness of equality as a social objective?

The economic advances were modest and uneven. The political advances of the 1960s—independence and recognition of civil rights—raised the hope that the end to political constraints would lead to substantial improvement in economic conditions for black people. Clearly there were many steps forward in the quality of life for black people in the intervening four decades, but they were not recorded in terms of sharply higher average incomes. From the vantage point of 2000, it seemed that new political power had not made a great difference to economic welfare. In making such comparisons, it is important to distinguish the economic discrepancies *between* nations from economic discrepancies *within* nations. Within almost every nation, the comfortable, affluent classes of blacks increased in number. Professional and public-service employment of blacks grew in every country, and ownership of landed property and buildings grew for a smaller portion of the population. Despite the great advances in education of the general population, however, unemployment levels remained significant and average incomes modest. [Black employment conditions advanced furthest in the public sector, while in the private sector blacks remained more vulnerable to discrimination or exclusion.] Other material and cultural conditions of black people advanced more substantially. The discrepancies in health and education, which earlier left blacks far behind the most privileged communities, declined remarkably, though black populations and Africans in particular remained low in international comparisons of health and education.

Perhaps the greatest advance was the least tangible: the widespread acceptance of social equality in principle. The new constitution of South Africa provided an outstanding statement of the expanded vision of equality. South Africa's constitutional convention drew an international assembly of lawyers in support of South African delegates. The resulting document, adopted in 1996, may well become a model for national constitutions throughout the world: the thirty-two sections of its Bill of Rights include explicit and thorough statements protecting social equality. Remarkably, the long campaign of the ANC (founded in 1913) for a parliamentary government based on citizenship and representation for all appears to have survived the transition to majority rule.

Another sort of equality is that brought by the rise of black people to levels of excellence and prestige in many areas of endeavor. The rise of black men and women in sports is perhaps the most obvious way to locate the recognition that can come with individual achievement. At least equally valued is the advance of blacks in almost every area of intellectual endeavor—in the professions, science, business, and cultural affairs. One way to describe this aspect of equality is to say that there are now fewer social arenas from which blacks are excluded. Yet equality cannot be measured by any single tool. The globalizing economy provides potential consumers with an astonishing range of goods and services, multiple communication networks, and opportunities to work or play endlessly. Social pressures encourage one to conform to powerful norms but also to seek the most individual of identities. What then is the definition of equality?

The sum of these dimensions of equality, while complex, suggests that the black campaign for social equality achieved significant if not measurable advancement by 2000. Nevertheless, while one can demonstrate the existence of a new philosophy of social equality and of powerful social movements and legal provisions in support of it, it remains true that the ideas about social life and social interaction change slowly. The habits of discrimination—by racial, sexual, religious, and other categorizations—are deeply ingrained. They do change, but the lifetime of an individual is only long enough to see a small part of the change.

Diaspora

Diasporas have long existed, but the growing level of migration and the increasing ability of diaspora communities to maintain contact with one another over distances means that diasporas have become a greater part of society in modern times than ever before. The notion of the African diaspora, first coined as a phrase in the 1970s, developed wide popularity in the 1990s; African-diaspora consciousness grew even further with time.[29] In addition to becoming a term of large-scale community identity, "diaspora" has become a concept for social-science analysis. In this volume, we have considered diaspora-wide interactions within black communities, with hegemonic powers, with non-African communities, and mixing of various sorts. Viewed in these conceptual terms, we can say that the African diaspora has been in existence for a long time, even though formal diaspora consciousness has taken hold increasingly only in recent years.

The changes in dress and personal appearance among black people reveals the increasing connections among the diaspora's regions and cultures. This story is invoked most directly through a look at hair styles. The practice of braiding and weaving the hair of black women goes far back and was practiced episodically throughout the diaspora. Burial remains show evidence of it in the Nile Valley over two thousand years ago. But an updated version of the style caught on in the 1980s, probably as hairdressers in West Africa found new materials for extensions and sharpened their skills in making long and tight braids. This style of braiding gained sudden popularity in many parts of Africa, North America, the Caribbean, and eventually South America. Innovations and modifications in braiding moved back and forth across this large area. Black men began adopting braids in North America and the Caribbean, though less so in Africa. At the same time, steady advances in technology made it easier to "relax" the hair of black women, and varying degrees of straight and curly hair were readily available to women throughout the continent and diaspora. A third tradition was that of dreadlocks, adopted by men and women alike from the era of reggae music. In addition, the common African pattern of women trimming their hair close to their heads appeared in the diaspora as well. In sum, black women and men shared a complex variety of hair styles, with new styles traveling long distances in short times and with a range of styles evident in any community.

The visual art of black artists underwent a creative explosion in the late twentieth century, going many directions at once. The continuing traditions of representational painting, picturing the life of black communities, were paralleled by metaphorical and abstract works in painting, sculpture, and installations. Visual artists traveled throughout the black world, exchanging ideas on forms and materials. The dramatic expansion of a multilayered market for painting and sculpture provided an outlet for schooled and unschooled artists. At the top end, new and old African sculpture gained an expanded place in museums and galleries, along with the works of academic African-American artists. At the middle layer, an international market for tourist art circulated the works of African, Caribbean, and North American artists to airports and galleries everywhere. The sudden popularity of soapstone sculpture from Zimbabwe is one example of these genres. At the local level, artists in Latin America and every other region produced works for home audiences. The quantity of this output and the range of experimentation raises the possibility that some major new developments in visual art may emerge.

The number of topics and participants in the various dimensions of black culture continued to expand. The expanding vision of "world music" allowed for broader recognition of local musical traditions: for instance, the *gnawa* music of Afro-Moroccans grew in popularity within Morocco and abroad (see figure 6.4). Religion and sports each saw substantial advances in the position and the accomplishments of black people. Public represen-

FIGURE 6.4 Master Mokhtar Gania

A 2005 photo of Mokhtar Gania, a noted performer in the Gnawa tradition of music and spiritualism in Morocco.

Source: Photo courtesy of Chouki El Hamel.

tations of the experience of blacks proliferated, for instance, with the creation of museums and historical exhibits on slavery in Liverpool, Nantes, Florida, Ouidah, Goree, Cape Coast, and New York. In one sense, these cultural developments confirmed the increasing contacts and interconnections among blacks everywhere. In another sense, they were the expression by black individuals and communities of cultural values shared with people of all ancestries.

The Scourge of HIV

In 1979, doctors in New York began identifying patients suffering from an unknown syndrome causing a range of symptoms including Karposi's sarcoma, a previously rare form of cancer. By 1982, the condition had been identified on every continent except Asia and Europe and came to be labeled "Acquired Immune Deficiency Syndrome," or AIDS (SIDA in French, Spanish, and Portuguese). It also became clear that AIDS could be transmitted sexually among men as well as by blood transfusions. For cases in Africa, the symptoms were also found to be conveyed by heterosexual contact.

The advent of this disease, as with earlier epidemics, created fear, blame, and guilt. The prevalence of AIDS among gay men fostered assertions of the disease being a retribution for deviance and sin or a consequence of promiscuity. The suggestion that the disease had African connections created fear of Africans and sparked debates about homosexuality within black communities. The gradual advance of medical knowledge about AIDS brought clarification and new problems. In 1983, Dr. Luc Montagnier of the Pasteur Institute in Paris isolated a virus that he labeled LAV. In 1984, Dr. Robert Gallo of the U.S. National Cancer Institute isolated a virus, labeled it HTLV-3, and announced that it was the AIDS virus. In 1986, an international commission affirmed that the two viruses were the same and labeled it HIV (human immunodeficiency virus).

Gallo went beyond his identification of the AIDS virus to assert a theory for its origin: African green monkeys. Gallo noted the presence of AIDS symptoms in Central Africa, among Haitians in Haiti and in the United States, and in American homosexual populations. He noted that viruses of a similar structure existed in monkeys and asserted that the AIDS virus had passed from African green monkeys to Central African populations, to Haitians, and then to gay American men. Because of the authority of his position, the theory spread widely. In effect, it blamed Africans for the disease. In subsequent attempts to set up HIV screening procedures, officials at the

Centers for Disease Control listed a set of risk factors; among them was Haitian nationality. This put further blame on Haitians.

In the fear and excitement of the epidemic's early stages, the use of medical categories gave way to social discrimination. Communities of Haitians, Africans, and gay men responded angrily to their being singled out, and ultimately their voice was heard. In particular, being of Haitian nationality should never have been listed as a risk factor. No matter how high the rate of infection among Haitians, the HIV virus recognizes only biological opportunities to propagate. Its dissemination has nothing to do with national identity. These biological criteria were later and more correctly defined as blood exchange through any of several mechanisms: hypodermic and surgical needles (used for blood transfusions, other medical purposes, and for injection of narcotic drugs), sex among males, and heterosexual contact. In addition, it was recognized that having multiple sex partners or poor levels of nutrition and general health boosted infection rates.

As the HIV/AIDS epidemic worsened, the medical system began to respond at national and international levels. By the end of 1986, eighty-five countries had reported 38,401 cases of AIDS to the World Health Organization: thirty-two thousand of these were in the Americas, four thousand in Europe, over two thousand in Africa, and smaller numbers elsewhere. The United States appeared to be the center of the epidemic, though African cases were surely underestimated for lack of adequate medical infrastructure. In 1987, Kenneth Kaunda, president of Zambia, announced that one of his sons had died of AIDS. Consequently, the disease began to be taken more seriously in Africa.

Tests for HIV infection began to be developed in 1985. The ELISA test, easily administered, tended to overestimate the number of HIV infections; the Western Blot test, more difficult to administer, was more conservative but also overestimated HIV infections. As testing expanded, figures began to be reported for HIV infection (most showed no symptoms) rather than AIDS symptoms. For the year 1990, over 307,000 AIDS cases were officially reported to the WHO, but the actual number was estimated to be closer to a million. Even assuming substantial underestimates for 1986, the 1990 figures assumed a growth in AIDS cases by a factor of ten or twenty over this four-year period. The 1990 AIDS cases reported were 156,000 for North America and 77,000 for Africa (though the estimated actual figures were 200,000 for North America and 650,000 for Africa). For 1990, the estimate of people infected with HIV worldwide was eight to ten million. Of the eight million, it was estimated that about five million were men and three million women. The estimated three million HIV-positive women were estimated to have given birth to about three million infants, of whom one-fourth were born infected with HIV. Kapita Bila, the physician who—in 1975 in the hospital he directed in his home town of Kinshasa—was probably first to encounter AIDS as an epidemic, wrote in 1988 of its growing implications: "The Aids of the late twentieth century judges our society, our morality, and the direction of our economic progress. Today's society seems to have attained the level of evolution required for its own destruction."[30]

The worst was yet to come. In North America, the epidemic peaked in 1990 and then slowly declined, though the number of black Americans infected continued to grow until later in the 1990s. (The high level of imprisonment of young black males spread the HIV virus through their sexual contact.) In later years, the virus spread disproportionately among African-American women. In Uganda, AIDS was first diagnosed in 1982 and was soon recognized to be spreading rapidly there and elsewhere in Central and East Central Africa. In 1986, President Museveni of Uganda proclaimed a national prevention campaign focusing on abstention and condoms. In 1991, official statistics based on HIV testing showed the prevalence of infection among pregnant women ages fifteen to twenty-four stood at a terrifying 21 percent. The year 1995 appeared to be the peak year of infections in Uganda, with a decline thereafter, though the rate of decrease was disputed.

While there was a great display of energy and imagination among those most concerned with combating the spread of HIV and treating those afflicted with AIDS, those with the power of the purse took little interest in the epidemic. In 1993, the World Bank reviewed its activities in Africa and decided that AIDS should not dominate its agenda on population, health, and nutrition issues. The World Bank believed AIDS would have little demographic effect but recognized it as a serious threat to health and economic development. With reference to blood screening, it was argued that this was costly and "might not be cost-effective under all circumstances." Meanwhile, the number of AIDS cases doubled from 1990 to 1993 and the number infected with HIV rose by five million (50 percent) to fourteen million total. Of the 2.5 million AIDS cases in 1993, 1.7 million were in sub-Saharan Africa, four hundred thousand in North America, three hundred thousand in Latin America and the Caribbean, and one hundred thousand in Europe.

In 1995, the number of deaths from AIDS in the United States began to decline. (The rate of HIV infection in the United States had peaked some years earlier.) Worldwide, however, and especially in Africa, HIV infection and AIDS symptoms continued to grow at alarming rates. An estimated 4.7 million new HIV infections occurred in 1995 worldwide. Of these, 2.5 million were in Southeast Asia and 1.9 million in sub-Saharan Africa. Approximately five hundred thousand children were born with HIV. As the 1990s proceeded, the number of new infections declined in Central Africa but grew rapidly in southern Africa.

The epidemic in southern Africa exceeded any preceding limits. The irony was that, at the very moment of the long-awaited transition to majority government and in the region of the continent with the most extensive network of health-care facilities, the HIV epidemic expanded with startling and unprecedented speed. For prenatal tests of women in South Africa, rates of HIV infection went from a tiny 0.8 percent of those tested in 1990 to 10.4 percent in 1995 and up to 24.8 percent in 2001. In Botswana, Namibia, Swaziland, and Zimbabwe, 1998 estimates showed that between 20 and 26 percent of people were living with HIV or AIDS. In July 2000, the Thirteenth International AIDS Conference was held in Durban, South Africa. This was the first time that such a conference took place in a developing country or in Africa. The conference voted to confirm that HIV was the cause of AIDS, countering doubts on that issue expressed by South African President Thabo Mbeki, yet the seriousness of the epidemic revealed that neither the analysis, diagnosis, nor treatment of the disease were yet fully understood.

In the early twenty-first century, deaths from AIDS were stable at twenty thousand per year in the United States and rising in Latin America with deaths of one hundred thousand per year. Infection rates remained high in Haiti and almost zero in Cuba. Death rates for Africa must have been over a million per year. Indeed, the effects of the HIV/AIDS epidemic were sufficient to have reversed all the improvements in life expectancy since 1960. For South Africa, average life expectancy fell from sixty-two years in 1990 to forty-eight in 2000, lower than the 1960 rate. For Zambia, life expectancy reached fifty years in 1990 and fell to thirty-eight years in 2000, well below the 1960 level.

In 2001, UN Secretary General Kofi Annan opened the UN General Assembly Special Session on HIV/AIDS in New York. This was the first-ever UN meeting devoted to a public-health issue. Yet the cost in life over the previous decade had been immense, and it has been borne very unequally. The epidemic showed that, as much as humans have gained control over their circumstances, there is much in nature they cannot manage. It also showed that social and economic discrimination among humans still has devastatingly unequal effects. People lacking great economic power—and commonly that includes black people—were too low a priority for big governments to address their needs. And medical science, despite the dedication of its practitioners, had not yet found the needed ways to link its expertise to the cultural specificity of local populations.

With the passage of time, the HIV/AIDS crisis, in Africa and worldwide, inched toward improved management of the disease and perhaps toward cure. Yet one must ask what price black people will pay for the loss in life and the high rates of dependency. What lessons will humans as a whole learn? Why have black people suffered disproportionately from HIV/AIDS? Why has a disproportionately small effort in the campaign against HIV/AIDS gone into healing of black people, especially in Africa? One does not know what to predict, except that the history of the African diaspora will continue to be one of interesting changes and developments.

What Happened to "Race"?

The first studies of human genetic history through mitochondrial DNA were published in 1985. These early tests of human genetic variation, using newly developed techniques for the analysis of DNA, suggested that the greatest genetic variation in humans was among black people, and therefore that humans had lived longer in Africa than anywhere else. By the early 1990s, ferocious scientific debates had confirmed these results: it was clear that anatomically modern humans had evolved in Africa some two hundred thousand years ago and had expanded to populate the world. Rather than a series of separate races, humans were now understood to be a single species, recently developed, that spread and differentiated across the planet.[31] The spread of humans out of Africa was later understood to have been limited to the past seventy thousand years, and the development of "racial" differences took place mostly within the last thirty thousand years, as humans occupied all the continents. This new scientific knowledge proved irrefutably the error of two centuries of scientific claims that human racial groups are sharply different from one another and that they can be placed in a hierarchy. Genetic change is slow, and humans are too new a species to have differentiated much from one another. The physical differences among us come precisely because our ancestors had the skills to occupy every environment, and groups in each region then developed superficial bodily changes in response to variation in weather and diet.

In short, scientific research of the 1990s rejected "the biological concept of race" among humans—we are all too much alike to be subdivided. At the same time, social practice over a longer period of time rejected "the social concept of race," according to which people can be classified by color and ranked in a hierarchy. Many and perhaps most people did not need biological tests to affirm human equality. Novelists and poets had long since documented the variety within each human group and the commonality of human struggles and dilemmas within every group.

Partly because of the new scientific results but mostly because of social changes, the term "race" tended to fall out of use in English and many other languages at the end of the twentieth century. In place of it came references to color, ethnicity, community, nation, and sometimes religion. One of the few areas where the term "race" continued to be used was in the increased use of "multiracial" to refer to people of "mixed" ancestry. Did this terminological change mean that racial thinking had ended? The advances in biological confirmation of the unity and similarity of all human populations, and the variety within human populations, reinforced this tendency to let "racial" thinking go. The historic form of color-based racial discrimination has now been discredited, if not entirely vanquished. But the impulse for prejudice and discrimination against groups identified by one criterion or another seems deeply built into human reasoning, even in an era where nondiscrimination is adopted as a principle. The growing conflicts between Christians and Muslims show that it is still possible to categorize and dismiss groups based on oversimplified thinking that assumes differences between groups to be bigger than differences within groups.

Is the goal of social equality a realistic one for people of the African diaspora? The notion of race is more seriously called into question than ever, yet the same physical differences among us remain, along with the impulse to categorize. Are we all the same? Biologically, yes. Is there a way to enable us all to be biologically and legally the same yet allow for social and cultural differences? This question, argued on both sides in Cuba and elsewhere more than a century ago, is still under debate. The generations to come will determine whether equality means uniformity, and how much of each they wish to have. Meanwhile, in a world proclaiming equality as its guiding principle, statistical analyses of every region of Africa and the diaspora show the continuing discrepancies in health, education, employment, and wealth.

Suggested Readings

The 1966 FESTAC gathering resulted in a conference volume in which many of the leading figures made brief contributions: Society of African Culture with the cooperation of UNESCO, *First World Festival of Negro Arts: Colloquium on Negro Art* (Paris: Présence Africains, 1968). At the festival, Aimé

Césaire produced his critical play, *La Tragédie du roi Christophe* (Paris: Présence Africaine, 1963)

High Tide in Politics and Culture: The 1960s

The dramatic black achievements of the 1960s in civil rights and national independence have been written up, primarily, as separate national episodes rather than as a global social movement. For an early summary at the level of the African continent, see Immanuel Wallerstein, *Africa: The Politics of Independence* (New York: Vintage, 1961). On politics of this era in Brazil, see George Reid Andrews, *Blacks and Whites in São Paulo, Brazil, 1888–1988* (Madison: University of Wisconsin Press, 1991). On the 1960s in Cuba, see Alejandro de la Fuente, *A Nation for All: Race, Inequality, and Politics in Twentieth-century Cuba* (Chapel Hill: University of North Carolina Press, 2001). For a thorough analysis of Congo-Kinshasa in the early 1960s, see Crawford Young, *Politics in the Congo: Decolonization and Independence* (Princeton, N.J.: Princeton University Press, 1965). On Martin Luther King Jr. in the United States, see Taylor Branch, *Pillar of Fire: America in the King Years, 1963–65* (New York: Simon and Schuster, 1998); and Taylor Branch, *At Canaan's Edge: America in the King Years, 1965–68* (New York: Simon and Schuster, 2005). On the Nation of Islam in the United States, see Louis E. Lomax's *When the Word Is Given: A Report on Elijah Muhammad, Malcolm X, and the Black Muslim World* (Westport, Conn.: Greenwood Press, 1979); and Alex Haley, *The Autobiography of Malcolm X* (New York: Grove Press, 1966).

New Inequalities, 1970–1988

For a broad survey of post-1960s black political movements, focusing especially on Anglophone societies, see Ronald W. Walters, *Pan Africanism in the African Diaspora: An Analysis of Modern Afrocentric Political Movements* (Detroit, Mich.: Wayne State University Press, 1993). On the rise of the Rastafarian movement in Jamaica and its consequences, see Leonard E. Barrett, *The Rastafarians: Sounds of Cultural Dissonance*, rev. ed. (Boston: Beacon Press, 1988); and Horace Campbell, *Rasta and Resistance: From Marcus Garvey to Walter Rodney* (Trenton, N.J.: Africa New World Press, 1987). On the black community in Britain, see Winston James and Clive Harris, eds., *Inside Babylon: The Caribbean Diaspora in Britain* (London: Verso, 1993); on ethnic mixes in North America, see Paul Spickard, *Mixed Blood: Intermarriage and Ethnic Identity in Twentieth-century America* (Madison: University of Wisconsin Press, 1989). On Thomas Sankara's campaign for self-reliance, see Alfred Sawadogo, *Le Président Thomas Sankara: Chef de la Revolution Burkinabé, 1983–1987* (Paris: L'Harmattan, 2001).

Mercer Cook was first to translate a work of Cheikh-Anta Diop into English: Cheikh Anta Diop, *The African Origin of Civilization: Myth or Reality*, trans. Mercer Cook (Westport, Conn.: L. Hill, 1974); additional works were translated thereafter and they gained attention in the United States that paralleled Diop's fame in French-speaking Africa. For other major statements in philosophy, art, and culture in the black world of the 1970s and 1980s, see Alex Haley, *Roots* (Garden City, N.Y.: Doubleday, 1976); Françoise Pfaff, *The Cinema of Ousmane Sembene, a Pioneer of African Film* (Westport, Conn.: Greenwood Press, 1984); Paulin Hountondji, *African Philosophy: Myth and Reality*, 2nd ed. (Bloomington: Indiana University Press, 1996); Sidney Littlefield Kasfir, *Contemporary African Art* (London: Thames and Hudson, 1999); Paul Berliner, *The Soul of Mbira: Music and Traditions of the Shona People of Zimbabwe* (Berkeley: University of California Press, 1978); Patrick Taylor, ed., *Nation Dance: Religion, Identity, and Cultural Difference in the Caribbean* (Bloomington: Indiana University Press, 2001); and Monique Taylor, *Harlem Between Heaven and Hell* (Minneapolis: University of Minnesota Press, 2002).

A key document in the World Bank's launching of restrictive "structural adjustment" programs in Africa, Asia, and Latin America was the "Berg Report," led by Harvard economist Elliott J. Berg: World Bank, *Towards Accelerated Development in Sub-Saharan Africa: An Agenda for Action* (Washington, D.C.: World Bank, 1981). For assessments of the effects of this policy, see Gerald K. Helleiner, ed., *Africa and the International Monetary Fund* (Washington, D.C.: International Monetary Fund, 1986); Rosemary Thorp, *Progress, Poverty, and Exclusion: An Economic History of Latin America in the Twentieth Century* (Baltimore, Md.: The Johns Hopkins University Press, 1998); and François Houtart, *Crisis del Neoliberalismo y Recreación de las Luches de los Pueblos* (Bogotá: Universidad Nacional de Colombia, 2003).

Democratization and Globalization, 1989–2000

The political transformation of South Africa is set in global context in James P. Barber, *Mandela's World: The International Dimension of South Africa's Political Revolution, 1990–1994* (Oxford: James Currey, 2004). On the national conferences of 1990–1994, see Patrick Manning, *Francophone Sub-Saharan Africa, 1880–1995*, 2nd ed. (Cambridge: Cambridge University Press, 1998). On the complex political trajectory of Haiti, see Robert Fatton,

Haiti's Predatory Republic: The Unending Transition to Democracy (Boulder, Colo.: Lynne Rienner, 2002). On the politics of genocide in the highlands of East Africa, see René Lemarchand, *Burundi: Ethnic Conflict and Genocide* (Cambridge: Cambridge University Press, 1996); Johan Pottier, *Reimagining Rwanda: Conflict, Survival, and Disinformation in the Late Twentieth Century* (Cambridge: Cambridge University Press, 2003); and Gérard Prunier, *Africa's World War: Congo, the Rwandan Genocide, and the Making of a Continental Catastrophe* (New York: Oxford University Press, 2008).

The economics of globalization had ramifications throughout the African diaspora. See, for example, M. Anne Pitcher, *Transforming Mozambique: The Politics of Privatization, 1975–2000* (Cambridge: Cambridge University Press, 2003); and Raneta Lawson Mack, *The Digital Divide: Standing at the Intersection of Race and Technology* (Durham, N.C.: Carolina Academic Press, 2001).

On South Africa's large-scale effort at national reconciliation, see Richard A. Wilson, *The Politics of Truth and Reconciliation in South Africa* (Cambridge: Cambridge University Press, 2001). More broadly on reconciliation and reparations, see John Torpey, ed., *Politics and the Past: On Repairing Historical Injustices* (Lanham, Md.: Rowman & Littlefield, 2003); Ronald W. Walters, *The Price of Racial Reconciliation* (Ann Arbor: University of Michigan Press, 2008).

The acceleration, in the late twentieth century, of visual and literary creativity among black artists worldwide is evident in the pages of summaries such as Richard J. Powell, *Black Art: A Cultural History* 2nd ed. (London: Thames and Hudson, 1999); and V. Y. Mudimbe, *The Idea of Africa* (Bloomington, Ind.: Indiana University Press, 1994).

The Scourge of HIV

The literature on the HIV/AIDS epidemic is growing in size and value. An outstanding work, because of the author's extensive knowledge of both African social conditions and medical history, is John Iliffe, *The African AIDS Epidemic: A History* (Oxford: James Currey, 2006). For other significant works on Africa, see Helen Epstein, *The Invisible Cure: Why We Are Losing the Fight Against AIDS in Africa* (New York: Farrar, Straus and Giroux, 2007); and Kyle Dean Kauffman, David L. Lindauer, and Desmond Tutu, *AIDS and South Africa: The Social Expression of a Pandemic* (New York: Palgrave Macmillan, 2004). On Latin America, see Tim Frasca, *AIDS in Latin America* (New York: Palgrave Macmillan, 2005). For a general study that gives ample attention to the United States and Europe, see Jonathan Engel, *The Epidemic: A Global History of AIDS* (New York: Smithsonian Books, 2006).

What Happened to "Race"?

For a video presentation that summarizes scientific and historical knowl-edge and also reflects contemporary changes in attitudes to "race," see Tracy Heather Strain, *Race: The Power of an Illusion* [videorecording] (San Francisco: California Newsreel, 2003). See also Troy Duster, "Race and Reification in Science" and other online articles in "Is Race 'Real'?: A Web Forum Organized by the Social Science Research Council" (http://raceand genomics.ssrc.org).

The Future of the African Diaspora

Three principal narratives have unfolded within these pages: the rise and fall of slavery, the social struggles of black communities, and the cultural representations of life and life's hardships produced in those communities. These braided stories convey the African diaspora's growth and change, especially during the past six centuries. Here, I pose and attempt to answer some very important interpretive questions prompted by this chronicle, three about the past and four about the future, as a way of stepping back for a broader closing perspective and to encourage further study and discussion.

The historian can rarely, if ever, answer such broad and deep questions precisely, yet the ongoing study of the past is of great use in refuting mistaken interpretations and narrowing the range of debate about the human condition. Interpretive summaries like the one I provide here can answer numerous small questions and more sharply define some of the bigger queries.

Why Did World Slavery Grow to Such an Extent in the Modern Era?

The practice of slavery has long existed. As far back as the time of Assyria, pharaonic Egypt, and Minoan Crete, slavery existed and grew in the Mediterranean and the Middle East. For the institution to expand, cultures eventually had to break their own laws and then make new ones, because enslavement required the theft or seizure of human beings and then the creation of a subordinate legal status for those enslaved. Hellenistic, Roman, Byzantine, and early Islamic societies inherited laws recognizing slavery from earlier times and so slavery continued as a central institution. Wars produced a cheap supply of captives who were set to work in agriculture, mining, transportation, and domestic service. In medieval times, slavery expanded and contracted in the Mediterranean and Middle East as the power of empires and profitability of commerce waxed and waned.

The economic boom of the newly opened Atlantic basin dramatically expanded slavery westward in the sixteenth and especially the seventeenth century. The boom only benefited some, however. In the same era, the indigenous population and the old economy of the Americas collapsed. European adventurers, who controlled Atlantic warfare and commerce, sought cheap labor to perform the heavy agricultural and mining tasks necessary for their profiteering. African laborers, relatively inexpensive when they could be obtained as captives, were preferred because they were available, hardy, and able to survive disease better than other populations. Racial discrimination by color, identifying Africans as likely slaves, emerged as a way of sustaining and expanding slavery.

Yet why did Atlantic-centered enslavement spread its influence so far, causing slavery in Africa and Asia to expand? Africa did not undergo an economic boom like the American colonies, though in Africa too a class of wealthy merchants and rulers emerged in a climate of overall economic decline. In the centuries of exposure to enslavement, many African legal systems changed to allow the practice and officially recognize slave status. Systems of seizure and delivery improved with time, perfected by raiders and merchants. In addition, enslavement spread by contagion: too often, people who had lost family to enslavement in turn enslaved their own enemies. Slavery became a global system of labor, expanding in many Old World regions as a key element of a steadily transforming economy.

The nineteenth century witnessed the peak and near collapse of slavery, its greatest expansion and most rapid contraction. The moral and political campaign against the institution was one main reason for its decline. The other was the rise of the industrial age, which saw the creation of steamships that enabled cheap, safe, transoceanic travel. As free people started migrating in large numbers, it became possible for labor-hungry business owners to abandon slavery.

What Have Been the Social Contributions
of Black Communities?

Throughout the era of slavery and in postemancipation years, black communities have produced, contributed, and innovated in ways that maintained and advanced their own societies as well as benefited human welfare more generally. In their home societies, the labors and investments of people of African descent enabled their communities to move forward step by step. As enslaved migrants and as wage workers, these individuals also provided valuable labor for other communities. At home and abroad, they developed techniques for resisting slavery and other forms of oppression. They created a broad, pan-African identity, providing local black communities with a sense of participation in a larger society. Black people developed flexible family structures to adapt to their complex social situations, structures that relied heavily on a time-tested vision of motherhood. They learned skills and created traditions appropriate for urban life. They also established governing philosophies and practices to administer their own communities, even though hegemonic powers could interfere at will. These kinds of social contributions all evolved in unique ways.

Africans, over a long history of travails and adventures, sustained, advanced, and, when necessary, rebuilt their societies. The travel and social interaction that were a part of their life fostered a web of connectivity within the continent and with the peoples of Asia and Europe. The pattern of expanding communication and investment, established long before the slavery boom, continued through the centuries of large-scale enslavement and still goes on today. Outside their own communities, black people built much of the modern world economy—perhaps more than their share. Especially in the era of slavery but also more recently through industrial labor, black workers have contributed substantially to global construction, production, and trade. The work has ranged from building colonial cities in the Americas to constructing railways on four continents; from harvesting sugar and cloves to extracting silver, gold, coal, diamonds, and petroleum; from operating hand looms to running textile mills; from hoisting sails and loading steamships to repairing aircraft; from carving the Suez and Panama canals to tunneling subways and bomb shelters; from blacksmithing and assembling automobiles to computer programming; and, always, cleaning house.

The oppression experienced by workers fostered individual resistance and larger social movements. Enslaved black people developed traditions of opposition to slave raiders, buyers, and owners that stand as major accomplishments in their own right. Individual resistance included escape, sabotage, the purchase of freedom for one's self or loved ones, and debate with slave owners and defenders of slavery. Group resistance included elaborate defenses against raiders, rebellions aboard ship or on plantations, and the formation of maroon escapee communities. Over time, black communities developed a balance of individual and group resistance and rebellion that significantly weakened slave systems and built a proud tradition of social struggle. In a word, slavery caused antislavery. Similar movements came about in response to forced labor under colonial rule and to work in prison gangs. Subsequent and broader campaigns for national liberation and civil rights were inspired and instructed by the earlier tactics of resistance to slavery.

Yet black people also became slave owners and exploiters, and in later times some became dictators and corrupt business moguls. From the fifteenth century, African warlords and merchants sold captives to purchasers along the Atlantic coast. Then in the eighteenth and especially the nineteenth centuries, black people of wealth and power, encouraged by global trends, bought expanded numbers of captives and put them to work. They did so in the Americas—especially in St.-Domingue and Brazil—and in Africa. Then from the 1960s, as black people began to regain political power, democracy turned to dictatorship in many countries, and expanded wealth somehow ended up concentrated in the hands of a few families. Black people have always faced the problem of how to handle such conflicts within their own communities.

Black people created themselves as a group: they developed and sustained a diaspora-wide identity, partly in response to the logic of "race." Far from an instinctive recognition of black unity, and equally far from a straightforward acceptance of racial categorization by whites, this common identity could only be a product of gradual, complex discussions. Black people thus found themselves struggling not only against enslavement but also against racial categorization. While rejecting racial hierarchy, black leaders developed a pan-African racial identity and with it launched some of the earliest efforts to build modern nations, most notably in Haiti and Sierra Leone. The recognition of multiethnic nations in Africa and of multiracial nations in the Americas led to new questions regarding how to sustain and best use black identity. With time, as improved media technology and political independence enabled greater flexibility, a transnational identity extended to much larger portions of black communities (see figure 7.1).

Black families developed new traditions, on the continent and in the diaspora, as economic and political conditions changed. The centrality of moth-

FIGURE 7.1 Oprah Winfrey and South African Youth

Oprah Winfrey, wealthy and prominent from her U.S. television show, invested time and money in care for South African youth, especially those whose parents had died of AIDS.

Source: Courtesy of Harpo Productions.

erhood in the family, deeply honored in Africa's ancestral times, gained new importance under the influence of slavery, colonization, emancipation, and industrialization. As the slave trade ripped African families apart and as slave owners exploited women who had no family to protect them, the individual strength of mothers grew in centrality. Legal systems discouraging slaves from marrying, in the diaspora and in Africa, loaded further child-rearing responsibility on women. Even after emancipation, migrant-labor systems split up family units and left women as the center of family life; today's prison systems do the same in some countries. This same set of pressures left black fathers frustrated and often marginalized in family life. One should not go too far with this generalization, since it is surely the case that most black children of recent centuries, in Africa and the diaspora, have grown up in the company of both mother and father. On the other hand, since contemporary discourse often presents female-headed black households as a defect and a failure of family life, it is worth emphasizing that the effectiveness of black mothers in raising their children stands as a major social accomplishment of the African diaspora.

Another significant contribution of black people has been in the physical and cultural construction of urban spaces. From the sixteenth to eighteenth centuries, Africans built capital cities such as Gao and Mbanza Kongo, port cities such as Elmina and Luanda, and American cities such as Havana, Lima, and Salvador. In the nineteenth century, African and Latin American cities languished, but Africans contributed to the expansion of Mecca, New York, and New Orleans. In the twentieth century, black people led in forming the popular culture of rapidly expanding metropolises in Latin America, North America, and Africa, as well as adding new character to the cities of Europe.

[Black traditions in government also reflect substantial achievements. Through strong debate among themselves, black communities and their leaders developed solid notions of proper government.] One great task was learning how to govern a community while under the thumb of hegemonic or imperial forces. Holding on to the idea of the beneficent African king— a person who was powerful, just, and deeply focused on the community's welfare—was one way to maintain political principles. A second tradition involved the messianic leader brought suddenly to prominence in times of crisis. A third and quite contradictory political tradition grew out of the long centuries of slavery and imperial subjugation. In this version, the king reigned with absolute power, demanding and receiving complete submission and frequent protestations of loyalty from his subjects.

In another vein, the many contributions of black people to the knowledge and technology of the modern world appear among the accomplishments of individual inventors who, among other things, improved transportation, medicine, agriculture, day-to-day domestic life, and manufacturing techniques, as well as developed new techniques in the arts and communication. While individual discoveries and inventions mark big changes in knowledge, the real driving force behind steady technological advance is the many small improvements made by anonymous thinkers that have been implemented and then passed on to succeeding generations. While many of the small breakthroughs came from untutored artisans who used good sense to solve the problems before them, formal education has become essential during the past century to advance innovative thinking in an increasingly complex world. For the peoples of Africa and the African diaspora, such education has made great strides, especially in the Arabic, English, French, Portuguese, and Spanish languages.

During the past four centuries, black people worldwide, in carrying out their social struggles, have played a significant role in colonization, industrialization, urbanization, and the advance of formal education, science, and technology. The global changes they participated in made life increasingly complex rather than simpler. Of the struggles carried out in earlier ages, none were complete at the end of the periods I identified: survival of black communities was not assured by 1800, emancipation had yet to reach many people in Africa or Afro-Eurasia by 1900, and all black peoples had by no means achieved citizenship in 1960. Similarly, blacks had not achieved equality by 2000. Indeed, this last objective seems in some ways the most elusive. The peoples of Africa and the diaspora have achieved big steps toward equality in a number of cultural areas but have fallen behind systematically in overall economic well being.

How Did Black Communities Create Their Cultural Advances?

African-diaspora communities turned local expressive cultures into a cosmopolitan cultural outpouring, taking advantage of newly forming audiences. In the nineteenth century, these audiences developed through social changes that expanded theatrical and musical venues for the general populace. In the twentieth century, technological change made it possible to reach greater numbers of people through print, sound recordings, film, radio, television, and many other forms of media.

The long oppression of slavery and racism led ironically to the flowering of black popular culture. The deprivation brought by slavery, racism, and colonialism denied Africans the opportunity to sustain powerful elites—on the continent and especially in the diaspora. As a result, the most talented artists, rather than be summoned by monarchs to palaces to create music and art aimed at praising great leaders, were left to entertain members of their own communities. As a result, throughout Africa and the diaspora, the work of individual artists and the broad traditions of popular culture gained prominence over the celebration of nobles and monarchs in elite courts. For individual artists, their specific accomplishments in storytelling, music, and dress developed in different directions because their audience was the community rather than the ruling class. For the art forms as a whole, the broad techniques of communicating with popular audiences were able to grow—emphasizing the basic issues of life and death with sensuality and mystery—

free from interference by royal authorities focused on their own interests and agendas. In an interesting twist, the *griots*, who sang praises for kings of the savanna and who were particular innovations of African royal art, now took on the task of sustaining the memory of the whole community; that is, they became an element of popular culture.

Black popular culture renewed itself repeatedly through new technology, new audiences, improvisation, and continued borrowing. Jazz music provides an outstanding metaphor in this regard, in that it formally treats improvisation as essential to the genre. In fact, improvisation and attention to new audiences or new techniques have characterized most genres within black popular culture.

The emergence of black artists who have gained wide recognition in elite cultures can also be understood in terms of popular culture and broad audiences. Leading writers, philosophers, singers, playwrights, composers, and actors have each had to develop technical and artistic proficiency meeting the highest standards of their field, but they have also relied on their ethnic links to black communities to reaffirm the social conscience of their cultural work. For example, tenor Roland Hayes's practice of including spirituals in his classical recitals made this point in one way. Among artists, the term "giving back" was sometimes used to describe such an act of recognizing their community. Many years later, another form of giving back involved a budding black academic who sought to contribute through his studies to a recognition of the African diaspora as including the Siddi community in South India (see figure 7.2).

How will changes in society and in patterns of culture influence the future of black popular culture? The very success of black artists in music, dance, literature, and other fields has altered the cultural landscape. New genres that began in black communities are now shared by many ethnic and racial groups. Hip-hop, for instance, has gained not only large cross-cultural audiences but major artists from beyond the black community across several continents. The steady crossover of black cultural innovations into broader audiences is ongoing, while the cultural creativity within black communities continues unabated.

Will Social Equality Ever Be Possible?

The ideal of achieving social equality has now gained wide support. In the last three centuries, slavery has been repudiated, ideas of democracy and

FIGURE 7.2 Researcher with Family of the Informant, Karnataka, India

In this multifaceted image of the Indian Ocean diaspora, members of an African-descended family of Hyderabad (Karnataka state) pose with a visiting anthropologist. The visitor, Ababu Minda Yimene of Ethiopia, was completing his doctoral studies at the University of Goettingen in Germany.

Source: Courtesy of Ababu Minda Yimene.

citizenship have challenged earlier notions of social hierarchy, racial and religious discrimination are now widely decried, and the United Nations has formally adopted the ideal of universal human rights. The twentieth-century expansion of literacy has given poor people a greater voice. In these senses, society has become more egalitarian. However, the struggle for the realistic achievement of social equality continues to occupy the people of Africa and the African diaspora.

Black individuals and communities have contributed much to the advance of egalitarian ideas. Their participation in campaigns against slavery and imperialism and their continuing criticism of other forms of oppression have done much to articulate the concerns of the poor and the underprivileged. In particular, the history of the African diaspora provides ample evidence of acts of individual strength and imagination that brought significant advances in the struggle for and attainment of social equality. The names Toussaint Louverture, Harriet Tubman, and Nelson Mandela are sufficient to illustrate this dimension of black achievement.

Popular culture has had a surprisingly great influence in spreading the idea of social equality. Music and dance convey the impression of such equality even where economic differences are large. Songs, dances, and other musical creations have restated and magnified joy, sadness, hope, despair, and above all a sense of community. These forms recognize leadership yet also show a healthy skepticism for hierarchy. The traditions of cultural representation, invented in earlier millennia in Africa, have been tested and reformulated over four centuries of broader interaction across the continent and diaspora. They comment on and become part of life in a way that has continuing relevance for black people. Perhaps of equal importance is that these traditions have also instructed and inspired many beyond the black population.

In contrast, however, economic inequality has grown over the past two centuries to an unprecedented and even threatening level. It separates rich nations from poor and wealthy individuals from the destitute. In turn, those who are well off and highly educated have great power to make decisions affecting all humanity, and they have access to a far greater range of cultural achievements and to better health conditions than ordinary people.

Some crises of inequality have become particularly severe. In the contemporary world, there remains particular concern about problems of poverty, inequality, and racial discrimination within black communities and in their relations with other communities. I think especially of South Africa and Zimbabwe, where the heritage of racial hierarchy has left patterns of inequity that have only begun to heal and where governance is collapsing in the latter. I think also of New Orleans, where the natural disaster of Hurricane Katrina and its aftermath revealed the poverty and racial inequality remaining in the world's most powerful nation. These examples reflect the global divide between the haves and have-nots, in which the poor must fend for themselves and face manipulation by private corporations, powerful government institutions, and the international capitalist economic order.

The question of social equality leaves us with a serious dilemma. While one can note many concrete steps toward defining and legislating basic equality for human societies, one dare not ignore the immense and growing gap in wealth and power that characterizes our age. To sort out this dilemma, we would be wise to draw deeply from the archive of experience our predecessors have stored over the last few centuries of history. That history can provide profound insights on which aspects of social change we can control and which we cannot.

Should Reparations Be Granted for Past Injustices?

Occasionally, victors in wars have forced losers to pay reparations for damages or evils done. After World War I, the Allies, especially Britain and France, required the German government to make payments, arguing that Germany was to blame for the conflict's destruction. British and French colonial authorities in Africa burned rebellious villages and then required the inhabitants to pay back taxes and the cost of the expeditions that subdued them. Following World War II and the Holocaust in Europe, East and West German governments agreed to compensate the state of Israel for Jewish loss of life. Sometimes the victors have been forced to pay. Decades after it won independence, Haiti paid France twenty-five million gold francs—a huge sum in the mid-nineteenth century—to compensate French planters for their losses. Parallel notions of reparations at an individual level accompanied the end of slavery. Former slave owners demanded recompense for their property loss and they received it from the British government in 1838 and in other cases. Freed slaves demanded payback for their loss of freedom and the theft of their labor. In the American South, victorious Union armies distributed land to thousands of black families, but in 1866, the federal government revoked these land titles and expelled the ex-slaves: their call for "forty acres and a mule" echoed for years thereafter. In recent decades, with the renunciation of the heritage of slavery and racism, black groups on all continents have called for reparations for the descendants of those enslaved and compensation for black societies that have suffered racial discrimination.[1]

While the hope for reparations is simple, implementing a workable plan is highly complex. Since it is impossible to grant payments to victims long dead, should support go to their descendants? Are the reparations due to descendants of slaves only in the diaspora or in Africa as well? To the degree that Africa as a whole was weakened by slavery, should general payments be made to the continent? Who should make the payments? Should compensation be demanded only from the descendants of slave owners? Should payments be made by all white people? Should everyone alive today make payment, given we have all benefited in some measure from the past exploitation of slaves? These and many more questions make clear why it has been difficult to proceed practically with the idea of reparations.

Despite its complexities, the notion opens the door to a more general concept: compensation for the past as a way of ensuring a better future. There is no way to undo previous inequities. Neither is there a way to compensate satisfactorily for past oppression, though some recompense may be better than none. Yet it seems worthwhile to think of more ways to respond in our own time to past discrimination, since any attempt to "forgive and forget" serves in practice to continue old divisions.

Creating *memory* is one device that can help make up for past oppression. To establish and strengthen memory of past events and processes, one may rely on songs, images, and stories. The formation of memory is as contentious as any area of history: governments rely on monuments and official textbooks to create historical memory. But the monuments and textbooks are usually made by and devoted to the victors: the Arc de Triomphe in Paris was built to commemorate Napoleon's military victories. Nevertheless, some countries have designated holidays to celebrate the emancipation of slaves and as a reminder of past oppression, and memorials to slaves are being constructed and are opening for view all around the Atlantic.[2]

A much more specific compensating device is *affirmative action*. With this policy, a society attempts to adjust the appointment of individuals for employment, education, and other benefits in an attempt to ensure that previously disadvantaged groups do not suffer exclusion. Affirmative action exists today in quite different forms in such countries as India, Canada, the United States, South Africa, and Malaysia. Here too the complications are considerable. Deciding which groups need or no longer need extra help is a difficult, contentious issue for any society and more so for humanity as a whole.

Meanwhile, the old inequities continue. A policy of "benign neglect" might appear to some as a neutral approach that neither adds to past oppression nor interferes with the social order, but in fact it necessarily continues to facilitate inequality.[3] Those people today who live in part on wealth created from the proceeds of past oppression need bear no individual guilt for their ancestors' actions. They do, however, bear particular responsibility for ensuring that new inequities are not propagated. The narrow considerations of profit, in the hands of unrepresentative bodies of decision makers, continue to cause discrimination in educational access, inequitable wages and prices in international trade, and, sadly, inequitable health services to the groups hardest hit by the HIV epidemic.

While the ideal of social equality requires action from all, each community must ultimately heal itself. This is another contentious issue. In public debates about inequality, one often hears calls for black communities in Africa and the diaspora to take more responsibility for self-improvement. One often hears the proverb, "Physician, heal thyself." The danger in such calls is they tend assume that black people have no record of successful self-improvement. The history of the African diaspora shows, in marked contrast, how black communities have healed and rebuilt time and again. The list of such campaigns is long: recreating African culture in the diaspora under slavery, gaining freedom from slavery as individuals and in groups, gaining land and building independent communities with emancipation, pursuing education relentlessly despite the consistent lack of governmental support, developing neighborhoods and community organizations for urban and industrial life, and creating cadres of highly skilled lawyers, bankers, and other professionals. Up to the twentieth century, the economic productivity of slaves generated growth in the Americas and helped sustain the economies of Africa. Nevertheless, the economic construction of Africa and of diaspora communities in the twentieth century, though substantial, failed to make up the ground lost to other communities. One cannot be sure, but it may be that complaints about economic inadequacies of blacks today are parallel to the complaints about cultural inadequacies of blacks a century ago. It may be that powerful responses to those critiques are well under way. The twenty-first century might bring surprises as big as those of the twentieth.

Regardless of these points about the past, there surely exists a widely shared responsibility to ensure that inequities are not propagated purposefully or unthinkingly into the future. Arguably, the world as a whole does owe something to black people of Africa and the diaspora—partly out of concern for equitable distribution of the benefits of human society and partly as recognition of the unfair price paid by black people in constructing the modern world. Today's response to the inequalities of race and slavery provides one great test for humanity. How well we perform on this test is fundamentally relevant to the more general problem of protecting our species and the environment in which we live.

Will Racism End?

There is hope that racism will end—or at least disappear in its present form. The campaign against racial discrimination has achieved remarkable successes. It will not do to deny the important changes that have taken place in what used to be called "race relations." A long list of social movements—campaigns against racism, anticolonial struggles, democratization movements, scholarly research, and protests in education, sport, politics, and on the job—have created a situation where public support for racial discrimination has become rare.

These warm campaigns of black struggle and of human solidarity have done something to melt the snows of social discrimination against people of African ancestry. But the melting snows reveal the enormous iceberg of prejudice and inequality that lies below the surface, an iceberg made solid by the compressed accretions of hierarchy and dispossession over the centuries. Sometimes the melting of one layer of prejudice reveals not the purity of equality but new forms of discrimination, as when color prejudice gives way to discrimination by religion or by language. One may hope and work for the ultimate disappearance of this iceberg, but no quick fix is likely to vaporize the lasting consequences of its existence.

Once we understand that racism is about color but *not only* about color, the difficulty of ending it becomes clearer. Color prejudice has been an outstanding form of social discrimination in recent centuries, but as long as other forms of prejudice remain significant, color prejudice can reappear at the height of some social controversy.

Sometimes it is suggested that society and government can become "colorblind." According to this view, we would take no account of racial differences, and by this act of will the heritage of past discrimination would soon fade away. To implement this view, governments, schools, private firms, and news media would cease to identify people by race or ethnicity. One great difficulty with this approach is that it cannot guarantee that everyone will act at once to halt the use of race or ethnicity as means of categorizing people. Another difficulty is that it asks people to cease recognizing the physical and social differences that our ancestors have noted for millennia.[4]

As a result, changes that are interpreted as the end of racial categorization may in fact be a revision of racial categorization. The early history of racial discrimination provides reminders on this point: "racial" differences were once seen to focus significantly on religious difference and on lineage, then the focus changed to emphasize phenotype and assumed genetic differences. These shifts moved individuals from one category to another but retained the idea of separate categories. One wants neither to deny the changes that have taken place nor to erect fantasies of a world devoid of conflict and prejudice. Perhaps it will be productive to ask what precise forms of social conflicts of the future will create new visions of "race."

Perhaps there is something to be learned by comparing racism with patriarchy. Patriarchy is the widespread—almost universal—practice and belief that places males as dominant in human society. For patriarchy as for race, the belief relies on the fundamental and erroneous assumption that the differences between groups (by race or by sex) are greater than the differences within groups. The phenotypical and biological differences between the sexes exceed those between the races: men and women have clear differences from each other. But the readiness of humans to categorize and then to exaggerate the validity of categories has created a sort of hierarchy and discrimination by gender that parallels discrimination by race. Scientists continue to test areas of similarity and difference between the sexes, and the social movement for women's equality has achieved many advances. Meanwhile, the category of biological racism has been more thoroughly tested and refuted than any other category, and this refutation will have its effects.

We can be sure that humans will continue to categorize and discriminate, using the logic of the "other" as a way to simplify complex social issues. Even when most individuals in a population emphasize human equality (meaning that the small differences among us are distributed almost randomly), a few people can make a difference. If they gain office or create disruptions, they may have the power to impose a program of social discrimination on the majority.

What Is the Future of Black Identity?

The heritage of slavery will count for less in the future than in the past. One may expect that the stigma but not the memory of slavery will pass away. But we also understand that slavery goes on even today, and in many societies, wherever some people are able to gain power over the bodies of others.

The differences we have labeled as "race" will also count for less in the future than they have in the past. The most recent discoveries in human biology show how tiny the variations between one "race" and another are, so that black identity cannot be seen as reflecting any deep and inherent dispar-

ity. Phenotypical "race" is now known to consist of a set of superficial differences in an overwhelmingly similar human population. The genetic differences among African populations are greater than those separating Africans
from other populations. By that logic, there is no such thing as racial purity.
By the same logic, "mixes" can no longer be treated as intermediate in biological terms.

These biological realities remind us that race is socially constructed—its
existence lies in the collective decisions of humans and not in nature. The
growing understanding of the genetic unity of mankind has done a great deal
to reduce actions and ideas of explicit racial discrimination. But people still
see the differences among them, however superficial they may be, and are
likely to act on them. Racial identity is not about to disappear.

By the same token, black identity is socially constructed—both by the
members of black communities and by the opinions of persons outside
the community. Black identity has only recently achieved widespread and
positive recognition from those outside black communities. Black people
have steadily built their range of self-concepts over recent centuries, so it is
most unlikely that they will give up this identity even if racial discrimination
ceases to put them on the defensive. In addition, the physical and phenotypical characteristics of black people reproduce themselves dependably every
generation.

Chéri Samba, the imaginative and self-centered painter from Kinshasa,
presents a truly thought-provoking assessment of black identity in his *J'aime
la couleur* (see figure 7.3). He presents an optimistic outlook both on color
in strictly chromatic terms and, not far below the surface, on the place of
people of color (in all their variety) in the world.

The identities of "mixed" people are socially constructed in different
ways by the same processes. It may be that the people who have been labeled
as "mixed," and who have therefore been left between categories, will gain
the most in security of identity out of the current biological advance and
social rethinking.

As in earlier times, the nature of black identity is linked to the nature of
human identity and human community. The problem of community is now
posed in a different fashion. There is no way to go back to the past. But just as
black people have worked to create larger communities—national communities and pan-African communities—so does humanity in general face the
need to define a human community. This need for community faces its greatest contradiction in the expanding economic inequality among humans.

In contrast to the unity and linkage of black communities, there are growing divisions within black communities. The recent rise of more black people

FIGURE 7.3 *J'aime la couleur*, by Cheri Samba, 2003

Cheri Samba, the prolific and argumentative painter of Kinshasa, usually paints himself at the center of his visual social commentaries. This 2003 painting, whose title translates as "I Like Color," is composed of acrylic and glitter on campus. Details of the text at the bottom left and right of the painting: *Left*: "La tête doit tourner un peu comme dans le sens d'une spirale afin de reconnaître ce qui nous entoure. J'AIME LA COULEUR." *Right*: "Tout ce qui nous entoure n'est autre que la couleur. On est soi-même couleur. La couleur c'est la vie. VIVE LA COULEUR Pour ne pas dire la peinture!!"

Source: Courtesy of Jean Pigozzi.

to positions of influence and wealth means that black communities will necessarily become more heterogeneous. The ideal of maintaining black unity and social cohesion will require, therefore, the creation of new means for establishing common identity across an increasingly wide social and economic range. It may be that the experience and process of sustaining and recreating a common identity across the African diaspora will provide some pointers on how to strengthen a sense of community among humans generally. Or it may be that conflicts within black communities will become more severe.

The previous experiments in defining black identity have run into their limits. The North American approach was to label the hierarchy of society with race at every turn, thereby formally denying black people the opportunity for social advancement. One "drop of black blood" was sufficient to deprive a person of the benefits of being white. The Latin American technique was to avoid labeling the hierarchy with race and thereby ignore the fact that unspoken discrimination was denying black people the opportunity for social progress. An intermediate experiment, particularly in the Caribbean, was to identify the range of colors and to rank the social hierarchy by shades of color. (All of these experiments have been applied, in varying ways, in Africa and in the Old World diaspora as well.)

In this fascinating mix of genetic similarities, cultural overlaps, and arbitrary social distinctions, some South American trends in black identity appear to be of particular interest. There are moves to abandon the region's old experiment—the ideology of "racial democracy," which meant ignoring or denying the inequality. The national cultures of Brazil, Venezuela, Colombia, and other countries are now recognizing formally both their African ancestry and the heritage of discrimination that goes with it. They are beginning to adjust their history and institutions to acknowledge this new thinking. Or perhaps one should say they are thinking up new ways of stating the relationships among black, brown, and white, since these were the previous Latin American categories. Of course, these changes come not out of the blue but in response to the steady demands and incremental advances of the people of African descent in those countries. The prospect is interesting: perhaps it will be possible to sustain a strong black identity even when differences in race or color are not set in a hierarchy. In addition, perhaps it will be possible to recognize all the "mixes" by which people choose to identify themselves. One need not expect to end social conflict or to eliminate racial difference as a factor in human life, but the next experiments in defining black identity may lead to a substantially new stage.

The Journey Continues

Linkages and interactions throughout the African diaspora have determined the path of history of black people for centuries. The expanded African Web has brought remarkable parallels to various parts of the black world. The links were guaranteed by long habits of migration and exchange, then by slavery, then by responses to racism, then by voluntary association. The connections among regions are probably now deeper than ever.

The experience of the African diaspora provides insights into the continuity of human history. The ideology of the nineteenth and early twentieth century taught people to think in terms of isolated nations as the containers within which history was made. The ideology of the early twenty-first century teaches us that global forces are now breaking down those earlier boundaries. In contrast to these simplifications of the past, the history of the African diaspora shows that interconnections and global patterns have been central to history for centuries, not just in the past decade. Even for those who were mostly subjects of empires rather than rulers, or subjects of nations rather than the chosen people, the connections of the African diaspora provide a deep heritage and a steady source of innovations. While every black community values its local traditions, it has the opportunity of drawing on shared experience over a wide area and a long time.

Notes

Preface

1. The version of sociologist Stuart Hall, while attentive to people of color, assumes that modernity began in Europe and slowly expanded, nation by nation. Historian C. A. Bayly, in his interpretation of the modern world, offers his only substantial discussion of the African diaspora late in his story: entitled "Slavery's Indian Summer," it rapidly recapitulates the history of slavery worldwide and wonders about the persistence of slavery at the end of the nineteenth century. (The cover illustration of Bayly's volume is a 1797 portrait of Jean-Baptiste Belley, a Haitian political leader, but the text offers concise examples rather than sustained argument on the place of blacks in the birth of the modern world.) Immanuel Wallerstein's three-volume analysis of "the modern world-system" from 1500 to the 1840s notes some details and debates on slave trade, slave labor, and the Haitian revolution but does not elevate these into a major theme. Michel Beaud's history of capitalism, in multiple editions, leaves out Africans and people of African descent except for cursory references to slave labor. Stuart Hall et al., eds., *Modernity: An Introduction to Modern Societies* (Cambridge, Mass.: Blackwell, 1996); C. A. Bayly, *The Birth of the Modern World, 1780–1914: Global Connections and Comparisons* (Oxford: Blackwell, 2004), 402–410; Immanuel Wallerstein, *The Modern World-System*, 3 vols. (New York: Academic Press, 1974, 1980, 1989); and Michel Beaud, *A History of Capitalism, 1500–2000*, trans. Tom Dickman and Anny Lefebvre (New York: Monthly Review Press, 2001). For other interpretations of the modern world, confirming the pattern of scant attention paid to the place of black people, see David Harvey, *The Condition of Postmodernity: An Enquiry into the Origins of Cultural Change* (Oxford: Blackwell, 1989); Anthony Giddens, *The Consequences of Modernity* (Stanford, Calif.: Stanford University Press, 1990); Anthony Giddens, *Modernity and Self-Identity: Self and Society in the Late Modern Age* (Stanford, Calif.: Stanford University Press, 1991); and Robert B. Marks, *The Origins of the Modern World: A Global and Ecological Narrative from the Fifteenth to the Twenty-first Century*, 2nd ed. (Lanham, Md.: Rowman and Littlefield, 2007).

2. James Baldwin, *The Fire Next Time* (New York: Dial Press, 1963); Cheikh-Anta Diop, *Black Africa: The Economic and Cultural Basis for a Federated State*, trans. Harold Salemson (Westport, Conn.: L. Hill, 1978); Aimé Césaire, *Discourse on Colonialism*, trans. Joan Pinkham (New York: Monthly Review Press, 1972); C. L. R. James, *A History of Negro Revolt* (New York: Haskell House, 1969); Walter Rodney, *How Europe Underdeveloped Africa*, rev. ed. (Washington, D.C.: Howard University Press, 1981); Ali A. Mazrui, *The Africans: A Triple Heritage* (London: BBC Publications, 1986); V. Y. Mudimbe, *The Invention of Africa: Gnosis, Philosophy, and the Order of Knowledge* (Bloomington: Indiana University Press, 1988); Anthony Appiah, *In My Father's House: Africa in the Philosophy of Culture* (New York: Oxford University Press, 1992). See also Chancellor Williams, *The Destruction of Black Civilization: Great Issues of a Race from 4500 BC to 2000 AD*, rev. ed. (Chicago: Third World Press, 1976). For a recent historical overview focusing on the United States, see Nell Irvin Painter, *Creating Black Americans: African-American History and Its Meanings, 1619 to the Present* (New York: Oxford University Press, 2007).

1. Diaspora

1. Robin Cohen, *Global Diasporas: An Introduction* (Seattle: University of Washington Press, 1997); see also Stephane Dufoix, *Diasporas*, trans. William Rodamor (Berkeley: University of California Press, 2008).

2. Terence O. Ranger, ed., *Emerging Themes in African History* (Nairobi: East African Publishing House, 1968); George Shepperson, "Introduction," in *The African Diaspora: Interpretive Essays*, ed. Martin L. Kilson and Robert I. Rotberg (Cambridge, Mass.: Harvard University Press, 1976), 2; Joseph E. Harris, "Introduction," in *Global Dimensions of the African Diaspora*, ed. Joseph E. Harris (Washington, D.C.: Howard University Press, 1982), 3.

3. Joseph Harris, Adell Patton, and their colleagues at Howard University taught a course on African-diaspora history beginning in the early 1980s. For an early text, see Vincent Bakpetu Thompson, *The Making of the African Diaspora in the Americas, 1441–1900* (New York: Longman, 1987); a later text was Michael L. Conniff and Thomas J. Davis, *Africans in the Americas: A History of the Black Diaspora* (New York: St. Martin's Press, 1994).

4. In 1976, Lawrence J. McCaffrey published *The Irish Diaspora in America* (Bloomington: Indiana University Press); otherwise, the term "Irish diaspora" began to be used in the 1990s. The term "Chinese diaspora" began to be used in the 1990s, especially with Lynn Pan, *Sons of the Yellow Emperor: A History of the Chinese Diaspora* (Boston: Little, Brown, 1990). Otherwise, the term "African diaspora" was used far more frequently in publications, especially after Thompson's 1987 *Making of the African Diaspora*.

5. Patrick Manning, "Africa and the African Diaspora: New Directions of Study," *Journal of African History* 44 (2003): 487–506.

6. Molefi Kete Asante, *Afrocentricity, the Theory of Social Change* (Buffalo, N.Y.: Amulefi Publishing Co., 1980); Molefi Kete Asante, *Afrocentricity*, new rev. ed. (Trenton, N.J.: Africa World Press, 1988).

7. Paul Gilroy, *The Black Atlantic: Modernity and Double Consciousness* (Cambridge, Mass.: Harvard University Press, 1993). In addition, *The Black Atlantic* is an intervention

on the topic of modernity—an attempt to gain recognition for the place of blacks in creating the modern world overall.

8. Edward Said, *Orientalism* (London: Routledge & Kegan Paul, 1978).

9. Gilroy, *The Black Atlantic*, 5–19, 99–103, 147–149.

10. John K. Thornton, *Africa and Africans in the Making of the Atlantic World, 1400–1680* (Cambridge: Cambridge University Press, 1992).

11. Patrick Manning, "Interactions and Connections: Locating and Managing Historical Complexity," *The History Teacher* 39 (2006).

12. W. E. B. Du Bois, *The Negro*, introduced by George Shepperson (1915; repr., London: Oxford University Press, 1970), 9.

13. National population figures—and worldwide comparisons of them—have become accurate only since 1950. African populations reached their lowest proportion of the global total in the period from about 1900 to 1950. For earlier times, recent analysis shows that the populations of Africa and other regions outside Europe and East Asia were somewhat larger than previously thought.

14. Frank Snowden, *Before Color Prejudice: The Ancient View of Blacks* (Cambridge, Mass.: Harvard University Press, 1991); and Frank Snowden, *Blacks in Antiquity: Ethiopians in the Greco-Roman Experience* (Cambridge, Mass.: Belknap Press, 2005). For a contrasting view, see Benjamin Isaac, *The Invention of Racism in Classical Antiquity* (Princeton, N.J.: Princeton University Press, 2004).

15. The key initial publication was R. L. Cann, M. Stoneking, and A. C. Wilson, "Mitochondrial DNA and Human Evolution," *Nature* 325 (1987): 31–36. See also Richard Dawkins, *River out of Eden* (New York: Basic Books, 1995); and Luigi Luca Cavalli-Sforza, *Genes, Peoples, and Languages*, trans. Mark Seielstad (New York: North Point Press, 2000).

16. George Fredrickson, *Racism: A Short History* (Princeton, N.J.: Princeton University Press, 2002).

17. Frantz Fanon, *Wretched of the Earth*, trans. Constance Farrington (New York: Grove, 1963); Martin Luther King Jr., *The Measure of a Man* (Philadelphia: Christian Education Press, 1959). Of the contemporaries of Fanon and King, Kwame Nkrumah stood out as a practitioner of electoral political mobilization, and Nelson Mandela became remarkable as one who, in his long life, relied on all three approaches.

18. The experience of slavery and emancipation reaffirmed the central role of mothers in diaspora societies yet put extra burdens on them, both in early days of slave societies, when women were so few in number, and in later slave societies, where mothers were commonly the heads of households. After emancipation, family structures again reaffirmed the maternal role, but mothers were often single, as the "free" labor market made it difficult for men to sustain marriages. (This is the story for free blacks during the time of slavery and for postemancipation black societies.)

19. The brass sculpture of the kingdom of Benin, showing royal guards but also Portuguese gunmen, is an exception.

2. Connections to 1600

1. A third term, "Kaffir" (from the Arabic term for "unbeliever"), came to be used as an ethnic label for people of African descent in Ceylon (modern Sri Lanka).

2. Jan Vansina, "The Bells of Kings," *Journal of African History* 10 (1969): 187–197; Eugenia W. Herbert, *Red Gold of Africa: Copper in Precolonial History and Culture* (Madison: University of Wisconsin Press, 1984).

3. Frances Wood, *The Silk Road: Two Thousand Years in the Heart of Asia* (Berkeley: University of California Press, 2002).

4. The Democratic Republic of Congo, with its capital at Kinshasa, lies east and south of the Republic of Congo, with its capital at Brazzaville. The two countries are often known as Congo-Kinshasa and Congo-Brazzaville. The two capitals face each other across the Congo River. Congo-Kinshasa (known as Zaire from 1975 to 1997) was a Belgian colony; Congo-Brazzaville was a French colony. Both gained independence in 1960.

5. Andrew Goudie, *Great Warm Deserts of the World: Landscapes and Evolution* (New York: Oxford University Press, 2002).

6. Further, the Niger-Congo languages are linked with the Kordofanian languages of the Republic of Sudan to form the Niger-Kordofanian phylum. This relationship suggests that the homeland for speakers of the language ancestral to all others in this group may also have been in the Nile Valley.

7. Khoisan languages are spoken by peoples of Khoi and San ethnicity, mostly in Namibia, and also by the Hadza and Sandawe peoples of Tanzania.

8. For a fine collection of sketches and photos of drums and musicians, mostly from West and West-Central Africa, see Esther A. Dagan, ed., *Drums: The Heartbeat of Africa* (Montreal: Galerie Amrad African Art Publications, 1993).

9. For an excellent historical study of textile production and consumption, see Colleen E. Kriger, *Cloth in West African History* (Lanham, Md.: AltaMira Press, 2006).

10. Christopher Ehret, *Civilizations of Africa* (Charlottesville: University Press of Virginia, 2002), 40–43, 49–51, 54–55; Christopher Ehret, *History and the Testimony of Language* (Berkeley: University of California Press, 2008).

11. Jan Vansina, *Paths in the Rainforests: Toward a History of Political Tradition in Equatorial Africa* (Madison: University of Wisconsin Press, 1990), 72–73, 274–275.

12. Archaeologist Peter Garlake has done a fine job of summarizing the work of many analysts to portray the processes responsible for these works. See Peter Garlake, *Great Zimbabwe*, rev. ed. (Harare: Zimbabwe Publishing House, 1985).

13. The language of the Benin Kingdom, Bini, is different from that of Ife and the other neighboring Yoruba peoples.

14. Benin Kingdom lies within the borders of modern Nigeria; Benin Republic is the modern state just to the west of Nigeria.

15. The early days of the Kuba kingdom are dated to the fifteenth century, and its proliferation of titles began in the late seventeenth century; the origins of Mangbetu kingdoms are dated with less certainty. Jan Vansina, *Kingdoms of the Savanna* (Madison: University of Wisconsin Press, 1968), 119–121; Jan Vansina, *The Children of Woot: A History of the Kuba Peoples* (Madison: University of Wisconsin Press, 1978); Herbert, *Red Gold of Africa*, 248–249.

16. René A. Bravmann, *Islam and Tribal Art in West Africa* (London: Cambridge University Press, 1980).

17. Thousands of Arabic-language documents, long held in private collections in Timbuktu, are now being accessed and catalogued in new libraries, notably the Fondo Kati

Library, with support from international donors. Professor John Hunwick of Northwestern University played a key role in drawing attention to this rich documentary collection on African history and life.

18. D. T. Niane, *Sundiata, an Epic of Old Mali*, trans. G. D. Pickett (Harlow: Longman, 1965). For the epic of Askia Sundiata, see Thomas A. Hale, *Scribe, Griot, and Novelist: Narrative Interpreters of the Songhay Empire* (Gainesville: University of Florida Press, 1990). See also Thomas A. Hale, *Griots and Griottes: Masters of Words and Music* (Bloomington: Indiana University Press, 1998);

19. John Thornton, *Africa and Africans in the Making of the Atlantic World, 1400–1680* (New York: Cambridge University Press, 1992), 74. Other aspects of Thornton's view of African involvement in Atlantic slave trade have been discussed earlier, in chapter 1.

20. Thornton, *Africa and Africans*, 84–85.

21. On the distinction of subordinates and slaves, see Joseph C. Miller, *Way of Death: Merchant Capital and the Angolan Slave Trade, 1730–1830* (Madison: University of Wisconsin Press, 1988), 42–53, 94–100; on the ownership of land, see J. E. Casely Hayford, *The Truth About the West African Land Question* (London: C. M. Phillips, 1913); on the scale of expansion in slave trade, see Patrick Manning, *Slavery and African Life: Occidental, Oriental, and African Slave Trades* (Cambridge: Cambridge University Press, 1990), 18–23, 32–37.

22. On orientalism, see Edward Said, *Orientalism* (New York: Vintage, 1979); see also the analysis of orientalism in the thinking of the French philosopher Montesquieu as developed by Roberto M. Dainotto, *Europe (in Theory)* (Durham, N.C.: Duke University Press, 2007).

23. Marcus Rediker, *The Slave Ship: A Human History* (New York: Viking, 2007); Emma Christopher, Cassandra Pybus, and Marcus Rediker, eds., *Many Middle Passages: Forced Migration and the Making of the Modern World* (Berkeley: University of California Press, 2007); Elizabeth Savage, *The Human Commodity: Perspectives on the Trans-Saharan Slave Trade* (London: Frank Cass, 1992).

24. Nehemia Levtzion and Randall L. Pouwels, eds., *The History of Islam in Africa* (Athens: Ohio University Press, 2000); in this volume, see especially Peter von Sivers, "Egypt and North Africa" (21–36); and M. N. Pearson, "The Indian Ocean and the Red Sea" (37–59). For Arab history up to the thirteenth century, see Philip K. Hitti, *The Arabs: A Short History* (Chicago: Gateway, 1970). On the Almoravids and Almohads, see Jamil M. Abun-Nasr, *A History of the Maghrib in the Islamic Period* (Cambridge: Cambridge University Press, 1987).

25. T. F. Earle and K. J. P. Lowe, *Black Africans in Renaissance Europe* (Cambridge: Cambridge University Press, 2005), 125–154; see 130 for Mantegna's 1492 painting *Judith and Her Maidservant*.

26. Patricia Seed has begun work on locating, documenting, and digitizing the initial Portuguese maps of the African coast. For discussion of these maps, see http://www.ruf.rice.edu/~feegi/maps.html.

27. A. C. de M. Saunders, *A Social History of Black Slaves and Freedmen in Portugal, 1441–1555* (Cambridge: Cambridge University Press, 1982).

28. Ivana Elbl, "The Volume of the Early Atlantic Slave Trade, 1450–1521," *Journal of African History* 38 (1997): 31–76.

29. Alfred W. Crosby, *The Columbian Exchange: Biological and Cultural Consequences of 1492* (Westport, Conn.: Prager, 2003).

30. Frederick Bowser, *The African Slave in Colonial Peru, 1524–1650* (Stanford, Calif.: Stanford University Press, 1974); and Colin A. Palmer, *Slaves of the White God: Blacks in Mexico, 1570–1650* (Cambridge, Mass.: Harvard University Press, 1976).

31. Ira Berlin, *Many Thousands Gone: The First Two Centuries of Slavery in North America* (Cambridge, Mass.: The Belknap Press, 1998), 17–46.

32. The greatest African gold deposits of all, in South Africa, were buried deeply and mixed in complex ores—they could only be exploited with the new technology of the late nineteenth century.

33. In the fifteenth century, the silks and porcelain of China and the cottons of India traveled the world along routes almost as extensive as those for silver.

34. In recent times, Nzinga has become a hero for Central African struggles for self-determination in response to European encroachment; such heroes are harder to locate for precolonial West Africa. Linda Heywood and John K. Thornton, *Central Africans, Atlantic Creoles, and the Foundation of the Americas, 1585–1660* (New York: Cambridge University Press, 2007).

3. Survival, 1600–1800

1. Thomas Hobbes, *Leviathan*, ed. Marshall Missner (New York: Pearson Longman, 2008), 83.

2. The "ton" was a measure of the capacity (not the weight) of ships used by European and American shippers. Measures of tonnage varied but, as measured in Dutch shipyards of the 1730s, a ship of one hundred feet in length had a capacity of 250 tons, while a ship of 130 feet in length had a capacity of six hundred tons. In the nineteenth century, the ton became standardized at one hundred cubic feet, or just under three cubic meters.

3. Johannes Postma, *The Dutch in the Atlantic Slave Trade, 1600–1815* (Cambridge: Cambridge University Press, 1990), 308–319.

4. Jean Mettas, *Répertoire des expeditions négrières françaises au XVIIIe siècle*, 2 vols. (Paris: Société Française d'Histoire d'Outre-Mer, 1975–1984), 1:24–35, 1:703–720.

5. Ibid. The fact that the average tonnage per slave increased does not necessarily mean that captives had more space; it may mean that more space was allocated to water and other stores.

6. George E. Brooks, *Eurafricans in Western Africa: Commerce, Social Status, Gender, and Religious Observance from the Sixteenth to the Eighteenth Century* (Athens: Ohio University Press, 2003), 198–249.

7. K. O. Dike, *Trade and Politics on the Niger Delta, 1830–1885: An Introduction to the Economic and Political History of Nigeria* (Oxford: Clarendon Press, 1956); T. O. Ranger, *Revolt in Southern Rhodesia, 1896–1897: A Study in African Resistance* (London: Heineman,1967).

8. Patrick Manning, *Slavery and African Life: Occidental, Oriental, and African Slave Trades* (Cambridge: Cambridge University Press, 1990). These arguments are documented in greater detail in Patrick Manning and Scott Nickleach, *African Population, 1650–1950: The Eras of Enslavement and Colonial Rule* (forthcoming).

9. "Those positing a strong impact on Africa from the Atlantic world must show that Atlantic trade somehow had an effect out of proportion to its size. In the case of the slave trade, this would require stressing the means by which slaves were assembled for export rather than the absolute or relative value of the traffic. Any other viewpoint risks implying that, in the face of limited amounts of overseas goods, African social and cultural resilience as well as economic efficiency was considerably less than the quantitative evidence suggests." David Eltis and Lawrence C. Jennings, "Trade Between Western Africa and the Atlantic World in the Pre-colonial Era," *American Historical Review* 93 (1988): 957–958.

10. Trevor Burnard, *Mastery, Tyranny, and Desire: Thomas Thistlewood and His Slaves in the Anglo-Jamaican World* (Chapel Hill: University of North Carolina Press, 2004), 156–164. Burnard describes Jamaican society as patriarchal rather than paternal, in that the owners ruled through terror.

11. Michael Gomez, *Exchanging Our Country Marks: The Transformation of African Identities in the Colonial and Antebellum South* (Chapel Hill: University of North Carolina Press, 1998); William D. Piersen, *Black Yankees: The Development of an Afro-American Subculture in Eighteenth-century New England* (Amherst: University of Massachusetts Press, 1988); Michael Gomez, *Black Crescent: The Experience and the Legacy of African Muslims in the Americas* (Cambridge: Cambridge University Press, 2005). In *Black Crescent*, Gomez notes the traces of literate Muslims among the slave populations of New York, the American South, several islands of the Caribbean, and Brazil.

12. John K. Thornton, "African Dimensions of the Stono Rebellion," *American Historical Review* 96 (1991): 1101–1113.

13. Four main approaches to cultural change—theses of dominance, survival, syncretism, and creolization—are advanced, respectively, in E. Franklin Frazier, *The Negro Family in the United States* (Chicago: University of Chicago Press, 1939); Melville J. Herskovits, *The Myth of the Negro Past* (New York: Harper & Bros., 1941); Charles Steward and Rosalind Shaw, eds., *Syncretism/Anti-syncretism: The Politics of Religious Synthesis* (London: Routledge, 1994); and Sidney Mintz and Richard Price, *An Anthropological Approach to the Afro-American Past: A Caribbean Perspective* (Philadelphia: Institute for the Study of Human Issues, 1976). For a proposal to revise these, see Kristin Mann, "Shifting Paradigms in the Study of the African Diaspora and of Atlantic History and Culture," in *Rethinking the African Diaspora: The Making of a Black Atlantic World in the Bight of Benin and Brazil*, ed. Kristin Mann and Edna G. Bay, 3–21 (London: Frank Cass, 2001). See also Edouard Glissant, *Creolization*, trans. Jeff Humphreys and Julec La Porte (Princeton, N.J.: Markus Wiener, 2001).

14. On brotherhoods, see João José Reis, *Death Is a Festival: Funeral Rites and Rebellion in Nineteenth-century Brazil*, trans. H. Sabrina Gledhill (Chapel Hill: University of North Carolina Press, 2003). On the caste regime, see George Reid Andrews, *Afro-Latin America, 1800–2000* (New York: Oxford University Press), 44–52.

15. Ralph A. Austen's estimates of the volume of slave trade across the Sahara and the Red Sea, though imprecise because of the nature of the sources, provide helpful indications. See Ralph Austen, "The Trans-Saharan Slave Trade: A Tentative Census," in *The Uncommon Market: Essays in the Economic History of the Atlantic Slave Trade*, ed. Henry A. Gemery and Jan S. Hogendorn, 23–76 (New York: Academic Press, 1979); and Ralph Aus-

ten, "The Islamic Red Sea Slave Trade: An Effort at Quantification," in *Proceedings of the Fifth International Conference on Ethiopian Studies*, ed. Robert L. Hess, 443–467 (Chicago: University of Illinois at Chicago Circle, 1979).

16. But it was possible to make refreshment stops in mid-voyage at ports along the Arabian coast.

17. Bernard Lewis, *Race and Slavery in the Middle East: An Historical Enquiry* (New York: Oxford University Press, 1990).

18. Allison Blakely, *Russia and the Negro: Blacks in Russian History and Thought* (Washington, D.C.: Howard University Press, 1986), 14–15, 19–25; Dieudonné Gnammankou, *Abraham Hannibal. L'Aieul noir de Pouchkine* (Paris: Présence Africaine, 1998).

19. He was a candidate for the directorship of the royal opera in 1775, though he was passed over. Claude Ribbe, *Le Chevalier de Saint-Georges* (Paris: Perrin, 2003).

20. Jacobus E. J. Capitein, *The Agony of Asar: A Thesis on Slavery by the Former Slave, Jacobus Elisa Johannes Capitein*, trans. Grant Parker (Princeton, N.J.: Markus Wiener, 2001); Ottobah Cugoano, *Thoughts and Sentiments on the Evil and Wicked Traffic of the Slavery and Commerce of the Human* (London, 1787); Olaudah Equiano, *The Interesting Narrative of the Life of Olaudah Equiano, or, Gustavus Vassa, the African* (London, 1789); Burchard Brenties, *Anton Wilhelm Amo: Der Schwarze Philosoph in Halle* (Leipzig: Koehler and Amelang, 1976).

21. "En veinte y siete de Mayo, Pasque de Pentecostes de mil setecientos noventa y dos . . . [two baptisms] . . . ytt seguidamente y con las misma solemnidad, bauticé a une niña Negra de Mr Lioto, nacida de dos años, venida de Guinea, se la puso por nombre Julia, hija naturel de Felipe y Madalena, Negros sin bautizar, del dicho Lioto: Padrinos Valentin Florez, y Julia, el primero Grifo esclavo de Madama Gaynard, la segunda Negra de Madama Mermiyon . . . Fr. Diego de Canniedo." Source: Archives of the Archdiocese of New Orleans, Black Baptisms for New Orleans [volume including 1792], 319, entry 1540.

22. Archives of the Archdiocese of New Orleans. Research into sales records of newly landed slaves revealed that Mr. Liotohad purchased an infant slave in 1789, though the child was given no more detailed identification.

23. Magali M. Carrera, *Imagining Identity in New Spain: Race, Lineage, and the Colonial Body in Portraiture and* Casta *Paintings* (Austin: University of Texas Press, 2003); Ilona Katzew, Casta *Painting: Images of Race in Eighteenth-century Mexico* (New Haven, Conn.: Yale University Press, 2004).

24. An exception is the Indian Ocean islands of Réunion and Mauritius, where those known as "creoles" or "black creoles" were of African ancestry.

25. In an early rationalization of race, a series of Spanish-born priests in seventeenth-century Mexico had used the science of the time, astrology, to show that Europeans were superior to Amerindians and needed to control their labor for the development of society. These ideas, however, died out with the decline of astrology. Jorge Cañizares-Esguerra, *How to Write the History of the New World: Histories, Epistemologies, and Identities in the Eighteenth-century Atlantic World* (Stanford, Calif.: Stanford University Press, 2001).

26. Linnaeus labeled subspecies by region, but that was following procedures he used in classifying plants and animals.

27. Long, *History of Jamaica*. See also Burnard, *Mastery, Tyranny, and Desire*, 130, 148.

28. Wallerstein's analysis put the black people of the Americas in the "semiperiphery" and the "periphery," in contrast to the European "core." Africa, the source of slaves and a region of expanding slavery, was labeled as "external" to the modern world-system.

29. Joseph E. Inikori, *Africans and the Industrial Revolution in England: A Study in International Trade and Economic Development* (Cambridge: Cambridge University Press, 2002). For earlier debates on the place of Africans and slavery in the industrial revolution, see Eric Williams, *Capitalism and Slavery* (Chapel Hill: University of North Carolina Press, 1944); and Barbara L. Solow and Stanley L. Engerman, eds., *British Capitalism and Caribbean Slavery: The Legacy of Eric Williams* (New York: Cambridge University Press, 1987).

30. David Nicholls, *From Dessalines to Duvalier: Race, Colour, and National Independence in Haiti* (London: Macmillan Caribbean, 1996), 30. Boisrond Tonnerre's outburst included West African symbolism: skulls of defeated kings and generals were exhibited by the victors.

4. Emancipation, 1800–1900

1. Mervyn Hiskett, *The Sword of Truth: The Life and Times of the Shehu Usuman dan Fodio* (New York: Oxford University Press), 56.

2. Murray Last, *The Sokoto Caliphate* (Harlow: Longmans, 1967).

3. Cassandra Pybus, *Epic Journeys of Freedom: Runaway Slaves of the American Revolution and Their Global Quest for Liberty* (Boston: Beacon Press, 2006).

4. Christopher Fyfe, *History of Sierra Leone* (London: Oxford University Press, 1962); Jean Herskovits Kopytoff, *A Preface to Modern Nigeria: The "Sierra Leonians" in Yoruba, 1830–1890* (Madison: University of Wisconsin Press, 1965).

5. Paul Lovejoy, focusing on African experiences, has called these "transformations" in slavery. See Paul Lovejoy, *Transformations in Slavery*, 2nd ed. (Cambridge: Cambridge University Press, 2000); see also Patrick Manning, *Slavery and African Life: Occidental, Oriental, and African Slave Trades* (Cambridge: Cambridge University Press, 1990), 147–164.

6. Fortunately, economic historians have recently begun to give more attention to the global and interactive dimensions of industrialization; what remains is for them to focus in greater depth on the place of the African diaspora in industrialization. See Joseph Inikori, *Africans and the Industrial Revolution in England: A Study in International Trade and Economic Development* (Cambridge: Cambridge University Press, 2002); Kevin H. O'Rourke and Jeffrey G. Williamson, *Globalization and History: The Evolution of a Nineteenth-century Atlantic Economy* (Cambridge, Mass.: The MIT Press, 1999); Andre Gunder Frank, *ReOrient: Global Economy in the Asian Age* (Berkeley: University of California Press, 1998); Kenneth L. Pomeranz, *The Great Divergence: China, Europe, and the Making of the Modern World Economy* (Princeton, N.J.: Princeton University Press, 2000).

7. Michael Gomez, *Exchanging Our Country Marks: The Transformation of African Identities in the Colonial and Antebellum South* (Chapel Hill: University of North Carolina Press, 1998); Michael Gomez, *Black Crescent: The Experience and Legacy of African Muslims in the Americas* (New York: Cambridge University Press, 2005); Sterling Stuckey,

Slave Culture: Nationalist Theory and the Foundations of Black America (New York: Oxford University Press, 1987); Kim D. Butler, *Freedoms Given, Freedoms Won: Afro-Brazilians in Postabolition São Paulo and Salvador* (New Brunswick, N.J.: Rutgers University Press, 1998).

8. The total provincial population of color in Minas Gerais grew steadily, and the number of free people grew through manumission. Laird W. Bergad, *Slavery and the Demographic and Economic History of Minas Gerais, Brazil, 1720–1888* (Cambridge: Cambridge University Press, 1999), 90.

9. The ideological and political campaign against slavery has been traced in detail, especially through the work of David Brion Davis and Seymour Drescher. David Brion Davis, *Inhuman Bondage: The Rise and Fall of Slavery in the New World* (New York: Oxford University Press, 2006); David Brion Davis, *The Problem of Slavery in Western Culture* (Ithaca, N.Y.: Cornell University Press, 1966); David Brion Davis, *The Problem of Slavery in the Age of Revolution* (Ithaca, N.Y.: Cornell University Press, 1975); Seymour Drescher, *Capitalism and Antislavery: British Mobilization in Comparative Perspective* (New York: Oxford University Press, 1987); Seymour Drescher, *The Mighty Experiment: Free Labor Versus Slavery in British Emancipation* (New York: Oxford University Press, 2002).

10. Kenneth S. Greenberg, ed., *The Confessions of Nat Turner and Related Documents* (Boston : Bedford Books, 1996); João José Reis, *Slave Rebellion in Brazil: The Muslim Uprising of 1835 in Bahia*, trans. Arthur Brakel (Baltimore, Md.: The Johns Hopkins University Press, 1993).

11. W. G. Clarence-Smith, *Islam and the Abolition of Slavery* (Oxford: Oxford University Press, 2006).

12. Ismail Rashid, "'A Devotion to the Idea of Liberty at Any Price': Rebellion and Antislavery in the Upper Guinea Coast in the Eighteenth and Nineteenth Centuries," in *Fighting the Slave Trade: West African Strategies*, ed. Sylviane Diouf, 144–147 (Athens: Ohio University Press, 2003).

13. Gwyn Campbell, *An Economic History of Imperial Madagascar, 1750–1895: The Rise and Fall of an Island Empire* (Cambridge: Cambridge University Press, 2005), 236–242.

14. Eric Williams, *Capitalism and Slavery* (Chapel Hill: University of North Carolina Press, 1944); Robin Blackburn, *The Overthrow of Colonial Slavery, 1776–1848* (London: Verso, 1988).

15. David Eltis, *Economic Growth and the Ending of the Transatlantic Slave Trade* (New York: Oxford University Press, 1987).

16. Toyin Falola and Matt D. Childs, eds., *The Yoruba Diaspora in the Atlantic World* (Bloomington: Indiana University Press, 2005); J. Lorand Matory, *Black Atlantic Religion: Tradition, Transnationalism, and Matriarchy in the Afro-Brazilian* Candomblé (Princeton, N.J.: Princeton University Press, 2005).

17. Maureen Warner-Lewis, *Central Africa in the Caribbean: Transcending Time, Transforming Cultures* (Kingston: University of the West Indies Press, 2003).

18. Ehud Toledano, *Slavery and Abolition in the Ottoman Middle East* (Seattle: University of Washington Press, 1998); William Gervase Clarence-Smith, ed., *The Economics of the Indian Ocean Slave Trade in the Nineteenth Century* (London: Frank Cass, 1989).

19. Abdul Sheriff, *Slaves, Spices and Ivory in Zanzibar: Integration of an East African Commercial Empire Into the World Economy, 1770–1873* (London: James Currey, 1987); Campbell, *Economic History of Imperial Madagascar*.

20. Robert Chaudenson with Salikoko S. Mufwene, *Creolization of Language and Culture*, trans. Sheri Pargman et al. (London: Routledge, 2001).

21. Patrick Manning and Scott Nickleach, *African Population, 1650–1950: The Eras of Enslavement and Colonial Rule* (forthcoming).

22. Claude Meillassoux, *Anthropology of Slavery: The Womb of Iron and Gold*, trans. Alide Dasnois (Chicago: University of Chicago Press, 1991); Martin A. Klein, *Slavery and Colonial Rule in French West Africa* (Cambridge: Cambridge University Press, 1998); Richard Roberts, *Warriors, Merchants, and Slaves: The State and the Economy in the Middle Niger Valley, 1700–1914* (Stanford, Calif.: Stanford University Press, 1987).

23. The practice of castrating young male captives and selling the survivors as eunuchs became especially developed in the states of Bagirmi and Wadai in the central Sudan. See Humphrey J. Fisher and Allan G. B. Fisher, *Slavery in the History of Muslim Black Africa* (New York: NYU Press, 2001), 284.

24. Ehud Toledano, *The Ottoman Slave Trade and Its Suppression: 1840–1890* (Princeton, N.J.: Princeton University Press, 1982), 43–54.

25. B. W. Higman, *Slave Population of the British Caribbean, 1807–1834* (Baltimore, Md.: The Johns Hopkins University Press, 1984). On global patterns in slavery without slave trade, see Patrick Manning, "The Anthropology of Slavery," *African Economic History* 17 (1988): 147–152.

26. For this and other dimensions of slavery in the Brazilian southeast, see Mary C. Karasch, *Slave Life in Rio de Janeiro, 1808–1850* (Princeton, N.J.: Princeton University Press, 1987), esp. 44–46.

27. Gomez, *Exchanging Our Country Marks*, 242–243.

28. Janet J. Ewald, "Crossers of the Sea: Slaves, Freedmen, and Other Migrants in the Northwestern Indian Ocean, c. 1750–1914," *American Historical Review* 105 (2000): 69–90.

29. Walter Rodney, *A History of the Guyanese Working People, 1881–1905* (Baltimore, Md.: The Johns Hopkins University Press, 1981).

30. Tom W. Schick, *Behold the Promised Land: A History of Afro-American Settler Society in Nineteenth-century Liberia* (Baltimore, Md.: The Johns Hopkins University Press, 1980); Antonio McDaniel, *Swing Low, Sweet Chariot: The Mortality Cost of Colonizing Liberia in the Nineteenth Century* (Chicago: University of Chicago Press, 1995).

31. George Reid Andrews, *Afro-Latin America, 1800–2000* (New York: Oxford University Press, 2004), 93, 97.

32. J. Lorand Matory, *Black Atlantic Religion: Tradition, Transnationalism, and Matriarchy in the Afro-Brazilian* Candomble (Princeton, N.J.: Princeton University Press, 2005); Monica Schuler, *"Alas, Alas, Kongo": A Social History of Indentured African Immigration Into Jamaica, 1841–1865* (Baltimore, Md.: The Johns Hopkins University Press, 1980).

33. Thomas C. Holt, *The Problem of Freedom: Race, Labor, and Politics in Jamaica and Britain, 1832–1938* (Baltimore, Md.: The Johns Hopkins University Press, 1992); Philip D. Curtin, *Two Jamaicas: The Role of Ideas in a Tropical Colony, 1830–1865* (Cambridge, Mass.: Harvard University Press, 1955).

34. Wilson Jeremiah Moses, *Alexander Crummell: A Study of Civilization and Discontent* (Amherst: University of Massachusetts Press, 1992); Jesse Page, *The Black Bishop: Samuel Adjai Crowther* (Westport, Conn.: Greenwood Press, 1979).

35. These included writers and artists of North Africa, the Ottoman Empire, and the Arabian peninsula.

36. David Livingstone, *Missionary Travels and Researches in South Africa* (London: John Murray, 1857); David Livingstone and Chalres Livingstone, *Narrative of an Expedition to the Zambesi and Its Tributaries* (London: John Murray, 1865); David Livingstone, *The Last Journals of David Livingstone in Central Africa*, ed. Horace Waller, 2 vols. (London: John Murray, 1874).

37. John Hope Franklin, *George Washington Williams, a Biography* (Chicago: University of Chicago Press, 1985).

38. Leo Spitzer, *Lives in Between: Assimilation and Marginality in Austria, Brazil, and West Africa, 1780–1945* (Cambridge: Cambridge University Press, 1989).

39. Patrick Balfour, Baron Kinross, *Between Two Seas: The Creation of the Suez Canal* (New York: Morrow, 1969); Brian Winston, *Media Technology and Society: A History from the Telegraph to the Internet* (London: Routledge, 1998).

40. Anténor Firmin, *The Equality of the Human Races (Positivist Anthropology)*, trans. Asselin Charles (New York: Garland, 2000).

41. Their reasoning followed Mendelian genetics, as it was just rediscovered. In this case, a whole trait, such as the color of human eyes or the color of sweet-pea flowers (in Mendel's case), is determined by a single gene. It is now understood that intelligence depends on a great many genes, so there can be no simple rules for the inheritance of intelligence.

42. Neil MacMaster, *Racism in Europe* (New York: Palgrave, 2001).

43. Brook Thomas, ed., *Plessy v. Ferguson: A Brief History with Documents* (Boston: Bedford Books, 1997).

44. Neil Parsons, *King Khama, Emperor Joe, and the Great White Queen: Victorian Britain Through African Eyes* (Chicago: University of Chicago Press, 1998).

5. Citizenship, 1900–1960

1. W. E. B. Du Bois, *The Souls of Black Folk* (Oxford: Oxford University Press, 2007).

2. Julian Bond and Sondra Kathryn Wilson, eds., *Lift Every Voice and Sing: A Celebration of the Negro National Anthem; 100 Years, 100 Voices* (New York: Random House, 2000).

3. Such claims to citizenship were not limited to English-speaking people of the African diaspora. For Lusophone activists, see Douglas L. Wheeler, "'Angola Is Whose House?' Early Stirrings of Angolan Nationalism and Protest, 1822–1910," *African Historical Studies* 2 (1969): 1–22. For Francophone activists, see Patrick Manning, "L'Affaire Adjovi: la bourgeoisie foncière naissante au Dahomey, face à l'administration." In *Entreprises et entrepreneurs en Afrique*, ed. Catherine Coquery-Vidrovitch, 1:241–262 (Paris: Harmattan, 1983).

4. On Warrick, see W. Fitzhugh Brundage, "Meta Warrick's 1907 'Negro Tableaux' and (re)Presenting African American Historical Memory," *Journal of American History* 89 (2003): 1368–1400. On the influence of Dan and Grebo sculpture on "white" artists, see William Rubin, *Primitivism in Twentieth-century Art* (New York: Museum of Modern Art, 1984) 1:13–21; Patrick Manning, "Primitive Art and Modern Times," *Radical History Review* 35 (1985): 165–181.

5. On Broca and Galton, see chapter 4, above; on Marr, see Neil MacMaster, *Racism in Europe, 1870–2000* (New York: Palgrave, 2001); Arthur de Gobineau, *The Inequality of Human Races*, trans. Adrian Collins (New York: G. P. Putnam's Sons, 1915); Herbert Spencer, *The Principles of Sociology*, 3 vols. (New York: D. Appleton & Co., 1880–1897); Antony Thomas, *Rhodes* (London: BBC Books, 1996).

6. Quinine use by anyone previously unexposed to malaria— Europeans, blacks from the Americas, and others—greatly reduced the immense death toll that previously carried off half of new arrivals within their first year in Africa. Africans did not gain access to quinine until late in the colonial period.

7. The French took Algeria, Tunisia, and Morocco in North Africa, plus Madagascar. The British took Egypt and several territories in South Arabia. Italy took Libya in 1911. In the wake of World War I, Saudi Arabia took the Hijaz from the Ottoman Empire. For the offshore regions of the African diaspora, the Atlantic islands remained under Portuguese and Spanish rule, the Sahara fell under European rule, and the Indian Ocean islands remained under European rule.

8. In addition, Jews were identified separately in French North Africa, and many gained French citizenship.

9. Alejandro de la Fuente, *A Nation for All: Race, Inequality, and Politics in Twentieth-century Cuba* (Chapel Hill: University of North Carolina Press, 1900).

10. Robin Dale Moore, *Nationalizing Blackness: Afrocubanismo and Artistic Revolution in Havana, 1920–1940* (Pittsburgh, Penn.: University of Pittsburgh Press, 1997).

11. Booker T. Washington, *Up from Slavery: An Autobiography* (Garden City, N.Y.: Doubleday & Co., 1901); W. E. B. Du Bois, "Of Mr. Booker T. Washington and Others," in *The Souls of Black Folk: Essays and Sketches* (Chicago: A. C. McClurg, 1903). In addition, Washington and Du Bois delivered two lectures each in 1908 as the William Levi Bull Lectures on Christian Sociology, in Philadelphia. Booker T. Washington and W. E. B. Du Bois, *The Negro in the South: His Economic Progress in Relation to His Moral and Religious Development* (Philadelphia, George W. Jacobs & Co., 1907).

12. Richard Roberts and Martin Klein, "The Banamba Slave Exodus of 1905 and the Decline of Slavery in the Western Sudan," *Journal of African History* 21 (1981): 375–394.

13. John Hope Franklin, *George Washington Williams, a Biography* (Chicago: University of Chicago Press, 1985); E. D. Morel, *Red Rubber: The Story of the Rubber Slave Trade That Flourished in Congo in the Year of Grace 1906* (London: T. F. Unwin, 1906).

14. Colonial officials were observing the African transition to "slavery without slave trade" (described in chapter 4) and convinced themselves that there were no abuses of the slaves.

15. The term "free womb" was earlier used in the 1871 Brazilian proclamation with the same purpose.

16. In 1924, Tovalou-Houénou traveled to New York to be installed as the patriarch of the Universal Negro Improvement Association.

17. W. C. Handy, *Negro Authors and Composers of the United States* (New York: Handy Brothers Music Co., 1938); W. C. Handy, ed., *Blues, an Anthology: Complete Words and Music of Fifty-three Great Songs*, rev. Jerry Silverman (New York: Da Capo Press, 1990).

18. Alan Lomax, *Mister Jelly Roll: The Fortunes of Jelly Roll Morton, New Orleans Creole and "Inventor of Jazz,"* 2nd ed. (Berkeley: University of California Press, 1973).

19. One might even argue that the two genres of music had different sorts of cross-over appeal: ragtime was arguably an accommodation to white standards, while jazz was more outspoken and aggressive.

20. For two interpretations of the development of spirituals, see Arthur Jones, *Wade in the Water: The Wisdom of the Spirituals* (Maryknoll, N.Y.: Orbis Books, 1993); and James H. Cone, *The Spirituals and the Blues: An Interpretation* (Maryknoll, N.Y.: Orbis Books, 1991).

21. Randall K. Burkett and Richard Newman, eds., *Black Apostles: Afro-American Clergy Confront the Twentieth Century* (Boston: G. K. Hall, 1978); A. C. Valdez with James F. Scheer, *Fire on Azusa Street* (Costa Mesa, Calif.: Gift Publications, c. 1980); Allan Anderson, *Spreading Fires: The Missionary Nature of Early Pentecostalism* (Maryknoll, N.Y.: Orbis Books, 2007).

22. Internet articles by Pentecostal ministers remain the most accessible source of information on the Pentecostal movement, though these articles give only minimal attention to the widespread adoption of Pentecostalism in many parts of Africa and the African diaspora. Gary E. Gilley, "A Brief History of Pentecostalism" (1989), available online at http://www.rapidnet.com/~jbeard/bdm/Psychology/char/abrief.htm.

23. George Reid Andrews, *Afro-Latin America, 1800–2000* (New York: Oxford University Press, 2004).

24. Harvey M. Feinberg, "The 1913 Natives Land Act in South Africa: Politics, Race, and Segregation in the Early Twentieth Century," *International Journal of African Historical Studies* 26 (1993): 65–109; Sol. T. Plaatje, *Native Life in South Africa, Before and Since the European War and the Boer Rebellion* (London: P. S. King & Son, 1915).

25. George Shepperson, *Independent Africa* (Edinburgh: Edinburgh University Press, 1958); Jean Suret-Canale, *French Colonialism in Tropical Africa, 1900–1945*, trans. Till Gottheiner (New York: Pica Press, 1971), 95–103.

26. Patrick Manning, *Francophone Sub-Saharan Africa, 1880–1995*, 2nd ed. (Cambridge: Cambridge University Press, 1998), 64–67.

27. Bridget Brereton, *A History of Modern Trinidad, 1783–1962* (Kingston: Heinemann, 1981), 158–176, 194.

28. Imanuel Geiss, *The Pan-African Movement: A History of Pan-Africanism in America, Europe, and Africa*, trans. Ann Keep (New York: Africana Publishers, 1968), 229–263; J. Ayodele Langley, *Pan-Africanism and Nationalism in West Africa, 1900–1945* (Oxford: Clarendon Press, 1973), 243–285.

29. Robert A. Hill, "General Introduction," in *The Marcus Garvey and Universal Negro Improvement Association Papers* (Berkeley: University of California Press, 1983), 1:lxvii–lxviii; Brereton, *History of Modern Trinidad*, 163.

30. Price suggests that this "centrality of margins" may be more general in patterns of changing fashion. Sally Price, "The Centrality of Margins: Art, Gender, and African-American Creativity," in *The African Diaspora: African Origins and New World Identities*, ed. Isidore Okpewho, Carole Boyce Davies, and Ali A. Mazrui, 204–227 (Bloomington: Indiana University Press, 2001).

31. Robert Farris Thompson, *Flash of the Spirit: African and Afro-American Art and Philosophy* (New York: Random House, 1983).

32. Sylvia Jacobs, *Black Americans and the Missionary Movement of Africa* (Westport, Conn.: Greenwood Press, 1982).

33. Much of the spread of Islam in Africa has been through the efforts of Sufi orders. Knut S. Vikor, "Sufi Brotherhoods in Africa," in *The History of Islam in Africa*, ed. Nehemia Levtzion and Randall L. Pouwels, 441–476 (Athens: Ohio University Press).

34. Well-established institutions such as al-Azhar University in Cairo and the University of Havana admitted some black students; recently founded institutions included the University of São Paulo (1934), the University of the West Indies (1948), and the University of Dakar (1957).

35. His earlier vision of blacks as having a "double consciousness," one black and one American, gave way to a more cosmopolitan recognition of the shadings and multiplicities of the black world. Du Bois, *Souls of Black Folk*; Robert Gregg and Madhavi Kale, "*The Negro* and the *Dark Princess*: Two Legacies of the Universal Races Congress," *Radical History Review* 92 (2005); Henry Louis Gates Jr., "The Close Reader; Both Sides Now," *New York Times Book Review* (May 4, 2003).

36. The records of the movement as a whole have been collected and published in a multivolume series: Robert A. Hill, ed., *The Marcus Garvey and Universal Negro Improvement Association Papers*, 9 vols. (Berkeley: University of California Press, 1983–).

37. P. L. Wickins, *The Industrial and Commercial Workers' Union of Africa* (Cape Town: Oxford University Press, 1978).

38. Brereton, *History of Modern Trinidad*, 148–175.

39. Paul E. Lovejoy and Jan S. Hogendorn, *Slow Death for Slavery: The Course of Abolition in Northern Nigeria, 1897–1936* (Cambridge: Cambridge University Press, 1993); Paul E. Lovejoy, "Concubinage and the Status of Women in Early Colonial Northern Nigeria," *Journal of African History* 29 (1988): 245–266; Ibrahim K. Sundiata, *Brothers and Strangers: Black Zion, Black Slavery, 1914–1940* (Durham, N.C.: Duke University Press, 2003).

40. Patrick Manning, *Slavery, Colonialism, and Economic Growth in Dahomey, 1640–1960* (Cambridge: Cambridge University Press, 1982), 267–275.

41. Bennetta Jules-Rosette, in a multifaceted analysis of Baker, concludes, "Baker manipulated primal imagery under a public gaze as a way of appealing to the fantasies and expectations of her audience. . . . Baker used the subversive spaces of primitivism to transform herself and live her dream, moving from bananas to fashions by Bertraux, Chanel, Dior, and Balenciaga." Jules-Rosette, *Josephine Baker in Art and Life: The Icon and the Image* (Urbana: University of Illinois Press, 2007).

42. Peter Wade, *Race, Music, and Nation: Música Tropical in Colombia* (Chicago: University of Chicago Press, 2000).

43. Phyllis M. Martin, *Leisure and Society in Colonial Brazzaville* (Cambridge: Cambridge University Press, 1995).

44. David H. Anthony III, "Culture and Society in a Town in Transition: A People's History of Dar Es Salaam, 1865–1939," Ph.D. diss., University of Wisconsin (1983), 10–14; Margaret Strobel, *Muslim Women in Mombasa, 1890–1975* (New Haven, Conn.: Yale University Press, 1979).

45. Strobel, *Muslim Women in Mombasa*.

46. C. L. R. James, *Beyond a Boundary* (London: Hutchinson, 1963); Floyd Merrell, *Capoeira and Candomblé: Conformity and Resistance Through Afro-Cuban Experience* (Princeton, N.J.: Markus Wiener, 2005).

47. Various versions of this song have developed over the years, with differences in wording and in spelling of the Xhosa text. I have relied principally on a version published on the Web site of Miriam Makeba.

48. Jacqueline Goggin, *Carter G. Woodson: A Life in Black History* (Baton Rouge: Louisiana State University Press, 1993).

49. Nathan Huggins, *Harlem Renaissance* (New York: Oxford University Press, 1973). Many writers since have deepened the understanding of the Harlem Renaissance, including A. B. Christa Schwarz, *Gay Voices of the Harlem Renaissance* (Bloomington: Indiana University Press, 2003). See also Nancy Cunard, ed., *Negro: An Anthology* (London: Continuum, 1996).

50. W. C. Handy, *Father of the Blues, an Autobiography* (New York: Macmillan, 1941).

51. Tim Niblock, *Class and Power in Sudan: The Dynamics of Sudanese Politics, 1989–1985* (Albany: State University of New York Press, 1987); Heather J. Sharkey, *Living with Colonialism: Nationalism and Culture in the Anglo-Egyptian Sudan* (Berkeley: University of California Press, 2003); Cecil Eprile, *War and Peace in the Sudan, 1955–1972* (Newton Abbot, U.K.: David & Charles, 1974). For earlier times in Sudan, see R. S. O'Fahey and J. L. Spaulding, *Kingdoms of the Sudan* (London: Methuen, 1974).

52. Alissandra Cummins, Allison Thompson, and Nick Whittle, *Art in Barbados: What Kind of Mirror Image?* (Kingston: Ian Randle, 1999).

53. Carolina Maria de Jesus, *Quarto de Despejo: Diário de uma favelada*, introd. Audálio Dantas (São Paulo: Livraria Francisco Alves, 1960). The literal translation of the title is "Neighborhood of Despair."

54. Carolina Maria de Jesus, *Child of the Dark: The Diary of Carolina Maria de Jesus*, trans. David St. Clair (New York: Mentor, 1962), 42; Robert M. Levine and José Carlos Sebe Bom Meihy, *The Life and Death of Carolina Maria de Jesus* (Albuquerque: University of New Mexico Press, 1995).

6. Equality, 1960–2000

1. Aimé Césaire, *La Tragédie du Roi Christophe* (Paris: Présence Africaine, 1963). In addition to the parallels to the realities of the Duvalier regime and the warnings offered by Frantz Fanon, one may note a parallel in the play to Eugene O'Neill's 1921 play *Emperor Jones*.

2. Countries of the Old World diaspora that gained independence after World War II included Syria, Lebanon, and Jordan (all 1946), Libya (1951), Tunisia (1956), Morocco (1956), Madagascar (1960), Algeria (1962), South Yemen (1967), Mauritius (1967), and later the Seychelles and Comoros. In the interwar years, independence came to Iraq (c. 1932) and Egypt (c. 1936). Saudi Arabia, Iran, Turkey, and most European countries avoided the experience of being colonized

3. Leading figures who proclaimed ideologies of African socialism during the 1960s included Léopold Sédar Senghor of Senegal, Ahmed Sékou Touré of Guinée, Modibo

Keita of Mali, Kwame Nkrumah of Ghana, and Julius Nyerere of Tanganyika (later Tanzania).

4. This breakdown paralleled what happened with two other federations of British colonies: the East African Common Market, which existed from 1967 to 1977, and the Central African Federation, which existed from 1953 to 1963. The latter came apart as Africans objected to white domination from Rhodesia. Zambia and Malawi gained independence in 1964, while the white government of Rhodesia made a unilateral declaration of independence in 1965 and held on for fifteen years.

5. The Highlander Folk School, founded in 1932, followed the nineteenth-century Danish tradition of folk schools. Zilphia Horton, wife of educational director Myles Horton, collected the song in Charleston and revised it; Pete Seeger followed with revisions. Guy Carawan of the school was active in spreading the song in the 1960s. The Student Nonviolent Coordinating Committee (SNCC) formed in 1960 after a Highlander college workshop. John M. Glen, *Highlander: No Ordinary School, 1932–1962* (Lexington: University Press of Kentucky, 1988), 2, 148. Philip Nel of Kansas State University reports that the lyrics derived from Charles Tindley's gospel song "I'll Overcome Some Day" (1900) and the melody from the nineteenth-century spiritual "No More Auction Block for Me."

6. Nelson Mandela, *No Easy Walk to Freedom* (London: Heinemann, 1965); Frantz Fanon, *Black Skin, White Masks*, trans. Charles Lam Markmann (1952; repr., New York: Grove Press, 1967); Frantz Fanon, *Wretched of the Earth*, trans. Constance Farrington (1961; repr., New York: Grove Press, 1963).

7. Similarly, the inhabitants of the former French territory of St.-Domingue gave a new name to their land when they declared independence, taking the Amerindian term "Haiti."

8. Paulo Freire, *Pedagogy of the Oppressed*, trans. Myra Bergman Ramos (New York: Herder and Herder, 1970).

9. The African Studies Association of the United States held its first annual conference in 1958; international conferences in African history met in Dakar in 1958 and Dar es-Salaam in 1965.

10. The National Council of Black Studies first met in 1975.

11. In Algeria, the war of national liberation began in 1954 and achieved the beginning of negotiations with France in 1958, but Algerian independence came only in 1962; by 1965, Algeria had its third government.

12. Hilda Bernstein, *The World That Was Ours: The Story of the Rivonia Trial* (London: Heinemann, 1967).

13. For the report that underlay this application of neoliberal policies to Africa, see *Accelerated Development in Sub-Saharan Africa* (Washington, D.C.: World Bank, 1981); the author of the report was Elliot Berg of Harvard University.

14. Gino J. Naldi, *The Organization of African Unity: An Analysis of Its Role*, 2nd ed. (London: Mansell, 1999).

15. Saad S. Khan, *Reasserting International Islam: A Focus on the Organization of the Islamic Conference and Other Islamic Institutions* (Karachi: Oxford University Press, 2001).

16. Richard Wright had used the term in 1956 in his critical assessment of Ghana as it gained independence. Wright, *Black Power: A Record of Reactions in a Land of Pathos* (New York: Harper, 1954).

17. Leonardo Boff, *Introducing Liberation Theology*, trans. Paul Burns (Maryknoll, N.Y.: Orbis Books, 1987); Gustavo Gutiérrez, *A Theology of Liberation: History, Politics, and Salvation*, trans. Sister Caridad Inda and John Eagleson (Maryknoll, N.Y.: Orbis Books, 1973).

18. Ganja (marijuana) was long an element of Rastafarian culture, and it came to be adopted more broadly as part of youth culture in urban areas; it held on in various rural areas. But conflicts occurred with the authorities over the use of this drug, and by degrees it got connected to various forms of heroin, which brought more corporate profits and more debilitating social effects.

19. Marley got close to articulating the philosophy of his artistry in his 1980 "Redemption Song," sung solo, accompanied by acoustic guitar:

> Old pirates, yes, they rob I;
> Sold I to the merchant ships,
> Minutes after they took I
> From the bottomless pit.
> But my hand was made strong
> By the 'and of the almighty.
> We forward in this generation
> Triumphantly.
> Won't you help to sing
> These songs of freedom?
> 'cause all I ever have:
> Redemption songs;
> Redemption songs.

20. In later stages of this process, the first Miss Universe from sub-Saharan Africa was Miss Botswana in 1998; the first Miss World from sub-Saharan Africa was Miss Nigeria in 2001.

21. Franco of Congo-Kinshasa, whose recording career began in the 1950s, is an example of an artist who often spoke rather than sang his lyrics.

22. The term "neoliberal" refers to economic policies emphasizing strict market orientation, the restriction of government regulation and economic activity, and the privatization of publicly owned enterprises; these policies were tied especially to the influence of economists Milton Friedman and Friedrich von Hayek. The term "neoconservative" refers to political movements allied to neoliberal economic policies and especially to the national governments of Margaret Thatcher in the United Kingdom and Ronald Reagan in the United States.

23. See Patrick Manning, *Francophone Sub-Saharan Africa, 1880–1985* (Cambridge: Cambridge University Press, 1988), for more on national conferences.

24. The military regime scrapped preparations for a bicentennial celebration to honor the August 1791 uprising that had ended slavery and created the Haitian nation.

25. Arif Dirlik, *Global Modernity: Modernity in the Age of Global Capitalism* (Boulder, Colo.: Paradigm Publishers, 2007).

26. In Central Africa, reverberations of the Rwandan events continued. Rwandan and other refugee groups in eastern Zaire gave rise to more militias. In 1997, forces loyal to Laurent Kabila but relying in practice on Ugandan and Rwandan army forces and Tutsi militias swept through eastern Zaire and moved toward the capital of Kinshasa. Mobutu, ailing from cancer, finally fled. Kabila's forces occupied the capital in May and he proclaimed the country would again be named the Democratic Republic of Congo. Within a year, however, Kabila had failed to establish a political consensus within the country and most of his allies broke away from him. The domestic struggle rapidly escalated into international confrontation, with Angola, Namibia, and Zimbabwe supporting Kabila and Uganda, Rwanda, and numerous Congolese groups opposing him. The confrontation continued until Kabila's January 2001 assassination by a bodyguard and his replacement by his son Joseph Kabila as president.

27. Charles Villa-Vicencio and Fanie du Toit, eds., *Truth and Reconciliation in South Africa: Ten Years On* (Claremont, South Africa: David Philip, 2006).

28. Fanon, *Wretched of the Earth*, 95–106.

29. Ineke van Kessel, "Conference Report: Goa Conference on the African Diaspora in Asia," *African Affairs* (2006). See also Shihan de Silva Jayasuriya and Richard Pankhurst, eds., *The African Diaspora in the Indian Ocean* (Trenton, N.J.: Africa World Press, 2003).

30. Kapita M. Bila, *Sida en Afrique: maladie et phénomène social* (Kinshasa: 1988), 58. Quoted in John Iliffe, *The African AIDS Epidemic: A History* (Oxford: James Currey, 2006), 97.

31. Chris Stringer, *African Exodus: The Origins of Modern Humanity* (New York: Henry Holt, 1997). For the original report on mitochondrial-DNA analysis of humans, see R. L. Cann, M. Stoneking, and A. C. Wilson, "Mitochondrial DNA and Human Evolution," *Nature* 325 (1987): 32–36.

Epilogue. The Future of the African Diaspora

1. Charles P. Henry, *Long Overdue: The Politics of Racial Reparations* (New York: New York University Press, 2007); Ronald P. Salzberger and Mary C. Turck, *Reparations for Slavery: A Reader* (Lanham, Md.: Rowman and Littlefield, 2004).

2. Slave-trade museums include those at the Merseyside Maritime Museum (Liverpool), Cape Coast Castle (Cape Coast, Ghana), the Mariners' Museum (Newport News, Virginia), and an exhibit based on the slave ship "Henrietta Marie" at the Mel Fisher Maritime Heritage Society (Key West, Florida). In addition, there are projects for slave-trade museums at Gorée, Senegal, and at Cartagena, Colombia. An exhibit in Nantes, "Les Anneaux de Mémoire," was in place from 1992 to 1994; a Web site survives it.

3. In the United States, sociologist (and later U.S. Senator) Daniel Patrick Moynihan took up the term "benign neglect" to propose that the best policy a government could follow to improve the social condition of poor and black families was to do very little at all.

374 ♦ Equality, 1960–2000

4. Eduardo Bonilla-Silva, *Racism Without Racists: Color-blind Racism and the Persistence of Racial Inequality in the United States* (Lanham, Md.: Rowman and Littlefield, 2003). The idea of a "color-blind" policy toward race today has some parallel with the 1843 decision of the East India Company to cease recognizing the institution of slavery. In declaring itself blind to slavery, the company stopped giving legal support to slavery but made no active effort to end slavery.

Index

Index

Price-Mars, Jean, 224, 252
prices, for slavery, 99, 109, 181
Price, Sally, 238
pride, 7; black pride, 290
primitivism, 266
Principe, 73
Protestant Christianity. *See* Christianity
Puerto Rico, 172, 197; son and, 265; United
    States and, 216
purity of blood, 14
Pushkin, Aleksandr, 192

Qajar Empire, 196
quadroon, 142
Querino, Manuel, 224
Quest of the Silver Fleece (Du Bois), 242
quilombos, 92, 94
quinine, 367*n*6
quinoa, 78

Rabah, Bilal ibn, 36
race, 11–16, 136–45; biology and, 13; catego-
    ries of, 225; changing definitions of,
    14–15; *vs.* community, 12; differences
    of, 12–13; 1400–1600, 84; genetics and,
    13, 14, 30, 329–30; Islam and, 39; Jews
    as, 12; science and, 200; theory of,
    144
racial discrimination, xvii, 13, 15, 30, 285;
    with Baker, 259; in Europe, 299
racial mixing, 15–16, 18–19, 350; Arabs and,
    225; in Europe, 5; identity and, 253;
    mestizo, 5, 15, 16, 214; métis, 142
racial purity, 15
racism, 11; biological, 14; emancipation
    and, 201; hierarchies and, 143; language
    of, 16; in 1960s, 290; possibilities for
    ending, 348–49; scientific, 15; skin
    color and, 144
Radiyya, 39
ragtime, 21, 230, 368*n*19
Rainbow Coalition, 312
Randolph, A. Philip, 245
rap music, 309
Rastafarians, 305–6, 372*n*18

Ravaton, "Ti-Frère" Alphonse, 306
Rawley, James Walvin, 101
re-Africanization, 142
Reagan, Ronald, 311
rebellion: against colonialism, 234; Nat
    Turner's, 165; from slavery, 146–47; on
    slave ships, 105; smallpox, 217; Stono,
    128, 153; Texas, 169
reconquest, 38
"Redemption Song" (Marley), 372*n*19
Rediker, Marcus, 101
Red Sea, 63–64
reflective culture, 21, 22
reggae, 305–6
religion: in 1900s, 232; in 1910s, 240; in
    1950s, 272–73, 273; phenotype and, 39;
    slavery and, 127. *See also* Christianity;
    Islam
Renamo, 310
reparations, 345–47
resistance, 10
return migration, 5
"Return to my Native Land" (Césaire),
    257
Réunion, 98; sugar in, 177
Revels, Hiram, 190
Rhodes, Cecil, 213
Rhodesia, 226
rice, 47
Rio de Janeiro, 110; smallpox rebellion
    in, 217
riots: after World War I, 237; rock and roll
    and, 270
Rivadavia, Bernardino, 190
Roberts, Richard, 180
Robeson, Paul, 257
Robinson, Randall, 312
Roca, Vicente, 190
Rochereau, 288, 307–8
rock and roll, 270
Rodney, Walter, 60, 187
roles, 23; in African societies, 22
Romani, 171, 262
Romans, 13
Roots (Haley), 290

Columbia Studies in International and Global History

Matthew Connelly and Adam McKeown, editors

The idea of "globalization" has become a commonplace, but we lack good histories that can explain the transnational and global processes that have shaped the contemporary world. Columbia Studies in International and Global History will encourage serious scholarship on international and global history with an eye to explaining the origins of the contemporary era. Grounded in empirical research, the titles in the series will also transcend the usual area boundaries and will address questions of how history can help us understand contemporary problems, including poverty, inequality, power, political violence, and accountability beyond the nation state.